The Struggle for Supremacy in the Middle East

Since 1979, few rivalries have affected Middle Eastern politics as much as the rivalry between Saudi Arabia and Iran. However, too often the rivalry has been framed purely in terms of 'proxy wars', sectarian difference, or the associated conflicts that have broken out in Iraq, Lebanon, Syria, Bahrain, and Yemen. In this book, Simon Mabon presents a more nuanced assessment of the rivalry, outlining its history and demonstrating its impact across the Middle East. Highlighting the significance of local groups, Mabon shows how regional politics have shaped and been shaped by the rivalry. The book draws from social theory and the work of Pierre Bourdieu to challenge problematic assumptions about 'proxy wars', the role of religion, and sectarianism. Exploring the changing political landscape of the Middle East as a whole and the implications for regional and international security, Mabon paints a complex picture of this frequently discussed but oft-misunderstood rivalry.

Simon Mabon is Professor of International Politics at Lancaster University. He is Director of SEPAD (the Sectarianism, Proxies and De-Sectarianization Project), which aims to trace the emergence and development of sectarian animosity in global politics. He has previously published *Saudi Arabia and Iran: Soft Power Rivalry in the Middle East* (2013), *The Origins of ISIS* (2016, co-author), and *Houses Built on Sand* (2020), along with several other edited collections. In 2016/17 he served as academic advisor to the House of Lords International Relations Committee's inquiry into the UK's relationship with the Middle East.

The Struggle for Supremacy in the Middle East

Saudi Arabia and Iran

Simon Mabon

Lancaster University

CAMBRIDGE
UNIVERSITY PRESS

Shaftesbury Road, Cambridge CB2 8EA, United Kingdom

One Liberty Plaza, 20th Floor, New York, NY 10006, USA

477 Williamstown Road, Port Melbourne, VIC 3207, Australia

314–321, 3rd Floor, Plot 3, Splendor Forum, Jasola District Centre,
New Delhi – 110025, India

103 Penang Road, #05–06/07, Visioncrest Commercial, Singapore 238467

Cambridge University Press is part of Cambridge University Press & Assessment,
a department of the University of Cambridge.

We share the University's mission to contribute to society through the pursuit of
education, learning and research at the highest international levels of excellence.

www.cambridge.org
Information on this title: www.cambridge.org/9781108473361

DOI: 10.1017/9781108603690

First published 2023

A catalogue record for this publication is available from the British Library.

Library of Congress Cataloging-in-Publication Data
Names: Mabon, Simon, author.
Title: The struggle for supremacy in the Middle East : Saudi Arabia and
Iran / Simon Mabon, Lancaster University.
Description: Cambridge ; New York, NY : Cambridge University Press, 2023. |
Includes bibliographical references.
Identifiers: LCCN 2022034946 | ISBN 9781108473361 (hardback) |
ISBN 9781108461443 (paperback) | ISBN 9781108603690 (ebook)
Subjects: LCSH: Saudi Arabia – Foreign relations – Iran. | Iran – Foreign
relations – Saudi Arabia. | Middle East – Politics and government – 1979–
Classification: LCC DS228.I7 M33 2023 | DDC 327.538055–dc23/eng/20221206
LC record available at https://lccn.loc.gov/2022034946

ISBN 978-1-108-47336-1 Hardback
ISBN 978-1-108-46144-3 Paperback

For Edward-Omi, an endless source
of love, happiness, and hope.

Contents

Acknowledgements

After the completion of my first book (based on my PhD thesis) on Saudi–Iranian relations in 2013, I thought I was done writing on the rivalry between Riyadh and Tehran. Like most, I felt uncomfortable with the ways in which I had developed ideas across the PhD and book, and I wanted to focus on other things, namely a burgeoning interest in sovereignty. Five years after *Saudi Arabia and Iran: Soft Power Rivalry in the Middle East* came out, I returned to the topic. The genesis of this book came at the same time the Sectarianism, Proxies and De-sectarianization (SEPAD) project was formed in early 2018. In putting together a grant application to the Carnegie Corporation, the seeds of an idea were forming that would allow me to combine my interests in sectarianism and political theory with a study on Saudi–Iranian relations. When we were lucky enough to be successful with our funding application, the project was born.

I must first thank the wonderful people at Cambridge University Press for being so supportive of me – and patient with me – while I navigated the challenges of finishing the book at a time of global pandemic and the birth of our son. In particular, I wish to thank Maria Marsh – my first editor at I.B. Tauris – who was so enthusiastic about the project when it first began and helped guide it to completion. Thanks must also go to Santhamurthy Ramamoorthy, Natasha Whelan, and Rachel Imrie for their continued support and patience during my more idiosyncratic moments.

Countless people have assisted me across this journey. I must thank Elias Ghazal, Adel Ruished, and Luiza Cerioli, who provided invaluable research assistance at different times during this book. All my colleagues in SEPAD have been an inspiration, offering critical and constructive feedback on arguments from the book, many of which were in their infancy when shared. The weekly work in progress sessions that began at the start of the Covid-19 lockdown served to keep me intellectually focused at a time when the world around us was in turmoil; adding to this chaos – in a truly wonderful way – was the arrival of our son, Edward-Omi, a mere two months into the UK lockdown. Conversations with SEPAD fellows gave me an intellectual focus at a time when it could easily have been lost.

A huge thanks must go to Edward 'Eddie' Wastnidge for his continued support and friendship. He has been a constant source of encour-
agement and intellectual stimulation, humouring my bizarre ideas and
encouraging their development; he is partly responsible for the spatial
turn in my research. Also, thanks to Elias, Staci Strobl, Vincent Durac,
Mustafa Menshawy, Javier Bordon, Hussein Kalout, and Adel Ruished
for reading draft chapters of this book and offering invaluable feedback.
If I have missed anyone, I sincerely apologize.

Thanks must also go to John Nagle, Staci, Morten Valborn, Vincent,
Kaveh Ehsani, and Ibrahim Halawi for ongoing conversations about these
ideas, academic life, and surviving its myriad challenges, particularly during the pandemic. I must thank Toby Dodge for introducing me to the
work of Pierre Bordieu through a process of osmosis at various SEPAD
and Project on Middle East Political Science (POMEPS) events across
the world. A particularly amusing memory was a discussion between
Toby, Bassel Salloukh, and myself at the Lebanese American University
in Beirut about the strengths of applied political theory – namely the
ideas of Bourdieu, Antonio Gramsci, and Giorgio Agamben – much to
the chagrin of Marc Lynch and others! Toby has been kind enough to
guide my immersion into the rich yet challenging world of Bourdieu,
providing feedback and resources. Greg Gause has been a long-standing
inspiration and during the past few years I have been lucky enough to
get to know him. It was a conversation with Greg about the nature of
hegemony that shaped much of what follows in this book.

I have been fortunate enough to present ideas from this book at a
range of places across the world, both in person and virtually. Thank you
to those at Harvard University, Brookings Institute, Georgetown University Doha, the London School of Economics, Durham University,
Lebanese American University, Doha Institute, and elsewhere.

Adam Hug at the Foreign Policy Centre continues to be supportive,
dating back to the time that I met him at Euston station in the summer of
2011. Adam and the FPC have hosted countless SEPAD events, many
of which focused on Saudi–Iranian relations and their impact across the
region. Fabian Blumberg and Mohammad Yaghi at the Konrad Ada-
neur Stiftung have been equally supportive, organizing workshops and
events looking at all manner of things pertaining to sectarianism, and
the Saudi–Iranian rivalry, particularly in the context of the Yemen crisis.

Of course, none of this would have been possible without the gener-
ous funding from the Carnegie Corporation. Hillary Weisner and Nehal
Amer at the Carnegie Corporation have offered immeasurable support
since that initial expression of interest, across countless email exchanges,
phone calls, zoom meetings, conversations about synaesthesia, and

engagement in workshops. I could not have imagined this level of support or critical engagement with the ideas that the book – and SEPAD more broadly – has produced; Hillary, Nehal, I am forever thankful to you both.

I must thank those who have taken time to be interviewed over the past six years. These interviews took place across the Middle East and remotely, via Skype, Zoom, and email. This book also draws from a period spent as academic advisor to the House of Lords International Relations Committee which, at the time, had a keen interest in Saudi–Iranian relations. That experience, while deeply frustrating, has provided useful material for this book. Supplementing this is material from the *Saudi Cables* and *US Diplomatic Cables*, both released by the Wikileaks organization. The book also dips a toe very lightly into the world of quantitative data collection, drawing material from a SEPAD survey run by Justin Gengler. I received support from my wonderful colleague Basia Yoxon, who helped guide me through the dark forest of quantitative analysis.

So many others have helped in ways that may not appear obvious to them, but matter to me. These include (but are not limited to) Mehran Kamrava, Geneive Abdo, Clive Jones, Bassel Salloukh, Robert Mason, Jawad Fairouz, Samira Nasirzadeh, Eyad Al Refai, Olivia Glombitza, Ana Maria Kumarasamy, Larry Rubin, Banafsheh Keynoush, Mariam Salehi and all the people I have spoken to for the SEPADPod podcast series, which has served as a source of endless aspiration at the amazing work people are doing.

Beyond the academy, family and friends have been a constant source of support across the darkest days of writing and the pandemic. Thanks to my parents, George and Sally, for their enthusiastic support and for all the help you gave us in the early months of Edward-Omi's life. A huge thank you to my wife Swarna, who endured her own challenges across this period yet still managed to keep me on the proverbial straight and narrow, providing love, tasty food, and emotional grounding. Finally, thank you to my son, Edward-Omi, to whom this book is dedicated. You have brought so much light into our lives and when things start to get a little too much, your cheeky smile cuts through all the *bakwas* of everyday life.

While many people have had an impact on my ideas, ultimately any errors remain mine alone.

Introduction

As I reached the end of my allotted 20 minutes, the hands began to rise. I was at Harvard University presenting research that would ultimately go into this book, focusing on the rivalry between Saudi Arabia and Iran after the Arab Uprisings. The first question came from a Shi'a cleric. Sporting the black turban worn by descendants of the Prophet Muhammad, the question asked why I focused on Saudi Arabia, given that the real rivalry was between Iran and the United States. Subsequent questions from the floor echoed this point, rejecting Saudi agency and framing the Kingdom as a stooge of the United States. In rejecting Saudi agency, the question – and those that followed – pointed to the complexity of a rivalry that is viewed in a range of ways by people across the Middle East[1] and the wider Muslim world yet continues to have a devastating impact on the lives of those in the region and beyond. Despite these claims, the rivalry between Riyadh and Tehran is regularly framed as central to much of the region's turmoil. From Iraq after the US-led invasion in 2003 to the ongoing devastation in Yemen, via Lebanon, Syria, and Bahrain, the rivalry has had a devastating impact on regional affairs, but the reverberations of the rivalry are felt far beyond the borders of the Middle East.

Relations between Saudi Arabia and Iran have typically been characterized by rivalry and suspicion since the establishment of the Islamic Republic of Iran in 1979. Political in nature yet couched in Islamic rhetoric, the rivalry is driven by a desire to ensure regime security and legitimacy along with increasing influence across the Middle East, albeit conditioned by regional context. This interplay of domestic and regional

---

[1] I use the term 'Middle East' after lengthy conversations with colleagues and friends from the region, many of whom rejected the use of other terms due to identifying with the concept of the Middle East and fearing a form of intellectual colonization with the imposition of other terms. While acknowledging the importance of decolonization, I cannot – in good faith – reject what friends and colleagues from the region have asked me to use.

factors allowed the relationship to oscillate between periods of outright hostility and apparent rapprochement, conditioned by developments in regional and international politics.

The influence of regional politics is perhaps best seen in the aftermath of the Arab Uprisings, where the fragmentation of political projects opened new arenas for competition between the two states who sought to increase their influence over regional affairs, often at the expense of the other.[2] In pursuit of this, both Riyadh and Tehran sought to deploy a mixture of material and ideational resources to cultivate relationships with actors across the region. While this often took place between groups who shared sectarian allegiances, this also involved the development of relationships between groups who shared visions of order. Understanding the way in which visions of order resonate across the Middle East is integral in analysing the impact of the rivalry between Saudi Arabia and Iran on the region; in pursuit of this, I use the ideas of the French social theorist Pierre Bourdieu.

Western media coverage has largely framed the rivalry between Saudi Arabia and Iran as a 'cold' or 'proxy' war, driven by 'ancient hatreds' pitting Sunni Muslims against their Shi'a counterparts.[3] Such views are overly simplistic, orientalist, and, in some cases, xenophobic. Indeed, the concept of the Cold War first coined by Bernard Baruch on 16 April 1947 bears little resemblance to contemporary events. Writing some years later, Ybigniew Brzezinkski defined the Cold War as 'warfare by other (non-lethal) means'.[4] This idea of *non-lethal* means shares little with the rivalry in the contemporary Middle East as Saudi war planes bomb targets across Yemen while Iranian military officials fight to support Bashar al-Assad in Syria.

While the rivalry between Saudi Arabia and Iran plays out regionally, conditioned by the interplay of local and global forces, it also plays out *within* states. The presence of shared normative environments, conditioned by religion, sectarian affinity, ethnicity, or ideology, helps Riyadh and Tehran to engage with groups found (predominantly, although not exclusively) within state borders. This engagement results in the

---

[2] Simon Mabon, *Houses Built on Sand: Violence, Sectarianism and Revolution in the Middle East* (Manchester: Manchester University Press, 2020).

[3] For example, amongst many others, see Dilip Hiro, *Cold War in the Islamic World: Saudi Arabia, Iran and the Struggle for Supremacy* (London: Hurst, 2019); Jeremy Cliffe, 'Iran and Saudi Arabia are Locked in a Cold War-Style Stand-Off – but the Situation is Even More Volatile', *The New Statesman* (08.01.20), www.newstatesman.com/world/2020/01/iran-and-saudi-arabia-are-locked-cold-war-style-stand-situation-even-more-volatile; France 24, 'Saudi-Iran "Proxy Wars" Play Out in Embattled Lebanon' (31.10.21), www.france24.com/en/live-news/20211031-saudi-iran-proxy-wars-play-out-in-embattled-lebanon.

[4] Ybigniew Brzezinkski, 'The Cold War and Its Aftermath', *Foreign Affairs* 81 (1991–3).

cultivation of relationships of a range of different forms, between states and non-state actors. Such relationships have regularly been referred to as 'proxy wars' and are deemed to play a central role in contemporary conflict, particularly in the context of the rivalry between Riyadh and Tehran.

As scholars such as Andrew Mumford observe, proxy wars are products of relationships between benefactors external to particular conflict arenas and local actors who are the conduits for the provision of weapons, funding, and training from the benefactor.[5] The proxy wars thesis operates on the premise of *indirect engagement* in an effort to conduct 'subversive operations' in pursuit of its goals. This point is developed further by Vladimir Rauta, who argues that proxy wars should be conceptualized as 'strategic bargains' in pursuit of coercion.[6] In lieu of the concept of 'proxy wars', the concept of 'proxy networks' has also been used in an effort to examine the nature of transnational relationships between actors across the region.

Conflict across the Middle East, including in Iraq, Libya, Syria, Yemen, has routinely been framed as a consequence of proxy wars, albeit playing out in different ways.[7] These proxy wars are often viewed as features of the rivalry between Saudi Arabia and Iran, yet the ways in which Saudi Arabia and Iran develop relationships with local actors points to a more complex set of linkages than the model typically understood within a 'proxy relationship'. Indeed, as work done by the Sectarianism, Proxies and De-sectarianization (SEPAD) project has observed, perhaps most clearly in a special issue edited by Edward Wastnidge and myself, trans-state relationships between states – in this case Saudi Arabia and Iran – and non-state actors are products of time and space, meaning that a range of factors influence the relationships, producing a number of different outcomes. This includes some local actors possessing far more agency than is often typically assumed, as observed by Amal Saad in the case of Hizbullah.[8] This ability to exert influence independent of the patron actor's wishes appears to push the borders of the concept.

[5] Andrew Mumford, 'Proxy Warfare and the Future of Conflict', *The RUSI Journal* 158:2 (2013), 40–6.

[6] Vladimir Rauta, 'Proxy Warfare and the Future of Conflict: Take Two', *The Rusi Journal* 165:2 (2020), 1–10.

[7] Benedetta Berti and Yoel Guzansky, 'Saudi Arabia's Foreign Policy on Iran and the Proxy War in Syria: Toward a New Chapter?', *Israel Journal of Foreign Affairs* 8:3 (2014), 25–34; Steven Heydemann, 'The Syrian Conflict: Proxy War, Pyrrhic Victory, and Power-Sharing Agreements', *Studies in Ethnicity and Nationalism* 20:2 (2020), 153–60; Ranj Alaaldin, 'Proxy War in Iraq', PWP Conflict Studies (2019).

[8] Amal Saad, 'Challenging the Sponsor-Proxy Model: The Iran-Hizbullah Relationship', *Global Discourse* 9:4 (2019), 627–50.

For Saad, the model of proxy wars is deeply problematic, emerging from a reductive and conceptual inadequacy, particularly when seeking to examine multi-dimensional relationships. This stems from its grounding within the Realist tradition of International Relations (IR), where 'alliance theory and the sponsor-proxy model provide insufficient and over simplistic explanations for relationships that are to an overwhelming extent bound by ideational factors such as identity, norms, values and discourse, reducing them to crude material considerations like military and economic power and interests'.[9]

Moreover, as the cultivation of cross-border relationships developed by Saudi Arabia and Iran reveal, these relationships are not uni-directional, but rather can also be driven by local actors seeking to find regional powers able to provide support. This has typically been bound up in assumptions about the location of power within sponsor–client relationships, typically taking place over state/non-state lines with the latter subordinate to the former. Moreover, as we shall see, these relationships play out differently across time and space, shaped by the complexities and contingencies of local context.

Relationships are not purely constructed with groups who use violence; instead, links can also be forged with political parties, tribes, religious groups, and clerical networks. While these relationships may be formal, they may also be transient, of the moment, which points to something more amorphous than the development of alliances. Although this appears counter-intuitive when reflecting on relationships during conflict, this need not necessarily result in war, but may be shaped by broader understandings of violence – such as those advocated by Johan Galtung – and inter-group tensions. Here, while violence erupts intermittently, the underlying social structures that condition daily life may not result in acts of direct violence but rather create a form of *stasis* wherein inter-group tension plays out within the fabric of the state without necessarily descending into conflict. Furthermore, these structures have facilitated the development of relationships between local and external actors in an effort to consolidate or expand influence. Acknowledging this complexity, I refer to transnational relationships rather than proxies or alliances. Underpinning the development of these relationships, I argue, are shared visions of order, either local or regional, that allows groups to come together on the grounds of shared belief or visions of order.

[9] Ibid., 628.

Understanding the Rivalry

Efforts to understand the rivalry between Saudi Arabia and Iran typically fall into three camps. The first argues that the rivalry emerges out of a struggle for regional supremacy, namely, geopolitical competition that is shaped by concerns about the organization of regional security.[10] The second argues that the rivalry is a consequence of centuries-old enmity within Islam, stemming from 'ancient hatreds' that pit Sunni against Shi'a. Adherents of such a primordialist view hold that the rivalry between Saudi Arabia and Iran stems from a contemporary manifestation of these religious tension. The third argues that religion has been used as a mechanism of control alongside and within geopolitical concerns, resulting in a rivalry that plays out across time and space, shaping – and being shaped by – local contexts.[11]

While there is much work on the nature of the rivalry, there is little systematic work looking at the impact of the rivalry across the region and beyond. The rivalry plays out across a range of different spaces, shaped by the complexities of local context. Understanding the ways in which life is organized in particular spaces is necessary in order to critically reflect on the impact of the rivalry between Saudi Arabia and Iran on those spaces. In many cases, this requires a reflection on the nature of the state and the governance mechanisms that regulate life, which condition particular forms of contestation. In Lebanon, for example, the rivalry is grounded within blocs found in the power-sharing system, albeit with broader repercussions. Amidst state fragmentation, however, the rivalry plays out in different forms, such as in Iraq, Syria, and Yemen, where Riyadh and Tehran provided support for militias and armed groups operating largely – although not exclusively – beyond the coercive capacity of the state.

While some argue that this struggle is one for hegemony, either across the Middle East or the Islamic world, hegemonic aspirations amongst actors in the Middle East are routinely doomed to fail, a point made by Gregory Gause. In an essay on the topic of hegemony in the Middle

---

[10] Henner Furtig, *Iran's Rivalry with Saudi Arabia between the Gulf Wars* (Reading: Ithaca Press, 2006); Shahram Chubin and Charles Tripp, *Iran-Saudi Arabia Relations and Regional Order* (London: OUP for IISS, 1996); Banafsheh Keynoush, *Saudi Arabia and Iran: Friends or Foes?* (London: Palgrave, 2016); and Robert Mason, *Foreign Policy in Iran and Saudi Arabia: Economics and Diplomacy in the Middle East* (London: I.B. Tauris, 2014).

[11] Simon Mabon, *Saudi Arabia and Iran: Soft Power Rivalry in the Middle East* (London: I.B. Tauris, 2013). See also Simon Mabon, 'Introduction: Saudi Arabia, Iran and the Struggle to Shape the Middle East', in Simon Mabon (ed.), *Saudi Arabia and Iran: The Struggle to Shape the Middle East* (London: Foreign Policy Centre, 2018).

East, Gause argues that the multi-polar nature of order, underpinned by both material and ideational capabilities, coupled with the penetration of regional politics by external actors, leaves hegemonic aspirations doomed to fail.[12] Similarly, a volume edited by Adham Saouli points to a region dominated by 'middle powers' in a range of different forms, who seek to exert influence on regional and global politics but this ability is conditioned by structural factors and relations with global powers.[13]

The increased involvement of the United States in the Middle East post-2003 supports such hypotheses, revealing a complex set of struggles between actors seeking to exert influence and shape the region in their image, albeit often struggling to do so due to other competing visions of order. For example, both Saudi Arabia and Iran seek to shape regional politics in accordance with particular political visions, yet so too do Turkey, Qatar, Israel, Hizbullah, Da'ish, the United States, and China, amongst others. In this complex mélange of interactions, each actor seeks to impose its own vision of order on the region through cultivating relationships with actors across the region in the form of political parties, militias, clerics, or broader popular support through media outlets. While relative power and influence differs between actors and across time and space, in such conditions, to speak of a quest for hegemony viewed in zero-sum terms appears misguided. Instead, as I shall endeavor to show, what is at play particularly in the case of the rivalry between Saudi Arabia and Iran is competition for order, between different visions of how (regional) politics *should* be organized.

Religion and State

For Fred Halliday and Ray Hinnebusch, two luminaries of the IR of the Middle East, understanding regional developments necessitates reflecting on domestic affairs and the impact of these machinations at a regional level. Indeed, as Halliday argued, the rivalry between Saudi Arabia and Iran 'is a product not so much of imperialist interference or of millennial and atavistic historical antagonisms, but of the two interrelated modern processes of state formation and the rise of nationalism'.[14] State formation and the development of nationalist identities required engagement with regional trends and

[12] F. Gregory Gause, *Saudi Arabia and Regional Leadership: The Impossibility of Hegemony* (Middle East Insights, No.243, 25.08.20).
[13] Adham Saouli (ed.), *Unfulfilled Aspirations* (London: Hurst, 2020).
[14] Fred Halliday, 'Arabs and Persians beyond the Geopolitics of the Gulf', *Cahiers d'etudes sur la Mediterranee orientale et le monde turo-iranien* [En ligne], 22 (1996), https://journals.openedition.org/cemoti/143?lang=fr#quotation.

ideologies such as pan-Arabism and Islamism, along with powerful anti-colonial movements. As Hinnebusch reflects, the strength of such ideologies meant that state borders lacked the 'impenetrability or sanctity of the Westphalian system', leaving regimes sensitive to the rhetoric and action of others.[15] A similar point is made by Paul Noble who observes the presence of a shared normative environment, described as an 'echo chamber' in which the presence of shared norms, identity, history, and culture mean that the actions of one are felt across this environment. The prominence of Islam within both states creates such an environment.

For Saudi Arabia and Iran, claims to Islamic leadership and legitimacy offer a means of increasing their power and influence across the region. While often seen in zero-sum ways, this competition means that gains made by one equate to losses for the other. In part, this importance stems from the position of Islam within the processes of state building and the very fabric of each state. Both Saudi Kingdom and Islamic Republic are run in accordance with the Shari'a while political activity is legitimized by clerical decree. Beyond Saudi Arabia and Iran, Islam is built into the fabric of other states across the region, meaning that those actors with religious capital are able to exert influence in a form of religious 'soft power'.[16] Although the Saudi Kingdom is a monarchy, the ruling Al Sa'ud family operates as the custodians of the two holy places, deriving Islamic legitimacy from protecting those who make *hajj* to Mecca and Medina. In the Islamic Republic of Iran, the system of *veleyat-e faqih* (the Regency of the Jurist) is in operation in the absence of the 12th Imam. Devised by Ruhollah Khomeini, *veleyat-e faqih* is a system of government that ensures compliance with Islam, with senior clerics overseeing all aspects of political life. Yet this proved to be a controversial decision, moving against traditional Shi'a views which called for a separation of religion and politics.

While clerics occupy a central role within the system of *veleyat-e faqih* overseeing governance at all stages, in the Kingdom of Saudi Arabia, clerics have historically provided theological support to the Al Sa'ud, legitimizing the actions of the ruling family in return for a prominent place within the Kingdom. The alliance between Al Sa'ud and clerics from the fundamentalist Wahhabi school that dates back to the eighteenth century serves as a source of legitimacy for both domestic and regional audiences. Although not all Saudis identify as Wahhabi, clerical

---

[15] Raymond Hinnebusch, *The International Politics of the Middle East* (Manchester: Manchester University Press, 2003), p. 3.
[16] Mabon, *Saudi Arabia and Iran*.

influence was integral in shaping the Kingdom's political life across the twentieth century.[17]

Although central to Saudi Arabia, Wahhabi thought is situated on the periphery of orthodox Sunni forms of Islam and, as Hamid Algar suggests, it is a movement 'without pedigree', lacking 'substantial precedent' across Islamic history'.[18] Anachronistic, preaching the oneness of God and a need to deny all other forms of worship, Wahhabism requires devotion and worship 'purely and exclusively to God'.[19] This premise positions Wahhabism as fundamentally opposed to Shi'a Islam with repercussions both for the Kingdom's own Shi'a population and for neighboring Iran. Across the century, Shi'a communities across Saudi Arabia faced widespread discrimination in political, social and economic realms, prompting expressions of concern from Reza Shah in Iran about the treatment of Shi'a groups.[20]

Latent structural violence prevented political empowerment amongst Shi'a communities as they were stopped from accessing state institutions. In the aftermath of the 1979 revolution, Shi'a communities were quickly framed as a security threat, seen as fifth columnists.[21] This framing of Shi'a communities as an existential threat results in widespread marginalization and discrimination in all forms of political and social life.[22] Here, violence is directed against particular groups, while also being structural in the institutionalization of discrimination.

Following the events of 1979, several clerics in Saudi Arabia issued *fatwas* against Shi'a Muslims, including denouncing the Shi'a as apostates and sanctioning the killing of members of the Shi'a community.[23] These tensions, although couched in theological terms, possess a clear political aspect, seeking to erode the legitimacy of the other. One consequence of the relationship was a vehemently anti-Shi'a position that is both theological and political, resulting in widespread discrimination of

---

[17] See David. D. Commins, *The Wahhabi Mission and Saudi Arabia* (London: I. B. Tauris, 2006); Hamid Algar, *Wahhabism: A Critical Essay* (New York: Islamic Publications International, 2002); Joseph Kostiner, 'On Instruments and Their Designers: The Ikhwan of Najd and the Emergence of the Saudi State', *Middle East Studies*, 21:3 (1985), 298–323; Joseph Kostiner, 'State, Islam and Opposition in Saudi Arabia: The post-Desert Storm Phase', *Middle East Review of International Affairs*, 1:2 (1997), 75–89.

[18] Algar, *Wahhabism*, p. 27.

[19] Ibid., p. 35.

[20] Keynoush, *Friends or Foes?*

[21] For an in-depth history of this, see Toby Matthiessen, *The Other Saudis: Shiism, Dissent and Sectarianism* (Cambridge: Cambridge University Press).

[22] See Mabon, *Houses Built on Sand*.

[23] Vali Nasr, *The Shi'a Revival: How Conflicts within Islam Will Shape the Future* (New York: W. W. Norton, 2007), p. 236.

the Kingdom's Shi'a population, producing anti-Shi'a sentiment across the Kingdom that has implications for Shi'a Muslims across the world.

After the execution of the Saudi Shi'a cleric Nimr al-Nimr in 2016, protests broke out across Iran and in other Shi'a communities in the Middle East and South Asia. During the course of these protests, the Saudi embassy in Tehran was set ablaze, prompting Saudi Arabia to give Iranian diplomats stationed in the Kingdom 48 hours to leave the country as diplomatic ties between the two were broken. The event highlights the intersection of politics and religion within the context of a complex and often vitriolic rivalry that is conditioned by the complexities of time and space.

The importance of Islam within Saudi Arabia meant that Iran's behaviour on the international stage post 1979 was a cause of great consternation in Riyadh and required a range of different strategies in response. From this, it is easy to see how religion has played an important role in shaping the nature of the rivalry, with the need to speak to domestic audiences having an impact upon external relations and external relations impacting upon domestic stability.

In Iran, the regime of Reza Pahlavi was toppled in early 1979 after months of violent clashes between the Shah's forces and protesters. The post-revolutionary landscape was quickly imbued with political meaning through a referendum that established Grand Ayatollah Ruhollah Khomeini's vision of *veleyat-e faqih* as the political system of the new state. *Veleyat-e faqih* enshrined and protected Shi'a Islam within the fabric of the state. From then, all aspects of government and life were run in accordance with the jurist's interpretation of the Shari'a. Khomeini's vision departed from traditional Shi'a positions, which separated politics and theology and this division is a source of tension within the Shi'a world.[24]

Shi'a ideas were a central part of revolutionary – and post-revolutionary – Iran. These ideas found traction following the Shah's fierce military responses to unrest in the preceding years which prompted parallels with the narratives of martyrdom in Shi'a history.[25] Ideas of sacrifice and resistance were a prominent feature of domestic and regional politics at this time, once again found in Shi'a thought. Although ethnically heterogeneous, the Islamic Republic relies upon a Shi'a narrative as a mechanism through which to keep its population unified.[26] Cultivating a 'Janus

[24] Nikki R. Keddie (ed.), *Religion and Politics in Iran: Shi'ism from Quietism to Revolution* (New Haven: Yale University Press, 1983).
[25] Rola El-Husseini, 'Hezbollah and the Axis of Refusal: Hamas, Iran and Syria', *Third World Quarterly*, 31: 5 (2010), 808–9.
[26] Mabon, *Saudi Arabia and Iran*.

faced' identity, building upon ideas of being the children and grandchildren of both Cyrus the Great and Muhammed, the Iranian state derives legitimacy from Islamic and nationalist history.[27] In spite of this, Iranian history is marked by periods of unrest, disunity, political conflict, and anti-imperialism. The revolution established an explicitly Islamic state in the Middle East, posing an existential challenge to the Al Sa'ud's claims to legitimacy and dramatically reformulated relations across the region.

The position of Islam within the political, social, and theological fabric of both Saudi Arabia and Iran is easily seen, yet as Nazih Ayubi suggests, it is difficult to monopolize Islam as a consequence of its shared belief and the myriad (often competing) visions and interpretations.[28] Instead, efforts to do so can exacerbate division, creating schisms within the community in response to particular claims to leadership. This adherence to Islam and performative claims to legitimacy positions the two states within a shared normative environment that is underpinned by theological beliefs but shaped by contingent factors and opportunities. These efforts to position claims to Islamic legitimacy within the fabric of political projects has clear repercussions for the construction of foreign policy. Moreover, these efforts leave states vulnerable to regional trends, impacting the formation of foreign and domestic policy.

A shared normative environment provides both states with access to – and in some cases influence over – groups and people. Once again, however, presence within a shared normative environment does not provide sufficient conditions for an actor to exert power over another; instead, we must place such relationships within their context. This normative environment is further shaped by the spread of sect-based identities across the region that are also associated with political projects belonging to the same sect. This points to the normative position of the *diacritical–normative* debate initially presented by Rogers Brubaker and applied to the study of sectarianism by Morten Valbjorn.[29] Reflecting on the role of religious identity in constructing difference, Brubaker suggests that two contrasting positions exist. The diacritical understanding of religion views it purely in terms of drawing boundaries between those included and those excluded from communal groupings. The boundaries are 'culturally empty', shaped purely by political and socio-economic context and

[27] Farideh Farhi, 'Creating a National Identity amidst Contentious Politics in Contemporary Iran', in Homa Katouzian and Hossein Shahidi (eds.), *Iran in the 21st Century, Politics, Economics and Conflict* (Oxon: Routledge, 2008), p. 13.
[28] Nazih N. Ayubi, *Political Islam: Religion and Politics in the Arab World* (London: Routledge, 1991), p. 120.
[29] Rogers Brubaker, 'Religious Dimensions of Political Conflict and Violence', *Sociological Theory*, 33:1 (2015), 1–19.

can, in principle, be replaced by other types of markers. In contrast, the normative ordering points to the presence of 'cultural stuff' within religious identities, associated with a particular worldview. This view has implications for self-identity, relations with the other, threats, appropriate behaviour and, as a result, is fundamentally about the desirable order for society and contemporary life.

The presence of 'cultural stuff' facilitates the existence of transborder relationships between those groups sharing the same form of 'cultural stuff'. Existing and operating an environment dominated by shared identities, ethnicities, language, religion, history, and culture creates conditions whereby actors across state borders may find affinity with one another, perhaps even more so than with others in their own borders. Yet this can also create the simplistic perception – supported by a survey conducted by Pew – that Saudi Arabia is seen more favourably by Sunni Muslims[30] while Iran is seen more favourably by Shi'a Muslims.[31] To reduce cross-border relationships to shared faith misses the nuance articulated by Broubaker in his normative understanding, failing to take into account the importance of myriad other factors in the construction of identity and worldview.

While Saudi Arabia has been able to capitalize on economic largesse in pursuit of influence, Iranian influence across the Middle East is exerted through a number of different mechanisms including but not restricted to cultural capital, religious linkages, and financial support. Since the revolution, Iranian officials have developed the narrative of resistance which has helped it transcend sectarian divisions. The so-called axis of resistance is one example of such an alignment, drawing upon Iran's nonaligned status and long-standing resistance to Israel. Support for groups such as Hizbullah and Hamas has only served to increase this popularity.

Consideration of the narrative of resistance reveals a strong Shi'a undercurrent, drawing upon the narrative of the Battle of Karbala, during which time Hussein and his infant son were killed. As a consequence, ideas of guilt and martyrdom inherent within Shi'a thought facilitate the cultivation of a narrative that finds traction amongst Shi'a

---

[30] In Jordan, 78 per cent were in favour of Saudi Arabia while only 8 per cent held favourable views of Iran. In Palestine, this gap was closer, 51–34 per cent perhaps reflecting Iranian support to Palestinian groups and strong anti-Israeli rhetoric. See Pew Research, *Wide Variation in Favorability of Saudi Aabia and Iran in the Middle East*, www.pewresearch.org/fact-tank/2016/01/07/the-middle-easts-sectarian-divide-on-views-of-saudi-arabia-iran/ft_16-01-06_saudiarabia_iran/.

[31] Pew Research, *Lebanese Split along Religious Lines in Views on Saudi Arabia and Iran* (06.01.16), www.pewresearch.org/fact-tank/2016/01/07/the-middle-easts-sectarian-divide-on-views-of-saudi-arabia-iran/ft_15-01-06_saudiarabia_iran_lebanon/.

communities across the world. In contrast, Saudi influence is predominantly achieved through financial methods, although it is supported by the proliferation of Wahhabi clerics and money to support infrastructural development.

While material and ideational capabilities have allowed Saudi Arabia and Iran to increase their influence across the region, more work is required to understand the ways in which the two states exert influence across the region and the conditions that facilitate such engagement. It is here, using the work of Pierre Bourdieu, that I seek to contribute to debates on the rivalry between Saudi Arabia and Iran, on sectarianism, on regional politics, and on the nature of the state.

Foreign Policy: Vision and Process

To understand the nature of the rivalry between Riyadh and Tehran, it is important to look at the ways in which the foreign policies of Saudi Arabia and Iran play out over the Middle East. Here, it is necessary to look at both the construction of foreign policy and the broader visions that condition action and behaviour. As an emerging literature on the foreign policies of Saudi Arabia and Iran (especially post-2011) can attest, visions of regional order have a key role to play in understanding Riyadh and Tehran's actions across the Middle East, but these visions of order are also conditioned by developments within each state. Despite political life being dominated by the supreme leader and the king, individuals and factions can shape the manifestation and essence of these visions of order.

Efforts to understand foreign policy decision making in both Saudi Arabia and Iran are often limited by a lack of transparency over process and the absence of omniscience concerning perception and awareness of domestic and regional developments. As a result, efforts to understand policy making processes are often heuristic, building on incomplete information of process and evidence. That being said, there is a general awareness of structural process in both states. The following section sets out a broad overview of foreign policy making processes in both states. This does not claim to be a comprehensive analysis of foreign policy making, but rather an overview of key processes and the role of individuals within these structures.

In Iran, policy making emerges from the interplay between religious considerations and political constraints. The foreign policy arena offers insight into the ways in which formal and informal institutions and processes interact in Iran. As Jalil Roshandel notes, the making of foreign policy involves the interplay of key sources of power and authority, namely:

1. The constitution, which sets out key principles of foreign relations.
2. The religious leadership, notably supreme leader, Expediency Council, and the Assembly of Experts.
3. The government, notably president, Council of Ministers, and Supreme Council for National Security.
4. The consultative assembly (*majlis*).
5. The Ministry of Foreign Affairs, responsible for the dual function of making and implementing policy.[32]

Although the foreign policy making process has been a site of contestation between different groups, a broad foreign policy strategy can be identified. This strategy fuses religious identity and geopolitical aspirations, bringing together an ideological commitment to supporting the *mostaz'afin* (downtrodden) of the Muslim world and a broader aspiration to secure Iranian influence in the region. Across the history of the Islamic Republic the second component of this strategy differs in application (between revolutionary expansionism and a more pragmatic restraint). Central to much of this is the development of relations with non-state actors, many of whom represented marginalized Shi'a communities. Across the following decades, a vision of order forged by narratives of resistance, supporting the *mostaz'afin*, and increasing influence across the region shaped Tehran's foreign policy strategy.[33] At the heart of the strategy was Khomeini's vision of a world

sharply divided into two warring classes—*tabaqat*: the *mostaz'afin*—oppressed—against the *mostakberin*—oppressors; the *foqara*—poor—against the *sarvatmandan*—rich; the *mellat-e mostaz'af*—oppressed nation—against the *hokumat-e shaytan*—Satan's government ... In the 1970s, however, he used [the term *mostaz'afin*] in almost every single speech and proclamation to depict the angry poor, the 'exploited people,' and the 'downtrodden masses.' After the revolution, he gradually broadened the term to bring in the propertied middle class, which actively supported the new order.[34]

Khomeini's vision was enshrined in Article 3.16 of the Islamic Republic's constitution, which expressed a 'fraternal commitment to all Muslims, and unsparing support to the *mostaz'afin* of the world'.[35] This commitment included the provision of ideological support, economic

---

[32] Jalil Roshandel, 'Iran's Foreign and Security Policies: How the Decisionmaking Process Evolved', *Security Dialogue*, 31:1 (2000), 105–17.
[33] Interview with Iranian scholar and foreign policy analysts.
[34] Ervand Abrahamian, *Khomeinism, Essays on the Islamic Republic* (Berkley: University of California Press, 1993), pp. 26–7.
[35] Iranian Constitution, Article 3.16, www.alaviandassociates.com/documents/constitution .pdf.

largesse, military aid (both tactical and weaponry) and, in times of great need, direct military intervention. For many, this vision of order became known as the 'axis of resistance', a loose grouping of actors that included Iran, Syria, Hizbullah, Iraqi Popular Mobilization Forces (PMFs), the Houthis, and Hamas (a Sunni outlier in an otherwise Shi'a collective).[36]

Much like other areas of Iranian politics, the office of the supreme leader dominates foreign policy decision making processes, supported by the Iranian Revolutionary Guards Corps. As a result, ideological and ideational factors have played a key role in the foreign policy making process. This structural arrangement allows those with the ability to exert influence to shape the nature of foreign policy. For example, under Khomeini, Iranian foreign policy was driven by revolutionary zeal yet other seemingly more pragmatic currents took precedence after his death.

In Iran, tensions over the ideological direction of the Islamic Republic also manifested in its foreign policy trajectory. For example, advocates of the exporting of revolutionary goals such as Mohammad Montazeri support the establishment of groups such as Hizbullah in Lebanon and Hizbullah al-Hijaz in Saudi Arabia. Such exponents of the system of *veleyat-e faqih* featured prominently in the early years of the Islamic Republic, yet after Khomeini's death, the influence of this ideological camp waned. In the following decades, a more pragmatic turn took place, with foreign policy becoming more compliant with the salience of Westphalian sovereignty as an ordering principle. 'Ali Khamenei, Khomeini's successor as supreme leader, initially struggled to assert the same level of influence across the Islamic Republic, allowing other political figures such as 'Ali Akbar Hashemi Rafsanjani to assert dominance. Over time, however, Khamenei and his key allies wretched control back and began to shape foreign policy according to their vision. Although sharing many of the hallmarks of Khomeini's vision, Iran's foreign policy under Khamenei fuses revolutionary zeal with a degree of pragmatism in an effort to deter attacks and to counter any containment efforts.[37] This dual strategy – as proposed by Mohsen Milani – sits neatly together in a strategy that is simultaneously concerned with articulation of vision and, pragmatically, survival. In contrast, for detractors of the Islamic Republic, Tehran's engagement with non-state actors across the region is reflective of hegemonic intent. As Shahram A kbarzadeh, William Gourlay, and Anoushiravan Ehteshami note, while the development of what is termed a 'forward-defence' strategy offers practical benefits,

---

[36] El-Husseini, 'Hezbollah and the Axis of Refusal'.
[37] Mohsen Milani, 'Tehran's Take', *Foreign Affairs*, 88:4 (2009), 88.

shaping realities on the ground across the region, the strategy ultimately feeds suspicion and hostility.[38]

In contrast, Saudi Arabia's foreign policy strategy has largely been driven by a desire to maintain the status quo and ultimately the survival of dynastic monarchies and authoritarian regimes. This desire to maintain regional order cuts across the turbulent decades of the twentieth and twenty-first centuries, notably the pan-Arab movements, pan-Islamist movements, Iraqi regional aspirations, and the Arab Uprisings. Ultimately, as one Saudi analyst observes, the Kingdom has 'no interest in undermining the regional order'. In contrast, Iran seeks to 'bring down the ruling order in the region'.[39] Status quo aspirations do, occasionally, create contradictory situations, such as the events of 2006 and the Hizbullah–Israel war.

Much like Iran, the Kingdom's domestic makeup has historically had a significant impact on foreign policy approaches with claims to Islamic legitimacy occupying a central role in external engagement. The proselytizing of Wahhabi values both financially and ideationally was central in the Kingdom's foreign policy across the second half of the twentieth century, reflecting Saudi Arabia's growing influence on the world stage. Post-9/11, however, Saudi foreign policy strategy sought to move away from a reliance on Sunni Islamism in an attempt to distance itself from the violent extremism of groups such as al-Qaʿida. In the formative years of the twenty-first century, the rising threats of violent Islamism and Iran dominated Saudi foreign policy calculations, with battle hardened diplomats such as Prince Bandar bin Sultan and Prince Sultan occupying prominent roles in the Kingdom's foreign policy machinery.

The most dramatic change in the Kingdom's foreign policy activity and vision of regional order emerged as a consequence of the 'unprecedented transformation' of Saudi Arabia under King Salman and his son, Crown Prince Mohammed bin Salman (MbS).[40] While previously the Kingdom's politics was in some ways conditioned by a form of power sharing amongst senior princes who offered checks and balances, under 'the Salmans'[41] an even more centralized, decisive, yet risky decision making process has emerged. King Salman gained credibility in the

[38] Shahram Akbarzadeh, William Gourlay, and Anoushiravan Ehteshami, 'Iranian Proxies in the Syrian Conflict: Tehran's "Forward-Defence" in Action', *Journal of Strategic Studies* (2022), 1–24.
[39] Interview with Saudi analyst.
[40] F. Gregory Gause, 'Fresh Prince: The Schemes and Dreams of Saudi Arabia's Next King', *Foreign Affairs* (May/June 2018), www.foreignaffairs.com/articles/middle-east/2018-03-19/fresh-prince.
[41] Madawi al-Rasheed (ed.), *Salman's Legacy. The Dilemmas of a New Era in Saudi Arabia* (London: Hurst, 2018).

Kingdom for overseeing the dramatic transformation of Riyadh while governor (1963–2011). Having identified similar energy in MbS, the two worked to transform the Kingdom. In part, as earlier studies of Saudi Arabia's foreign policy have demonstrated, domestic developments play an important role in shaping the Kingdom's foreign policy,[42] yet the crown prince's bombastic nationalist and populist rhetoric at home exacerbated an already assertive foreign policy.[43]

At the heart of the crown prince's vision for regional politics was a desire to curtail the twin ambitions of Iran and Islamist movements. This vision manifested in action on 26 March 2015 with the decision to intervene in Yemen, a decision supported by the king albeit against the wishes of Mohammad bin Nayef (MbN), the minister of interior and erstwhile crown prince; clashes over Yemen between MbS and MbN ultimately led to the 'Royal Coup' of 22 June 2017 which saw hundreds of prominent Saudis detained in the Ritz Carlton hotel in Riyadh in what was framed as an anti-corruption crackdown.[44] In the years that followed, MbS played a leading role in the production of Saudi foreign policy, tacitly supported by the king who retains the final say on the Kingdom's foreign policy activities. This vision – one similar to that presented by Mohammad bin Zayed of the United Arab Emirates (UAE) – depicts Iran as a significant threat to the Kingdom and regional order through its relations with regional actors, while also framing Islamist groups as a substantial threat. In some cases, Islamist groups offered a means to counter Iranian gains (such as in Yemen and Bahrain), posing significant dilemmas to Riyadh and Abu Dhabi.

In Saudi Arabia, much like Iran, foreign policy decision making is dominated by those in positions of power. The distribution of political portfolios across the Saudi state is carefully designed to consolidate power, meaning that those loyal to the king are often put in prominent positions, including in the foreign and defence ministries. While individuals matter, in the Kingdom the king remains the final arbiter of power, with decision making highly centralized, reflecting the widespread dominance of the Saudi state by the Salmans.

---

[42] Joseph Kostiner (ed.), *Middle East Monarchies: The Challenge of Modernity* (London: Lynne Rienner, 2000); Fred Halliday, *The Middle East in International Relations: Power, Politics and Ideology* (Cambridge: Cambridge University Press, 2005).

[43] Fatiha Dazi-Héni, 'The New Saudi Leadership and Its Impact on Regional Policy', *The International Spectator*, 56:4 (2021), 49–65.

[44] Stephen Kalin, 'Saudi Arabia Winds Down 15-Month Anti-Corruption Campaign', Reuters (30.01.19), www.reuters.com/article/us-saudi-arrests-idUSKCN1PO2O1.

Despite the dominance of leaders, there is scope for individuals to exert agency in both states, albeit within structural confines set out by the supreme leader and king (and crown prince), who typically dominate such processes. Those individuals able to demonstrate particular skills or credentials have a role to play in making real the visions articulated by the leaders. This, of course, poses challenges to those wanting to gain a greater awareness of foreign policy making, limiting knowledge to a select few.

In Saudi Arabia, the royal court provides a structural framework within which key officials operate. A degree of consistency emerges here, with the court serving broadly guiding the foreign policy making process. Of course, the make-up of the court then becomes a site of contestation, with officials seeking to populate it with their own allies.[45] Similarly, in Iran, the supreme leader and religious leadership offers a structural framework guiding Iranian foreign policy. While there are substantial differences in the foreign policies of erstwhile presidents (best seen comparing the tenures of Ahmadinejad and Rouhani), the parameters of such processes are established by the supreme leader and the broader religious leadership.

Despite the existence of foreign policy visions of regional order, there are several moments of disjuncture in relations between the two states. While 1979 served as a key moment in reshaping regional relations, the rivalry between the Saudis and the Iranians can, as Chapter 2 demonstrates, be viewed across five periods. Understanding foreign policy dynamics across these periods is one of the aims of this book, demonstrating that while regional developments play a prominent role in the evolution of the rivalry, foreign policy goals and objectives are also conditioned by developments within states. Such observations reveal the importance of agency and the capacity of individuals to operate, albeit within parameters set out by the institutional fabric of the state. Significant changes in policy trajectory reveal the strength of actors and their domestic influence, alongside the weakness of structural factors. As a result, individuals may have a key role to play in the foreign policy making of both states allowing the cultivation of bilateral relationships with ministerial or official equivalents to supplement official relationships.

Overview

In seeking to understand the ways in which the rivalry between Saudi Arabia and Iran shapes local and regional politics across the Middle East,

---

[45] Neil Partrick, *Saudi Arabian Foreign Policy: Conflict and Cooperation* (London: I. B. Tauris, 2016). p. 12.

I cut across discussions of regional security and order, identity politics, sectarianism, sectarianization, relations between religion and politics, and the broader trajectory of political life in five case study countries. Focusing on the impact of Saudi and Iranian involvement in divided societies in Iraq, Bahrain, Lebanon, Syria and Yemen allows for detailed analysis of the ways in which regional rivalries between states adhering to different sectarian identities and possessing different visions of order shapes local politics, and vice versa. The case study countries have been selected as states regularly identified as arenas of competition between Saudi Arabia and Iran. Superficial analysis typically assumes that Saudi Arabia and Iran cultivate relationships with local actors on the basis of shared sectarian affinity, resulting in 'proxy relationships' between regional and domestic groups. Interrogating the ways in which regional actors shape local politics – and the ways in which local actors seek to derive support from regional powers – along with working towards a better understanding of the conditions that allow for particular forms of rivalry to emerge are the main aims of this book. In pursuit of this, I reflect on the following questions:

• What impact has the rivalry between Saudi Arabia and Iran had on states across the Middle East?
• How does the rivalry differ across time and space?
• What factors condition the interplay between domestic and regional politics?

In seeking to explore the rivalry and its impact on the region – and vice versa – I engage in a comparative approach along *most similar* lines. Each of the five case study states (Iraq, Bahrain, Lebanon, Syria, and Yemen) has been identified as an arena of rivalry between Saudi Arabia and Iran. Rejecting the label of proxy conflicts, I first seek to trace relations between Riyadh and Tehran and case study states before exploring how the organisation of political life in case study countries has provided opportunities for competition. In doing this, we are able to get a better sense of the impact of the rivalry upon different parts of the Middle East while also placing the conflict within the context of local struggles, bringing agency back into a discussion that is all too quick to deny it.

The book draws on interviews conducted over the past decade with officials, activists, scholars, and journalists, along with testimony gained during my time as academic advisor to the House of Lords International Relations Committee.[46] These interviews took place during time

---

[46] No material was used that was not officially disclosed as testimony in the final report.

spent across the region, over the phone, via email, and over skype and zoom. All names have been removed to preserve anonymity. As many who work on the Gulf will attest, access to information is often limited, particularly when dealing with questions of security and foreign policy; the adage 'those who know don't talk' certainly rings true here. At the time of writing, the two states were engaged in a complex and sensitive series of track II diplomatic efforts, once again limiting access. When I have been unable to get interview data, I have relied on material from WikiLeaks or public statements; in a number of cases, however, material is not in the public sphere. While not ideal, this data offers some eviden-tial support to aid the analysis.

The book is organized across seven chapters with five case study chapters that provide detailed reflections of the ways in which the rivalry plays out within the context of political life. The first chapter offers an introduction to the rivalry between the two states and the way in which IR approaches seek to approach the rivalry. In doing this, I focus on efforts to explain the rivalry in terms of religion, geopolitics, or a constructivist approach that focuses on an interplay between the two identities, contextualized across time and space. The chapter then reflects on the ways in which the rivalry plays out across regional politics, seeking to offer a new account of transnational relationships predicated on shared visions of order.

Chapter 2 traces the rivalry between the two states since the turn of the twentieth century until the present day. It breaks the rivalry down into five distinct periods which oscillate between times of hostility and burgeoning rapprochement. These dynamics shift according to a range of factors, notably the changing political structures in Iran after the revolution, or the shifting international currents during the War on Terror. In tracing this history, I seek to offer an overview of the rivalry which helps to map onto the case study chapters.

Chapter 3 explores the way in which the rivalry plays out in Iraq. It traces the history of Iraqi politics from the creation of the state in 1921 until the present day, reflecting on how the evolution of local politics creates moments of possibility for both Riyadh and Tehran to exert influence on Iraqi politics. Chapter 4 looks at the rivalry in Bahrain. While predominantly focusing on the post-independence period, it grounds this analysis in the emergence and development of political organization under the British protectorate. The chapter focuses on the ways in which regional developments have shaped Bahraini politics and how protest and the contestation of Al-Khalifa sovereign power is seen to create possibilities for regional manipulation.

Chapter 5 considers the rivalry in Lebanon, which serves as a different form of competition, predominantly playing out in political, economic, and communal ways. The organization of political life across Lebanon along sectarian lines has provided opportunities for external players to exert influence across the state. Chapter 6 looks at the rivalry in Syria. While a great deal of the chapter reflects on events after 2011, it also considers the historical role of Syria in the organization of regional politics and the numerous efforts from Riyadh and Tehran to exert influence over local politics. Chapter 7 explores the way in which the rivalry has shaped Yemeni politics. Much like the preceding chapter, a great deal of the focus is on contemporary events, reflecting on the extent to which tensions between Riyadh and Tehran – which manifest in broader geopolitical currents – have shaped local politics in Yemen.

Fundamentally, the book seeks to demonstrate that while the rivalry between Saudi Arabia and Iran plays a prominent role in the (re)construction of regional politics and security, the parameters of this competition are set not only in the corridors of power in Riyadh and Tehran, but also in contestation of political, social, economic, and religious fields found in states across the region.

1   States, Sects, and Order

According to an International Crisis Group list of '10 Conflicts to Watch in 2018', the rivalry between Saudi Arabia and Iran – with the added complexity of the United States – was ranked second after only the North Korean situation. In the report, the rivalry was 'enabled and exacerbated by three parallel developments: the consolidation of the authority of Mohammed bin Salman, Saudi Arabia's assertive Crown Prince; the Trump Administration's more aggressive strategy toward Iran; and the end of the Islamic State's territorial control in Iraq and Syria, which allows Washington and Riyadh to aim the spotlight more firmly on Iran'.[1] The report bemoaned the lack of diplomacy, concluding that 'the risk of an escalatory cycle is great', meaning that any move 'could trigger a broader confrontation'. In the years that followed, leaders in both states were able to navigate several incendiary moments to reach a point where diplomatic initiatives began to find traction, albeit with serious hurdles to be overcome.

At the turn of the millennium, such diplomatic moves appeared unlikely. Following the US-led invasion of Iraq in 2003, the rivalry between Saudi Arabia and Iran became increasingly influential in shaping the nature of Middle Eastern politics. For F. Gregory Gause, one of the foremost scholars of contemporary Gulf politics, opportunities emerging from the hollowing out of the Iraqi state post-2003 increased the intensity of the rivalry between the two states.[2] In the years that followed, and particularly after the Arab Uprisings of 2011, the fragmentation of states across the region provided additional opportunities for the two to continue their rivalry, with devastating repercussions in Syria, Bahrain, Yemen, and Lebanon. For Adel bin Ahmed al-Jubeir, the Saudi foreign minister and an outspoken critic of the Islamic Republic, Iran

[1] International Crisis Group, 10 Conflicts to Watch in 2018 (02.01.18), www.crisisgroup.org/global/10-conflicts-watch-2018.
[2] F. Gregory Gause, *Beyond Sectarianism: The New Middle East Cold War* (Washington DC: Brookings Doha Centre, 2014).

was responsible for regional upheaval and sought to 'obscure its dangerous sectarian and expansionist policies, as well as its support for terrorism, by levelling unsubstantiated charges against the Kingdom of Saudi Arabia'.[3] For al-Jubeir, Iran was 'the single-most-belligerent-actor in the region, and its actions display both a commitment to regional hegemony and a deeply held view that conciliatory gestures signal weakness either on Iran's part or on the part of its adversaries'.[4]

Underpinning al-Jubeir's remarks were concerns about Iran's ability to manipulate and mobilize groups across the region, with fears that Iran would exploit societal divisions in pursuit of greater influence on regional politics. These aspirations date back to the formation of the Islamic Republic, where clauses in the new constitution professed support to the 'downtrodden' of the Muslim world. In the years that followed, Iranian foreign policy included financial, ideological, and military support to Shi'a groups across the region, capitalizing on local divisions in pursuit of influence, much to the chagrin of many.

Such concerns were perhaps best characterized by King Abdullah of Jordan, who referred to a 'Shi'a Crescent'[5] suggesting that the region's Shi'a populations were fifth columns under the control of Tehran. Of course, such comments fail to take into account the complex nature of identity politics across many Middle Eastern states, where identities intersect with a range of issues. As a result, we must consider identities in terms of their specific context, a point stressed by Gause who – in lieu of a Shi'a Crescent – refers to an 'arc of state weakness'.[6] Although a number of states were affected by the Arab Uprisings, demographic factors in Bahrain, Syria, and Yemen meant that they presented ample opportunities for Riyadh and Tehran to exert influence. Moreover, in certain arenas competition was seen as an extension of a state's sovereign territory, perhaps best highlighted by the case of Bahrain and the claims made by both Riyadh and Tehran over the sovereignty of the archipelago. Given the range of factors at play within and across states, it is perhaps hardly surprising that the rivalry has played out in different ways across the region, capitalizing on the organization of life in particular spaces, along with the melange of identities interacting at those times.

This chapter seeks to ground what follows in debates within the IR of the Middle East, with a particular focus on how scholars have sought to

[3] Adel bin Ahmed al-Jubeir, 'Can Iran Change?', *New York Times* (19.01.16), www.nytimes.com/2016/01/19/opinion/saudi-arabia-can-iran-change.html?_r=2.
[4] Ibid.
[5] 'Hardball with Chris Matthews: King Abdullah II of Jordan', *NBC News* (07.12.08). Event occurs at 02:06. See also 06RIYADH3312, 'The Saudi Shi'a: Where do their loyalties lie?' (02.05.06), https://wikileaks.org/plusd/cables/06RIYADH3312_a.html.
[6] Gause, *Beyond Sectarianism*, p. 10.

characterize the rivalry between Riyadh and Tehran. In a departure from these debates, the chapter then seeks to understand Saudi and Iranian efforts to exert order over space. Lastly, it brings together geopolitical, ideational, and spatial analysis to set out a (comparative) framework to understand the impact of the rivalry between Saudi Arabia and Iran on local politics, and vice versa.

Understanding Regional Politics

Within the IR of the Middle East, conventional approaches tend to dominate efforts to understand regional politics given the prevalence of state actors, conflict, instability, and military spending. Although realism and constructivism have long occupied central roles in the way in which scholars seek to interrogate events across the region, alternative approaches located broadly within historical sociology and critical theory have also found vocal exponents in recent years.[7] At a regional level, a great deal of work focuses on the role of material and ideational factors in conditioning both behaviour and threat perception. More recently, scholarship has begun to offer a more nuanced reading of the development of alliances and relationships between state and non-state actors that reflects the complexity of regional politics.[8]

Across the past century, the development of political projects in the Middle East created conditions in which domestic and geopolitical forces routinely overlapped. This overlapping is seen in the competition over regional order in the 1950s and 1960s,[9] Iraq's invasion of Kuwait in 1990, the 2003 invasion of Iraq, the 2006 war between Hizbullah and Israel, and the Arab Uprisings that eviscerated regime–society relations across the region.[10] These conditions are pertinently acknowledged by Bassel Salloukh and Rex Brynen as 'a set of overlapping domestic and trans-regional challenges that collectively underscored the domestic challenges facing authoritarian regimes, and the explosion of transnational non-state actors'.[11] As Salloukh later argues, this premise also applies to the post-Arab Uprisings region,

---

[7] For example, see Ewan Stein, *International Relations in the Middle East* (Cambridge: Cambridge University Press, 2020).

[8] May Darwich, 'The Saudi Intervention in Yemen: Struggling for Status', *Insight Turkey* (Special issue: The Gulf on the Verge: Global Challenges and Regional Dynamics) 20:2 (2018), 125–42.

[9] Michael Barnett, *Dialogues in Arab Politics: Negotiations in Regional Order* (New York: Columbia, 1998).

[10] Mabon, *Houses Built on Sand.*

[11] Bassel F. Salloukh and Rex Brynen, '"Pondering Permeability": Some Introductory Explorations', in Bassel F. Salloukh and Rex Brynen (eds.), *Persistent Permeability: Regionalism, Localism and Globalization in the Middle East* (London: Ashgate, 2004), pp. 1–14.

where regional affairs can only be understood through exploring links between domestic contexts, transnational affinity, and state ambition.[12]

Scholars have typically sought to conceptualize the interaction of these factors through ideas of permeability, facilitated by (the legacy of) colonialism, state formation, Islam and its cultural impact and ethnolinguistic connections, creating a context wherein ideology and events reverberate across borders.[13] For Paul Noble, this situation resulted in a 'vast sound chamber in which information, ideas, and opinions have resonated with little regard for state frontiers'.[14] The complexity of this context is exacerbated by the forces of globalization, the cultivation of civil society, the evolution of ruling bargains, and an evolving regional security environment. In such conditions, relations between local, national, and regional identities become increasingly fluid, with repercussions felt across state borders. As Noble outlines, 'the Arab system resembled a set of interconnected organisms separated only by porous membranes or, alternatively, a large-scale domestic system divided into compartments of varying degrees of permeability. This gave rise to a transnational political process encompassing not only governments but also groups as well as individuals across the system.'[15]

While such conditions shape what Malcolm Kerr termed 'The Arab Cold War', which documented an ideological struggle for order in the Arab world, as many scholars are keen to stress, these systemic attributes remain central to understanding regional politics today, perhaps most notably in the rivalry between Riyadh and Tehran. Indeed, Salloukh and others argue that amidst a grand geopolitical struggle, referred to by Gause as a 'new Middle East Cold War',[16] the rivalry between Saudi Arabia and Iran plays out beyond the traditional Realist confrontations in a form of ideational competition that draws upon networks of transnational actors across space, leading to the formation of alliances between actors at both a regional and a local level.

In the broad Realist tradition, ideas of *bandwagoning*, *balancing*, *omnibalancing*, and *underbalancing* have all been used to explain the formation – or lack thereof – of alliances across the region.[17] Yet beyond this,

---

[12] Bassel F. Salloukh, 'The Arab Uprisings and the Geopolitics of the Middle East', *The International Spectator* 48:2 (2013), 32–46.

[13] Salloukh and Brynen, 'Pondering Permeability', p. 1.

[14] Paul Noble, 'The Arab System: Pressures, Constraints, and Opportunities', in Bahgat Korany and Ali E. Hillal Dessouki (eds.), *The Foreign Policies of Arab States* (Boulder: Westview, 1991), p. 57.

[15] Ibid.

[16] Gause, *Beyond Sectarianism*.

[17] Stephen R. David, 'Explaining Third World Alignments', *World Politics*, 43:2 (1991), 233–56; F. Gregory Gause, 'Ideologies, Alliances, and Underbalancing in the New

ideas found in constructivism[18] and political economy[19] highlight other variables that drive the creation of alliances, including ideology, identity, and economic capacity. Perhaps more persuasive is work by Curtis Ryan and May Darwich, arguing that regime survival is central to alliance building – which, as Ryan acknowledges, allows for theoretical eclecticism[20] – a position that is also endorsed by Darwich, through the concept of ontological security.[21] As Darwich argues, the creation of alliances – and, conversely, the identification of threats – stems from how – and when – regimes prioritize ideational or material factors.[22]

The rivalry between the two regional powers builds on a number of existing divisions, notably ethnicity, sect, vision of regional order, and relationship with external powers. From these divisions, relationships have been cultivated amongst actors who share similar outlooks to either Riyadh or Tehran. Often viewed as a sectarian struggle, such an approach hints at the formation of a 'Sunni bloc' to counter the 'Shi'a bloc', bringing together amongst others, Saudi Arabia, Qatar, and Turkey. Similarly, if viewed purely through the lens of power politics, a Saudi–Turkey–Israel alliance would have been forged to counter the threat posed by Iran. Yet fears about ideological acceptability amongst possible partners has prevented either from occurring, reflecting broader concerns about regional order which appear to trump alliance building.[23]

Middle East Cold War', in *International Relations Theory and a Changing Middle East*, Project on Middle East Political Science (POMEPS) Studies 16 (2015), 16–20; F. Gregory Gause, 'Balancing What? Threat Perceptions and Alliance Choice in the Gulf', *Security Studies* 13:2 (2003/4), 273–305; Mark L. Haas, 'Ideological Polarity and Balancing in Great Power Politics', *Security Studies* 23:4 (2014), 715–53; Richard Harknett and Jeffrey Vandenberg, 'Alignment Theory and Interrelated Threats: Jordan and the Persian Gulf Crisis', *Security Studies* 6:3 (1997), 112–53; Randall Schweller, 'Unanswered Threats: A Neoclassical Realist Theory of Underbalancing', *International Security* 29:2 (2004), 159–201; Stephen M. Walt, *The Origins of Alliances* (Ithaca: Cornell University Press, 1987).

[18] Barnett, *Dialogues in Arab Politics*.

[19] Jamie Allinson, *The Struggle for the State in Jordan: The Social Origins of Alliances in the Middle East* (London: I.B. Tauris, 2016).

[20] Curtis Ryan, 'Shifting Alliances and Shifting Theories in the Middle East', *Theorizing Structural Change in Shifting Global Politics and the Middle East*, Project on Middle East Political Science (POMEPS) Studies 34 (2019), 7–13; Curtis Ryan, *Inter-Arab Alliances: Regime Security and Jordanian Foreign Policy* (Gainesville: University Press of Florida, 2009); Curtis Ryan, 'Inter-Arab Relations and the Regional System', in Marc Lynch (ed.), *The Arab Uprisings Explained: New Contentious Politics in the Middle East* (New York: Columbia University Press, 2014), pp. 110–23; Curtis Ryan, 'The New Arab Cold War and the Struggle for Syria', *Middle East Report* 262 (2012), 28–31.

[21] Darwich, *Threats and Alliances in the Middle East: Saudi and Syrian Policies in a Turbulent Region* (Cambridge: Cambridge University Press, 2019).

[22] Ibid.

[23] See Haas, 'Ideological Polarity and Balancing', p. 729 and Gause, 'Ideologies, Alliances and Underbalancing'.

Although certainly compelling, focusing on alliances or threat perception only gets us so far. Given the complex jigsaw of relations cutting across an increasingly permeable region, it is important to focus on the broader processes at play. Indeed, while alliances are cultivated out of shared concerns or aspirations – often viewed in a direct causal chain – in the case of the rivalry between Saudi Arabia and Iran, the development of transnational relationships is often undertaken in an attempt to balance against actors who are aligned with others deemed unpalatable, albeit often under balancing with other obvious allies. Here we see regional powers seeking to cultivate a sense of order across the Middle East, working with local actors who share a vision of order that will curtail the influence of local groups, and their regional sponsors. These alliances may not necessarily be with state actors – as explored by Darwich – but rather cut across different levels of analysis, reflecting engagement, shared visions of order and security, and competition both regionally and locally.

Supplementing the cultivation of transnational relationships are broader efforts to frame the other as a threat to regional stability. Sharing many of the hallmarks of the securitization thesis presented by Barry Buzan, Ole Wæver, and Jaap de Wilde, discursive framings take place in a range of guises, yet typically involve the depiction of particular groups as existential threats to regional stability and security, in a number of cases even invoking calls for military action.[24] Perhaps the best examples of this include the narrative of the 'Shi'a Crescent' which framed Shi'a groups from Bahrain to Lebanon as fifth columnists doing the bidding of Iran, and calls from King Abdullah of Saudi Arabia to 'cut off the head of the snake', essentially demanding a US military strike against the Iranian regime.[25] Beyond the realm of high politics, such processes also took place locally through regime efforts to depict particular groups as subversive, a tactic ultimately designed to ensure survival and particular visions of order, locally, nationally, and internationally.

The permeability of local politics coupled with the regional ambitions of both states allows tensions between Saudi Arabia and Iran to interact with domestic and subregional rivalries. Through this process, relationships are formed between state and non-state actors which take on a range of different forms, from the transient to the formal, yet what is of note here – which pushes our enquiry beyond discussions of alliances – are the factors that condition the establishment of such relationships and

[24] Barry Buzan, Ole Waever and Jaap de Wilde, *Security: A New Framework for Analysis* (Boulder: Lynne Rienner, 1998).
[25] Simon Mabon, 'Muting the Trumpets of Sabotage: Saudi Arabia, the US and the Quest to Securitize Iran', *British Journal of Middle Eastern Studies* 45:5 (2018), 742–59.

their repercussions for local and regional politics. In this way, the character of these transnational – and sometimes transactional – relationships is contingent upon the context in which they take place, with state capacity, regional context, power relations, and content (ideological, economic, material) all shaping relationships. Of course, this results in different outcomes across space, which prompts questions as to why – and how – the repercussions of this rivalry differ across time and space.

As a consequence of this, and put in the language of IR theory, the rivalry between Saudi Arabia and Iran and its impact on the region is (re)shaped through a multi-level, multi-dimensional, and multi-causal set of interactions between a range of different actors operating across the region. Such behaviour is contingent not only upon the ways in which actors are able to operate within regional structures but also the extent to which external actors are able to exert influence over their domestic counterparts. The acknowledgment of the nexus of domestic and foreign politics has been the central concern of a number of scholars working on the region who seek to integrate domestic politics and IR, often drawing from comparative politics in the process.[26] As Noble suggests, this interaction of domestic and regional politics has had serious repercussions for regional politics. Indeed, the weakness of Arab states in their early years of independence – coupled with dramatic changes in societal organization – led to chronic instability in politics across the region, exacerbated by commonalities across state borders.[27] In the decades that followed, this pattern continued, with Arabism and Islamism offering ideational causes that could compete with states, leaving the residue for future transnational engagement.

Contesting Regional Order

Debate about regional order, both conceptually and when applied to the Middle East, has provoked a vast body of literature seeking to both theorize and map the concept and its implications.[28] While a thorough engagement with such debates is beyond the scope of this project, it is important to observe a number of key themes within discussion about

---

[26] See Bassel Salloukh, 'Regime Autonomy and Regional Foreign Policy Choices in the Middle East: A Theoretical Exploration', in Sallouk and Brynen (eds.), *Persistent Permeability*; James A. Caporaso, 'Across the Great Divide: Integrating Comparative and International Politics', *International Studies Quarterly* 41:4 (1997), 563–92.

[27] Paul C. Noble, 'The Arab System: Pressures, Constraints and Opportunities', in Bahgat Korany and Ali E. Hillal Dessouki (eds.), *The Foreign Policies of Arab States*, 2nd ed. (Boulder: Westview Press, 1991).

[28] In IR Theory, such questions are typically found in the English School, notably the work of Hedley Bull.

and competition over regional order, notably sovereignty, sectarianism, and transnational relationships.

Within the study of IR, order is typically understood as an arrangement between particular actors in a given time and space, conditioned by what Barry Buzan and George Lawson describe as a

smorgasbord of dynamics that are said to be disrupting the smooth functioning of international order: globalization, US militarism, dynamics of revolution and counter-revolution, finance capital, climate change, the rise of non-state actors, new security threats, the dislocating effects of information and communication technologies (ICTs), and more.[29]

Within this, more localized manifestations of competition play out. For some, such as Barry Buzan and Ole Wæver, order (or disorder) plays out within the context of 'regional security complexes', defined as a 'set of units whose major processes of securitisation, desecuritisation, or both are so interlinked that their security problems cannot reasonably be analysed or resolved apart from one another'.[30] Within this is a struggle over the ideational factors that shape the processes identified earlier. Here, as Barnett observes, dialogue and negotiation over meaning can also have material implications at local and regional levels. Indeed, importance should be given to the durable norms and institutions of regional politics which give structure to relations between actors across the region. Yet the struggle over norms, institutions and practice are themselves contested, which shapes the nature of regional order.

Over the course of the past century, order across the Middle East has been characterized – and determined by – a number of key factors shaping relations between rulers and ruled, notably around pan-Arabism, decolonization, Arab–Israeli wars, the British withdrawal, state consolidation, pan-Islamism, *Pax Americana*, global capitalism, non-state actors, debate over Political Islam(s), and state fragmentation.[31] These factors simultaneously impose a form of order, but are also contested as ordering principles amidst the range of different visions and interpretations at play, perhaps best seen in the pan-Arab and

---

[29] Barry Buzan and George Lawson, 'Capitalism and the Emergent World Order', *International Affairs* 90:1 (2014), p. 71.

[30] Barry Buzan and Ole Wæver, *Regions and Powers* (Cambridge: Cambridge University Press, 2003), p. 44.

[31] For example, see Malcolm Kerr, *The Arab Cold War 1958–1964: A Study of Ideology in Politics* (London: Royal Institute of International Affairs/Oxford University Press, 1965); Fred Halliday, *The Middle East in International Relations: Power, Politics and Ideology* (Cambridge: Cambridge University Press, 2005); Raymond Hinnebusch, *The International Politics of the Middle East* (Manchester: Manchester University Press, 2003); amongst others.

pan-Islamist visions of order. Conversely, dissent from articulations of order and the emerging fractures between rulers and ruled can increase permeability and, more broadly, instability. After the 2003 invasion of Iraq, sectarian difference – previously taboo within the realm of foreign policy – has become increasingly prevalent in regional politics.[32] While couched in the language of communal difference, understanding regional order after 2003 is perhaps better seen as the constellation of a number of parabolic and intersecting forces, of which sectarian difference is but one visible manifestation. Indeed, this constellation brings together regime insecurity, changing dynamics of polarity, precarious relations between rulers and ruled, state fragmentation, economic challenges, and increasing xenophobia, resulting in increased penetration of political projects.

While sovereignty was previously observed as an ordering principle amongst states in the Middle East,[33] the fragmentation of state projects posed serious questions to both regional order and intellectual engagement with the region. This weakening of state structures is often believed to prompt communities to turn elsewhere for protection, either amongst other substate actors or to more powerful regional patrons. These relationships are often propped up by shared ideational factors, or visions for regional order, with sectarian and ethnic identities playing an important role amidst the contestation and fragmentation of political organization. In societies shaped by communal division, the presence of norms which cut across state borders can bring about new forms of rivalry through increased penetration and permeability.

In such contexts, the interaction of domestic and regional politics can increase, particularly given the cross-border nature of sectarian identities. It is in these conditions that Saudi Arabia and Iran seek to exert influence, occupying the leading roles in a broader regional struggle for influence and power, using ideational and material capacities as a means of cultivating relationships in pursuit of influence and order, beyond traditional power politics.[34] Indeed, as Gause observes, regional instability is more about 'a struggle over the direction of the Middle East's domestic politics than purely a military contest'.[35]

---

[32] I do not seek to position sectarian difference as a driving force, but rather, the construction of division plays a prominent role in shaping regional affairs.

[33] F. Gregory Gause, 'Sovereignty, Statecraft, and Stability in the Middle East', *Journal of International Affairs* 45 (Winter 1992), 441–67.

[34] Lawrence Rubin, *Islam in the Balance: Ideational Threats in Arab Politics* (Stanford: Stanford Security Studies, 2014).

[35] Gause, *Beyond Sectarianism*, p. 3.

Amidst this regional struggle, Gause identifies similar conditions to those documented in Kerr's 'Arab Cold War', albeit transcending the Arab world to draw in Iran, Turkey, and Israel, yet focusing on the ability to shape domestic affairs across the region.[36] Here we see simultaneously movement *between* and *across* levels of analysis, bringing together local contexts with regional forces, resulting in a plethora of interactions amidst a quest for legitimacy, power, and order.[37] Of course, in raising the idea of *order*, one raises questions about both the *concept* of *order* and the *underlying principles* of order. As a consequence, material and ideational factors that cross borders and shape the ordering of life take on increasing significance. With the contestation of political projects, communal identities took on increasing salience.

The acknowledgement of sectarian difference as a key feature of regional order post-2003 brings with it a focus on other aspects of this constellation, perhaps most obviously seen in the challenge posed to states by transnational movements. State fragmentation exacerbates domestic and regional instability, leaving individuals facing precarious political, social, economic, or legal conditions. Indeed, the deployment of sectarian identity politics has facilitated transnational mobilization by state and non-state actors alike, providing ample opportunities for intervention and manipulation. While this constellation has predominantly resulted in geopolitically charged sectarian tensions, both domestically and regionally, the shifting dynamics of polarity have also resulted in intra-sectarian tensions, most notably seen in tensions between Saudi Arabia, Qatar, and Turkey which have played into ideas of 'underbalancing', a point reinforced by Gause in 2017.[38] Here, the failure to create a 'grand Sunni alliance' to tackle the perceived threat from Iran serves as a strong rebuttal to those seeking to reduce the struggle over regional order to sectarian difference.

Sectarian identities offer one such form of ordering given the salience of sects within political identity, particularly as these identities may offer an alternative to national identity. Much has been written on the emergence of sectarian difference in the Middle East, typically grouped into three camps.[39] The first, the primordialist, privileges sectarian difference above

[36] Ibid., pp. 3–4.
[37] Bulent Aras and Emirhan Yorulmazlar, 'Mideast Geopolitics: The Struggle for a New Order', *Middle East Policy* 24:2 (2017), 57–69
[38] F. Gregory Gause, 'Ideologies, Alignments, and Underbalancing in the New Middle East Cold War', *PS: Political Science & Politics* 50:3 (2017), 672–5.
[39] For more on this, see Morten Valbjørn, 'Beyond the beyond(s): On the (Many) Third Way(s) beyond Primordialism and Instrumentalism in the Study of Sectarianism', *Nations and Nationalism* 26:1 (2020), 91–107.

all other explanations, reducing political, ideological, socio-economic, ethnic, or geographic difference to a simplistic binary, in what is commonly referred to as a consequence of 'ancient hatreds'. This essentialist account of sectarian difference presents an *ahistoric* account of religious tensions dating back to the seventh century, resulting in static identities reproduced almost biologically over generations, with little scope for change. Deeply problematic, this essentialist view of sectarian difference is fundamentally Orientalist.[40] The second camp is the instrumentalist, who suggests that sectarian identities are malleable, amorphous entities that are subjected to the manipulation of 'entrepreneurs' acting in pursuit of their own interests. For the instrumentalist, identities are transient and products of their environment. Put another way, for the instrumentalist, sectarianism is more about politics than piety. The third approach is the constructivist, which holds that religion (and other identity markers) matter, but they are socially constructed, contingent upon the complexities of time and space.

Fundamentally, it is context that helps determine the salience of sectarian identities, notably state politics and regional affairs. Central to this context are concerns about regime security and the impact of transnational ideology on domestic politics, often resulting in transient or transactional relationships predicated on shared identities, ideologies, or visions of order, spanning across regions and levels of analysis. In many cases, political instability is also the epicentre of the interaction of transnational identities, be they sectarian, ethnic, ideological, or political. These epicentres are also often sites where regional powers are involved in pursuit of foreign policy goals, resulting in the cultivation of relationships which may (not) result in formal alliances, predicated on a combination of material and ideational factors and underpinned by visions of order.

Acknowledging this, the rivalry between Saudi Arabia and Iran plays out in different ways across time and space, oscillating between periods of outright hostility and apparent rapprochement as we shall see in Chapter 2. Within this broader rivalry, however, are complex and relational interactions between regional and domestic actors which cut across identity markers, ideology, and material interests. Put another way, the dominance of ideational forces allows actors to position themselves within broader geopolitical currents and to capitalize on political uncertainty by demonstrating their ideational credentials.[41] Of course,

---

[40] See the work of Vali Nasr for primordial accounts of sectarian difference.

[41] Bassel Salloukh, 'Overlapping Contests and Middle East International Relations: The Return of the Weak Arab State', *PS: Political Science & Politics* 50:3 (2017), 660–3.

the resonance of ideational forces means that they can also be used by actors in an instrumental manner, often to devastating effect.[42]

Consideration of the characteristics of a rivalry typically requires reflecting on a number of areas, including the way in which power operates between the actors involved; the history behind tensions; the political, social, and economic factors that drive tensions; understandings of security; and the role of other actors in exacerbating or mitigating tensions. This is particularly evident in discussion about rivalries across the Middle East, yet little attention has been paid to the spaces in which rivalries play out. In part, this perhaps reflects the dominance of the Westphalian model of political organization which privileges states, but when spaces of rivalry are discussed, they are typically referred to as zones of 'proxy conflict', removing local agency and locating events within the context of broader regional currents.

Framing regional developments through the lens of proxy conflicts is deeply problematic. Although initially seductive, this approach falsely depicts conflict as devoid of direct external intervention and purely as a result of internal conflict, albeit with external support. Closer examination of the cases of Syria, Yemen, and Iraq paint different pictures, with direct military engagement from either Saudi Arabia or Iran, in contravention of the main premise of the proxy wars thesis. Instead, complex transnational relationships are in operation that condition particular types of action contingent upon context specific factors. These relationships vary in their nature, from formal alliances to more transient and amorphous relationships underpinned by shared visions of regional order but conditioned by the contingencies of local politics.

By their very nature, transnational identities transcend state borders and play out in different ways contingent upon the complexities of time and space. Understanding the way in which these identities operate – and are mobilized – has been the subject of serious discussion, particularly in the years after the Arab Uprisings, amidst a collapsing distinction between internal and external.[43] Such exploration typically focuses upon the ways in which regional powers have mobilized and deployed (sectarian) identity and ideology across the region, often akin to traditional patron–client relationships, yet such an approach belies the complexity of these relationships.

[42] Christopher Phillips and Morten Valbjørn, '"What Is in a Name?": The Role of (Different) Identities in the Multiple Proxy Wars in Syria', *Small Wars & Insurgencies*, 29:3 (2018), 414–33.
[43] Mabon, *Houses Built on Sand.*

Those who derive legitimacy through recourse to Islamic rhetoric also position themselves within a normative environment that is shaped through the interactions of its constituent parts. For those states invested in both, geopolitical and religious environments operate in a dialectic manner, shaping domestic and foreign policy. In addition to efforts to exert influence and derive legitimacy from the Islamic world, Saudi Arabia and Iran have attempted to exert geopolitical influence across the Middle East. While Realist approaches to exploring the Middle East have tended to focus upon the latter while ignoring the former, as we have seen, this is both analytically problematic and empirically difficult. Instead, the prominence of Islam within the fabric of both states merges theological and political questions while being underpinned by myriad conceptions of security. Moving beyond the traditional statist approach allows us to shift the referent object of security to consider the interaction of politics, religion, and regional security.

This is commonly understood as the sectarianization of geopolitics where geopolitical agendas were undertaken under the veneer of sectarian difference, capitalizing on and manipulating schisms across the Middle East for political ends. In the aftermath of the Arab Uprisings, schisms between regimes and societies emerged that created opportunities for external actors to exert influence across the region, capitalizing on local instability in an effort to increase their influence. Conversely, precarious domestic conditions often prompted local groups to turn to external sponsors in pursuit of material resources deemed essential to meet their needs. In such conditions, local and regional politics began to interact in a parabolic cycle, facilitated by material and ideational capabilities, and exacerbated by local and regional context.

While it is easy to propagate narratives that members of *sect X* find support from *external sponsor Y* as a consequence of membership of particular sectarian communities the reality is far murkier. Although there is undeniably a degree of sectarian affinity, there also remains the observation that religion provides little more than a 'fig leaf' for other interests by groups espousing shared ideology in pursuit of material support.[44] Yet much like debates in sectarianism, it is important not to reduce such relations to pure instrumentalist views. Instead, as Staci Strobl has observed, sectarian identities have a 'stickiness' that allows them to resonate and to gain traction.[45] Moreover, while sectarian identities are undeniably important, other factors shape the construction of

[44] Phillips and Valbjørn, "'What's Is in a Name?'".
[45] Staci Strobl, *Sectarian Order in Bahrain: The Social and Colonial Origins of Criminal Justice* (London: Lexington Books, 2018), p. 117.

relationships and alliances, as seen in the case of Iranian support for Hamas. Here, visions of order comprising sectarian affinity, ideological outlook, political context, economic factors, and social capital are fundamental in understanding the cultivation of relationships, conditioned – and facilitated – by spatial context.

The Contingencies of Space

The complexity of human life and the interaction of myriad features of contemporary society poses problems for singular disciplinary approaches. The study of the rivalry between Saudi Arabia and Iran, for example, is one such case that is predominantly – although not exclusively – grounded within IR, in spite of a range of other factors that could facilitate more nuanced analysis. Those seeking to understand the Middle East have drawn from a range of disparate (sub)disciplines including IR, political science, geography, anthropology, sociology, law, and urban studies to name but a few. In a number of cases, disciplinary borders are eroded, leading to important scholarly work that is both multi- and inter-disciplinary. Yet much like the field of IR more broadly Middle Eastern IR has often struggled to move beyond what Justin Rosenberg has termed the 'prison of Political Science'.[46]

What remains counter-intuitively absent in contemporary debates on both regional politics and sectarianism is an exploration of the ways in which geopolitical rivalries play out in and across space, along with reflection of how local actors shape broader rivalries. Such an approach is essential in terms of reflecting on both the nature of regional politics and the forces that condition the behaviour of local, national, and regional actors, a point which becomes increasingly salient given the importance of state fragmentation in geopolitical rivalries.

Although largely equipped to deal with a plethora of contemporary issues, IR approaches typically struggle to address space and the causal relationships between different actors that play out across both time and space. For John Agnew, a leading geographer, the supremacy of the national and international in contemporary politics reveals the dominant perception of the nature of power, which stems from the ability to make others do the will of the state as a consequence of a range of different factors. It also emerges from the dominance of the nation-state as the traditional unit of analysis, both politically and intellectually.[47] As Agnew has elsewhere

---

[46] Justin Rosenberg, 'International Relations in the Prison of Political Science', *International Relations* 30:2 (2016), 127–53.

[47] John Agnew, 'Disputing the Nature of the International', *Geographische Zeitschrift* 89 (2001), 1–16.

argued, a fundamental problem with political science and IR is the unchallenged acceptance of existing territorial borders, in what he termed the 'territorial trap'. Predicated on three assumptions – (a) states are fixed units of sovereign space, (b) a distinction can be drawn between domestic and foreign affairs, and (c) states are containers for societies – Agnew's argument articulates fundamental flaws in approaches to international politics that represent modern states as exclusively territorial entities.[48]

Traditional approaches to IR hold the state to be central to their inquiry, as territorially grounded and largely fixed, allowing for a clear separation of domestic and international but, as Daniel Neep articulates – with a nod to John Agnew – in falling into the territorial trap, these approaches 'lock us into a world vision that unintentionally reflects a partial and incomplete perspective on the nature of the state within that world'.[49] Indeed, those focusing on state sovereignty are (perhaps implicitly) engaging in questions about security and territory.[50] More recently, states have been challenged by the complexity of contemporary life:

Regions, religions and ethnicity everywhere challenge territorial states as the loci of political identity. In many countries social classes and established ideologies appealing to 'class interest' have lost their value as sources of identity. Increasingly, the links between the places of everyday life in which political commitments are forged, and the territorial states that have structured them and channelled political activities, are under stress. New loyalties everywhere undermine state political monopolies.[51]

This is particularly true for the contemporary Middle East where cross-border interactions in all their forms take place in a context where ideational forces have regularly circumvented loyalties to states and given rise to efforts to contest the ordering of political life.[52]

In spite of this, as John O'Loughlin asserts, the study of IR typically takes place amidst a geographic vacuum where spatial context is often ignored. This, for O'Loughlin, typifies a broader schism between IR and Political Science on the one hand and Geography on the other, charging scholars with 'talking past each other'.[53] O'Loughlin's calls were echoed

---

[48] John Agnew, 'The Territorial Trap', *Review of International Political Economy* 1:1 (1994), 53–80.
[49] Daniel Neep, 'State-Space beyond Territory: Wormholes, Gravitational Fields, and Entanglement', *Journal of Historical Sociology* 30:3 (2017), 479.
[50] John Agnew and Stuart Corbridge, *Mastering Space: Hegemony, Territory and International Political Economy* (London: Routledge, 1995), p. 85.
[51] Ibid., p. 97.
[52] See Barnett, *Dialogues in Arab Politics*, and Simon Mabon, 'The World Is a Garden: Nomos, Sovereignty and the (Contested) Ordering of Life', *Review of International Studies* 45:5 (2019), 870–90.
[53] John O'Loughlin, 'Geography as Space and Geography as Place: The Divide between Political Science and Political Geography Continues', *Geopolitics* 5:3 (2000), 126–37.

by geographers such as Simon Dalby who point out the convergence of questions asked by scholars working in Political Geography and IR.[54]

In a special issue of the journal *Geopolitics*, Virginie Mamadouh and Gertjan Dijkink explore the reasons for the tension between IR and Geography (and Geopolitics as a peripheral subdiscipline in particular), suggesting that perhaps the most compelling reason for this disjuncture emerges from theoretical and ontological tensions. In mainstream IR, discussion forms around debate between realism, liberalism and constructivism, yet geographical approaches tend not to match their IR counterparts.[55] Moreover, while IR and geography share a common object of study – world politics – this focus prompts a range of different questions, methodologies, and subjects.[56] These tensions serve to deepen disciplinary schisms between IR and Geography, in spite of shared aspirations and starting points.[57] Indeed, as Harvey Starr acknowledges in the opening line of *On Geopolitics: Spaces and Places*, IR as a discipline – along with international and world politics – 'sits at the convergence of human inquiry that crosses both time and space'.[58] Understanding this convergence is of paramount importance to our task in this book.

Another key tension concerns the importance of context. For Political Geographers, context and contextual elements play an important role in the actions of individuals. In contrast, for scholars of IR – perhaps Political Science more specifically – the absence of context in analysis is lamentable.[59] It is easy to see why those IR scholars concerned with the ordering of international politics and the international system in particular would reject these assertions. Yet one of the key contributions

Writing nineteen years later, O'Loughlin suggests that the gap between disciplines of Political Science and Political Geography are widening. Moreover, in the same piece, O'Loughlin states that 'the main reason why papers from political scientists did not get accepted in Political Geography during my tenure as editor was due to their narrow and outmoded conception of space'.

[54] Simon Dalby, 'Crossing Disciplinary Boundaries: Political Geography and International Relations after the Cold War', in Eleonore Kofman and Gillian Youngs (eds.), *Globalization: Theory and Practice* (London and New York: Pinter, 1996). See also Burak Kadercan, 'Triangulating Territory: A Case for Pragmatic Interaction between Political Science, Political Geography and Critical IR', *International Theory* 17:1 (2015), 125–61.

[55] Virginie Mamadouh and Gertjan Dijkink, 'Geopolitics, International Relations and Political Geography: The Politics of Geopolitical Discourse', *Geopolitics* 11:3 (2006), 349–66.

[56] K. Dodds, *Global Geopolitics: A Critical Introduction* (Harlow: Pearson Education 2005).

[57] It should be noted that what collaboration exists does so from critical positions.

[58] Harvey Starr, 'On Geopolitics: Spaces and Places', International Studies Quarterly 57:3 (2013), 433.

[59] John O'Loughlin, 'Responses: Geography as Space and Geography as Place: The Divide between Political Science and Political Geography Continues', *Geopolitics* 5:3 (2000), 126–37.

made by geographers to IR is to contest the 'taken-for-granted nature of the territorial state and stable boundaries', a point that quickly emerges when considering the way in which ideas of the state and territory serve as 'natural containers' of political community.[60] It is here that geographers can help IR by focusing analysis on the complexity of flows and fractures that transcend state borders.

Yet these flows and fractures do not occur in a vacuum; rather, as O'Loughlin and Dalby stress, context is key. Environmental considerations play a prominent role in shaping the capacity of an actor to exert agency, contingent upon the world around them. Of course, environments differ depending on the actor, from the individual to the state, yet each actor operates within and across space. Geographers such as Edward Soja, part of a postmodern turn, sought to re-theorize spatiality, emerging from 'a reconstructed *ontology* of human society'.[61] In pursuit of this, Soja re-imagines relations between the social and the spatial, bringing agency to the fore in a move that demonstrates the fluid nature of space, contingent upon agency and social relations.[62]

Similar points are made by Doreen Massey whose seminal work *For Space* sets out three propositions for those seeking to undertake a spatial analysis. First, space is shaped through the interaction of myriad forces and actors, from the hegemonic global forces of contemporary capitalism to the 'intimately tiny'. Second, space is a sphere of possibility, multiplicity, and heterogeneity. Third, space is constantly (re)shaped.[63] Writing with John Allen and Allan Cochrane, Massey notes that space – along with place and region – is 'constituted out of spatialized social relations – and narratives about them – which not only lay down ever-new regional geographies, but also work to reshape social and cultural identities and how they are represented'.[64]

From this, it is easy to see how space is shaped in our inquiry through the interaction of regional and international forces with the intimately tiny machinations of local politics.[65] Here, the rivalry between Saudi

---

[60] Dalby, 'Crossing Disciplinary Boundaries', pp. 35–6.

[61] Edward W. Soja, 'Regions in Context: Spatiality, Periodicity, and the Historical Geography of the Regional Question', *Environment and Planning D: Society and Space* 3 (1985), 176 (italics in original).

[62] Ibid. See also Edward W. Soja, *Postmodern Geographies: The Reassertion of Space in Critical Theory* (London: Verso: 1980); Edward W. Soja, 'The Socio-Spatial Dialectic', *Annals of the Association of American Geographers* 70 (1980), 207–25.

[63] Doreen Massey, *For Space* (London: Sage, 2005), pp. 9–11.

[64] John Allen, Doreen Massey, and Allan Cochrane, *Rethinking the Region* (London: Routledge, 1998), pp. 1–2.

[65] In what follows, I do not seek to offer an explicitly spatial analysis of the rivalry between Saudi Arabia and Iran but rather to draw on ideas stemming from political geographers

Arabia and Iran plays out in myriad ways across different spaces as a consequence of the interaction between (often) unique intimately tiny forces and their relation to – and often with – Riyadh and Tehran. For example, competition in Beirut can draw in both Saudi Arabia and Iran due to relations with local political actors. Yet the relations between these political actors and local constituencies can differ before considering the ways in which local communities relate to regional powers. Of course, this differs across time and space as a consequence of the ways in which local politics interacts with regional forces, along with the ways in which regional powers perceive these spaces. For example, Bahrain and Yemen are of paramount importance for Saudi Arabia as a consequence of their geographical position, leading to a particular set of strategies that interact with local contexts. Yet questions remain about the ways in which space is shaped by actors seeking to exert influence, and here the work of the French social theorist Pierre Bourdieu aids our project.

(Transnational) Fields and Capital

While the state has typically been viewed as the dominant unit of political organization in the IR of the Middle East, responsible for regulating space within its (territorial) borders, increasing permeability has challenged Weberian ideas of a *given territory*.[66] Yet we should not view territory as an ontologically prior-bounded space waiting to be controlled. Instead, it is historically contingent, a product of its environment and the organization and categorization of forces that impose particular logics, technologies, and forms of expertise.[67] Put simply, the modern state does not simply acquire territory but rather produces what we recognize as territory. From this, some historical sociologists reject the premise that the state operates as the 'natural unit' of analysis in the social sciences. Indeed, the state itself becomes an area of competition, a site of contestation.

Moreover, as a nascent body of literature observes, the fragmentation of the (neo)Weberian model has allowed actors to occupy *hybrid* positions between states and non-state actors. Here, groups such as

---

to understand the nature of flows and fractures of transnational politics with a focus on how ideas and capital resonate across state borders. In doing this, I create opportunities to better understand the ways in which local and external actors interact, while also seeking to offer greater analytical clarity to ideas of state weakness which, as Gause and others have identified, are often heralded as central features of the rivalry between Saudi Arabia and Iran.

[66] Neep, 'State-Space beyond Territory'.

[67] Henri Lefebvre, *The Production of Space* (Oxford: Blackwell, 1991), pp. 9–30.

Hizbullah, Hamas, al-Hashd al-Sha'bi – PMFs – are positioned between the formal institutional structures of the state and of non-state actors, occupying a hybrid role. Accepting this allows us to better understand relationships between different actors, both endogenous and exogenous. Thus, while states seek to regulate their territory, other efforts to impose logics and order over space stemming from ideational or material positions of power creates conditions of permeability and contestation, conditioned by the relational interplay of actors involved.

Social theorists have extensively documented the widespread nature of contestation and the processes through which spatial transformations occur, including administrative, legal, economic, technological, and economic practices – manifesting in the emergence of biopolitical technologies of control – and that the development of the state and its infrastructure serves to re-order society into its own categories of knowledge.[68] What is at stake for our inquiry is the extent to which these processes are contested, positioned within competing claims for control which often bypass the formal institutions and infrastructure of the state in an effort to create new spatial orderings. These spaces may be territorial or non-territorial, defined in terms of ideas, norms and transactions that are themselves underpinned by formal or informal structures. Yet as we have begun to see, political organization, community membership, and the sovereign state are not necessarily coeval.

One of the more persuasive approaches to understanding the operation of political power within the state is put forward by Pierre Bourdieu, a French social theorist, who offers an approach that gives credence to both structure and agency. While many across Iraq, Lebanon, and Yemen may empathize with the claim *ma fi dawla* ('there is no state'), the approach put forward by Bourdieu allows us to move beyond the more formal institutions advocated by the (neo)Weberian model of statehood and move towards a relational struggle over both formal and informal modes of power and their resonance.

Combining ideas of field, habitus, forms of capital, and symbolic violence, Bourdieu provides a compelling account of interactions which shape the construction and operation of power, the state, and social order. Such a combination is necessary, for Bourdieu, given that the endeavour of thinking about the state risks being consumed by existing thoughts of the state or, put another way, 'applying to the state categories of thought produced and guaranteed by the state and hence to misrecognize its most

---

[68] See the work of Pierre Bourdieu, Michel Foucault, Achille Mbembe, Giorgio Agamben, Antonio Gramsci, and Hannah Arendt amongst others. SEPAD has produced a report on social theory in the Middle East, available at www.sepad.org.uk.

profound truth'.[69] To circumvent such challenges, Bourdieu proposes an approach that espouses the need for greater knowledge of the social world and the ways in which this knowledge is used to order social life.

In pursuit of this, Bourdieu adds the category of symbolic violence to Max Weber's famous formula of a state being defined as that which successfully claims the monopoly of the legitimate use of physical force over a clearly defined territory. This addition is fundamental in that it points to the ability of a state to incarnate itself both objectively and subjectively in institutional structures and mental structures, respectively. To reach this point, the state is the culmination of '*a process of concentration of different species of capital*'.[70] Such an acknowledgement demonstrates an awareness of the different forms of capital – and their competition – along with their reproduction. As such, Bourdieu's approach creates an environment to bring together different forms of interests and their competition for domination.

Competition over different forms of capital takes place within fields which, for Bourdieu, are 'relatively autonomous social microcosms'.[71] For Bourdieu, the field is fundamentally relational, formed through the interaction of objective relations between positions which are

objectively defined, in their existence and in the determinations they impose upon their occupants, agents or institutions, by their present and potential situation (*situs*) in the structure of the distribution of species of power (or capital) whose possession commands access to the specific profits that are at stake in the field, as well as by their objective relation to other positions[72]

The field is a space of relational forces, both active and potential. Beyond this it is also a site of struggle, as relational positions seek to preserve or transform the configuration of positions. Although interrelated – or 'homologuous' – fields are differentiated from one another by the nature of competitors and the struggle that follows; it is through this competition that the boundaries of the field are defined. It must be stressed, however, that the relational dimension of fields allows for an analysis that is fluid and evolves over time. Acknowledging this point, Emirbayer and Johnson argue that a field may also be understood as 'a temporary state of power relations within what is an ongoing struggle for domination'.[73]

---

[69] Pierre Bourdieu, 'Rethinking the State: Genesis and Structure of the Bureaucratic Field', *Sociological Theory* 12:1 (1994), 1. In addition, SEPAD's report on applied social theory may also be of interest.

[70] Ibid., 4, italics in original.

[71] Pierre Bourdieu and Loïc J. D. Wacquant, *An Invitation to Reflexive Sociology* (Cambridge: Polity Press, 1992), p. 97.

[72] Ibid., p. 97.

[73] M. Emirbayer and V. Johnson, 'Bourdieu and Organizational Analysis', *Theoretical Sociology* 37 (2008), 6.

As Toby Dodge acknowledges, critically reflecting on the political field is a task that must not be done *a historically* for fear of reifying competing identities operating within these fields; indeed, principles of vision and division evolve over time, shaped by the complexities of local contexts. For Dodge

Pierre Bourdieu's key analytical concepts of 'field' and different forms of 'capital' allow for this type of examination, stressing the political field's fluid and competitive nature. His relational sociology draws attention to the mutually defining competition between those attempting to impose different conceptions of Iraq's political identity. His focus on symbolic violence stresses the fact that this competition is ultimately about a struggle to impose one dominant vision of what Iraq is and who Iraqis are on the whole political field.[74]

As Dodge argues, the power of Bourdieu's approach is seen when exploring how 'competition for dominance within a field shape both the nature of that field and the value of the capital being fought over'. Thus, Bourdieu proposes a relational approach in which actors – individuals, groups, and states – are 'interdependent units involved in competitive struggles'.[75]

The state is a product of the interaction of these various fields, albeit dominated by the political field, where the struggle to amass symbolic capital and impose visions of order shape the nature of both the field and the state. For Bourdieu, the political field is one of importance due to its ability to define the social world in its totality through defining the social 'principles of vision and division'. Here, the ideas of elites resonate and harden through their adoption by people and groups in society. It is in the political field where the universe of political discourse is limited, and boundaries are imposed as to what is politically thinkable.[76] Although some accuse Bourdieu of methodological nationalism given an apparent focus upon the state, as we shall see shortly, field theory does not preclude a focus upon transnational dynamics, which is of particular importance for our inquiry.

While actors compete within fields, they do so in pursuit of habitus, understood as the cumulative sum of an individual's socialization, from birth to their role in society which subconsciously impacts cognition and physical action.[77] The concept of habitus is 'a system of schema [that] constantly orient choices, which though not deliberate, are nonetheless systematic; which without being arranged and organized expressly according

---

[74] Toby Dodge, '"Bourdieu Goes to Baghdad": Explaining Hybrid Political Identities in Iraq', *Journal of Historical Sociology* 31 (2018), 29.
[75] Ibid., 27.
[76] Pierre Bourdieu, *Language and Symbolic Power* (Cambridge: Polity, 1991), p. 172.
[77] Pierre Bourdieu, *The Logic of Practice* (Stanford: Stanford University Press, 1980), p. 56.

to an ultimate end, are nonetheless imbued with a sort of finality that reveals itself only *post festum*.[78] An individual's habitus shapes their engagement with the world around them and helps determine their actions.

Within any field, power is determined by relational arrangements of actors within the field and the different forms of capital each actor is able to deploy in their quest for domination. Different forms of capital vary in value from field to field, conditioned by the very nature of the struggle.[79] For Bourdieu, capital can take three main forms: economic, the ability to deploy financial resources; cultural, which has a stratifying power in society; and social, which emerges from the networks that an actor can draw upon. Social capital warrants further examination, particularly given the position of religion within social capital. For Bourdieu, social capital

Is the aggregate of the actual or potential resources which are linked to possession of a durable network of more or less institutionalized relationships of mutual acquaintance and recognition – or in other words, to membership in a group – which provides each of its members with the backing of the collectively-owned capital, a 'credential' which entitles them to credit, in the various sense of the word.[80]

Here, social capital is conferred from a group to an individual while also serving as a form of symbolic capital, stemming from the acknowledgement of credit, a point stressed in *The Logic of Practice*, where social capital is referred to as symbolic capital: 'symbolic capital is credit, but in the broadest sense, a kind of advance, a credence, that only the group's belief can grant'.[81] From this, religion possesses a form of organizationally dispensed capital, found in institutions and figures able to legitimize and (re)produce social hierarchies.

The ability to claim symbolic capital – and, in some cases, symbolic power – is central to those wishing to dominate and impose order over a field. Symbolic capital serves to legitimize power relations, allow actors to (re)shape social order through structuring 'the common sense operating in any given field and across society as a whole'.[82] Symbolic capital, for Bourdieu, is 'the power to constitute the given by stating it, to act

[78] Pierre Bourdieu, 'Postface', in Erwin Panofsky, *Architecture gothique et pensée scolastique* (Paris: Editions de Minuit, 1967), p. 161.

[79] Dodge, '"Bourdieu Goes to Bagdahd"', 30.

[80] Pierre Bourdieu, 'The Forms of Capital', in J. Richardson (ed.), *Handbook of Theory and Research for the Sociology of Education* (New York: Greenwood, 1986), p. 286.

[81] Pierre Bourdieu, *The Logic of Practice* (Cambridge: Polity Press 1990), p. 120.

[82] Toby Dodge, 'Beyond Structure and Agency: Rethinking Political Identities in Iraq after 2003', *Nations and Nationalism* 26:1 (2000), 111.

upon the world by acting upon the representation of the world'.[83] It is the ability to draw distinctions and establish hierarchies, to impose classifications that would dominate common sense and be seen as legitimate. In doing so, those wielding symbolic capital are able to shape the habitus, imposing a vision of order – and 'common sense' – over the field in the process.

The political field is central to understanding relations between different fields and with the state itself. Like other fields, the political field is an arena where actors compete to amass symbolic capital and to impose visions as the dominant common sense. Yet unlike other fields, the political field resonates across the social world in its totality, prompting Bourdieu to label competing definitions as the 'principles of vision and division'.[84] The political field tends to dominate society through its capacity to censor, placing boundaries on the (un)thinkable, and 'limiting the universe of political discourse'.[85]

Nomos and the Transnational Field

Reflection on the ways in which political fields are shaped by actors from beyond the borders of the state is of paramount importance, given the salience of shared norms, beliefs, and security concerns. Although Bourdieu proposed field theory to aid analysis of the state – prompting some to identify aspects of methodological nationalism[86] – this does not preclude analysis of international politics; in recent years there have been moves to examine the ways in which global or transnational fields exist and allow for competition. The existence of a transnational field opens up new lines of methodological inquiry about the nature of international politics but in the case of field theory, it raises questions about the ways in which fields at different levels of analysis interact. Here, a hierarchy of fields can emerge, given the organizational distribution of power within and across such fields. The concept of nesting allows us to better grasp this idea.

Accepting the existence of transnational fields adds an additional layer of complexity to contestation in the domestic field as the state is 'embedded in an ensemble of transnational fields'.[87] As a result, the nature of

---

[83] Bourdieu and Wacquant, *An Invitation*, p. 148.
[84] Bourdieu, 'Rethinking the State', 13.
[85] Bourdieu, *Language and Symbolic Power*, p. 172.
[86] Andreas Wimmer and Nina Glick Schiller, 'Methodological Nationalism, the Social Sciences, and the Study of Migration: An Essay in Historical Epistemology', *The International Migration Review*, 37: 3 (2003), 576–610.
[87] Monika Krause, 'How Transnational Fields Vary', paper delivered at the IR Theory Seminar, International Relations Department, London School of Economics and Political Science, 12 March, 2018, p. 4.

the domestic political field is contingent upon its position within and relationship to the transnational field. If the domestic political field is dominated by external actors who bring their own logics and visions, this may change the nature of actors within the field, providing them with hybrid characteristics conditioned not only by the logics of their own field but also by logics from other fields.[88]

Yet norms are not restricted to state borders, meaning that contestation over fields and capital within them is not necessarily restricted to domestic actors. Instead, normative values found in history and religion facilitate regulation of both territorially grounded and non-territorially grounded spaces. Such values may be codified into constitutions, guiding actions through adherence to a set of beliefs that have historically been accepted. Although some aspects of such beliefs may be contested – the severity of which may lead to schisms within communities – there are generally a set of fundamental principles to which all members of a community adhere. Of course, communities need not be grounded within sovereign states; indeed, religious membership traditionally transcends territorial borders – often encouraged by religious leaders – and normative values find traction in myriad different territorial contexts, while they may also be shaped by material considerations.

As Bourdieu and others acknowledge, there are fundamental principles that regulate the functioning of a field or society,[89] termed *nomos*. This *nomos* is irreducible and foundational, a regulatory principle which orders a field, but is not transcendental or eternal; rather, for Bourdieu, it is a product of time and space, reflecting the interests of groups within a dominant position in a field. In *The Sacred Canopy*, Peter Berger argues that a *nomos* is an 'ordering of experience ... imposed upon the discrete experiences and meanings of individuals';[90] a social construction that gives meaning to myriad interpretations and identities; a space for individuals or groups to perform their identity through word and deed. Put another way:

The socially established nomos may thus be understood, perhaps in its most important aspect, as a shield against terror. Put differently, the most important function of society is nominization. The anthropological presupposition for this is a human craving for meaning that appears to have the force of instinct. Men are congenitally compelled to impose meaningful order upon reality. This order, however, presupposes the social enterprise of ordering world construction.[91]

---

[88] Yves Dezalay and Bryant G. Garth, 'Hegemonic Battles, Professional Rivalries, and the International Division of Labor in the Market for the Import and Export of State-Governing Expertise', *International Political Sociology* 5 (2011), 277.

[89] Pierre Bourdieu, *Pascalian Meditations* (Cambridge: Polity Press, 1997), p. 96.

[90] Peter Berger, *The Sacred Canopy* (New York: Doubleday, 1967), p. 3.

[91] Ibid., p. 22.

Fundamentally, the *nomos* is concerned with the ordering of space through the interaction of people which, as Hannah Arendt argues, gives meaning to the world.[92] Competing visions of order – competing *nomoi* – thus gives rise to tensions between different groups. Yet what is of importance to our inquiry is not only the ordering of society but also the ordering of a region, beyond states and operating transnationally. In the context of field theory, a *nomos* operates as the fundamental principle ordering a field yet is not necessarily a product of that *specific* field; rather, *nomos* can emerge from the transnational field to shape domestic political fields.

In *The Human Condition*, Hannah Arendt talks of how 'each man is as much an inhabitant of the earth as he is an inhabitant of his country'. It is easy to see how individuals can then simultaneously inhabit two – or more – communities, which need not necessarily neatly coalesce with state projects or each other. Moreover, inhabitation stems from meaning and, as Berger argues, *the social enterprise of ordering world construction*. Meaning is then derived from a range of different processes which facilitate the ordering of world construction. Here, the ordering of world construction can transcend state borders to cultivate a set of relationships that emerge from membership of a shared *nomos*.

Observing the centrifugal interplay between domestic political fields and transnational fields, the logics conditioning political activity may not be all that different, underpinned by shared norms and practices which serve as the fundamental mechanisms of ordering relations. Norms and practices facilitate the manifestation of *nomos*, shaping visions of how the world *ought* to be, yet are open to interpretation and contestation. It is this process of dialogue and competition between competing visions of order – between competing *nomoi* – that determines the nature of the field. As Catherine Goetze surmises, *nomos* 'represents the deontology that morally justifies binding these norms together into a coherent and intelligible whole ... By normatively defining what is right or wrong in a field, the *nomos* reflects relative power positions in the field.'[93] This intelligible whole cuts across state borders, creating a *nomos* that is simultaneously found within the transnational field and domestic political fields. One consequence of cutting across fields, however, is that *nomoi* often encounter one another, with the results of that encounter shaped by context.

---

[92] Arendt, *Hannah, The Human Condition* (Chicago: Chicago University Press, 1998), p. 207.
[93] Catherine Goetze, *The Distinction of Peace: A Social Analysis of Peacebuilding* (Michigan: University of Michigan Press), pp. 195–6.

As a result, logics driving the actions of actors in different fields may be similar. Efforts to exert capital and impose principles of vision on a domestic field are conditioned by the organization of the transnational field and, in some cases, also the direct involvement of actors from the transnational field. Visions of order bound up in a particular *nomos* shape the actions of actors within particular fields. Fields then become sites of contestation between competing visions of order, both nationally and transnationally. For the purpose of this study, the transnational field is one that is shaped by the interaction of regional security concerns and religious competition. Here, questions of security, stability, and order are conditioned by interplay with actors laying claim to politicized forms of religious competition, playing out across states that are themselves sites of contestation and tension.

These tensions are quickly apparent when considering the competition between states, sects, and questions about geopolitically charged religious belonging across the region, manifesting in the emergence of a transnational field.[94] For example, a fundamental tension emerges when considering how the concept of the *umma* relates to the *dawla*, the territorially defined concept of a state. Amidst this shared *nomos*, efforts to lay claim to Islamic legitimacy are often seen as 'zero sum' ways by Saudi Arabia and Iran. As both Riyadh and Tehran rely upon Islam as a source of regime legitimacy, the use of Islamic rhetoric in an attempt to increase legitimacy poses serious challenges across the Gulf.

Closer examination of twentieth-century history across the Arab and Muslim world provides a range of examples of completion between different *nomoi*. Indeed, these ideas have been discussed at length by Michael Barnett, whose *Dialogues in Arab Politics* explores the power of the pan-Arab collective, and Fouad Ajami, who critically reflects on the interplay of the state and the *umma arabiyya wahida dhat risala khalida* (the 'one Arab nation with an immortal mission').[95] For Barnett, membership of a shared community gave states the power to resist the harsh realities of anarchic international politics. Words became powerful tools in the armouries of regimes across the region that deployed Arab Nationalism against Israel and the United States, but also pursued their own agendas.[96] As Bassam Tibi notes, pan-Arab rhetoric was the prevailing pretension in intra-Arab politics at this time, becoming a site of contestation itself.[97] Indeed, as both Tibi and Barnett address, competition over the deployment of pan-Arab

[94] Mabon, 'The World Is a Garden'.
[95] Fouad Ajami, 'The End of Pan-Arabism', *Foreign Affairs* (Winter 1978/79), 355–73.
[96] Barnett. *Dialogues in Arab Politics*
[97] Bassam Tibi, *Arab Nationalism: Between Islam and the Nation State* (New York: St Martin's Press, 1997).

rhetoric within intra-Arab politics would ultimately be detrimental to the broader cause, helping erode the legitimacy of the movement albeit also affected by devastating military losses to Israel.

Religion was used by a number of regional powers as a means of contesting the power of the pan-Arab movement, with pan-Islam 'heir apparent' following the demise of Nasser and pan-Arabism. At the vanguard of efforts to curtail Nasser's influence across the region, Saudi Arabia sought to proselytize its Wahhabist vision, facilitated by its vast petro dollars. In support of this, training and funding was provided to Imams from across the world at the Islamic University of Medina.[98] Yet much like its precursor, pan-Islamism also became an arena for (geo)political competition amidst fracturing visions of order and questions of leadership.[99]

One arena of competing claims to Islamic legitimacy is the Organization of the Islamic Conference/Co-Operation (OIC), which, as Shahram Akbarzadeh and Kylie Connor suggest, 'lays claim to the mantle of Islamic legitimacy and presents itself as working for the benefit of the transnational *umma*'.[100] In spite of this lofty ambition, the organization has been plagued by infighting, operating amidst competing claims and interpretations of Islam and legitimacy.[101] Thirteen years after the publication of Akbarzadeh and Connor's piece, Akbarzadeh and Zahid Shahab Ahmed added to this analysis with a damning indictment of the organization as one that is doing the bidding of Saudi Arabia whose position evolved from one of leadership to hegemony within the organization.[102]

The case of the OIC demonstrates the complexity of speaking about Muslim unity in contemporary political life, particularly amidst the dominance and apparent incompatibility of the sovereign nation-state acting in pursuit of national interest. It also illustrates the legitimizing power of religion amidst competition within the organization over support for political agendas, perhaps best seen amidst increasingly vitriolic sectarian difference and the rivalry between Saudi Arabia and Iran.[103]

---

[98] Michael Farquar, *Circuits of Faith: Migration, Education, and the Wahhabi Mission* (Stanford: Stanford University Press, 2016); Michael Farquhar, 'Saudi Petrodollars, Spiritual Capital, and the Islamic University of Medina: A Wahhabi Missionary Project in Transnational Perspective', *International Journal of Middle East Studies* 47:4 (2015), 701–21.

[99] Mabon, 'The World Is a Garden'.

[100] Shahram Akbarzadeh and Kylie Connor, 'The Organization of the Islamic Conference: Sharing an Illusion', *Middle East Policy* 12:2 (2005), 79.

[101] Sohail H. Hashmi, "International Society and Its Islamic Malcontents," The Fletcher Forum of World Affairs, Vol. 13, 1996, p. 23.

[102] Shahram Akbarzadeh and Zahid Shahab Ahmed, 'Impacts of Saudi Hegemony on the Organization of Islamic Cooperation (OIC)', *International Journal of Politics, Culture and Society* 31 (2018), 297–311.

[103] Mabon, *Saudi Arabia and Iran*, pp. 51–2.

For example, Saudi Arabia's Grand Mufti Abdul Aziz al-Sheikh argued that 'We must understand these are not Muslims. Their main enemies are the followers of Sunnah'. These are the sons of the Magi [Zoroastrians] and their hostility towards Muslims is an old one, especially with the people of the Tradition [Sunnis]'[104] while Iranian officials sought to reject the Al Sa'ud's responsibility as the protectors of the two holy places of Islam. Following the deaths of over 2,000 people on the 2015 *hajj* – including around 500 Iranians – the Iranian supreme leader, 'Ali Khamenei, rejected the Al Sa'ud's position as the custodians of the two holy places and, with it, challenged one of the main pillars of Saudi legitimacy:

The heartless and murderous Saudis locked up the injured with the dead in containers – instead of providing medical treatment and helping them or at least quenching their thirst. They murdered them ... The world of Islam, including Muslim governments and peoples, must familiarize themselves with the Saudi rulers and correctly understand their blasphemous, faithless, dependent, and materialistic nature. They must not let those rulers escape responsibility for the crimes they have caused throughout the world of Islam.[105]

This form of politically charged religious competition can be traced back to the establishment of the Islamic Republic of Iran in 1979, which positioned Islamic competition firmly within the construction of regional affairs.

Since the formal establishment of the Saudi state in 1932, Islam played a prominent role in daily life, contained within the fabric of institutions, with the Shahada represented on the nation's flag, facilitating the cultivation of legitimacy for both the nascent state and its ruling family. This fusion was a central tenet of the Al Sa'ud's power and legitimacy: to rebel against the family was to go against the state and, with it, God. Moreover, through serving as the protectors of the two holy places of Islam, the mosques of Mecca and Medina, the Al Sa'ud gained legitimacy across the broader Islamic *umma*, responsible for protecting those making *hajj* and *umra*.

It was hardly surprising then that revolutionary events in Iran would have a dramatic impact on regional politics. In the formative stages of the new republic, officials were keen to express Islamic unity. In the aftermath of the revolution, both Grand Ayatollah Khomeini and his

---

[104] Dahlia Nehme, 'Top Saudi Cleric Says Iran Leaders Not Muslims as haj Row Mounts', Reuters (07.09.16), www.reuters.com/article/us-saudi-iran-mufti/top-saudi-cleric-says-iran-leaders-not-muslims-as-haj-row-mounts-idUSKCN11D0HV.

[105] 'Hajj Hijacked by Oppressors, Muslims Should Reconsider Management of Hajj: Ayatollah Khamenei', *Tehran Times* (05.09.16), www.tehrantimes.com/news/406107/Hajj-hijacked-by-oppressors-Muslims-should-reconsider-management.

successor, Ayatollah Khameini, sought to demonstrate unity between Sunni and Shi'a, as we shall see in the following chapter. In spite of these expressions of unity, the Al Sa'ud quickly sought to secure their position by framing the revolution as both Shi'a and Persian, seeking to deny the nascent Islamic Republic broader cross-sectarian legitimacy by diminishing the appeal to Sunni Arabs across the Middle East and beyond. While the salience of religion waned over time, there is little doubt that those wielding religious capital have the capacity to exert influence over the transnational field.

Moving Forward

Understanding the ways in which the rivalry between Saudi Arabia and Iran plays out across the Middle East requires reflecting on the interaction of a number of different factors at different levels of analysis. The rivalry is shaped by the interplay of competition to shape domestic fields across different states and competition to shape the transnational field. As prominent actors in the transnational field with vast reserves of capital, yet competing principles of vision, the struggle between Saudi Arabia and Iran is central in shaping the transnational field.

Central to this competition are efforts to shape the political fields of states operating within the transnational field. For example, the imposition of principles of vision within a domestic field can determine the nature of relations that a state has within the transnational field. Thus, shaping domestic political fields is a key feature of a competition to shape the transnational field. Of particular interest to this project is the struggle to shape the political field after 2003, yet in many cases, to understand the interplay between different actors requires tracing contestation across the *longue durée* to avoid *ahistoricizing* events.

In such spaces, regional actors – in this case Saudi Arabia and Iran – seek to exert influence through the deployment of different forms of capital to impose principles of vision either directly or through relationships with local parts. This coming together may be through formal alliances or more transient, casual relationships, underpinned by shared principles of vision. This approach helps us to combine geopolitical aspirations, religion, competing *nomoi*, ideology, socio-economic forces, and the rhythms of everyday life to understand the way in which the rivalry plays out across time and space.

To understand the ways in which the competition between Saudi Arabia and Iran plays out across the transnational field, I embark on a study of efforts to shape domestic political fields across Iraq, Bahrain, Lebanon, Syria, and Yemen. To do this, I deploy a Historical Sociology approach to examine competition to shape domestic political fields across the *longue durée* and, with it, the opportunities and mechanisms through which contestation plays out. Here, local actors deploy different forms of capital in an effort to impose symbolic capital and principles of vision. At times, the nature of the transnational field will prompt regional powers to become involved in this contestation, either directly through deploying capital, or through the cultivation of relations with local actors. Similarly, local actors may seek to boost their reserves of capital by cultivating relations with regional actors or drawing on capital from the transnational field.

Although regional states can deploy reserves of capital within the domestic political field and local actors can deploy capital derived from the transnational field, movement across fields can erode reserves of capital. As such, to better understand the ways in which the rivalry between Saudi Arabia and Iran plays out across the region it is imperative to reflect on the ways in which capital operates across fields and with other forms of capital. What follows is influenced by spatial analysis, rejecting the existence of 'taken-for-granted' territorial states and stable boundaries, along with seeking to bring agency to the fore in shaping political life. Central to this understanding of space is contingency, where local socioeconomic factors shape the nature of events and the reserves of capital deployed by regional powers. It also calls for an exploration of the ways in which local identities are shaped by state-building processes, contestation of the political field, and the dynamics of the transnational field.

Chapters looking at contestation over the political field are structured in a similar genealogical manner shaped by a desire to examine contestation of the political field over the *longue durée*. In doing this, I weave together, when appropriate, the ways in which each state has formally engaged with Saudi Arabia and Iran over this period, before the struggle to shape political fields intensifies. This requires reflecting on both the contestation of political fields and the position of states within transnational fields, before exploring the parabolic interplay between different fields, actors, and principles of vision and division.

2   The Story of a Kingdom and a Republic

In what has since become a classic of the discipline, Malcolm Kerr's *The Arab Cold War* tells the story of competition for influence across the Arab world as a number of powerful states lay claim to leadership of the pan-Arab movement. More recently, the rivalry between Saudi Arabia and Iran has been viewed centrally within regional politics, described by some as a 'new Middle East Cold War'. For Shahram Chubin and Charles Tripp, understanding the rivalry between Riyadh and Tehran 'is the key' to understanding regional security.[1] Building on Chubin and Tripp's claim, I argue that the rivalry between Riyadh and Tehran plays a prominent role in shaping the transnational field as two states wielding vast reserves of political, religious, economic, and social capital which reverberates within those states located within the transnational field.

The modern history of Saudi–Iranian relations (dating back to the formation of the Saudi state in 1932) can be characterized broadly into five distinct phases.[2] The first is between 1932 and 1979, which is defined by regional distrust yet a willingness for the two states to engage with each other. The second period, 1979–91, is the period after the revolution until three years after the end of the Iran–Iraq War – where a catastrophic earthquake provided an opportunity to reset relations – which was driven by existential concerns about the nature of political organization and competition over Islamic legitimacy. The ensuing period from 1991 to 2003 was one in which a burgeoning rapprochement began to unfold, driven by domestic factors across the Gulf. The fourth period ran roughly from 2003 to 2011, in which the bombastic nationalism of Mahmoud Ahmadinejad, the Iranian president (2005–13) ran up against the belligerent 'Axis of Evil' narrative within the US War on Terror.

The fifth period emerged after the Arab Uprisings in 2011, providing the two states with opportunities to exert influence across the Middle

---

[1] Chubin and Tripp, *Iran-Saudi*, p. 3.
[2] The exact dates of these periods may be contested, particularly the boundary line between third and fourth.

East through the provision of support to groups across the region. The events of the Arab Uprisings provided further opportunities to increase their influence, particularly in those states where regime–society relations began to fragment. In what follows, I offer a brief genealogy of relations between Saudi Arabia and Iran with a focus on the construction of competing *nomoi* – visions of regional order – which play out across the transnational field and resonate within states.

A Kingdom is Formed

The Middle East's transnational field – emerging from the interplay of regional security calculations and competition over religious legitimacy – has its contemporary roots in the formation of the modern states system after the fall of the Ottoman Empire. In the formative years of this transnational field, Saudi Arabia and Iran did not play a central role in defining the principles of vision and division, yet Saudi Arabia's position as protectors of the two holy places of Islam (and responsibility to protect those who made *hajj*) meant it was able to deploy religious capital in the formative decades of the century. In contrast, *Persia* was able to draw upon social capital stemming from its long history, albeit reserves that did not easily manifest in the transnational field given the suspicions of other states and colonial actors present in the region.

Across the 1920s, both Persia and Saudi Arabia were engaged in processes of state formation. The *3 Esfand 1299 (1921)* established the Pahlavi monarchy in 1925 while the Saudi state was formally declared in 1932. Security concerns – fundamentally about survival – were prominent in the minds of the Shah and Ibn Sa'ud, and a friendship treaty was signed between the two in 1929 following dialogue and the visit of a Persian delegation to Mecca. As a consequence of security concerns, scant attention was paid to broader regional trends, although there was a long-standing suspicion of the ethnic 'other', which fed into mutual suspicion. One former Iranian official reflecting on relations with Saudi Arabia during this period described it as a 'secret' or 'hidden' rivalry.[3]

Although the détente was punctured by a number of territorial questions,[4] it was largely tranquil until the establishment of the state of Israel in 1948, which pitted Iran on the opposite side of an issue that would bring about the existential transformation of regional politics. In spite of such divisions, US president Richard Nixon sought to establish a twin

---

[3] Interview with former Iranian official, 2020.
[4] Richard Young, 'Equitable Solutions for Offshore Bundaries: The 1968 Saudi-Iran Agreement', *The American Journal of International Law* 64:1 (1970).

pillar regional security approach in the Persian Gulf built upon a relationship between Saudi Arabia and Iran but underpinned by mutual suspicion of the military capacity and intentions of the Ba'ath regime in Iraq.[5] Such concerns were exacerbated by the burgeoning Arab nationalist movement that played a prominent role in regional politics across the 1950s and 1960s. At this time, a seemingly revolutionary socialism threatened the stability of the conservative regional order, defined by Saudi Arabia and Iran. Such fears prompted military support from Iran, Saudi Arabia, and Jordan for the royalist partisans of the Mutawakkilite Kingdom in the Yemen civil war, pitting them against Egypt, Iraq and other Arab Republics who supported the Yemen Arab Republic.

At this point, an opposition cleric by the name of Ruhollah Khomeini was expelled from Iran, first seeking refuge in Iraq before being exiled in Paris.[6] Across this period of displacement, Khomeini refined his ideas of the role of clerics within political life, gaining widespread popularity in exile as conditions deteriorated in Iran. Despite not being physically present in the Iranian political field, Khomeini exerted a growing social and religious capital, prompting his expulsion. Yet the role of Islam during this period was largely secondary to Arab nationalism and the struggle between Arab republics and their monarchical counterparts.

Following the British decision to withdraw from 'East of Suez' in 1971, a new space emerged for political action, seen in the establishment of the UAE, Bahrain, and Qatar. Yet the British withdrawal also created space for increased Iranian activity and the resurgence of historical claims to Iranian ownership of Bahrain which were ended by a UN endorsed plebiscite.[7] At this point, an uneasy peace took hold across the Gulf, underpinned by geopolitical suspicions and long-standing tensions between Arabs and Persians, as the 'hidden' rivalry became a little more apparent.

The growing empowerment of Shi'a groups across the region played into such currents. Indeed, the establishment of the Movement for the Vanguards Missionaries (MVM), under the spiritual guidance of the Iranian ayatollah Sayyid Mohammad Mahdi al-Shirazi. The MVM established branches across the region, prompting protest and aiding the political empowerment of Shi'a groups, including in

---

[5] Fred Halliday, *Nation and Religion in the Middle East* (London: Saqi Books, 2000), p. 118.

[6] Ruhollah Khomeini, *Islam and Revolution: Writing and Declarations of Imam Khomeini*, translated and annotated by Hamid Algar (Berkely: Mizan Press, 1981).

[7] Roham Alvandi, 'Muhammad Reza Pahlavi and the Bahrain Question, 1968–1970', *British Journal of Middle East Studies* 37:2 (2010), 159–77.

Saudi Arabia.[8] Speaking in 1978 in an effort to circumvent such tensions, Crown Prince Fahd observed that 'the Arab states will have to support Iran and the Shah, because the stability of that country is important to the region ... and any radical change will upset its security balance'.[9] In the months that followed, the gravity of Fahd's warning became increasingly apparent.

The Revolutionary Transformation of the Transnational Field

After the relative calm of the preceding years, the events of 1979 dramatically altered the *nomoi* articulated by Saudi Arabia and Iran and, with it, the principles of vision and division ordering the transnational field. Three incidents in particular occurred that had direct – and severe – repercussions for the ordering of the region. First came the Soviet invasion of Afghanistan, which added a militant dimension to Islamism, positioning it against a secular other; second, was the revolution in Iran; and third, the seizure of the Grand Mosque in Saudi Arabia. The interplay of these three events positioned Islam centrally within the *nomoi* of Saudi Arabia and the nascent Islamic Republic, resonating across the transnational field in the process.

The revolution had a dramatic impact on Shi'a communities across the Middle East, strengthening arguments made by the MVM and inspiring protest in several states. The leadership of the MVM were taken to Iran where they developed close relations with the leadership of the nascent Islamic Republic and the Revolutionary Guards Corps (IRGC), demonstrating an apparent commitment to exporting the revolutionary goals of the Islamic Republic, which were quickly enshrined within the constitution of the state:

The Constitution of the Islamic Republic of Iran advances the cultural, social, political, and economic institutions of Iranian society based on Islamic principles and norms, which represent an honest aspiration of the Islamic Umma. This aspiration was exemplified by the nature of the great Islamic Revolution of Iran, and by the course of the Muslim people's struggle, from its beginning until victory, as reflected in the decisive and forceful calls raised by all segments of the population. Now, at the threshold of this great victory, our nation, with all its beings, seeks its fulfillment.[10]

---

[8] Toby Matthiesen, 'Hizbullah al-Hijaz: A History of the Most Radical Saudi Shi'a Opposition Group', *The Middle East Journal* 64:2 (2010), 179–97.

[9] Cited in Stephen Walt, *Revolution and War* (Cambridge: Cambridge University Press, 1992), p. 253.

[10] Iranian Constitution, www.constituteproject.org/constitution/Iran_1989.pdf?lang=en.

The explicitly Islamic aspect of the new republic was documented in Article 3.16, which clearly stated that foreign policy must be 'based on Islamic criteria, fraternal commitment to all Muslims, and unrestrained support for the impoverished people of the world'. Unsurprisingly, the declaration of the Islamic Republic was met with much consternation in the Kingdom, where many expressed concerns that Khomeini's regime would destroy the regional status quo.

In spite of these fears, King Khalid welcomed the establishment of the new state, stressing that

It gives me great pleasure that the new republic is based on Islamic principles which are a powerful bulwark for Islam and Muslim peoples who aspire to prosperity, dignity, and well-being. I pray the Almighty to guide you to the forefront of those who strive for the upholding of Islam and Muslims, and I wish the Iranian people progress, prosperity, and stability.[11]

Khomeini also sought to demonstrate unity:

There is no difference between Muslims who speak different languages, for instance the Arabs and the Persians. It is very probable that such problems have been created by those who do not wish the Muslim countries to be united ... They create the issues of nationalism, of pan-Iranianism, pan-Turkism, and such isms, which are contrary to Islamic doctrines. Their plan is to destroy Islam and Islamic philosophy.[12]

Yet this period of unity would not last, as political and theological differences began to manifest. As relations soured, the two states became increasingly vitriolic towards one another. Khomeini quickly articulated his desire to

export our experiences to the whole world and present the outcome of our struggles against tyrants to those who are struggling along the path of God, without expecting the slightest reward. The result of this exportation will certainly result in the blooming of the buds of victory and independence and in the implementation of Islamic teachings among the enslaved nations.[13]

Khomeini's comments were a source of deep concern to many across the region who feared that the new Islamic Republic would dramatically alter the balance of power. Such fears were shared by many. As Anoushiravan Ehteshami argues, the revolution 'disrupted the regional order and also ended the slowly emerging alliances of moderate forces

---

[11] Rubin, *Islam in the Balance*, 52.
[12] Amirahmadi Hooshang and Nader Entessar (eds.), *Iran and the Arab World* (Basingstoke: Macmillan, 1993), p. 3.
[13] 'Excerpts from Khomeini Speeches', *New York Times* (4 August 1987), www.nytimes.com/1987/08/04/world/excerpts-from-khomeini-speeches.html.

in the Middle East'.[14] The revolution put an end to Nixon's twin pillar approach and ushered in a new era across the Middle East, defined by competition for Islamic legitimacy.

At the centre of this competition was a war of words between Khomeini and the Al Sa'ud, each seeking to denounce the credentials of the other. In addition to its Islamic credentials, Khomeini's system of *veleyat-e faqih* was also anti-monarchist, positioning the Al Sa'ud as an obvious target:

If we wanted to prove to the world that the Saudi Government, these vile and ungodly Saudis, are like daggers that have always pierced the heart of the Moslems from the back, we would not have been able to do it as well as has been demonstrated by these inept and spineless leaders of the Saudi Government.[15]

Khomeini later condemned the Al Sa'ud as 'corrupt and unworthy to be the guardians of Mecca and Medina'[16] and referred to them as 'traitors to the two holy shrines',[17] calling on pilgrims to go from 'holy *Hajj* to holy *jihad* by bathing yourselves in blood and martyrdom'.[18]

For King Fahd – who succeeded his brother in 1982 – the Iranian regime was full of 'hypocrites and pretenders who are using Islam to undermine and destabilise other countries', in a marked shift on his earlier comments.[19] Fahd warned that attempts to demonstrate on the *hajj* would create an atmosphere of 'chaos and upset the peace', and would not be tolerated.[20] In addition, Saudi officials suggested that Khomeini was creating parallels with God, seen in banners on the *hajj* stating that 'God is Great, Khomeini is Great; We obey Khomeini', along with watches worn by his supporters that were inscribed with the 'Call of Khomeini'.[21] Khomeini later referred to King Fahd as a 'traitor to God' and to Wahhabism as a 'superstitious faith' while his successor depicted the Al Sa'ud as 'evil'.[22] The vitriol directed at the Al Sa'ud

---

[14] Anoushiravan Ehteshami, 'The Foreign Policy of Iran', in Raymond Hinnebusch and Anoushiravan Ehteshami (eds.), *The Middle East in the International System* (London: Lynne Reiner, 2002), p. 284.

[15] 'Excerpts from Khomeini Speeches'.

[16] Con Coughlin, *Khomeini's Ghost* (London: Macmillan, 2009), p. 274.

[17] 'Excerpts from Khomeini Speeches'.

[18] Jacob Goldberg, 'The Saudi Arabian Kingdom', in Itovar Rabinovich and Haim Shaked (eds.), *Middle East Contemporary Survey Volume XI: 1987* (Boulder: Westview Press, 1987), p. 589.

[19] Ibid.

[20] Ibid.

[21] Ibid., p. 602. Nasr, *The Shi'a Revival*, p. 236. See also Baqer Moin, *Khomeini: Life of the Ayatollah* (London: I.B. Tauris, 1999), p. 305.

[22] Frederick Wehrey, Theodore W. Karasik, Alireza Nader, Jeremy Ghez, Lydia Hansell, and Robert A. Guffrey, *Saudi-Iranian Relations since the Fall of Saddam: Rivalry, Cooperation, and Implications for U.S. Policy* (Santa Monica, CA: RAND Corporation, 2009). p. 38.

continued after Khomeini's death. Khomeini's will stated that Muslims 'should curse tyrants, including the Saudi royal family, these traitors to God's great shrine, may God's curse and that of his prophets and angels be upon them'.[23]

In the immediate aftermath of the revolution Iran sought to stress its Islamic credentials, attempting to transcend an association with Shi'a communities and to speak to the global *umma*. Demographic concerns were central to this strategy with Shi'a Muslims totaling only 15 per cent of the total Muslim population. As a consequence, Tehran sought to articulate a *nomos* that was anti-status quo, defined by resistance against the United States, Israel, and corrupt monarchies. It was hardly surprising when Saudi officials began to frame the revolution as one with Shi'a characteristics, immediately reducing its appeal to the much larger Sunni community.

Although the revolution enshrined ideological competition between the two states over leadership of the Islamic world, this rhetoric clouds strong nationalist sentiment.[24] The rivalry over leadership of the Islamic world played out within the OIC, the forum for Muslim states, shaped by the reserves of religious capital that Saudi Arabia and Iran were able to draw upon. As Peter Mandaville suggests, the OIC serves as a 'useful vantage point from which to observe the evolution of relations between the "core" and "periphery" of the Muslim world, and the competition for influence of various Muslim powers'.[25] In the months after the revolution, the OIC became increasingly political, a vantage point from which to view competition over the transnational field. Historically, the OIC had been used by Saudi Arabia to counter the power of pan-Arabism in the 1960s through demonstrating their legitimacy.[26] After the revolution, a similar strategy was deployed to counter the threat from Iran by demonstrating the legitimacy of Saudi claims to Islamic leadership.

As Martin Kramer notes, 'Iran conducted a vigorous campaign against Saudi Arabia's claim to organize the consensus of Islam. For a decade Iran virtually ignored the OIC, and convened frequent conferences of its own clients and supporters from abroad.'[27] A major part of such claims was the Al Sa'ud's responsibility to protect those who made *hajj* or *umra* in the Kingdom. As a consequence, when tragedy befell pilgrims, the Al

[23] Cited in Moin, *Khomeini: Life of the Ayatollah*, p. 305.
[24] Chubin and Tripp, *Iran-Saudi*, p. 15. See also the work of Fred Halliday, who stresses the importance of nationalism within regional politics across several texts.
[25] Peter Mandaville, *Global Political Islam* (Oxon: Routledge, 2007), p. 287.
[26] Ibid.
[27] Martin Kramer, 'Muslim Congresses', in John L. Esperito (ed.), *The Oxford Encyclopedia of the Modern Islamic World* (Oxford: Oxford University Press, 1995), p. 309.

Sa'ud was criticized for its inability to protect pilgrims. Yet the behaviour of the Al Sa'ud more broadly provided ample material for critics to use – both internally and externally – notably allegations of corruption and alliances with the West. Reflecting concerns at the challenge to the Kingdom's legitimacy, King Fahd changed the title of the monarch to the Custodian of the Two Holy Places; this came as a surprise to many given Fahd's colourful past, but it revealed how seriously the Saudi leadership was taking the threat from Iran.[28]

Others across the region viewed the revolution more favourably. The Kuwaiti newspaper *Al-Ra'i Al-Amm* remarked that the revolution prompted calls for 'admiration', suggesting that it was 'obviously clear that Iran has no claims against the Arabs and Tehran knows well that the Arabs have no claims against Iran'.[29] Another Kuwait paper, *Al-Qabas*, took a different line, concluding that while Iran 'clearly emerges that to don the garb of tolerant Islam, [Tehran] cannot mask imperialist and expansionist intentions'.[30] While some Iranian officials espoused conciliatory remarks, they were coupled with condemnation of regional elites and the suggestion that 'people are no more ready to be exploited'.[31]

In the following years, the transnational field became increasingly shaped by the interplay of religious competition and security concerns as actors struggled to locate themselves in the post-revolutionary order. The most obvious fallout from the revolution was the Iran–Iraq War (1980–88) which was driven by Iraqi desires to prevent the proliferation of revolutionary ideas beyond the borders of Iran. Although the Ba'ath regime of Saddam Hussein was deeply unpopular across the Middle East, fears about Iranian expansionism meant that Saudi Arabia, the United States, and other Gulf states supported Iraq in the war, much to the chagrin of Iran.

At this time Iran became increasingly pro-active across the Middle East, providing financial, ideological, and logistical support to a number of groups across the region, perhaps most notably Hizbullah, the Lebanese Party of God, and the Islamic Front for the Liberation of Bahrain (IFLB). Iran's *nomos*, driven by narratives of resistance and support for the *mostaz'afin* of the Muslim world, resonated across these communities, supported by the provision of financial and logistical aid.[32] Iranian

---

[28] Paul Wood, 'Life and Legacy of King Fahd', BBC (1 August 2005), http://news.bbc.co.uk/1/hi/world/middle_east/4734505.stm.

[29] *Al-Ra'i al-Amm*, 13 February and 4 June 1974,.

[30] *Al-Qabas*, 23 March 1980,.

[31] Barry Rubin, 'The Gulf States and the Iran-Iraq War', in E. Karsh (ed.) *The Iran-Iraq War* (New York: Palgrave Macmillan, 1989), pp. 13–26.

[32] Augustus R. Norton, *Amal and the Shi'a: Struggle for the Soul of Lebanon* (Austin: University of Texas Press, 1987).

capital amongst many was conditioned by ideas of resistance, shaped by collective Shi'a memory, most notably events at Karbala. For Khomeini, the world was

> sharply divided into two warring classes—*tabaqat*: the *mostaz'afin*—oppressed—against the *mostakberin*—oppressors; the *foqara*—poor—against the *sarvatmandan*—rich; the *mellat-e mostaz'af*—oppressed nation—against the *hokumat-e shaytan*—Satan's government … In the 1970s, however, he used [the term *mostaz'afin*] in almost every single speech and proclamation to depict the angry poor, the 'exploited people,' and the 'downtrodden masses.' After the revolution, he gradually broadened the term to bring in the propertied middle class, which actively supported the new order.[33]

This vision was articulated in the new Iranian Constitution, where Article 3.16 – which dealt with foreign policy – expressed a 'fraternal commitment to all Muslims, and unsparing support to the *mostaz'afin* of the world',[34] post-evident in support to Hizbullah. The Party of God was forged out of a time of great uncertainty, anger, and foment in Shi'a communities in Lebanon,[35] underpinned by a spirit of resistance inspired by Iran's revolutionary activity and the legacy of Karbala.[36] Support was also provided to the Assad regime in Syria, which facilitated the backing of the Party of God but also resulted in what became known as the 'axis of resistance',[37] giving Iran a foothold on the Mediterranean coast and occupying a prominent position in the transnational field.

For one Saudi official, Iranian foreign policy is the source of much frustration in the Kingdom.[38] Iranian actions in Lebanon provoked much concern in Saudi Arabia, prompting fears about discontent in neighbouring Bahrain. The demographic balance of the Al-Khalifa-run kingdom left it vulnerable to unrest, particularly amidst the historical marginalization of Shi'a communities. With revolutionary fever emanating from Iran, it was hardly surprising that the IFLB sought to topple the Al-Khalifa, with support from Iran.[39] Although unsuccessful – thwarted before it could begin – the actions of the IFLB resonated

---

[33] Abrahamian, *Khomeinism, Essays on the Islamic Republic*, pp. 26–7.
[34] Iranian Constitution, Article 3.16, www.alaviandassociates.com/documents/constitution.pdf.
[35] Augustus R. Norton, *Hezbollah* (Princeton: Princeton University Press, 2007), p. 29.
[36] Mabon, 'The Circle of Bare Life: Hizballah, Muqawamah and Rejecting "Being Thus"', *Politics, Religion & Ideology* 18:1 (2017), 1–22.
[37] El-Husseini, 'Hezbollah and the Axis of Refusal'.
[38] Interview with Saudi official, 2018.
[39] Hasan Alhasan, 'The Role of Iran in the Failed Coup of 1981: The IFLB in Bahrain', *Middle East Journal* 65:4 (2011), 603–17.

across the Gulf, creating a narrative that frames Shi'a unrest as a consequence of nefarious Iranian meddling. Fearing ongoing pernicious Iranian activity, the Gulf Co-Operation Council (GCC) was established in 1981 in an effort to secure rulers. Supporting this was the development of the King Fahd causeway – linking Saudi Arabia and Bahrain – ostensibly to cultivate stronger economic ties between the two states but also providing the means for a security force to access Bahrain at speed, if needed.[40]

At this point, the transnational field was contested by a range of actors deploying different forms of capital. Although Saudi Arabia and other Gulf states were opposed to an Iranian victory during the Iran–Iraq War – fearing the spread of revolutionary ideas – they were equally concerned about an increase in Iraqi power given their own military weaknesses;[41] while many feared the expansionist vision of Khomeini's Islamic Republic, they were equally wary of Saddam's Ba'athism. Despite these concerns, when Iraq positioned itself as the 'shield of the Arabs', this was reluctantly accepted by the other Gulf states.[42] During the war, cautious support was given to Iraq, and while Saudi Arabia attempted to stay neutral, a range of complex issues came to a head in the 'tanker war', resulting in a number of casualties and escalating tensions.

A fortnight before the end of the war, Hashemi Rafsanjani, then commander in chief of the Iranian military, suggested that Iran's strategic priority was to end the international isolation:

One of the wrong things we did in the revolutionary atmosphere was to constantly make enemies. We pushed those who could be neutral into hostility and did not do anything to attract those who could become friends. It is part of the new plan that in foreign policy we should behave in a way not to needlessly leave ground to the enemy.[43]

Such comments hint at what was to follow. While the war ended in stalemate, Saudi Arabia found itself caught between the secular Ba'ath vision of Saddam Hussein and the expansionist ideas of Ayatollah Ruhollah Khomeini. At this point, as Barry Rubin notes, the Gulf states – including Saudi Arabia – began to consider working with Iran as a counterweight to Iraq.[44] At the same time, as a US diplomatic cable

---

[40] Simon Mabon, 'The Battle for Bahrain', *Middle East Policy* 19:2 (2012), 84–97.

[41] Rubin, 'The Gulf States'. See also May Darwich, *Threats and Alliances*.

[42] 'Voice of the Masses Radio' (Baghdad) (04.03.80), in *FBIS* (06.03.80): Saddam Hussein quoted by the Iraqi News Agency (26.03.80), in *FBIS* (25.04.80).

[43] 'Excerpts from Khomeini Speeches', 4 August 1987.

[44] Rubin, 'The Gulf States'.

released by Wikileaks notes, Iran sought to improve relations with Saudi Arabia but suspicion remained, stemming from Iranian actions in Bahrain and claims to Abu Musa and the Greater and Lesser Tunbs. For one Iranian official, this suspicion ultimately stemmed from fear of Iranian history and civilization.[45]

The war had a dramatic impact on the Iranian psyche, with many in the higher echelons of power in Tehran bearing the scars of a devastating conflict. The war serves as an example of the sacrifice required to preserve the revolution, a point that provides a great deal of the IRGC's legitimacy, reinforcing the Iranian *nomos* of resistance in the process.[46] In the years to come this *nomos* would manifest in the principles of vision articulated in the transnational field and across states.

A Possible Rapprochement?

In the years after the Iran–Iraq War, a new era of relations between the Kingdom and the Islamic Republic emerged, characterized by moves towards rapprochement. A number of factors facilitated this rapprochement, notably shared security concerns about Saddam Hussein's Iraq, along with a devastating earthquake in Iran that killed an estimated 30,000 people, creating a transnational field that was conducive to a thaw in relations. In response to this catastrophe, Saudi Arabia sent aid to the Islamic Republic, resulting in the restoration of diplomatic ties.

In addition to regional developments, domestic desires for a thaw in diplomatic relations emerged, initially through the work of Hashemi Rafsanjani but matched by Crown Prince Abdullah in Saudi Arabia. After the death of Ruhollah Khomeini, power in Iran passed to Ayatollah 'Ali Khamenei, a somewhat surprising choice as supreme leader given an apparent lack of legitimacy in the clerical establishment, creating opportunities for the president to exert greater influence. Under the leadership of Hashami Rafsanjani, diplomatic relations between Saudi Arabia and Iran were restored as leadership from both states embarked on visits. In 1999 President Khatami visited Riyadh in the first visit to the Kingdom from an Iranian president since the revolution. In response, Crown Prince Abdullah visited Iran for a meeting of the OIC, prompting the signing of a number of bi-lateral deals between the two states.

In spite of this, security concerns remained, with both Riyadh and Tehran worried about the regional aspirations of Iraq whose belligerence

---

[45] Interview with Iranian official, 2020.
[46] Wehrey et al., *Saudi-Iranian Relations*.

posed a great challenge to other Gulf states. While Crown Prince Abdullah appeared open to improving relations with Iran, and vice versa, the position of US troops in the Kingdom remained a thorny issue for both the Al Sa'ud and the Islamic Republic, with the former concerned about the consequences of the presence of US forces on the Arabian Peninsula and the latter under US sanctions. Moreover, criticism from domestic actors in Saudi Arabia and Iran meant that achieving more formal relations would prove difficult.

Dialogue between Abdullah, King Fahd (albeit briefly), and representatives of the Islamic Republic remained positive, however, with the two states sharing concerns about Iraq under Saddam Hussein. This period of dialogue helped defuse tensions from a number of issues including unrest in Bahrain, competing claims over the Greater and Lesser Tunbs, and violent attacks on the Saudi state. The Khobar Towers attack outside a US army residential base on 25 June 1996 threatened to derail a thaw in relations, with Washington laying blame on Tehran for the death of nineteen US servicemen. In the immediate aftermath, Saudi Arabia refused to blame Iran, privately acknowledging the culpability of its citizens, which revealed the severity of tensions between rulers and ruled in the Kingdom but also that improvement in relations with Iran was deemed to be of strategic importance. Despite this, for many Saudis, an Iranian hand was behind the attacks, amidst Tehran's ongoing efforts to support militias and militant groups in the Kingdom at this time.[47] Over time, some in the Kingdom viewed the Khobar Towers attack as further proof about the broader essence of the Islamic Republic and its fundamental rejection of regional order in its current form.[48]

The challenges facing rulers in Riyadh and Tehran during the postwar period were such that it would have been easy to reject any further dialogue, stemming from domestic criticism and regional turmoil, particularly within divided societies. Yet the years after the Iran–Iraq War and before the 2003 Iraq War demonstrate the importance of building trust within seemingly intractable situations, revealing the capacity of the two states to work together in the face of seemingly endemic structural challenges. It is a period that also exposes the power of individual agency in shaping events.[49]

---

[47] Interview with Saudi official, 2018.

[48] This point came out in conversations with Saudi officials and analysts.

[49] Those interested in this period would be well served by reading Banafsheh Keynoush's excellent book *Saudi Arabia and Iran: Friends or Foes?* that has a detailed exploration of the domestic and regional machinations.

The Return of Principles of Division:
Sectarianization and the Shi'a Crescent

As al-Qa'ida operatives flew planes into targets across the east coast of the United States, few realized the seismic impact of the attacks. While the international community was firmly behind the American military response in Afghanistan, when strategists turned to Iraq, that popular support rapidly dissipated. The United States-led invasion of Iraq in 2003 dramatically altered Middle Eastern politics, changing the nature of the transnational field and its dominant principles of vision and division in the process. In Iraq, the removal of Saddam Hussein and the Ba'ath Party existentially altered the public sphere. The decision to remove all traces of the Ba'ath Party was done not only to prevent the revival of the movement but also to create space for political negotiations between Shi'a and Kurdish groups who had long endured repression by the Ba'athists. The Coalition Provisional Authority decision left hundreds of thousands unemployed as all party members were fired from public service employment. This move changed the contours of Iraqi politics: gone was the all-powerful Ba'ath regime, replaced by an occupying force and weak institutions, creating space for the emergence of powerful militias, a number of whom received financial support from Tehran.

The invasion of Iraq dramatically altered regional security calculations, creating a space for c Saudi Arabia and Iran to compete for local and regional influence. The establishment of a Shi'a-led government in Baghdad coincided with increased Iranian involvement across Iraq, much to the chagrin of many in Saudi Arabia who regularly expressed their concerns to their US counterparts, while also urging them to 'cut off the head of the snake'. Coeval to increased Iranian involvement in Iraq was the empowerment of the 'Axis of Resistance' – comprising Iran, Hizbullah, Hamas and Syria – which gave Tehran greater access to the Arab world and the sources of legitimacy that come with it. The fragmentation of sovereign projects created space and opportunities for actors to exert influence across the region, using a range of different strategies dependent upon context. In Iraq, according to US officials, Iranian actors deployed a range of 'unconventional' approaches to wage 'a multidimensional campaign to shape the geopolitical dynamic in central and southern Iraq.'[50] The fragmentation of Iraq created conditions of uncertainty and spaces of opportunity that were rapidly capitalized

---

[50] 05BAGHDAD3015_a, 'Building a House on Shifting Sands – Iran's Influence in Iraq's Center-South' (20.07.2005), www.wikileaks.org/plusd/cables/05BAGHDAD3015_a.html.

upon by Iranian actors, drawing on pre-existing political and religious ties. Hesitancy from other states from the region helped facilitate this transformation, much to the chagrin of many.

The struggle in Iraq was a key part of a broader geopolitical tussle to shape the region. After the toppling of Saddam Hussein, new alliances were created that drew upon shared ethno-sectarian identities but were driven by shared *nomoi*. A key component of this strategy was the securitizing of Iran, framing the Islamic Republic as an 'existential threat' to regional order. Central to this securitizing process was the narrative of the 'Shi'a Crescent', a term first used by King Abdullah II of Jordan, to denote an apparent arc of Iranian influence stretching from Damascus via Baghdad to Tehran.

In an interview with The Washington Post, Abdullah II stressed that

if pro-Iran parties or politicians dominate the new Iraqi government, he said, a new 'crescent' of dominant *Shi'ite* movements or governments stretching from Iran into Iraq, Syria and Lebanon could emerge, alter the traditional balance of power between the two main Islamic sects and pose new challenges to U.S. interests and allies … Abdullah, a prominent Sunni leader, said the creation of a new Shiite crescent would particularly destabilize Gulf countries with *Shi'ite* populations. 'Even Saudi Arabia is not immune from this. It would be a major problem. And then that would propel the possibility of a *Shi'ite*-Sunni conflict even more, as you're taking it out of the borders of Iraq.'[51]

The narrative of the Shi'a crescent was strengthened by comments from a number of the region's leaders. Central to these comments were fears about nefarious Iranian activity and the manipulation of Shi'a minorities. Reflecting such concerns, Abdullah II stressed that 'Iran should stop seeking to destabilize Palestine, Lebanon and Iraq or any other country so that we can build constructive relations'. In another interview, with the Israeli newspaper *Ha'aretz*, Abdullah argued that 'through Hamas, Iran has been able to buy itself a seat at the table in talking about the Palestinian issue'.[52] Fears about Iranian activity and Tehran's capacity to shape political organization quickly began to spread beyond Iraq. Supporting King Abdullah's comments about the Shi'a Crescent, former Egyptian president Hosni Mubarak suggested that 'Iraq belongs to the Shi'a … Shi'a form 65% of the Iraqis and there are Shi'a in large proportion of these [Arab] states and Shi'a are always loyal to Iran. Most of

---

[51] Robin Wright and Peter Baker, 'Iraq, Jordan See Threat to Election from Iran: Leaders Warn against Forming Religious State', *Washington Post* (8 December 2004), www.washingtonpost.com/wp-dyn/articles/A43980-2004Dec7.html.

[52] Both quotes are cited in Ian Black, 'Fear of a *Shi'a* Full Moon', *The Guardian* (26.01.07), www.theguardian.com/world/2007/jan/26/worlddispatch.ianblack.

them have allegiance to Iran and not to their states.'[53] Of course such a view offered a simplistic reading of regional events, but it became a view that found traction across the region.

In the aftermath of the US invasion of Iraq and ensuing fragmentation of the Iraqi state, the interplay between transnational fields and domestic political fields, demonstrating the importance and salience of particular ideas across the region. The emergence of the Shi'a Crescent narrative was driven by concern about political developments within states and the broader transnational field amidst the fragmentation of political projects. Central to this was the manipulation and cultivation of sectarian divisions. As Abdullah II articulated, 'if sectarianism deepens and spreads, its destructive effect will reflect on everyone. It will foster division, polarisation and isolationism. Our region will drown in a conflict whose outcome cannot be foreseen.'[54] This narrative fed into the domestic policies traditionally deployed by the Al Sa'ud as a mechanism of control. Clerics, including Abdul-Aziz Bin Baz, the Kingdom's leading Wahhabi cleric, issued *fatwas* against Shi'a Muslims and denounced them as apostates, while Abdullah ibn Jibrin sanctioned the killing of members of the Shi'a community.[55]

As Iraq descended into violent conflict, so too did Lebanon. In the summer of 2006, a thirty-four-day war broke out across southern Lebanon, between the Israeli Defence Forces (IDF) and Hizbullah. While Dahiyeh, a Hizbullah stronghold in south Beirut, was ultimately destroyed, the Party of God gained considerable capital across the region for standing up to the IDF in a broad demonstration of the power of the resistance axis. The events of 2006 posed a strategic dilemma for Saudi Arabia and other Sunni Arab states: should the Kingdom provide support to the Party of God in an effort to cultivate capital by opposing Israel, or should it do nothing, weakening a key Iranian ally in the process but looking impotent in the broader struggle against Israel? A central part of Saudi concerns was the Wahhabi *'ulama*'s condemnation of Shi'a groups, yet broader questions about legitimacy continued to play a prominent role in political decisions. In a move against the 'Arab game of politics', Saudi Arabia, Jordan, and Egypt all publicly condemned Hizbullah's decision to go to war with Israel, fearing the Party of God's rising popularity across the region.[56]

[53] Terrence Jeffrey, 'The Sunni-Shi'ite Cold War or Worse', *Human Events* (16.08. 2006), http://findarticles.com/p/articles/mi_qa3827/is_200610/ai_n17196736.

[54] Black, 'Fear of a *Shi'a* Full Moon'.

[55] Nasr, *The Shi'a Revival*, p. 236.

[56] Shibley Telhami, *Anwar Sadat Chair for Peace and Development University of Maryland/ Zogby International 2006 Annual Arab Public Opinion Survey* (08.02.2007).

The destruction of Dahiyeh required massive financial investment to facilitate the reconstruction process. Ultimately, while Iran provided $120 million for the rebuilding efforts, Saudi Arabia provided $1.2 billion.[57] The same year, Saudi Arabia and Kuwait donated $1.5 billion to the Lebanese Central Bank in an effort to boost the country's currency chest, and a further $1billion two years later to help peg the Lebanese pound to the dollar. Although Iran had secured the support of Hizbullah, Saudi Arabia continued to support the other dominant alliance in Lebanese politics – March 14 – and offered support to the formal institutions of the state.

Regional security in the years that followed was equally precarious. In 2008, at the Manama Dialogue, the proposal of an integrated regional security organization including the GCC, Arab League, Israel, Iran, and Turkey was swiftly rejected by Mahmoud Ahmadinejad, who refused to engage in an organization that included Israel.[58] Ahmadinejad also expressed disappointment at the lack of broader regional engagement, particularly with the Saudis. He claimed to have visited the Kingdom on several occasions, yet there had been no return visit, prompting laughter in Riyadh.[59] The following year, Manochehr Mottaki, the Iranian foreign minister, travelled to Riyadh in an attempt to improve relations. While meeting the king, Abdullah is alleged to have said 'it is not acceptable for friends to say one thing and do another'. When questioned about Iranian involvement with Hamas, Mottaki proclaimed 'these are Muslims'. In response, Abdullah declared 'You as Persians have no business meddling in Arab matters.'[60] During the meeting, Mottaki invited the king to Iran. In response, Abdullah claimed to have retorted, 'all I want is for you to spare us your evil'.[61]

Competing Principles of Vision: Fragmentation and Opportunism

These tensions reached a zenith at in the early months of 2011. The emergence of protest movements across the Middle East and North Africa rocked political organization across the region when long-established regimes were toppled while others were able to survive in the face

---

[57] Wehrey et al., *Saudi-Iranian Relations*, pp. 81–2.
[58] 08MANAMA835_a, 'Iran: Bahraini Foreign Minister's Visit to Tehran' (28.12.08) www.wikileaks.org/plusd/cables/08MANAMA835_a.html.
[59] Ibid.
[60] 09RIYADH447_a, 'Counterterrorism Adviser Brennan's Meeting with Saudi King Abdullah' (22.03.09), https://wikileaks.org/plusd/cables/09RIYADH447_a.html.
[61] Ibid.

of powerful currents of change. The protest groups were shaped by local context and grievances, but a number of common themes can be identified around frustration at a lack of political accountability, economic disenfranchisement, and seemingly existential frustration at daily life. Amidst such conditions, political organization began to fragment as sovereign power was contested and schisms between regimes and societies began to emerge.[62] In such conditions, Riyadh and Tehran were presented with opportunities to redraw the region in accordance with their geopolitical vision, countering the influence of the other in the process.

In states typically considered to be 'deeply divided societies' – such as Iraq, Bahrain, Lebanon, Syria and Yemen – the protests had serious repercussions, opening up opportunities for regional powers to exert influence, capitalizing on shared identities and underpinned by shared *nomoi*. The fragmentation of political life created space for external actors to manipulate domestic politics, resulting in the emergence of conflicts shaped by the complex interplay of local and regional factors. In Bahrain, Syria, and Yemen, protest quickly became constructed in an exclusionary manner – much like in Iraq and Lebanon – where different identity markers were used to close off communities against an other, a process which was exacerbated by the involvement of regional actors. Historical experience fed into the construction of *nomoi*, fears of nefarious activity, and principles of vision that played out across political fields. In a climate of fear, regimes sought to securitize protest groups along communal lines, drawing upon historical experience to ensure support from domestic populations and both regional and international actors.

In Bahrain, protesters from across society took to the streets demanding political reform, but the protest movement was quickly framed along sectarian lines, underpinned by a narrative of perfidious Iranian involvement.[63] In spite of wide-ranging allegations of Iranian involvement, the well-regarded Bassiouni Independent Commission Inquiry found 'no evidence of Iran's involvement in the 2011 events and no Iranian role in Bahrain's political crisis'.[64] Upon receiving the report, senior members of the Al-Khalifa rejected the findings, once again blaming Iranian agents for manipulating events.[65] In support of this, the regime's narrative was supported by Sunni theologians and politicians who reinforced the idea that the protesters were predominantly Shi'a and doing the

---

[62] For a detailed discussion of this, see Mabon, *Houses Built on Sand.*

[63] Simon Mabon, 'The End of the Battle of Bahrain and the Securitization of Bahraini Shi'a', *The Middle East Journal* 73:1 (2019), 29–50.

[64] Bahrain Independent Commission of Inquiry, *Report of the Bahrain Independent Commission of Inquiry* (10.12.11), www.bici.org.bh/BICIreportEN.pdf.

[65] Mabon, 'The End of the Battle of Bahrain'.

bidding of Iran. Taking the argument a step further, when reflecting on the Iranian presence in Bahrain, one Bahraini businessman declared that 'the Persians are everywhere', reasserting ethnic difference as another line of exclusion.[66]

In such a climate of fear, the Shi'a Crescent narrative once again gained traction. In the coming years, Iranian officials would brag about increased influence across the region. 'Ali Reza Zakani, Tehran's representative to the Iranian parliament and a close confident of the supreme leader, declared that the Arab capitals of Baghdad, Beirut, and Damascus 'have today ended up in the hands of Iran and belong to the Islamic Iranian revolution', while presciently suggesting that Sanaa was soon to follow.[67] Hyperbolic comments along similar lines were later made by Mohammed bin Salman in 2017, who declared that Iran was seeking to 'control the Islamic world'.[68] Central to these competing agendas was the manipulation of lines of exclusion and the mobilization of identities – often along sectarian lines – which had become increasingly vitriolic in the years after the invasion of Iraq. As Fanar Haddad suggests 'Shiites who used to be accused of ethnic otherness are now being cast as outside the Muslim community itself. Exclusion on doctrinal grounds was a mostly Saudi exception in the framing of Shiism. It is now increasingly becoming the regional rule.'[69]

This process of exclusion, typically understood as sectarianization took on an important role in the construction of regional politics. As we saw in the previous chapter, this process is driven by elites seeking to secure political goals through the mobilization of popular sentiment and the manipulation of identity markers.[70] These processes cut across state borders, resonating not only within domestic political fields but also across the transnational field. As a consequence, the increasingly vitriolic process of sectarianization had serious implications for the(re)organization of spatial dynamics across the region.

In the years that followed, conflict became framed, viewed, and reduced to a neo-Orientalist argument about 'ancient hatreds' stemming

---

[66] Interview with Bahraini businessman, Manama, 2014.

[67] 'Sanaa Is the Fourth Arab Capital to Join the Iranian Revolution', *Middle East Monitor* (27.09.14), www.middleeastmonitor.com/20140927-sanaa-is-the-fourth-arab-capital-to-join-the-iranian-revolution/.

[68] 'Iran Is Seeking "to Control Islamic World", Says Saudi Arabian Prince', *Associated Press* (02.05.17), www.theguardian.com/world/2017/may/02/iran-is-seeking-to-control-islamic-world-says-saudi-arabian-prince.

[69] Fanar Haddad. 'The Language of anti-*Shi'ism*', *Foreign Policy* (09.08.2013), https://foreignpolicy.com/2013/08/09/the-language-of-anti-shiism/.

[70] Nader Hashemi and Danny Postel, 'Sectarianization: Mapping the New Politics of the Middle East', *The Review of Faith & International Affairs* 15:3 (2017), 3.

from a centuries old struggle between Sunni and Shi'a, neglecting the socio-economic contingencies that shape human behaviour. The narrative gained traction when applied by regimes in an effort to engender their survival by denying political agency to protesters and reducing unrest to perfidious Iranian involvement. Supporting such a view, Adel al-Jubeir declared that Iran was responsible for the region's turmoil due to Tehran's efforts to 'obscure its dangerous sectarian and expansionist policies, as well as its support for terrorism, by levelling unsubstantiated charges against the Kingdom of Saudi Arabia'.[71] Later, al-Jubeir stressed that Iran is 'the single-most-belligerent-actor in the region, and its actions display both a commitment to regional hegemony and a deeply held view that conciliatory gestures signal weakness either on Iran's part or on the part of its adversaries'.[72] While the transition from the bombastic tenure of Mahmoud Ahmadinejad to the more diplomatically minded Hassan Rouhani appeared to present an opportunity for improving relations between Saudi Arabia and Iran – and Iran's relations with other states in the region more broadly – this was largely premature.[73]

Reflecting an awareness of the dangers posed by sectarian difference, Javad Zarif referred to it as 'the most serious security threat not only to the region but to the world at large'. Zarif was also vocal in criticizing those guilty of exacerbating this difference: 'Nobody should try to fan the flames of sectarian violence. We should reign it in, bring it to a close, try to avoid a conflict that would be detrimental to everybody's security.'[74] In response, Saudi officials were outspoken in their condemnation of Iran as the region's largest state sponsor of terrorism. It was hardly surprising that such fears were strongly rebuked by a range of Iranian officials, once again seeking to demonstrate their appeal across the Muslim world. Hassan Rouhani, the president of Iran, suggested that 'There is neither a Shiite nor a Sunni crescent. We have an Islamic moon. We, Muslims, are in a world where we must be united.'[75]

Vitriolic rhetoric once again became a prominent feature of relations between the two states. In the aftermath of the execution of Sheikh Nimr al-Nimr, a leading Shi'a cleric in Saudi Arabia in January 2016, 'Ali Khamenei called for 'divine vengeance' while others referred to it as a

---

[71] al-Jubeir, 'Can Iran Change?'.
[72] Ibid.
[73] This perhaps also reflects the source of power within the structure of the Islamic Republic that lies with the supreme leader rather than the president.
[74] 'Iran FM: Sectarian Strife is Worst Threat in World', *BBC News* (11.11.13), www.bbc .co.uk/news/world-middle-east-24893808.
[75] 'Iran's Rouhani Urges Muslim Countries to Unite', *EuroNews* (27.12.15), www .euronews.com/2015/12/27/iran-s-rouhani-urges-muslim-countries-to-unite.

political error on the part of the Saudi regime claiming that 'God will
not relinquish [avenging] the blood of the innocent. The blood spilled
unjustly will rapidly deliver a blow to the politicians and officials of
this [Saudi] regime.'[76] The execution of al-Nimr also prompted protests across the region including the storming of the Saudi consulate in
Tehran.

Senior ayatollahs in Iran had earlier condemned Saudi Arabia and Wahhabism for escalating tensions across the region. Grand Ayatollah Naser
Makarem Shirazi, a member of the Assembly of Experts, declared that

Wahhabism is a tool for the enemies, and Muslims should stay away from the
heretical Wahhabism … The disagreements and conflicts among Muslims
have today risen to an unprecedented level. In Syria, Egypt, Iraq, Yemen, and
Bahrain … the heretical Wahhabism is the chief cause of conflict. For hundreds of
years, Shi'ites, Sunnis, Alawites, and Christians lived together in Syria, but when
they [i.e. Wahhabi elements] entered [the arena] – look at the wars and bloodshed
that began. Several Arab countries have become tools for the U.S. and Israel.[77]

The IRGC weekly *Sobh-e Sadeq* was vocal in its condemnation of the Al
Sa'ud and the family's links with terrorists, suggesting that the 'hands of
the Al Sa'ud family [are] behind the crimes of these murderous terrorist
groups', also calling for a 'decisive and crushing response – a response
that will cause the Al Sa'ud family to regret its continuing hostility to
Iran'.[78] Writing in the *New York Times*, Foreign Minister Javad Zarif
argued that the 'extremist ideology promoted by Saudi Arabia' was
responsible for the region's ills, referring to Wahhabism as a 'theological
perversion' and a 'death cult'. In the article, Zarif also claimed that the
Saudi Kingdom 'spent tens of billions of dollars exporting Wahhabism
through thousands of mosques and madrassas across the world' over the
past thirty years.[79]

Saudi responses were equally unequivocal:

the statements of the Iranian regime expose its true [character], as expressed
by [its] support for terror, and continue the policy of undermining the security

---

[76] 'Iran Furious over Saudi Arabia's Execution of Shi'ite Sheikh Nimr al-Nimr' *Memri*
(04.01.16), www.memri.org/reports/iran-furious-over-saudi-arabias-execution-shiite-
sheikh-nimr-al-nimr.
[77] *Mehr* (Iran), 15 January 2014, cited in A. Savyon, Yossi Mansharof, E. Kharrazi,
and Y. Lahat, 'Iran Calls for Violent *Shi'ite* Reaction against Saudi Arabia', *MEMRI*
(12.02.2014), www.memri.org/reports/iran-calls-violent-shiite-reaction-against-saudi-
arabia.
[78] *Sobh-e Sadeq* (Iran), 26 January 2014.
[79] Mohammad Javad Zarif, 'Let Us Rid the World of Wahhabism', *New York Times*
(13.09.16), www.nytimes.com/2016/09/14/opinion/mohammad-javad-zarif-let-us-rid-
the-world-of-wahhabism.html.

and stability of the region's countries ... By defending the actions of terrorists and justifying them, the Iranian regime becomes a partner to their crimes, and it bears full responsibility for its policy of incitement and escalation.[80]

In the years that followed, the tit-for-tat rhetoric continued, shaped by regional developments. After the deaths of over 2,200 pilgrims on the 2015 *hajj*, events Khamenei criticized the Al Sa'ud for failing in their responsibilities as the Custodians of the Two Holy Places:

The incompetence of the Saudis and the insecurity imposed by them against the Hajj pilgrims to the House of God indeed demonstrated that this government is not qualified to manage the Two Holy Mosques and this reality must be spread in the Muslim world and be understood.[81]

Once again, Iranian officials sought to delegitimize the Al Sa'ud for failing to uphold their responsibilities to protect all Muslims during the *hajj*. Despite the tensions, dialogue over the *hajj* continued, with Saudi and Iranian officials regularly meeting to discuss the allocation of places to those wishing to make the pilgrimage along with addressing any possible security concerns. The existence of this dialogue, despite broader political pressures which occasionally erupt on the *hajj*, perhaps reflects a broader sense that the pilgrimage should be *apolitical*, a space for spirituality.[82]

Shifting Contours: Trump, MbS, and Biden

Exacerbating Saudi concerns about Iranian activity was an uncertainty about its relationship with the United State during the Obama presidency stemming from Washington's diplomatic engagement with Iran – notably the signing of the deeply unpopular nuclear deal (Joint Comprehensive Plan of Action [JCPOA]) – and vision of a regional security. In an interview between President Obama and *The Atlantic*'s Jeffrey Goldberg, Obama clearly articulated his view of the rivalry between the Saudis and the Iranians:

---

[80] 'Iran Furious over Saudi Arabia's Execution', *Memri*.
[81] 'Saudis Not Competent to Run Islam's Holy Mosques', *The Office of the Supreme Leader* (07.09. 16), www.leader.ir/en/content/16203/The-Leader's-meeting-with-families-of-Mina-and-Grand-Mosque-tragedies-in-Saudi-Arabia.
[82] Interview with cleric based at Al Azhar, Cairo. Skype, 2020. For more, see Simon Mabon and Lucia Ardovini, 'The Politics of Pilgrimage: Exploring the Hajj as a Site for Dialogue between Saudi Arabia and Iran', Luigi Narbone and Abdolrasool Divsallar (eds.) *Stepping Away from the Abyss: A Gradual Approach towards a New Security System in the Persian Gulf* (San Domenico, Italy: MEI, 2021), pp. 153–62, https://cadmus.eui .eu/bitstream/handle/1814/71221/QM-02-21-606-EN-N.pdf.

The competition between the Saudis and the Iranians—which has helped to feed proxy wars and chaos in Syria and Iraq and Yemen—requires us to say to our friends as well as to the Iranians that they need to find an effective way to share the neighborhood and institute some sort of cold peace.[83]

Unsurprisingly, Obama's words were not well received in Riyadh. In response, Prince Turki al-Saud rejected the accusation of being 'free riders', comparing

the Kingdom's 80 years of constant friendship with America to an Iranian leadership that continues to describe America as the biggest enemy, that continues to arm, fund and support sectarian militias in the Arab and Muslim world, that continues to harbor and host al-Qaʿida leaders, that continues to prevent the election of a Lebanese president through Hezbollah, which is identified by your government as a terrorist organization, that continues to kill the Syrian Arab people in league with Bashar Assad?[84]

Obama's inaction in Syria and inertia in Egypt angered many. As a result, the end of the Obama presidency was welcomed by a number of the Arab states who had invested in both candidates of the 2016 election. When Donald Trump was declared the victor, Gulf states were particularly optimistic, especially after the US withdrawal from the JCPOA and imposition of a campaign of 'maximum pressure' on Iran. For many, Trump was a leader who understood the importance of personal relationships, whose business acumen would allow them to work in a manner free from the constraints of diplomatic protocol. Additionally, Trump's administration was comprised of several anti-Iranian figures including John Bolton and Mike Pompeo whose views on Iran had been shaped by experience of the Iraq War. As a consequence, it was hardly surprising that the administration's Middle East policy was focused on curtailing the influence of Iran. As one official recalled: 'Our plan was to annihilate the physical caliphate of *isis* in Iraq and Syria – not attrition, annihilation – and to roll back the Persians. And force the Gulf states to stop funding radical Islam.'[85]

Writing in the *New Yorker*, Dexter Filkins offers prescient insight into how the Trump White House saw the Middle East:

Surveying the region, they concluded that the northern tier of the Middle East had been lost to Iran. In Lebanon, Hezbollah, an Iranian proxy, controlled the

---

[83] Jeffrey Goldberg, 'The Obama Doctrine', *The Atlantic* (2016), www.theatlantic.com/magazine/archive/2016/04/the-obama-doctrine/471525/#5.

[84] Turki al-Faysal, 'Mr. Obama, We Are Not "Free Riders"', *Arab News* (14.03.16), www.arabnews.com/columns/news/894826.

[85] Dexter Filkins, 'A Saudi Prince's Quest to Remake the Middle East', *New Yorker* (02.04.18), www.newyorker.com/magazine/2018/04/09/a-saudi-princes-quest-to-remake-the-middle-east.

government. In Syria, Iran had helped save President Bashar al-Assad from military disaster and was now bolstering his political future. In Iraq, the government, nominally pro-American, was also under the sway of Tehran. 'We kind of set those to the side,' the official told me. 'We thought, So then what? Our anchors were Israel and Saudi Arabia. We can't be successful in the Gulf without Saudi Arabia.'[86]

Fundamental to this strategy was the emergence of a young Saudi prince, viewed by many in Washington as perhaps the most influential actor in the Middle East; as one official recounted, 'We were going to embrace him as the change agent.'[87]

The son of King Salman, Mohammed bin Salman – commonly known as MbS – was named minister of defence after his father took the throne in January 2015. During this time, MbS sought to prevent the Houthi resurgence in Yemen, driven by a desire to curtail the influence of the Islamic Republic across the Middle East. After being named crown prince in 2017, MbS took on a more prominent role in the Kingdom, facilitating a process of rapid socio-economic transformation at a time when the Kingdom was engaged in a costly war in Yemen. Speaking to Jeffrey Goldberg on a fundraising trip to the United State, MbS was critical of the Iranian regime, suggesting that the supreme leader 'makes Hitler look good'. He later added that 'Hitler didn't do what the supreme leader is trying to do. Hitler tried to conquer Europe … The supreme leader is trying to conquer the world.'[88]

Under the Salmans, decision-making power became increasingly centralized, restricted to the king and crown prince. Despite his prominence in the Kingdom's political field, MbS was not known for his foreign policy acumen, and it was of little surprise that Saudi foreign policy was beset by a number of serious challenges. The most devastating of these remains the conflict in Yemen where Saudi and Emirati forces engaged in a bombing campaign targeted against Houthi rebels but with a destructive humanitarian impact that left 22.8 million people in dire need of humanitarian assistance. Beyond war in Yemen, MbS also struggled to address crises in Lebanon, best seen in the Saad Hariri incident which was prompted by a desire to curtail Iranian support for Hizbullah. Having agreed to work with the Party of God in the Lebanese government, Hariri was summoned to Riyadh on 3 November 2017 and immediately

---

[86] Ibid.
[87] Ibid.
[88] Jeffrey Goldberg, 'Saudi Crown Prince: Iran's Supreme Leader "Makes Hitler Look Good"', *The Atlantic* (02.04.18), www.theatlantic.com/international/archive/2018/04/mohammed-bin-salman-iran-israel/557036/; see also Filkins, 'A Saudi Prince's Quest to Remake the Middle East'.

placed under house arrest; a day later he resigned. During this time, missiles were fired from Yemen at targets across the Kingdom. After the interjection of French president Emmanuel Macron facilitated Hariri's release, he returned to Lebanon where he rescinded his resignation, continuing to work with Hizbullah.[89]

MbS was also a strong advocate of a desire to move towards a 'more tolerant' form of Islam, threatening a crackdown against members of the *'ulama'* who opposed his reform agenda and stressing a desire to 'destroy' extremist ideologies. This agenda had a foreign policy component, stemming from the Saudi *nomos* which was predicated on an anti-Iranian vision of order that also sought to exclude Islamist groups such as the Muslim Brotherhood. A systematic campaign was undertaken that sought to enforce this vision, both domestically and regionally, including the killing of Saudi critic and Islamist Jamal Khashoggi, an act that many believe was ordered by the crown prince.

With tensions across the region increasing, attacks on the Saudi state became more common. While missiles were routinely launched at strategic sites in the Kingdom, the most dramatic attacks came in 2019 and included a missile attack on the Khurais oilfield and Abqaiq refinery. The Khurais–Abqaiq attack was seen as a dramatic escalation, a serious strike against the Kingdom's oil infrastructure. Though the Houthis were quick to claim responsibility, the sophistication of the attacks pointed to some form of Iranian involvement. Although Donald Trump tweeted that his government was 'locked and loaded' but 'waiting to hear from the Kingdom' as to their desired course of action, Saudi officials were more restrained. Although firm in their condemnation of the attack, Saudi officials declared an intention to wait for the results of an inquiry before acting. Speaking with CNN in the wake of the Khurais–Abqaiq attack, Javad Zarif asserted that while Iran would seek to prevent all-out war, he was of the opinion that Saudi Arabia was willing to fight Iran 'to the last American'.[90]

The election of Joe Biden as the 46th president of the United States in autumn 2020 provoked a great deal of concern amongst many across the Gulf, who feared a return to a form of Obama-era engagement with Iran. Concern at what a possible Biden administration could mean for regional politics prompted several Gulf states to formalize relations with Israel in what became known as the Abraham Accords, yet while not formally normalizing relations, Saudi Arabia continued to retain tacit

[89] Filkins, 'A Saudi Prince's Quest to Remake the Middle East'.
[90] Reuters Staff, 'Iran's Zarif Says Saudi, UAE Want "to Fight Iran to the Last American"' *Reuters* (20.09.19).

relations with Israel.[91] Following his inauguration in early 2021, Biden sought to revive the Joint Comprehensive Plan of Action (JCPOA) and, alongside it, to end the war in Yemen.

At this time, officials from Saudi Arabia and Iran were taking part in a range of track II diplomatic initiatives organized by a number of international organizations. Designed to improve relations between the two states, track II processes gained traction over 2020, resulting in a formal diplomatic initiative hosted by Iraq in summer 2021 which sought to reintegrate Iran into regional affairs, albeit without a resolution to the Yemen War. These processes began with dialogue between academics to more cultural sets of activities aimed at reintegrating the two rivals. Such efforts had been taking place in the preceding years, with a series of initiatives operating across the world in an effort to de-escalate tensions. While some were more serious than others, all were conditioned by the complexities of international politics. Some initiatives even failed to begin as a consequence of a shifting global context, notably the actions of erstwhile US President Donald Trump, whose campaign of 'maximum pressure' – one which had a devastating impact on the Iranian economy – left Saudi officials less inclined to engage in dialogue with their Iranian counterparts.[92]

By 2022, however, global developments dramatically shaped the transnational field. Russia's invasion of Ukraine posed serious challenges to international politics, albeit in the face of vocal criticism from other members of the international community. Aside from challenging the salience of norms of sovereignty, the invasion also placed additional pressures on international efforts to resolve the Iranian nuclear question, with Russia involved as one of the members of the UN Security Council.

Conclusions

Despite the presence of dialogue between Saudi Arabia and Iran, challenges remain. As interactions in the transnational field become

---

[91] Clive Jones and Yoal Guzansky, *Fraternal Enemies* (London: Hurst, 2020).

[92] This author has spoken to several people involved in different initiatives and explored the possibility of establishing such an initiative under the SEPAD umbrella. Further details have been withheld to avoid disclosing sensitive information. One such initiative that has published information about its activities is CARPO: https://carpo-bonn.org/en/iran-saudi-dialogue-initiative/. The sensitivity of such processes also impacted on broader track II efforts, including cultural engagement. One such effort involved musicians from both sides of the Persian Gulf coming together to record an album. Yet concerns about political sensitivity – predominantly amongst Arab musicians – ultimately made such efforts futile. For more information on track II processes between Saudi Arabia and Iran, see Ibrahim Fraihat's excellent book on the topic. Ibrahim Fraihat, *Iran and Saudi Arabia: Taming a Chaotic Conflict* (Edinburgh: Edinburgh University Press, 2020).

increasingly fractious, hostility resonates across states in the transnational field, particularly those comprising divided societies and with groups who subscribe to the *nomoi* of regional powers. Such divisions are exacerbated by processes of sectarianization – shaped by geopolitical factors – which were then imbued with dehumanizing meaning, condemning *the other* and becoming a prominent part of the everyday lexicon. Such comments transcend the high politics of public officials and find traction amongst the populations of states across the region, aided by social media and the ability to stream speeches and sermons from across the world.

Tracing the rivalry between Saudi Arabia and Iran goes some way to dismissing the 'ancient hatreds' thesis that pits the two major Gulf powers against one another in a primordialist battle that threatens to consume the Muslim world. While spirals of rhetoric between the two states have become commonplace, these are not solely driven by religious difference but instead find traction amidst political crises, most notably after the revolution of 1979 and after the Arab Uprisings. Much like the view put forward by Michael Barnett in *Dialogues in Arab Politics*, political events and incidents provide opportunities to mould the region in pursuit of geopolitical agendas. Thus, if one looks at the rivalry between Riyadh and Tehran, we can see that at times of crisis the rivalry is redrawn, often in a negative manner but also with the capacity for positive change, as seen in the aftermath of the 1990 earthquake.

Much like the construction of space, the rivalry is shaped by global forces and the intimately tiny intricacies of domestic politics. It is a rivalry that is a product of the contingencies of time and space, constructed through the interaction of myriad factors. After the establishment of the Islamic Republic of Iran in 1979, the rivalry played an important role in shaping the transnational field. At this time, religious capital became increasingly important in defining principles of vision, further embedding domestic political fields within the transnational field. The interplay of religious, political, social, cultural, and economic capital shaped the nature of political fields as actors sought to define principles of vision in pursuit of their *nomos*.

3   Iraq

In the early hours of 3 January 2020, a US drone strike close to Baghdad International Airport killed Iranian general Qassim Suleimani, the leader of the Quds force, and Abu Mahdi al-Muhandis, the de facto leader of the PMF. The attack was prompted by fears about the rising influence of Suleimani and Iran across Iraq and the wider region. Al-Muhandis appeared to be in the wrong place at the wrong time, yet the repercussions of his killing continue to be felt as the PMF organization splinters and struggles to vie for influence across Iraq's already decimated political field. The continuation of the *Tishreen* protests into 2022 reflects the depth of anger held by protesters at endemic corruption, bureaucratic inertia, and the presence of foreign actors in Iraqi politics.

Since the US-led invasion in 2003 which removed Saddam Hussein from power, Iraq's political field has been a site of widespread contestation between actors seeking to assert principles of vision. Yet Iraq's position in the post-2003 transnational field left it a prominent arena of competition between Saudi Arabia and Iran. Sharing land borders with the Kingdom and the Islamic Republic, with a society divided along ethno-sectarian lines, Iraq possesses strategic importance for both Saudi Arabia and Iran. While formerly a prominent actor in regional politics, the post-2003 landscape was such that Iran – in particular – was able to exert vast influence across Iraq's political, economic, and religious fields, much to the chagrin of Saudi Arabia. Over time, Saudi Arabia sought to combat Iranian gains but the legacy of violent Sunni Islamism, first in the guise of al-Qaʻida then Daʼish left Sunni groups struggling to exert political capital, prompting the Kingdom to find creative approaches beyond supporting tribal or sectarian kin. Continued Iranian influence in support of a corrupt elite became a source of frustration for many Iraqis, prompting widespread protests from 2019 onwards. Yet at this time, Iraq began to reassert itself on the regional stage, hosting a series of diplomatic efforts designed to improve relations between Saudi Arabia and Iran.

To understand the ways in which Saudi Arabia and Iran have engaged with Iraqi politics and sought to define the principles of vision within Iraq's political field, one must understand the structural factors conditioning and curtailing the deployment of capital. Here, tracing the evolution of Iraq's political field is essential as a means of understanding the actions of Riyadh and Tehran. This tracing involves reflecting on identity politics and the interplay between communal groups and the state. The nature of this interplay, in turn, allows for the development of relations with regional powers, both on an individual and group level.

The Quest for Order and Iraq in the Transnational Field

The quest to shape Iraq's political field has its roots in the formation of the modern state. Across the following decades, efforts to impose visions of order onto Iraq's social world were conditioned by actors laying claim to different forms of capital and principles of vision and division – privileging ethnicity, nationalism, tribe, and sect at various points in space and time – all underpinned by the position of Iraq within the transnational field. Iraq's position within this transnational field and the nature of contestation within its own political field has positioned it prominently within the struggle between Saudi Arabia and Iran. Its geographical location, ethno-sectarian demographic makeup and, post-2003, the *muhassasa* system of power sharing created deep-rooted permeability which gave ample opportunities for external powers to exert influence.

While principles of vision privileging sectarian identity offer an obvious means through which transnational relationships were developed, these are conditioned by a range of other factors, including the symbiotic relationship with national identity, socio-economic factors, and clerical legitimacy. The importance of Iraq's position within the transnational field meant that developments within the country's political field resonate across the transnational field, prompting external actors to become directly involved in domestic politics in an effort to shape the political and transnational fields. External actors seeking to exert influence in Iraq were thus able to draw on capital from both the transnational field and Iraq's political, economic, and religious fields.

The provision of safe haven and political support to Shi'a figures who fled Iraq under Saddam Hussein gave Tehran a great deal of social and economic capital in the post-2003 political field, particularly amidst a principle of vision that ordered politics along communal lines. Relationships with political elites and the organizational structure of political life in Iraq gave Iran a range of opportunities for influence. In contrast, Saudi Arabia viewed the Iraqi leadership with much trepidation and also struggled to make inroads into the Sunni political bloc, meaning that what little influence the Kingdom was able to exercise predominantly took place informally and through tribal links.

Over time, rising frustration at levels of corruption across the state gave the Kingdom opportunities to cultivate relations with Shi'a parties, prioritizing ethnicity over sectarian difference. The emergence of an alternative principle of vision predicated on Iraqi nationalism and anti-corruption manifested in widespread protests across the state against politicians, the PMFs, and Iran itself. At this point, Saudi Arabia was able to exert greater social and economic capital having worked to cultivate relationships with tribal and political elites.

State Formation and Development

The contemporary contestation of Iraq's political field can be traced to the formative years of the state and British involvement in the Middle East during the First World War. Modern Iraq began life as a British mandate in 1921 – enacted the following year – with Faysal ibn Hussein, son of the sherif of Mecca as king. Seen to be a popular Arab leader, Faysal appeared to be the obvious choice, yet the challenge facing him in creating the state was clear

There is still – and I say this with a heart full of sorrow – no Iraqi people but unimaginable masses of human beings, devoid of any patriotic idea, imbued with religious traditions and absurdities, connected by no common tie, giving ear to evil, prone to anarchy, and perpetually ready to rise against any government whatsoever.[1]

In a similar vein, Hanna Batatu argues that the Arabs of Iraq were 'congeries of distinct, discordant, self-involved societies', plagued by divisions along class lines, most notably playing out in tensions between urban and rural societies.[2] As Adeed Dawisha acknowledges:

no Shi'ite was accepted in the military college or in the bureaucracy, except on very rare occasions. There were all kinds of hurdles preventing Shi'ites from even entering high schools. The State did not think of the Shi'ite community as part of it, and the Shi'ites did not consider themselves to be part of the state.[3]

---

[1] T.E. Lawrence, 'Faysal's Table Talk', report to Colonel Wilson, 8 January 1917, FO 686/6, p. 121. Faysal's remarks are also quoted in Hanna Batatu, *The Old Social Classes and the Revolutionary Movements in Iraq* (Princeton: Princeton University Press, 1978), pp. 25–6.

[2] Batatu, *The Old Social Classes*, p. 13.

[3] Adeeda Dawisha, *Iraq: A Political History from Independence to Occupation* (Princeton: Princeton University Press, 2013), p. 72.

In the formative stages of the state, debate over the political, social, economic, theological, and tribal vision of the political project manifested in schism along different lines and the process of state building that was employed shaped the relationship between regimes and communities across the state.

Suspicion at the loyalty of the various groups across the state played a prominent role in the political machinations of those in power. A key advisor to the new king, Gertrude Bell, stated

The proximity of Persia and the existence in Mesopotamia of Karbala and Najaf, two of the most holy shrines of the Shi'a sect, to which the Persians belong, with the resulting influx of Persian pilgrims, have brought the country much under Persian influences. Nomad Arabia belongs wholly to the Sunni half of Islam, yet the tribes settled in Mesopotamia have embraced, almost without exception, the Shi'a faith. Those, however, who maintain purely nomadic habits, 'people of the Camel' as they proudly call themselves, have kept as a rule to the desert doctrine and are almost invariably Sunni.[4]

Tribal, sectarian, and economic divisions created parabolic forces undermining political stability. Although Faysal sought to create conditions that would facilitate the development of the political project, this ultimately embedded such tensions within the institutional fabric of the state. Indeed, in an attempt to create some semblance of stability, a land settlement law was passed seeking to safeguard tribal influence and protect tribal leaders who had informally occupied such positions. It was hardly surprising, therefore, when wealthy tribal elites and urban bourgeois were able to exploit this decision, often at the expense of the Shi'a of the south. This development of political life across Iraq enshrined difference and fear in the new state and across its communities.

Although political organization matured, a complex melange of identity politics regulated by neo-patrimonialism posed a serious challenge to political stability. Instability fermented with latent discrimination manifesting in a number of incidents where particular groups sought to express their dissatisfaction with political elites. The deployment of capital – in a range of forms – by those in power had a devastating impact on marginalized communities, while the continued presence of the British colonial masters served to exacerbate the situation.

The development of infrastructural projects provided elites with the means through which to circumvent political dissent amongst Shi'a groups, marginalizing Shi'a communities through institutional structures

---

[4] Gertrude Bell, *A Woman in Arabia: The Writings of the Queen of the Desert* (New York: Penguin, 2015), p. 169.

and privileging a vision of Iraqi identity that was Sunni, Arab, and predominantly urban. At this time, it was common practice to deny Shi'a
entry to military colleges and bureaucracy.[5] Moreover, accessing high
school posed serious challenges for Iraqi Shi'a.[6] It was hardly surprising that this cultivated feelings of dissent amongst these communities.[7]
This practice of discrimination resulted in the emergence of an array
of visions of what the Iraqi state would look like, best documented in
Hanna Batatu's magisterial study of Iraq.[8] Processes of state formation
embedded – and exacerbated – divisions within the fabric of the state
and the individual's habitus, which would become manipulated in the
years that followed by domestic and regional actors seeking to increase
their influence.

Over time, it was hardly surprising that developments in the transnational field began to resonate in Iraq's political field and, vice versa.
From US efforts to counter Soviet gains in the Middle East through the
short-lived Baghdad Pact to the emergence of pan-Arabism, Iraq featured centrally in these developments.[9] Bureaucratic institutions sought
to embed such sentiments within their structures as a means of engender-
ing legitimacy and loyalty amongst an increasingly restless population.
The establishment of Ba'athist dominance– and the ensuing emergence
of Saddam Hussein as leader – brought about a violent and exclusionary
set of principles of vision which dramatically deepened divisions between
Iraq's communal groups.

Suspicion and War

Following revolution in Iran, the outbreak of war between Iraq and Iran
in late September 1980 had a seismic impact on regional relations, dramatically altering the balance of power across the Gulf. The war posed
serious challenges to strategists across the region, but perhaps none more
seriously than Saudi Arabia. While previously the Kingdom had cultivated relations with both states in an effort to balance against the interests of the other, the war prompted the Al Sa'ud to pick a side. As May
Darwich pertinently notes, the Saudi decision to support a militarily

---

[5] By 1958, Sunnis made up 70 per cent of all officers, while Shi'a comprised 20 per cent
and Kurds and other minorities 10 per cent. See Ahmed S. Hashim, 'Military Power and
State Formation in Modern Iraq', *Middle East Policy*, x:4 (2003), 29.

[6] Dawisha, *Iraq: A Political History*, p. 72.

[7] Ibid., p. 72.

[8] Batatu, *The Old Social Classes*.

[9] Jeffrey Karam, *The Middle East in 1958: Reimaging a Revolutionary Year* (London: I.B.
Tauris, 2021).

superior Iraq against a weakened Iran – brought about by the disband-ment of the Iranian army after the revolution – appears at odds with conventional understandings of alliance building in IR theory.[10] Under-pinning this decision, Darwich argues, was a broader concern about ontological security and a challenge from the Islamic Republic to the Kingdom's legitimacy.

The revolution and outbreak of war shaped both the transnational field and the domestic affairs of a number of Middle Eastern states, par-ticularly their relationship with Shi'a communities who became increas-ingly viewed with suspicion in Sunni-dominated states. Many in Tehran, buoyed by revolutionary zeal, thought that Iraq's Shi'a population would side with their sectarian kin against the 'Godless Ba'athists', ignoring the importance of nationalism in both the habitus and Saddam Hus-sein's symbolic capital. Across eight years, the conflict decimated the two states, resulting in the death of a generation of Iranians and injury to many others.

The war exacerbated Iraq's communal tensions. At this point, the big-gest threat to Saddam's rule was seen to be from the Shi'a groups across the south of Iraq, best represented by al-Da'wa and al-Mujahidin.[11] Although the groups drew support from different constituencies and advocated different visions of order – the former largely from Shi'a cler-ics and those excluded from mainstream politics[12] while the latter found favour amongst religious graduates – both groups had been inspired by the work of Muhammad Baqir al-Sadr, an Iraqi cleric from the shrine city of Najaf. In 1980, al-Sadr was executed by Saddam Hussein amidst fears of an insurgent Shi'a population across the south. Such fears had been exacerbated by events in Iran a year earlier, leading to suspicion across the region's divided societies that Shi'a groups were fifth col-umnists whose loyalty lay with Iran. Shortly after al-Sadr's execution, regime officials began a crackdown on al-Da'wa, which ultimately served to force key figures and other Shi'a opposition groups into exile in Iran.

Amidst the presence of a large and politically active Iraqi diaspora in Iran, the Supreme Council for the Islamic Revolution (SCIRI) was established which sought to bring these disparate figures together.[13]

---

[10] May Darwich, *Threats and Alliances.*

[11] Hanna Batatu, 'Iraq's Underground Shi'a Movements' (MER102, 1981), www.merip .org/mer/mer102/iraqs-underground-shii-movements.

[12] Soren Schmidt, 'The Role of Religion in Politics. The Case of Shi'a-Islamism in Iraq', *Nordic Journal of Religion and Society*, xxii:2 (2009), 129.

[13] Ibid., p. 128. In 2007 SCIRI became known as the Islamic Supreme Council of Iraq (ISCI) as the group sought to distance itself from Iran. For more on this, see p. 80.

Established by Ayatollah Khomeini under the auspices of a desire to export revolutionary goals, this nascent community of Iraqi political figures in exile in Iran was replete with ideological and political difference, not least over the role of clerical leaders in political life. Rhetoric from Tehran about exporting the revolution had a dramatic impact on their neighbours. Iraqi Shi'a routinely crossed the border into Iran, meaning intermarriage and cultural exchange was common, while many Iraqis had grandparents who were Iranian.

Reflecting fears about the loyalty of Shi'a Muslims, Saddam issued Decision 666 on 26 May 1980, which declared that any Iraqi of *foreign* origins – primarily Iranian – was no longer considered a citizen if they were found to be disloyal in any way.[14] In an interview with the Kuwaiti newspaper *al-Thawra*, Saddam suggested that Arab Shi'a sought to blend in with the population until the time came to reveal their 'sinister' Persian identity, once again creating a vision of order in which the fusion of Shi'a and Persian was a threat. Across the following decade, a spate of investigations into family lineages resulted in forced deportations of those with Iranian origins who were seen to be disloyal to Iraq.[15] This investigation posed an existential challenge to Iraq's Arab Shi'a population, where a small connection to Iran was used to justify deportation and the erosion of their identity. At this time a great number of Iraqis fled to Iran in search of refugee where they were initially placed in camps but a large number were able to improve their situation by joining groups such as al-Da'wa or SCIRI.[16] Despite Saddam's suspicions, the outbreak of war between Iraq and Iran witnessed Shi'a Iraqis fighting against their fellow Shi'a in a display of nationalist loyalty to Iraq.

While the war between Iran and Iraq had pitted two of Saudi Arabia's regional rivals against one another, the fears of many Saudis were realized in the summer of 1990 when 700 tanks and 100,000 soldiers from the Iraqi army crossed the border into Kuwait. In response, King Fahd closed the Kingdom's border with Iraq, broke off diplomatic relations and quickly turned to its largest arms dealer for protection, unabashedly welcoming half a million members of the US armed forces into the

---

[14] National Legislative Bodies/National Authorities, Iraq: Resolution No. 666 of 1980 (nationality), 26 May 1980, www.refworld.org/docid/3ae6b51d28.html.

[15] Ali Babakhan, 'The Deportation of Shi'a during the Iran-Iraq War: Causes and Consequences', in Faleh Abdul-Jabar (ed.), *Ayatollahs, Sufis, and Ideologues: State, religion, and Social Movements in Iraq* (London: Saqi Books, 2002), pp. 183–210.

[16] Some estimates place the number of refugees as high as 100,000. See: ill Ricotta 'The Arab Shi'a Nexus: Understanding Iran's Influence in the Arab World', *Washington Quarterly* 39:2 (2016), 144.

Kingdom.[17] During this period, the Kingdom was required to enhance its diplomatic credentials both to shore up an anti-Iraq alliance and to host diplomatic exchanges aimed at shaping the future of the region after the war.

After the invasion of Kuwait, Iraqi troops returned home where long-standing social, economic, and political grievances – particularly amongst Shi'a groups – once again began to resonate, resulting in rebellion across the south of the state which was put down violently by the Iraqi military. Reports from the 1991 rebellion recall members of the Iraqi armed forces chanting *la shi'a b'ad alyoum*, translated as 'no Shi'a after today'. Such remarks only served to exacerbate fears amongst Shi'a communities, shaping perceptions of persecution that would erupt in the decades to come.[18]

The Fragmentation of the State

Operation Iraqi Freedom, which began on 19March 2003 as part of US president George W. Bush's 'War on Terror', emerged after a prolonged period of diplomatic crisis and resulted in a swift military victory for coalition forces against their Iraqi counterparts. The fall of Baghdad took place a mere three weeks after the beginning of the war, resulting in Bush's premature declaration of victory on the deck of the USS *Abraham Lincoln* under a banner reading 'Mission Accomplished'.[19] In the months that followed, previously exiled figures began to return to Iraq, integrating themselves with US officials in an attempt to cultivate influence and situate themselves prominently within political decision-making processes.[20]

The post-invasion period was shaped by fear and uncertainty amongst Iraqis and regional powers. In creating the conditions to allow Iraqis to determine their own future as noted in UNSCR 1511, it was deemed necessary to prevent the re-emergence of Ba'athism. The ensuing process of de-Ba'athification sought to create conditions of political possibility, although little consideration was given to the all-encompassing

---

[17] Rachel Bronson, 'Understanding US-Saudi Relations', in Paul Aarts and Gerd Nonneman (eds.), *Saudi Arabia in the Balance: Political Economy, Society, Foreign Affairs* (London: Hurst 2005), p. 385.

[18] See Fanar Haddad, *Sectarianism in Iraq: Antagonistic Views of Reality* (New York: Columbia University Press, 2011).

[19] 'Text of Bush Speech', *CBS News* (01.05.03), www.cbsnews.com/news/text-of-bush-speech-01-05-2003/. Seven months later, Saddam Hussein was captured and executed in 2006.

[20] Charles Tripp, *A History of Iraq* (Cambridge: Cambridge University Press, 2007), p. 280.

nature of Ba'athism and the extent to which Saddam had eviscerated political opposition under his rule.

Post-2003, politics in Iraq was shaped by competing visions of order. As Fanar Haddad observed, sectarian identities was viewed as the 'mutually antagonistic other of national identity',[21] an alternative principle of vision. In the following years, discrimination and exclusion was reversed within a climate of extreme insecurity and fear. Power relations were re-organized, leading to the establishment of a form of the tyranny of the majority, of Shi'a over Sunni. Complicating matters was the presence of a coalition military force which exacerbated instability and violence. With rising violence from al-Qaʻida and affiliated groups, Sunni Iraqis were increasingly caught between accusations of being a terrorist or being a Ba'athist.[22] A number of accounts from Sunni Muslims document the violence of Shi'a militias. Amidst such conditions of exclusion, marginalization, and persecution, facing an array of socio-economic challenges and lacking a form of political expression, Sunnis faced increasingly precarious futures, with little support or protection.[23]

In an attempt to facilitate the de-Ba'athification process, coalition forces created the Coalition Provisional Authority which, through a number of orders, embarked on the process of removing all traces of the Ba'ath Party. As Charles Tripp notes, the process had a devastating impact on Iraqi society, eradicating large parts of state infrastructure and making 30,000 Ba'athists redundant. Beyond this, a further 300,000 armed young men were made unemployed, while the pensions of tens of thousands of others were stopped and prominent administrators were purged from key government ministries.[24]

The extent of the damage done by the de-Ba'athification process was later shown by the Chilcot Inquiry, the British inquest into the Iraq War, which noted that the process 'made the task of reconstructing Iraq more difficult, both by reducing the pool of Iraqi administrators and by adding to the pool of the unemployed and disaffected, which in turn fed insurgent activity'.[25] The report also refers to a discussion between David

---

[21] Fanar Haddad, 'Sectarian Relations in Arab Iraq: Contextualising the Civil War of 2006–2007', *British Journal of Middle Eastern Studies*, xl:2 (2013), 115–38.

[22] International Crisis Group interview with a young Sunni.

[23] See Mabon, *Houses Built on Sand*; Simon Mabon and Ana Maria Kuramasamy, 'Da'ish, Stasis and Bare Life in Iraq', in Jacob Erikson and Ahmed Khaleel (eds.), *Iraq after ISIS* (New York: Palgrave Macmillan, 2018); and Simon Mabon, 'The Apocalyptic and the Sectarian', in Tim Clack and Rob Johnson (eds.), *Upstream Operations* (New York: Palgrave Macmillan, 2018).

[24] Tripp, *A History of Iraq*, p. 282.

[25] John Chilcot, *The Iraq Inquiry*, vol. 8 (2016), p. 8.

Manning and Paul Bremer in Baghdad, which acknowledged that the de
Ba'athification process was responsible for creating a 'new reservoir of
angry men' and an increasingly unstable environment.[26]

In such conditions, the Iraqi state was largely impotent, unable to exert
sovereign control over territory or people, leaving it open to the actions
of regional rivals. Iraq's political field became a site of violent contestation between actors with competing principles of vision and division,
albeit playing out in the context of the newly implemented Iraqi constitution and the *muhassasa* system. Amidst instability and uncertainty, a
number of groups emerged using violence as a means of protecting their
own constituents, often with the support of regional powers. This perilous terrain became increasingly fractious with the mobilization of sectarian identity markers, deepening communal divisions in the process. For
Iran, a shared sectarian identity allowed it to circumvent ethnic divisions
which had previously thwarted Tehran's efforts to challenge Saddam
Hussein in the halcyon days of the Islamic Republic.

The US invasion – in the context of the war on terror – also served as
a catalyst for empowering Sunni militants who flocked to Iraq to fight
against the Americans. In the months that followed, fighters from across
the region travelled to Iraq to join the forces of a local al-Qaʿida franchise,
led by the Jordanian Abu Musab al-Zarqawi, a vociferously anti-Shi'a
figure whose actions later inspired Da'ish. Al-Zarqawi's actions included
the targeting of Shi'a Muslims and shrines, including a car bomb attack
outside the Imam ʿAli Mosque in August 2003 which killed Ayatollah
Muhammad Baqr al-Hakim, the leader of SCIRI, prompting reciprocal
attacks and the escalation of tensions between Sunni and Shi'a.

Such events had a dramatic impact on relations between Sunni and
Shi'a communities in Iraq and across the region (as other chapters will
demonstrate). Samarra, a city home to both sects, became plagued by
sectarian violence after the 2003 invasion. In recent memory, the city had
been largely secular, with a Sunni majority, yet amidst increasing Iranian
influence, many feared efforts to 'fundamentally alter the city's character', transforming it from largely secular into a devout Shi'a locale.[27]
In fighting between the different groups, the city's Golden Mosque –
a site of great importance for Shi'a Muslims[28] – was damaged, along

[26] Ibid., p. 14.
[27] 08BAGHDAD3994_a '(C) PRT Salah ad Din: Iranian Involvement in Samarra'
(21.12.08), https://wikileaks.org/plusd/cables/08BAGHDAD3994_a.html. See also
Simon Mabon and Stephen Royle, *The Origins of ISIS: The Collapse of Nations and
Revolution in the Middle East* (London: I.B. Tauris, 2016).
[28] The mosque is said to be the burial place of the 10th and 11th Imams and the site of the
12th Imam's occulation and return as Mahdi.

with other parts of the city's infrastructure. The reconstruction process was also beset by tensions and controversy as the Golden Mosque was repaired before basic infrastructure was rebuilt.[29]

Relations between these groups became increasingly complex as socio-economic issues shaped the struggle between sect and national identity. Coalition efforts to regulate life through divide and rule strategies embedded a sense of institutional difference within the fabric of the state which was routinely adopted by Iraqi rulers. The US-led invasion of 2003 created possibility for identities routinely subjected to structural violence and institutional discrimination to exert political agency. In such conditions of uncertainty with many facing precarious futures, Iraq also became a site of increased competition between Saudi Arabia and Iran. In the years that followed, communal tensions within Iraq drew in regional actors seeking to shape the political field and strengthen the capital of their local allies. Yet as the struggle to shape Iraq's political field intensified, the transnational field increasingly became a site of vitriolic contestation, as we shall see.

The Struggle for Principles of Vision

Following the removal of Saddam Hussein, the struggle to dominate Iraq's political field was shaped by the interplay of a range of different principles of vision and division, including articulations of ethno-sectarian communal difference, Iraqi nationalism, and tribalism.[30] The dominance of Saddam's Ba'athist principle of vision and evisceration of civil society left few individuals within Iraq able to exert capital. While clerics such as Grand Ayatollah 'Ali Sistani and others in Najaf and Karbala or popular leaders like Muqtada al-Sadr were able to exert social capital, the post-2003 political field was dominated by the return of previously exiled figures from Iran, which created an environment of instability and tension as they clashed with actors who had remained in Iraq.

With this came increased Iranian influence in Iraq. Initially characterized by close security cooperation and good relations, over time Iranian influence began to include economic and cultural engagement, and efforts to demonstrate influence in the transnational field. Between 2003 and 2014, Iraq was Iran's second largest export market,[31] while Iranian investment in Iraq dramatically increased

---

[29] 08BAGHDAD3994_a, '(C) PRT Salah ad Din'.

[30] Dodge, 'Bourdieu Goes to Baghdad'.

[31] 'I. R. Iran's Main Export Destinations in 2013', *Iran Trade Statistics in Brief 2013*, Iranian Trade Planning Office, http://eng.tpo.ir/uploads/2013statictic_word_tabdil_be_pdf_7454.pdf.

through tourism to Iraq's shrine cities of Najaf and Karbala. As Edward Wastnidge observes, the importance of the shrine cities for Iran offers a 'powerful incentive and justification' for Tehran's actions and *nomos*.[32]

In contrast, Saudi actions were driven by a concern at increased Iranian influence across the state and Tehran's dominance of Iraq's political field.[33] Although Riyadh had articulated its concerns to Washington about an invasion, the presence of the United States in Iraq post-2003 helped to assuage broader concerns about Iranian influence regionally. Dialogue between officials in Riyadh and their US counterparts regularly stressed the need for the United States to remain in Iraq to prevent it falling into Iran's sphere of influence.

Although reliant on Washington, Saudi strategy also sought to cultivate relationships with Iraqi actors. While difficult to accurately document, the Iraq Study Group identified the involvement of Saudi figures in funding the Sunni insurgency in Iraq, a claim also made by Iranian media outlets.[34] In the years that followed, Saudi Arabia sought to counter Iranian gains through material support for predominantly tribal Sunni groups, albeit with little success. Similarly, unlike their Iranian counterparts – as we shall see shortly – the cultivation of relations with local actors proved less successful, unable – and often, during the initial post-Saddam years, unwilling – to cultivate relations with Shi'a groups. Instead, Riyadh focused on engaging with Sunni tribes from the Anbar province in an effort to balance against Shi'a elites dominating Iraqi politics.

The evisceration of the Iraqi state posed serious strategic challenges to Riyadh, removing one actor with the capacity to balance against Iran.[35] Moreover, the invasion – which took place against the advice of Washington's Arab allies – opened up opportunities for Iran to operate with strategic depth. Moreover, as Iraq no longer occupied a 'container' role with regard to Iran, Tehran would have unhindered access to allies in Syria and Lebanon, exposing Saudi vulnerabilities and fears.

Yet while Iran was able to deploy social, economic, and religious capital both individually and through relationships with officials occupying

---

[32] Edward Wastnidge, 'Iran's Own "War on Terror": Iranian Foreign Policy Towards Syria and Iraq during the Rouhani Era,' in *Foreign Policy of Iran under President Hassan Rouhani's First Term (2013-2017)* (Singapore: Palgrave Macmillan), pp. 107–29.

[33] See Katherine Harvey, *A Self-Fulfilling Prophecy: The Saudi Struggle for Iraq* (London: Hurst, 2021).

[34] Wehrey et al., *Saudi-Iranian Relations*, pp. 63–7.

[35] Dina Badie, *After Saddam: American Foreign Policy and the Destruction of Secularism in the Middle East* (New York and London: Lexington Books, 2017).

prominent political portfolios, broader issues remained. Although there are strong religious links between Shi'a counterparts in Iraq and Iran, a number of theological and political differences placed checks on Tehran's religious capital, stemming from the clerical authority of Grand Ayatollah 'Ali Sistani, whose quietist position is contrary to the ideas of *veleyat-e faqih*. Moreover, there was suspicion amongst many at Iran's efforts to exert religious and political influence amongst Iraqis. A 2007 poll found 62 per cent of Shi'a Iraqis believed that the Iranian government advocated sectarian violence.[36] Three years later, 48 per cent of the same constituency held a negative view of Iranian relationships with Iraqi political elites.[37]

Political instability had a devastating impact on the already decimated Iraqi economy, leaving people in need of financial assistance and the state open to external penetration. While Sunnis gained support from tribal networks, Shi'a communities found support from local groups who simultaneously provided food and fulfilled social roles, while also protecting them against multifarious threats. It was in this climate that groups such as the Sadrists, led by Muqtada al-Sadr (the grandson of Grand Ayatollah Sayyid Mohammad Mohammd Sadiq al-Sadr) gained prominence.

Increasing Shi'a influence across Iraq and beyond was a source of great consternation for many Sunni Arab rulers who were worried about rising Iranian influence across the region. These fears were routinely articulated by Saudi officials to their US counterparts. In one such conversation, it was stressed that the United States

should not leave Iraq until its sovereignty has been restored, otherwise it will be vulnerable to the Iranians. He said the Saudis will not support one Iraqi group over the others and that the Kingdom is working for a united Iraq. However, he warned that, if the U.S. leaves precipitously, the Saudis will stand with the Sunnis.[38]

In this environment, it was hardly surprising that regional rivalries began to play out across Iraqi politics, finding traction through the various forms of capital garnered by Riyadh and Tehran over the years that followed.

---

[36] Michael Eisenstadt, Michael Knights, and Ahmed Ali, *Iran's Influence in Iraq: Countering Tehran's Whole-of-Government Approach* (Washington, DC: Washington Institute for Near East Policy, 2011).

[37] David Pollock and Ahmed Ali, 'Iran Gets Negative Reviews in Iraq, Even from *Shi'ites*', Policywatch blog, Washington Institute for Near East Policy, Policy #1653 (04.05.10), www.washingtoninstitute.org/policy-analysis/view/iran-gets-negative-reviews-in-iraq-even-from-shi'ites.

[38] 06RIYADH9175_a 'Saudi Moi Head Says if U.S. Leaves Iraq, Saudi Arabia Will Stand with Sunnis' (26.12.06), https://wikileaks.org/plusd/cables/06RIYADH9175_a.html.

The Muhassasa *System: Ethno-Sectarian Power Sharing*

Efforts to regulate political life through democratic processes in Iraq require addressing the challenging ethno-religious divisions that have plagued the state's history. The system of *Muhassasa Tai'fiyya* (sectarian apportionment) was established in 2003 in an attempt to empower individuals from all facets of society, born out of a conference held by exiles in 1992. The return of these exiles were a key part of this system, becoming its new elite and, with it, giving external actors access to positions of influence. In 2005, elections were held across Iraq that saw the United Iraqi Alliance – a group defined by Shi'a solidarity – win a majority and the group's leader, Ibrahim al-Jaafari, nominated to be prime minister. Quickly seen as ineffective, al-Jaafari resigned in April 2006 to be replaced by Nouri al-Maliki, a member of al-Da'wa and a long-standing critic of Saddam Hussein who had spent time in Iran.

Central to the *muhassasa* system was the allocation of positions according to the principles of 'Salah al-Din', which divided jobs along ethno-religious lines. Identities were central to the heart of the agreement which sought representation from groups across the different communities.[39] Yet the development of a system that exacerbates and enshrines division is seen to have fundamentally weakened a political system, much like other criticisms of consociational rule, enshrining divisions within society but also creating an environment that facilitated endemic corruption.[40]

Although the Shi'a bloc dominated the electoral process, political divisions within Shi'a groups and parties posed a number of serious challenges to governing and intra-communal unity. The existence of schisms was hardly surprising, with the bloc divided along political, economic, and theological lines resulting in difference between SCIRI, al Da'wa, the Sadrists, the 'quietist' clerical establishment, amongst others. As a consequence, the various groups sought to impose a dominant principle of vision across Iraq's political field, using a range of forms of capital in the process.

---

[39] See Fanar Haddad, 'From Existential Struggle to Political Banality: The Politics of Sect in Post-2003 Iraq', *The Review of Faith & International Affairs*, 18:1 (2020), 70–86; Toby Dodge and Renad Mansour, 'Sectarianization and De-sectarianization in the Struggle for Iraq's Political Field', *The Review of Faith & International Affairs*, 18:1 (2020), 58–69; Toby Dodge, 'The Failure of Peacebuilding in Iraq: The Role of Consociationalism and Political Settlements', *Journal of Intervention and Statebuilding*, 15:4 (2021), 459–75. Ibrahim Nawar, 'Untying the Knot', *al-Ahram Weekly*, no. 625 (February 2003), http://weekly.ahram.org.eg/archive/2003/625/sc5.htm.

[40] Toby Dodge, 'Iraq and Muhassasa Tai'fiyya: The External Imposition of Sectarian Politics', in Mabon (ed.), *Saudi Arabia and Iran*.

While Sadr's reserves of capital were built upon the fusion of Shi'a piety, populism, and a nationalist agenda underpinned by claims that he was *ibn al-balad* (a son of the soil), SCIRI sought to solidify its support base across the south of Iraq through the Badr Brigades, which became the de facto government in the run up to the 2005 elections. While the Sadrists were fighting against coalition forces, SCIRI sought to capitalize on the opportunity to expand their influence with the help of both Iran and Hizbullah. A focus on the south, notably around Basra, paid dividends in the 2005 election, winning six out of eight of the Shi'a majority governorates while also coming first in Baghdad with 40 per cent of the vote. The elections gave SCIRI access to the much-coveted Interior Ministry and, with it, gave the Badr Brigades access to the police. As a consequence, reciprocal sectarian attacks began to shape the Iraqi political landscape, prompting the deputy governor of Diyala, Ouf Rahmoumi, to refer to the beginning of 'a sectarian war'.[41]

While Shi'a groups had great success in the elections, this spawned intense rivalry across Iraq. Across the post-election political landscape, a debate took place about the new Constitution, yet a parallel debate took place between Shi'a groups about the nature of the 'future Shi'a state'. While the government in Baghdad expressed a more pluralist position, the governorates in the south were more devout, enforcing religious laws, particularly with regard to dress codes and the sale of alcohol. The southern landscape quickly began to reflect the Iranian influence, with streets adorned with the images of Khomeini and Khamenei.

Despite serving consecutive terms as prime minister, al-Maliki proved to be deeply unpopular, overseeing rampant corruption and serious intercommunal violence. Distrust of al-Maliki was not limited to Iraqis, as documented in a US diplomatic cable released by Wikileaks:

The King said he had 'no confidence whatsoever in (Iraqi PM) Maliki, and the Ambassador (Fraker) is well aware of my views.' The King affirmed that he had refused former President Bush's entreaties that he meet with Maliki. The King said he had met Maliki early in Maliki's term of office, and the Iraqi had given him a written list of commitments for reconciliation in Iraq, but had failed to follow through on any of them. For this reason, the King said, Maliki had no credibility. 'I don't trust this man,' the King stated, 'He's an Iranian agent.' The King said he had told both Bush and former Vice president Cheney 'how can I meet with someone I don't trust?' Maliki has 'opened the door for Iranian influence in Iraq' since taking power, the King said, and he was 'not hopeful at all' for Maliki, 'or I would have met with him.'[42]

[41] Mariam Fam, 'Militias Growing in Power in Iraq', Associated Press (7.11.05), www.washingtonpost.com/wp-dyn/content/article/2005/11/07/AR2005110700977_pf.html.
[42] 09RIYADH447_a, 'Brennan's Meeting with Saudi King Abdullah'.

Such views were exacerbated by al-Maliki's political behaviour, which helped to enshrine sectarian difference within the political, social, and economic fabric of the new Iraqi state. An International Crisis Group report from 2013 observed that

Prime Minister Nouri al-Maliki has implemented a divide-and-conquer strategy that has neutered any credible Sunni Arab leadership. The authorities also have taken steps that reinforce perceptions of a sectarian agenda. Prominent officials – predominantly Sunni – have been cast aside pursuant to the Justice and Accountability Law on the basis of alleged senior-level affiliation to the former Baath party. Federal security forces have disproportionately deployed in Baghdad's Sunni neighbourhoods as well as Sunni-populated governorates (Anbar, Salah al-Din, Ninew, Kirkuk and Diyala). Al-Iraqiya, the political movement to which Sunni Arabs most readily related, slowly came apart due to internal rivalries even as Maliki resorted to both legal and extra-judicial means to consolidate power.[43]

While the army continued to be plagued by sectarian bias, with one official suggesting that the armed forces were 99 per cent Shi'a,[44] other security institutions fared no better. The police service also endured both sectarian divisions and a lack of capability. A 2006 Iraq Study Group report noted that

It has neither the training nor legal authority to conduct criminal investigations, nor the firepower to take on organized crime, insurgents, or militias … Iraqi police cannot control crime, and they routinely engage in sectarian violence, including the unnecessary detention, torture, and targeted execution of Sunni Arab civilians. The police are organized under the Ministry of the Interior, which is confronted by corruption and militia infiltration and lacks control over police in the provinces.[45]

This ineptitude was exacerbated by the penetration of the Ministry of Interior by members of the Badr Brigade and the Madhi Army, which then also dissuaded Sunnis from joining such institutions.[46] Fundamentally, the dominance of Iraq's political field by actors espousing a vehemently anti-Sunni principle of vision – in contravention of what

---

[43] International Crisis Group, 'Make or Break: Iraq's *Sunnis* and the State', Middle *East Report*, 144 (2013), www.crisisgroup.org/~/media/Files/Middle%20East%20North%20Africa/Iraq% 20Syria%20Lebanon/Iraq/144-make-or-break-iraq-s-sunnis-and-the-state.pdf.

[44] Edward Wong, 'U.S. Faces Latest Trouble with Iraqi Forces: Loyalty', *New York Times* (6 March 2006), www.nytimes.com/2006/03/06/world/americas/06iht-military .html?pagewanted=all.

[45] Iraq Study Group Report, December 2006.

[46] Walter Pincus, 'US Military Urging Iraq to Rein in Guard Force', *Washington Post* (25.12.06), www.washingtonpost.com/wp-dyn/content/article/2006/12/24/AR2006122400551 .html.

came before – shaped the habitus of individuals through the deployment of different forms of capital, many of whom were supported by Iran.

Iranian Capital in Operation

The fragmentation of the Iraqi state after 2003 created an environment that was conducive to the involvement of external actors, most immediately Iran, who deployed cultural, financial, and coercive capital in pursuit of their aims. Much of this Iranian activity was co-ordinated by Qassim Suleimani, whose efforts had a dramatic impact on the physical landscape of southern Iraq.[47] One senior advisor to the Ministry of Interior referred to Basra as an 'Iranian city'[48] while another senior advisor told US officials that police brigades in Karbala, Diwaniyah, and Nasiriyah were under the control of SCIRI and Badr officials.[49] From 2004, the Quds force provided Shi'a militias across Iraq with weapons that resulted in around 20 per cent of US deaths at the time. Supported by Hizbullah, the Quds force also provided training for Shi'a militias, which involved not only training in combat but also ideological and religious classes in support of Tehran's vision.[50]

Capitalizing on a stagnant Iraqi economy and a divided Shi'a community, Suleimani was able to wield a great deal of influence.[51] Suleimani's influence in Iraq dates back to 2005 elections, where he led a public relations campaign for pro-Iranian parties, providing them with printing presses, consultancy, and broadcast equipment necessary to exert influence.[52] In 2006, amidst a dispute over selection of the first prime minister, Suleimani snuck into Baghdad's Green Zone, amidst tight security, to broker a deal that ultimately brought Nouri al-Maliki to power.[53] He later helped negotiate peace between the Sadrists and government in Baghdad. In the aftermath of elections in 2010, Suleiman helped to negotiate a deal that returned al-Maliki as prime minister in spite of Iyad

---

[47] 05BAGHDAD3015_a, 'Building a House on Shifting Sands'.
[48] 08BAGHDAD239_a '"The Street Is Stronger than Parliament": Sadrist Vows Opposition to LTSR' (27.01.08), https://wikileaks.org/plusd/cables/08BAGHDAD239_a.html.
[49] Ibid.
[50] Joseph Felter and Brian Fishman, *Iranian Strategy in Iraq: Politics and 'Other Means'* (West Point, NY: Combatting Terrorism Center, 2008).
[51] 'Iran's Deadly Puppet Master', *Foreign Policy Magazine* (Winter 2019), https://foreignpolicy .com/gt-essay/irans-deadly-puppet-master-qassem-suleimani/.
[52] Hannah Allam, Jonathan S. Landay, and Warren P. Strobel, 'Iranian Outmaneuvers U.S. in Iraq', *McClatchy Newspapers* (28.04.08), www.mcclatchydc.com/2008/04/28/35146/ iranian-outmaneuvers-us-in-iraq.html.
[53] Ibid.

Alawi's successes in the election. Iranian actors were later instrumental in forcing al-Maliki from power in 2014.

The deployment of economic capital resulted in the provision of an estimated $100 million to SCIRI and $45 million to Badr, yet a legacy of distrust towards Iran had an impact on Shi'a Iraqi groups, with SCIRI subjected to criticism – alongside al-Da'wa – for siding with Iran during the Iran–Iraq War.[54] In 2007, the group sought to distance itself from Iran, changing its name from the Supreme Council for the Islamic Revolution in Iraq to the Islamic Supreme Council of Iraq (ISCI), and proclaiming allegiance to Sistani in an attempt to increase its legitimacy in the eyes of Iraqi Shi'a.[55]

In contrast, Iranian relations with the Sadrists were more complex, stemming from the group's strong nationalist sentiment and perception that Muqtada al-Sadr was too independent. Unlike other militias, Sadrists declare Muqtada as their religious leader, rather than Ayatollah Khamenei, drawing on the former's family credentials.[56] Additionally, Sadr's populism positioned him as key player in Iraqi politics. In 2003, through support from Hizbullah, the Jaish al-Mahdi (JAM) was formed to fight coalition forces, supported by the Quds force. Sadr was named by an Iranian ayatollah Kazem Haeri as his representative in Iraq which, although viewed cynically by some, resulted in Sadr studying in a Qom seminary over those in Najaf. JAM later splintered over tensions concerning Sadr's relationship with Baghdad, resulting in the creation of the Peace Brigades in 2014, which subsequently played a key role in the fight against Da'ish.

One of the groups that splintered from JAM was Asa'ib Ahl Haq, referred to by the US government as a 'direct action' arm of their Quds force, with strong similarities with Hizbullah in Lebanon. Haq is explicitly loyal to *veleyat-e faqih*, also following Iranian ayatollahs Shahroudi and Haeri.[57] Standing as a nationalist party, it won seats in the 2014 elections in the al-Sadiqon Bloc, also included in Maliki's State of Law Coalition. Beyond Haq, other groups splintered from JAM, including Katai'b Hizbullah, established by Quds force officials in early 2007. Much like Haq, Katai'b Hizbullah is also considered a 'direct action' arm of the IRGC.

[54] 05BAGHDAD3015_a, 'Building a House on Shifting Sands'.
[55] Felter and Fishman, *Iranian Strategy in Iraq*; see 05BAGHDAD3015_a, 'Building a House on Shifting Sands'.
[56] Visser Reidar, 'Religious Allegiances among Pro-Iranian Special Groups in Iraq', *CTC Sentinel*, 4:9 (September 2011), 5–8.
[57] 'Nokhostin Mosaahebe-ye Tafsili-ye Rahbaraan-e Asa'ib Ahl Haq Dar Iran' ['First Detailed Interview of Asa'ib Ahl Haq Leaders in Iran'], *Fars News Agency* (02.09.14), www.farsnews.com/newstext.php?nn=13930811000718.

Financial might allowed ISCI and Badr officials to recruit Sadrists who were later paid a monthly stipend to fight against rival militias, coalition forces, and Iraqi government security forces on behalf of Iran.[58] Yet intra-Shi'a tensions were common, stemming from disparate long-term goals. Moreover, frustrations also grew amongst local populations frustrated by violence, prompting Iran to shift its strategy towards cultivating relations with political figures and to increase its economic influence, playing a key role in the provision of support to the estimated one million religious visitors to Karbala from Iran.[59] Myriad channels were cultivated to exert influence across the state, such as the Shamsah Travel and Tourism group, an umbrella organization operating in Karbala, comprising an estimated 2,500 Iranian companies with ties to the government and described as the 'soft arm' of the Quds force.

The penetration of Iraq by Iranian actors was widespread. Yet while Tehran wielded vast reserves of economic, social, and coercive capital, there was a growing sense of unease amongst the Iraqi population. While the *marja'iyyah* typically refrained from commentary on Iranian influence in Iraq, clerical frustration at Iranian activity was rife, amidst concerns at the propagation of *veleyat-e faqih* across Iraq.[60] In the years to come, this unease and frustration would erupt.

Shifting Capital: Da'ish, Riyadh, and Tishreen

In spite of growing anger, the 2011 protests that became known as the Arab Uprisings failed to find serious traction in Iraq. At this time, prominent Iraqis spoke out in support of protesters across the region. 'Ali Sistani endorsed the protesters, while Muqtada al-Sadr urged followers to mobilize in support of their Bahraini kin, echoing the support that Bahrainis had declared to their Iraqi counterparts in 2003. In Basra and across the south, three days of protests took place with a crowd of over 20,000 condemning GCC intervention, burning effigies of the Al Sa'ud and Al-Khalifa.[61]

---

[58] 08BAGHDAD239_a, '"The Street Is Stronger than Parliament"'.
[59] 08BAGHDAD2812_a, 'Karbala: Iran Exerts Heavy Influence through Tourism Industry' (02.08.08), https://wikileaks.org/plusd/cables/08BAGHDAD2812_a.html.
[60] 10BAGHDAD22_a, 'Iraqi Views on Events in Iran and Impact on Iraq' (05.01.10), https://wikileaks.org/plusd/cables/10BAGHDAD22_a.html.
[61] 'Iraq's Sadr Calls for Protest against Bahrain Deaths', *World Bulletin* (16.03.011), www.worldbulletin.net/?aType=haber&ArticleID=71168; 'Iraq's Zealous Sons March in Support of Downtrodden Bahraini People' (in English), *al-Amarah News Network* (16.03.11), http://al3marh.net/news (al-Amarah News Network is affiliated with al-Sadr). 'Thousands across Iraq Protest Bahrain Crackdown', Agence France Presse and *NOW Lebanon* (18.03.11).

The emergence of Da'ish, the Islamic State of Iraq and al-Sham in the summer of 2014 posed an existential challenge to the Iraqi state. The group seized control of large swathes of territory and conducted a spate of attacks against a range of targets across the state. Central to their ideological vision was a vitriolic hatred of Shi'a who were framed as *rawafed* ('rejectionists'). Widely condemned, the group quickly gained control of large parts of Iraq and Syria and conducted violent attacks against a wide range of targets in the Middle East and beyond.

Recognizing the challenges posed by the group, Iranian president Hasan Rouhani declared that

Iran has taken huge steps to safeguard security and stability in the region ... The Islamic Republic ... has had the greatest contribution in saving the people of Iraq—in [Iraq's] south, west, east and north—its Kurds, its Sunni-dominated [areas], Shi'a-dominated [cities] in the whole country. Iran has rendered greatest service to establish relative security and stability in Iraq.[62]

These dangers were also recognized by other states. By December 2015, Saudi Arabia had declared the establishment of the Islamic Military Alliance which brought together thirty-four Muslim states, yet not Iran. At this point, with other global powers also working to defeat Da'ish, Saudi Arabia and its Islamic Alliance was working towards the same aims as the United States, Russia, Iran, and Israel.

At the vanguard of the fight against Da'ish in Iraq were the PMFs, a collection of fluid networks typically operating in horizontal leadership structure with vertical ties to a social base in Iraq, while some possessed close relations with Iran. The PMFs occupied a symbiotic relationship with the state – notably the security services, political figures, and the economy – integrated into Iraqi politics with strong reserves of cultural and coercive capital, yet not always manifesting in political capital or formal engagement in government.[63] In summer 2014, thousands of Iraqis joined the PMFs in the fight against Da'ish, urged on by a *fatwa* from Grand Ayatollah 'Ali al-Sistani, yet rather than joining the Iraqi Army, most joined the PMFs. The PMFs were integral in the fight against Da'ish, yet after the military defeat, the existence of PMFs with the ability to operate independent of the state and with vast reserves of capital posed a challenge to the very existence of the state and those seeking to dominate its political field. Iranian support for certain PMFs was a source of

[62] 'Rouhani Praises Iran's Role in Ensuring Security in Iraq', speech given by Hassan Rouhani at shrine of Imam Reza, Mashhad, *Islamic Republic of Iran News Network/BBC Monitoring* (06.09.14).

[63] Renad Mansour, *Networks of Power: The Popular Mobilization Forces and the State in Iraq* (London: Chatham House, 2021).

anger for some, with many having 'given blood' for Iraq yet their leaders received support from external sources.[64] This sentiment was exacerbated by a general belief at this time that 'perennial Iranian involvement was a big burden',[65] yet the heterogeneity of the PMF meant that subparts of the PMF operated in pursuit of different agendas. While the existence of the PMFs was not new, after the military defeat of Da'ish they gained a great deal more capital.

Post-2014, Iraq set out on a process of post-conflict reconstruction, seeking both to mend the infrastructural damage caused by Da'ish and to heal the schisms that continued to plague the state. Efforts to bring the PMFs into the institutional fabric of the Iraqi state ultimately proved futile, with groups continuing to operate beyond the formal aspects of state power, wielding vast reserves of social capital due to their ability to speak to social bases. In the years that followed, the PMFs played a prominent role in shaping the political landscape, mobilizing their support base in support of particular candidates, serving as a means of brokering political negotiations. The consolidation of this support allowed PMF actors to cut across local government institutions and civil society organizations, and deliver state services. In such a climate, endemic corruption was hardly surprising.

The election of Haider al-Abadi was viewed as a positive step in addressing these tensions. Moreover, it was also a turning point in Iraqi relations with Saudi Arabia. While al-Maliki was viewed with suspicion, al-Abadi's efforts to position himself as an Iraqi first and foremost – and with it, an effort to demonstrate independence from Iran – meant that the Kingdom viewed him more positively, ultimately aiding the re-opening of its embassy in Baghdad in December 2016. The opening of the Arar border crossing quickly followed, as did the resumption of flights between the two states. Central to this was a Saudi strategy that was ostensibly designed to strengthen the Iraqi state while also eroding Iranian influence.

Under al-Abadi's leadership, economic investment was secured from a range of sources including the 2018 reconstruction donors conference hosted in Kuwait. Al-Abadi's political capital amongst the Gulf Arab states was increased in his efforts to bring the PMF under state control, with political elites across the region viewing an albeit disparate collection of units as an 'Iranian front'.[66] This economic investment came at a

[64] Interview with Iraqi journalist.
[65] Ibid.
[66] *Saudi Arabia: Back to Baghdad*, International Crisis Group (22.05.18), p. 5, https://d2071andvip0wj.cloudfront.net/186-saudi-arabia-back-to-baghdad%20(1).pdf.

time when financial commitments from Western governments began to be rolled back, creating space for Gulf states to act, yet socio-economic challenges remained. Moreover, frustration at seemingly endemic corruption which resulted in spates of protest across the state in 2018 and 2019 was in part driven by frustration at Iranian actions across the state.

Amidst the protest movement, Saudi Arabia sensed an opportunity to increase its capital in Iraq's political field, initially through the deployment of economic capital, providing material support to many across the state. Economic investment in the formal institutions of the state was coupled with the development of relationships with Shi'a elites – driven predominantly by the Kingdom's relationship with al-Abadi – and cultivation of cross-confessional relationships. For many Iraqis, a relationship with Saudi Arabia offered much, albeit with a concern that their country was a pawn in a broader regional game, and Riyadh's goal was to erode Tehran's influence rather than witness a flourishing Iraq.

Under MbS, the Kingdom's strategy with regard to Iran was more direct. Speaking with *The Atlantic*, the crown prince declared that the Kingdom was

pushing back on these Iranian moves. We've done this in Africa, Asia, in Malaysia, in Sudan, in Iraq, Yemen, Lebanon. We believe that after push back, the problems will move inside Iran. We don't know if the regime will collapse or not – it's not the target, but if it collapses, great, it's their problem. We have a war scenario in the Middle East right now. This is very dangerous for the world. We cannot take the risk here. We have to take serious painful decisions now to avoid painful decisions later.[67]

Fundamental to this was a shift in policy towards Iraq. In countering Iranian influence in Iraq, Riyadh faced two key challenges. First, in the years after the 2003 invasion Iraq's economy had been dominated by Iran, with the consumer market flooded with Iranian goods. With sanctions hitting the Iranian economy hard, access to Iraq provide invaluable, with the Iranian Trade Promotion Organization estimating that non-oil exports to Baghdad increased dramatically from $2.3 billion in 2008 to $6.2 billion by 2015.[68] As the fight against Da'ish intensified, Iran benefitted as trade routes between Iraq and Turkey were cut. Moreover, as geopolitical tensions between Iraq and others increased, Iran was able to capitalize.[69] While Tehran was able to increase trade, it struggled amidst

[67] Goldberg, 'Saudi Crown Prince'.
[68] Tamer Badawi, 'Iran's Iraqi Market', Carnegie Endowment for International Peace (27.07.16), https://carnegieendowment.org/sada/64187.
[69] Mehdi Bahranipour, 'Iraq's Determination to Replace Iranian and Saudi Goods with Iranian Goods', Mehr News Agency (n.d.), www.mehrnews.com/news/2350491/
شلمچه-دروازه-طلایی-تجارت-عزم-عراق-برای-جایگزینی-کالای-ایرانی.

rising anti-Iranian sentiment from 2016 onwards, resulting in protectionist measures being imposed on selected Iranian imports.[70]

Second, Saudi Arabia had to address the legacy of sectarian tensions which had long shaped the Kingdom's relations with Iraqi Shi'a actors amidst fears that such groups were inextricably tied to Iran. Such suspicions had historical roots, dating back to the time of Gertrude Bell, while also being shaped by broader regional developments. The institutionalization of sectarian difference and broader framing of links between Shi'a and Iran left Saudi efforts to circumvent sectarian schisms difficult; adding to this challenge was a general suspicion towards Saudi Arabia. Until 2018, the Saudis had even struggled to gain the support of Sunni tribal groups across Iraq.[71]

Yet a series of events which took place across Iraq allowed for a strategic shift in policy and a thaw in relations between the Kingdom and Iraq. The military defeat of Da'ish came at an economic and infrastructural cost, not only providing opportunities for the Kingdom to gain economically, but also eroding Iranian influence in the process. Removing Iraq from Iran's sphere of influence was no easy task for Saudi decision makers. Indeed, a multifaceted approach was necessary to counter the influence of Tehran, which had cultivated military and security relations with the government of Iraq,[72] the Kurdish regional government,[73] and the PMFs, along with developing economic relationships with local actors and businesses.

Central to this strategy was the courtship of Shi'a figures including Muqtada al-Sadr. While al-Sadr's Shi'a legacy is well known, the decision to cultivate ties points to an attempt to circumvent Iranian influence by speaking to an Iraqi and Arab nationalism, pushing back against a *Persian* influence. On 30 July 2017, MbS met Muqtada al-Sadr in Jeddah, a meeting that came only a month since the crown prince had met Haider al-Abadi. Documented by photos showing MbS seemingly at ease with his eyes closed but al-Sadr more suspicious of the camera, the meeting brought together two seemingly implausible allies in a shared desire to counter Iranian influence.[74] Of course, for al-Sadr a desire to

---

[70] 'Reduction of Iranian exports to Iraq due to increase in customs tariffs'; *AA* (08.06.16), www.aa.com.tr/fa/586400/کمرکی-های-تعرفه-افزایش-دلیل-به-عراق-به-ایران-صادرات-کاهش/ایران.

[71] Interview with Iraqi journalist.

[72] Michael R. Gordon and Eric Schmitt, 'Iran Secretly Sending Drones and Supplies Into Iraq, U.S. Officials Say', *New York Times* (26.06.14), www.nytimes.com/2014/06/26/world/middleeast/iran-iraq.html.

[73] 'Iran Provide Watpons to Iraq's Kurds: Barani', *Middle East Eye* (12.02.15), www.middleeasteye.net/news/iran-provided-weapons-iraqs-kurds-barzani.

[74] 'Riyadh Pushing for a Strong Independent Iraq', *Reuters* (17.08.17), https://gulfnews.com/world/mena/riyadh-pushing-for-a-strong-independent-iraq-1.2075708.

paint a more nationalist image ahead of impending elections required a clear articulation of Arab identity and distance from Iran. At the same time as al-Sadr was meeting MbS, al-Abadi was in Tehran, meeting with senior Iranian officials.[75]

For MbS and the Saudis, the meeting with al-Sadr was the start of an effort to cultivate local allies in Iraq from different sectarian backgrounds with the goal of establishing a strong and independent Iraq free from Iranian influence. In support of this, the Kingdom offered financial support for post-conflict reconstruction, backed by joint trade commissions and the opening of the border. In the years that followed, the establishment of a portfolio of economic investments in the Iraqi economy highlighted improvements in relations between the two, ranging from consumer markets to natural resources.

At the same time, latent anger at Iranian involvement in Iraqi politics began to manifest, resulting in a spate of protests across the state. The *tishreen* protesters were driven by a frustration at the widespread corruption that had become endemic in Iraqi politics and also included expressions of anger directed at groups affiliated with Iran, which was seen to be acting against the national interests of Iraq. Much like protests in Lebanon that emerged in 2019, Iraqi protesters expressed anger at the *muhassasa* power sharing system that allocated seats in accordance with an ethno-sectarian quota system. Part of this anger emerged from growing frustrations at the actions of Iran in Iraqi politics and the ongoing support for elites whose actions exacerbated corruption and division between rulers and ruled. In this environment, the struggle over capital and principles of vision became increasingly violent, as the government and prominent militias sought to ensure their dominance in an increasingly precarious political field. At this time, voices critical of PMF influence in Iraq were silenced and, in the case of Hisham al-Hashimi (and others), killed.[76]

Despite the domestic turmoil, Iraq sought to position itself as an influential actor in Middle Eastern politics by hosting track II talks between Saudi Arabia and Iran. Prime Minister Mustafa al-Kazimi's efforts reveal a desire to use its geographical proximity, historical importance, and identity makeup as a means of improving regional relations. There is little doubt that Iraq has suffered as a consequence of the rivalry

---

[75] 'Iraqi Prime Minister Meets with the Leader of the Revolution', *Khamenei.IR* (n.d.), https://farsi.khamenei.ir/news-content?id=36913.

[76] Renad Mansour, 'In Life and Death, Iraq's Hisham al-Hashimi', *Chatham House* (01.08.20), www.chathamhouse.org/publications/the-world-today/2020-08/life-and-death-iraqs-hisham-al-hashimi.

between Riyadh and Tehran, both of whom have sought to dominate Iraq's political field at the expense of the other and, often, at a cost to Iraqis. The track II process was largely viewed as a success, despite a diplomatic faux pas from Iran's chief diplomat Hossein Amir-Abdoullahian, who broke protocol to stand with heads of state at the front of a photograph, rather than with foreign ministers including Faysal bin Farhan al-Saud in the second row.[77]

Conclusions

In the early hours of 7 November 2021, a drone attack launched from near the Republic Bridge on the River Tigris was carried out on Prime Minister Mustafa al-Kazimi's residence in Baghdad, injuring six bodyguards but leaving al-Kazimi unhurt. The drone was fitted with explosives, which reports claim were Iranian made.[78] Coming less than a month after Iraqis went to the polls, the drone attack reflects the ongoing tensions within Iraq's political field and efforts of particular groups to assert coercive capital and define principles of vision.

Competing *nomoi* manifested prominently in competition to shape Iraq's political field. Efforts to impose symbolic capital over Iraq's political field have faced an array of challenges since the formation of the state, resulting in the dramatic evolution of habitus and principles of vision, from Arab nationalism through sectarian difference, to the reassertion of an Iraqi nationalism, albeit struggling to assert itself in the face of corruption and violence from the PMFs. These challenges have been exacerbated by the evolution of the transnational field, given Iraq's demographic makeup, meaning that reverberations from events in Iran in 1979 were keenly felt. Yet Iraq's position of prominence within the transnational field meant that the US-led 2003 invasion and ensuing toppling of Saddam Hussein resonated across the transnational field. In what followed, Iraq's political field was shaped by the complex interaction of local and regional actors wielding different forms of capital in an effort to impose principles of vision and symbolic capital.

The evolution of Iraq from a regional power to a state offering to mediate between Saudi Arabia and Iran reveals a great deal about the

[77] 'Exclusive: Despite Baghdad Photo Blunder, Iran-Saudi Talks Set to Resume', *Amwaj* (08.09.21), https://amwaj.media/article/exclusive-despite-baghdad-photo-blunder-iran-saudi-talks-set-to-resume.
[78] 'Iran-backed Militia Staged Drone Attack on Iraqi PM – Officials', *Reuters* (08.11.21), www.reuters.com/world/middle-east/iran-backed-militia-behind-attack-iraqi-pm-sources-2021-11-08/.

realignment of power in the transnational field post-2003. Central to these developments is the collision of domestic politics and regional rivalries, with tensions between Iran and Saudi Arabia – and the United States – playing out across a divided Iraqi state where political, social, economic, tribal, and religious divisions and grievances remain prevalent. While in some instances this presented opportunities for regional powers to develop relationships with local actors in pursuit of increased influence, it also allowed domestic actors to derive support from regional powers.

Iran's influence in Iraq was initially facilitated by the deployment of religious and cultural capital which evolved over time into economic and coercive capital, reflecting the organization of the political field at this time. The weakness of the Iraqi state and inability to assert coercive capital and create a habitus predicated on autonomy free of external interference, meant that the principles of vision and habitus were defined by actors either with allegiance or sympathies to Iran. Over time, however, the translation of Iranian capital from the transnational field to Iraq's political field began to find less traction. In part, this reflects a shifting habitus and contested principles of vision that emerged after the military defeat of Da'ish, manifesting in widespread popular protest in 2019. Yet it perhaps also reflects the growing influence of Saudi Arabia's economic capital and cultural capital, predicated upon shared Arab identity.

4   Bahrain

On a summer's day in Riyadh, four months after the start of protests that engulfed Bahrain in February 2011, Khalid bin Hamad Al-Khalifa, the fifth son of King Hamad, married Princess Sahab bint Abdullah Al Sa'ud. The marriage of Khalid and Sahab – who was said to be the favourite daughter of the erstwhile Saudi King, Abdullah – strengthened relations between the two neighbouring kingdoms. Vast disparities between the two states manifested in the dominance of the Saudi Kingdom over their Bahraini counterparts, shaping not only on the foreign policy of the latter but also their treatment of domestic populations, particularly those opposing the Al-Khalifa's *nomos*.

Despite its diminutive size, the archipelago of Bahrain[1] occupies a prominent role in Gulf politics. Relations between the ruling family and Shi'a communities is situated within a broader set of political, social, and economic issues that shapes life on an archipelago with a population of just over 1.7 million people. It occupies an important geopolitical position and has a society divided along sectarian lines. Located 16 kilometres off the eastern coast of Saudi Arabia but only 300 kilometres off the Western coast of Iran, it is hardly surprising that the Kingdom of Bahrain is viewed by many as the 'epicentre' of both a geopolitical and a sectarian conflict. In the immediate aftermath of the Arab Uprisings, it became a scene of political repression as the Saudi-backed Al-Khalifa ruling family sought to maintain power.

Prima facia exploration of Bahraini politics leads to assumptions that the state is divided along sectarian lines and that this division maps onto broader geopolitical rivalries. This results in what Omar AlShehabi terms the 'ethno-sectarian gaze' which privileges primordialist accounts of religious difference, above all other factors.[2] Yet the reality

---

[1] Historically, Bahrain was an archipelago of thirty-three islands but in recent years it is typically referred to as the island of Bahrain, named after the largest of the thirty-three.

[2] Omar H. AlShehabi, *Contested Modernity: Sectarianism, Nationalism and Colonialism in Bahrain* (London: Oneworld, 2019).

of life across the island is somewhat different. Amidst a long history of protest, often viewed along sectarian lines, political life has been characterized by many as a paradigmatic example of the *sectarianization* thesis, the mobilization of religious identities in pursuit of regime survival.[3] Yet this position also possesses some issues, seemingly ignoring what Staci Strobl terms the 'cultural practice' of sectarian identities.[4]

Deeper reflection of Bahrain's political field, however, reveals that the contestation over principles of vision and division fed into the emergence of a habitus that reinforces a form of sect-based politics, underpinned by concerns about regime survival and Iranian expansionism. This is not solely a consequence of those in power selecting a strategy that best ensures their survival, but rather a product of a state-building process that appropriated, institutionalized, and marginalized identities mobilized across the twentieth century. Indeed, as Strobl observes, the organization of political life across Bahrain 'reflects a deeper interplay of more socially and culturally embedded notions of sectarian identity that developed historically, and then were appropriated, modified and institutionalised during the colonial experience'.[5] For Sophia Pandya, this is the creation of a 'Sunni-normative environment' framed against the Shi'a other which is historically associated with Iran.[6] As Kristin Diwan Smith asserts, sectarian identities in Bahrain are shaped by broader political, geopolitical, and economic contexts, heightening tensions and exacerbating discord across the island.[7]

Put another way, the struggle to define Bahrain's political field and its social world more broadly plays out between regional, national, and local actors deploying capital to impose categories and meaning. Over time, this struggle involved the deployment of economic, social, religious, and coercive capital – in the form of nationalist, religious, sectarian, and tribal identities and narratives – shaping the individual's habitus and imposing meaning on the social world more broadly. Central to this is a *nomos* shaped by a position in a transnational politico-religious field determined by the complexities of the rivalry between Saudi Arabia and Iran.

Despite the Al-Khalifa's overwhelming monopoly of economic and coercive capital, the social and religious capital of other actors allowed

---

[3] Toby Matthiessen, *Sectarian Gulf: Bahrain, Saudi Arabia and the Arab Spring That Wasn't* (Stanford: Stanford University Press, 2013). Mabon, 'The End of the Battle of Bahrain'.

[4] Strobl, *Sectarian Order*, p. xiii.

[5] Ibid., p. xiv.

[6] Sophia Pandya, 'Women's Shi'a Ma'atim in Bahrain', *Journal of Middle East Women's Studies* 6:2 (2010), 40.

[7] Kristin Diwan Smith, 'Sectarian Politics in the Persian Gulf', in Lawrence Potter (ed.), *Sectarian Politics in the Persian Gulf* (London: Hurst, 2013), p. 144.

them to present alternative principles of vision to order the political field, in contrast to that put forward by the ruling family. The interplay of these competing principles of vision and division shaped Bahrain's political field, particularly in the period after independence in 1971.

This chapter explores efforts to determine Bahrain's political field and the ways in which its politically charged geographical location as the 'epicentre' of the struggle for supremacy between Riyadh and Tehran shapes these efforts. It explores the struggle for Bahrain's political field and its social reality which has allowed a range of domestic and regional actors to become involved in the contestation over principles of vision and division, deploying economic, political, and religious capital in the process. Central to this are a number of networks and relationships that shape perceptions and behaviour, along tribal, ethnic, and religious lines. As Saudi and Iranian efforts to impose order on the region focused on Bahrain, they coalesced with a complex set of intersectional phenomena bringing together tensions between rulers and ruled over social, economic, and political issues, all of which play out in the context of the transnational field.

The Quest for Order and Bahrain in the Transnational Field

Bahrain's political field in the years after independence has been dominated by the ruling Al-Khalifa family who have utilized different forms of capital to exert dominance and control. Although economic capital is central to much of the Al-Khalifa's actions, social, cultural, and religious capital have all been used at various points in an attempt to dominate the political field, limiting the universe of political discourse in the process. In doing so, the Al-Khalifa have drawn support from Saudi Arabia – whose economic capital in Bahrain is perhaps more powerful than that of the Al-Khalifa – to support efforts to dominate society, underscoring economic capital and broader claims to social and religious capital, particularly in the context of a challenge to regional order from Iran.

The principles of vision and division that play out in efforts to define Bahrain's political field are products of time and space, evolving from competing visions of democracy as an ordering principle in the 1970s to fears of sectarian division which increased after the Iranian revolution of 1979. In the years after the revolution, fears of Shi'a unrest, supported – and incited – by Iran became a key concern, prompting the ruling family to deploy its coercive capital to impose order and regulate the political field. While political unrest continued in the years that followed, much of this unrest was driven by alternative principles of vision to that proposed by the ruling Al-Khalifa, culminating in promises of political reform in 1999 when Hamad came to power, initially as emir then king. Despite these promises, little reform occurred and dissent continued.

After the Arab Uprisings, Bahrain's political field became shaped by regional currents and, once again, substantive fears about Iranian manipulation. At this time, the Al-Khalifa and their Saudi backers deployed economic, social, and coercive capital in pursuit of their vision of order. Although the individual's habitus had long been conditioned by the securitization of Iranian and Shi'a activities, by 2011 this dramatically increased as a vision of order was imposed upon Bahrain's political field – and the social world broadly – that sought to marginalize Shi'a communities. While the Al-Khalifa were prompted to act by increased fears about Iranian action across the region, opposition groups in Bahrain took solace in the gains made by counterparts in Iraq, along with expressions of support from Lebanon. The construction of a politically charged form of sectarian difference across Bahrain shaped the habitus of the majority of Sunni Bahrainis, reflected in aspects of socialization, while also setting the parameters of engagement for those Shi'a expressing loyalty to the regime.

The transnational nature of Islam and the religiously tinged political competition over regional order means that Bahrain's political field is also shaped by developments within the transnational field. Here, Bahrain's position within the transnational field is conditioned by the interplay of different actors seeking to exert symbolic violence across that field, dominated by Saudi Arabia and Iran. Yet the position of Bahrain within this transnational field makes it a site of importance for regional actors who also seek to exert influence in its political field. Bahrain's size and demographic makeup have left it vulnerable to broader regional currents. This external involvement in political life has been shaped by top-down processes with external actors seeking to shape domestic politics, yet despite the Al-Khalifa – and their Saudi backers – imposing principles of vision and symbolic capital, the social capital of opposition groups posed challenges to regime power (and survival) across the *longue durée*.

For rulers across the Gulf, ensuring the survival of the Al-Khalifa was of paramount importance, closely followed by the belief that the ruling family should not make concessions to allow an elected second chamber which would empower Shi'a groups across the Middle East. What quickly followed was a concerted effort by the Bahraini regime and their regional backers to locate the protests within a broader struggle against Iran. Key officials within the Peninsula Shield force declared that there was 'no doubt' of Iranian complicity in events.[8] These claims were supported by media outlets across the Gulf, who reported Iranian involvement in the smuggling of weaponry into Bahrain.[9]

Parallels were drawn between the political party al-Wifaq and Hizbullah,[10] while a number of Bahrainis were found guilty of spying for Iran, and others guilty of efforts to topple the regime.[11] Similar claims were made by regime officials including Mohammad Abd al-Ghaffar, who declared that 'Bahrain has been suffering for a long time from the Iranian interference in its internal affairs.'[12] Yet the actions of the Al-Khalifa and their Saudi backers had repercussions in divided societies across the Middle East, prompting an escalation in sect-based tensions with an explicitly geopolitical agenda. Unsurprisingly, Iranian officials were quick to condemn the Saudi actions,[13] while their Saudi counterparts accused Iran of playing 'the sectarian game'.[14]

Regional events have had a profound impact on Bahraini politics since independence. The Iranian revolution, the Iraq War, the 2006 Hizbullah–Israeli conflict, Syrian War, Yemen War, and rise of Da'ish all had an impact on sectarian identities across Bahrain, prompting groups to defend their nationalist positions against accusation of loyalty to external others. In some cases, these events were used by actors to galvanize support amongst sectarian kin, such as the Salafi use of events in Syria to strengthen Sunni support. In others, regional events were framed in such a way to view the sectarian other as a threat, such as the framing of Iranian meddling in Iraq as further evidence of pernicious intent with regard to Bahrain's Shi'a community.

---

[8] Quoted in Ethan Bronner and Michael Slackman, 'Saudi Troops Enter Bahrain to Help Put Down Unrest', *New York Times* (14.03.11), https://nyti.ms/2Kr5UWt.

[9] Maha El Dahan and William Maclean, 'Bahrain Says Foils Arms Smuggling Bid, Recalls Iran Envoy', *Reuters* (25.07.11), https://reut.rs/2Fe3MR1.

[10] 'Bahrain Accuses Foreign Media of Exaggeration', *Al Jazeera* (02.05.12), www.aljazeera.com/news/middleeast/2012/05/20125220628139601.html.

[11] Agence France–Presse, 'Bahrain Jails Three for Spying for Iran: Report', *Gulf News* (06.07.11), https://gulfnews.com/world/gulf/bahrain/bahrain-jails-three-for-spying-for-iran-report-1.833932. See also 'Bahrain Sentences 12 People for Life for Spying, Iran Links', *Reuters* (22.04.14), https://reut.rs/2Wandkp; 'Bahrain Jails 19 Shi'a Accused of Spying for Iran', *New Arab* (30.10.17), www.alaraby.co.uk/english/news/2017/10/30/bahrain-jails-19-shias-accused-of-spying-for-iran.

[12] Quoted in Yasser al-Chazli, 'Adviser to Bahrain King: GCC Basis of Balance in Region', *al-Monitor* (4.11.13), http://almon.co/2olf.

[13] 'Iran's FM Voices Concern about Bahrain in Letters to UN, OIC, Arab League', *Fars News Agency* (17.03.11), www.farsnews.ir/en/news/14010201000183/Iran-Vices-Deep-Cncern-ver-Israeli-Crimes-in-Leers-UN-OIC-Mslim-FMs and 'Learn Lesson from Saddam's Fate: Ahmadinejad', *Mehr News* (16.03.11), https://en.mehrnews.com/news/45204/Learn-lesson-from-Saddam-s-fate-Ahmadinejad.

[14] Moussa Mahmoud al-Jamal and Sonia Farid, 'Is Iran "Sectarianizing" Bahrain Conflict?' *al-'Arabiya* (20.04.11), http://english.alarabiya.net/articles/2011/04/20/146144.html.

Consideration of Bahrain's political field at this time suggests that the hard-line elements in the Al-Khalifa – operating with Saudi backing – sought to co-opt Sunni anger at regional developments and harness this acrimony in a struggle with the Shi'a groups believed to be operating in alliance with Iran. In spite of myriad claims to the contrary, there is little convincing evidence of direct Iranian involvement across Bahrain. Yet the Al-Khalifa's symbolic capital – conditioned by political, social, and coercive capital and shaped by historical experience, shared normative environments, and regional concerns – meant that the habitus of many was constructed along such lines.

Bahrain and was Its 'Sectarian Gaze'

The modern history of Bahrain is replete with contestation within the political field, shaped by competing forms of social, cultural, and economic capital, which has manifested in political and religious unrest across the state. Reflecting on Bahraini politics across the *longue durée*, socio-economic and political disenfranchisement appear embedded within the structures of the state. With Shi'a groups traditionally found in rural parts of the state and thus – amidst rapid urbanization – often failing to benefit from socio-economic developments, Bahrain's political history is punctured by unrest amongst Shi'a groups. This suggests that there is a long history of sectarian tension across the island, yet such a conclusion is problematic. Instead, a more nuanced approach is required, similar to that made by Fanar Haddad in the case of Iraq, which explores how socio-economic unrest across Bahrain's history has hit Shi'a communities disproportionately.

The history of Bahrain is one characterized by a struggle to define the political field and, as a consequence, to ensure the survival of a particular vision of society that privileges the ruling Al-Khalifa tribe and its supporters to the detriment of indigenous groups and the Shi'a majority. Prior to the formation of the modern state of Bahrain, however, it was social, religious, and cultural capital in the form of ethnic and religious identity that was central in shaping the political field. Bahrain's history is driven by a fusion of kinship – *asabiyya* – and religion – *al-Din* – underpinned by a history of trade-driven immigration, resulting in a mélange of identities, ideologies, and political agendas.[15] Here, a habitus was forged out of a shared system of schemes and

---

[15] Nelida Fuccaro, *Histories of City and State in the Persian Gulf: Manama since 1800* (Cambridge: Cambridge University Press, 2009), p. 9.

action predicated on tribal norms, Islam, and trade related to pearl diving.

Before the establishment of states across the Arabian Peninsula, Shi'a groups living in Eastern Arabia were inhabitants of a shared political community, spanning from Oman in the south to Basra in the north. Known as Baharna, these inhabitants had embraced Shi'ism in the formative stages of Islam – predating formal adherence to Shi'a Islam in Persia in 1501 – and lived a simple yet largely harmonious life until powerful Sunni tribes conquered the land and because of their virulent rejection of Shi'ism, sought to decimate indigenous communal organization. Along with Jabal Amil in Lebanon and Najaf and Kufa in Iraq, Bahrain was an important theological centre for Arab Shi'a and became a centre of learning for the Safavid state as it sought to educate clerics. In the formative years of the Safavid dynasty, rulers sought clerical approval from Bahraini clerics, which served as the source of allegations that Bahraini Shi'a are 'Safavid loyalists'.

Narratives surrounding state formation in Bahrain reveal a great deal about tensions between different communal groups. The history of Bahrain is replete with contestation and power struggles, beginning with accounts of state formation. The modern state of Bahrain was founded in 1783 by the Al-Khalifa dynasty who defeated the Al-Madhkur, the archipelago's previous rulers who had controlled Bahrain as a vassal of the Persian Empire. Yet the narrative of conquest is disputed, serving as a means of legitimizing rule and substantiating political positions.[16] The official narrative propagated by the Al-Khalifa is a liberation narrative, freeing Bahrainis from Persian rule and re-integrating the state into the Arab nation.[17]

For many of the island's Shi'a population, this narrative wilfully disregards the dominance of the indigenous Baharna over the island, which they claim had been populated by Shi'a Muslims since the Prophet Muhammad's death. For those who support this position, the Al-Khalifa and other Sunnis are 'no less than alien invaders'.[18] Such narratives are supported by a range of intellectual and activist voices who have sought to support these claims and counter the social capital of the ruling

---

[16] Nader al-Kadhem, *Isti'malat al-dhakira fi mujtama 'ta 'taduddi mubtala bi al-tarikh* [*Uses of Memory in a Multicultural Scoiety Buyrdened with History*] (Manama Bahrain: Maktaba Fakhrawi, 2008). See also Laurence Louër, *Transnational* Shi'a *Politics: Religious and Political Networks in the Gulf* (New York: Columbia University Press, 2008).

[17] Yitzhak Nakash, *Reaching for Power: The Shi'a in the Modern Arab World* (Princeton: Princeton University Press, 2006), pp. 7–8.

[18] Laurence Louër, 'The State and Sectarian Identities in the Persian Gulf Monarchies: Bahrain, Saudi Arabia and Kuwait in Comparative Perspective', in Potter (ed.), *Sectarian Politics*, p. 118.

Al-Khalifa. To many of the Baharna, Bahrain's tribal elite are viewed as foreign usurpers who came to power through conquest and later drew on a complex web of socio-economic, tribal, and religious factors to deploy symbolic power and violence. Maintaining this neo-patrimonial system of privilege has been a key factor in ensuring the survival of the ruling Al-Khalifa family, yet it has also been coupled with efforts to curtail the influence of members of the Baharna whose cultural capital posed a challenge to the Al-Khalifa's dominance of the political field.[19]

In light of this, Bahrain's political field – and with it, religion and social history – was forged through the interaction of indigenous social factors with military conquest, which often possessed a religious dimension. Thus, social cleavages emerged along a number of lines which were overcome by what Fuad Khuri referred to as a 'feudal estate system' that created a number of fiefdoms under the tutelage of prominent Al-Khalifa figures and their allies.[20] Members of other sects were able to retain possessions subject to heavy taxes that most were unable to cover, which were then appropriated, perhaps most notably the pearl trade. As Khuri documents, Shi'a pearling tribes were tightly regulated while their Sunni counterparts enjoyed vast freedoms in a policy that was not explicitly sect based, but rather an attempt to 'reward' the conquerors and ensure their presence in Bahrain. The deployment of economic capital helped not only to consolidate Al-Khalifa rule but also to shape the political field, creating hierarchies of order, symbolic power and violence in the process.[21]

In the formative stages of the Bahraini state, members of the Al-Khalifa – ably supported by their British allies – sought to move away from indigenous forms of governance on the archipelago and establish a single governmental body under Al-Khalifa leadership. A key component of this strategy was to prevent the emergence of intra-Sunni contestation, but it also served to reinforce sectarian difference. For Staci Strobl, this is not purely a consequence of self interest but rather it reflects 'a deeper interplay of more socially and culturally embedded notions of sectarian identity that developed historically, and then were appropriated, modified and institutionalized during the colonial experience'.[22]

Supported by British gunboat diplomacy, the Al-Khalifa was able to forge an independent path in spite of competing pressures from the

---

[19] AlShehabi, *Contested Modernity.*

[20] Fuad I. Khuri, *Tribe and State in Bahrain: The Transformation of Social and Political Authority in an Arab State* (Chicago: University of Chicago Press, 1980), p. 35.

[21] Ibid.

[22] Strobl, *Sectarian Order*, p. xiv.

emerging Saudi state and Persia, both of whom sought control and influence over Bahrain. Regulating life in the early decades of the twentieth century posed challenges given the competing loyalties of many across Bahrain, with Najdis seen as unreliable due to perceived ties to the Al Sa'ud, Shi'a – notably those of Persian descent – unreliable due to perceived ties with Persia, and Baharna deemed unreliable due to Charles Belgrave, the British agent's racially driven prejudice.[23] Violence stemming from the state security apparatus was widespread but prompted complaints from Baharna and Shi'a communities. These complaints drew anger from Persia about the treatment of the Shi'a in Bahrain – much like that expressed against Saudi Arabia at this time. As a consequence, the Al-Khalifa and their British backers had to negotiate Persian concerns and the anger of Ibn Sa'ud, who remained fearful of Persian aggression.[24] When clashes took place between different facets of the security apparatus and local populations, a difficult balancing act took place between the competing pressures of not only Bahrainis but also the Al Sa'ud and Persia, demonstrating Bahrain's vulnerability to shifting geopolitical currents.

Much like the other GCC states, Bahrain's Shi'a population are in a position of political weakness, although unlike their larger counterparts, the Shi'a population are a demographic majority. As a consequence, Shi'a unrest has typically been a source of concern for the ruling Al-Khalifa, particularly when combined with long-standing concerns about the loyalty of Shi'a communities across the region. Like most other societies, to speak of a singular Bahraini Shi'a community is problematic; indeed, in Bahrain, ethnic, theological, class, and political divisions create differences amongst the Shi'a community that passed across generations. What unites many of these groups, however, is a fundamental tension between national loyalty and transnational relationships.

Such structural marginalization has been pertinently captured by Strobl in a magisterial account of sect-based discrimination of Shi'a groups in the state's criminal justice system.[25] In an approach grounded in Critical Criminology, Strobl's account of criminal justice in Bahrain sheds light on political, legal, and social inequality embedded within the

---

[23] As Marc Owen Jones observes, Belgrave rejected the Baharna on the grounds of 'their physique and eyesight ... not being as good as that of the Arabs and men of African origin'. Marc Owen Jones, *Political Repression in Bahrain* (Cambridge: Cambridge University Press, 2020), p. 150. Citing Belgrave's Annual Report for Year 1357, p. 14.
[24] This is documented in ibid., p. 138.
[25] Strobl, *Sectarian Order*.

fabric of the state. Examining Bahrain's colonial history, Strobl documents historical cases of violence, both direct and structural, against Shi'a communities, with a particular focus on the role of the political agent. While many referred to Bahrain as a peaceful place in the early years of the twentieth century, Strobl paints a different picture, suggesting that 'the country was safe for Sunni Arab men and expatriates, less so for Shi'a and women'.[26]

Beginning her account in 1900, Strobl recounts a tribal struggle that created opportunities for the Al-Khalifa to replace violent responses with administrative structures that would regulate life – albeit with British colonial support – in a manner akin to the bureaucratic procedures of the sovereign state. From that point, tribal skirmishes were regulated through law while efforts to impose social order would 'increasingly centre on subjugating Shi'a'.[27] Tribal networks imbued the Al-Khalifa with reserves of social capital in their efforts to dominate the political field, later reinforced by reserves of economic and coercive capital. Yet religious capital – in the form of social and cultural capital – continued to offer a means through which to challenge the ruling family and its foreign backers.

Exit London; Enter Riyadh

It came as no surprise that the vacuum created by the British withdrawal from Bahrain as part of the London's 'East of Suez' recalibration of international engagement was swiftly filled by Riyadh. Seeking to ensure the survival of the Al-Khalifa monarchy and prevent democratization, Saudi Arabia capitalized on financial largesse to exert influence across their island neighbours. At this point in time, concern at perfidious Iranian manipulation of Shi'a populations was limited, but Iran's interest in Bahrain was far grander, amidst claims to ownership of the archipelago after the British withdrawal.

At the United Nations, Secretary General U Thant argued that 'the overwhelming majority of the people of Bahrain wish to gain recognition of their identity in a fully independent and sovereign State free to decide for itself its relations with other States'.[28] The leader of a UN mission exploring questions of Bahraini sovereignty, Vittorio Winspeare, noted that 'the overwhelming majority of the people of Bahrain wish to gain

---

[26] Ibid., p. xxvi.
[27] Ibid., p. 4.
[28] Note by the Secretary-General, United Nations Security Council, 30 April 1970, S/9772, p. 13.

recognition of their identity in a fully independent and sovereign State free to decide for itself its relations with other States'.[29] While Iranian claims to Bahrain continued under the shah, they took on more of a symbolic nature, to be revived once more after the establishment of the Islamic Republic.[30]

It is perhaps unsurprising that in the absence of the British, Saudi Arabia began to exert greater influence in Bahrain's political field. This relationship between Bahrain and Saudi – underpinned by financial support, joint ownership of the Abu Safah oilfield, and shared security concerns – had been partially concocted by Ian Henderson, the British colonial police officer guilty of atrocities in the name of counterinsurgency during the Mau Mau rebellion. Henderson advocated a 'treaty of friendship' predicated on law and order and welfare spending, underpinned by a desire to ensure Al-Khalifa survival. Ultimately, however, this reliance on Saudi patronage created a power disparity that eroded Bahraini autonomy. In the years that followed, Bahrain's political field became dominated by Saudi Arabia whose vision of order was shared by the ruling Al-Khalifa.

In the absence of the British, the Al-Khalifa's Saudi backers covered costs accrued both by the state and by the Sheikhs to help consolidate power in the ruling family. The 1973 oil crisis emboldened the Saudis financially which, in turn, allowed the Al-Khalifa to retreat to the politics of rentierism and patronage with the aim of preventing moves towards democratization. With the provision of financial largesse, however, came increasing influence on both the domestic and foreign policies of Bahrain. Fundamental to Saudi interests at this time was a desire to prevent democratization amidst fears of possible repercussions across within the Saudi Kingdom. While this had a dramatic impact on Shi'a groups, it also affected other civil society groups and political identities including Islamists, Arab Nationalists, Communists, and Salafists who were seen to challenge the regime.

In the early years of independence, Shi'a groups possessed religious freedom, with rulers displaying a degree of tolerance towards the expression of Shi'a religiosity and, at times, using the institutions of state as an ally against opposition forces, most notably the Marxist and pan-Arab nationalist movements of the mid-twentieth century.[31] This was perhaps best seen in the 1973 constitution, the country's first, which adopted the ninth and tenth days of Muharram as public holidays in respect to the

---

[29] Ibid.
[30] Christin Marschall, *Iran's Persian Gulf Policy: From Khomeini to Khatami* (London: Routledge, 2003), p. 27.
[31] Louër, 'State and Sectarian Identities', pp. 120–1.

Shi'a festival of Ashura and once again Shi'a holy days became outlets for political expression. After independence, the decision was taken to hold parliamentary elections and in 1973 Bahrainis took to the polls, returning Marxists and Arab nationalists as the dominant force in the assembly. At this time, it was hardly surprising that Shi'a movements became a key facet of opposition across Bahrain, shaped by domestic and regional events, coalescing around competing networks of Shi'a authority in Iraq. As the rivalry between al-Da'wa, a party with strong links to the *Marja'iyyah* of Najaf and the Shirazi network increased, it began to shape events in Bahrain;[32] once again, developments across the transnational field began to resonate locally.

Amidst rising instability across the archipelago, the decision was taken to impose emergency legislation, which remained in place until 2001. At the time of imposition, the sovereign decision was supported by the State Security Law and State Security Court, and while deeply unpopular, it went some way to curtailing political opposition.[33] It gave the ruling elite the ability to take a range of often draconian measures in support of regime survival. This portfolio of mechanisms of control is documented extensively by Marc Owen Jones, who identifies strategies ranging from the cultivation of loyalty through networks of patronage and rentierism to institutional exclusion and abandonment.[34] The ensuing dissolution of parliament had a seismic impact on the political landscape, prompting a more radical agenda from the Shiraziyyin, a number of whose members travelled to Lebanon to train with the Palestinian Liberation Organization and Amal, a Shi'a militia.

Following the dramatic rise in oil prices across the 1970s, the Al-Khalifa moved into a form of clientelist rule, underpinned by Saudi sponsorship but driven by the prime minister (and his key allies) who capitalized on personal relationships to make a vast fortune. The cultivation of the rentier project was not explicitly sectarian, with individuals from both sects incorporated into clientelist networks in a pragmatic manner in pursuit of regime survival and the betterment of its members. Yet differences between the sects manifested in several ways, perhaps most obviously in the urban/rural divisions that were exacerbated by the rapid transformation of urban centres.[35]

[32] Louër, *Transnational* Shi'a *Politics*, pp. 89–99.

[33] Abdulhadi Khalaf, 'Contentious Politics in Bahrain: From Ethnic to National and Vice Versa', *The Fourth Nordic Conference on Middle Eastern Studies, 'The Middle East in a Globalizing World'*, Oslo, 13–16, 1998, https://org.uib.no/smi/pao/khalaf.html.

[34] Jones, *Political Repression*.

[35] Fuccaro, *Histories of City and State in the Persian Gulf*. See also Simon Mabon, 'Sects and the City', in Simon Mabon and John Nagle (eds.), *Urban Spaces and Sectarian Contestation* (Lancaster: SEPAD, 2020).

While relations between Shi'a communities and the regime became increasingly fractious, the transnational field entered a turbulent phase following the establishment of the Islamic Republic of Iran which resonated domestically through Tehran's desire to export the revolution. The religious capital of Shi'a figures in Bahrain increased dramatically in the aftermath of the revolution as many were emboldened by developments across the Gulf. Shi'a groups in Bahrain were quick to pay homage to Khomeini and the new regime in Tehran, and the Shiraziyyin – who had maintained positive relations with Khomeini over the previous decade – sought to engender revolution in Bahrain, albeit without the support of the more influential al-Da'wa.[36] In 1981, the IFLB – led by the previously expelled Hadi al-Mudarrisi – planned a *coup d'état* against the Al-Khalifa, albeit in vain as the plotters were arrested in transit. In response, the regime embarked on a crackdown on Shi'a groups, with the legacy of this event continuing to shape the habitus, fuelling perceptions of nefarious Iranian activity.

It was hardly surprising that the attempted coup resulted in a marked shift in the Al-Khalifa regime's threat perception – particularly towards Shi'a communities – which Laurence Louër suggests began to be defined 'in sectarian terms',[37] yet as Strobl and others have documented, this is perhaps better understood as the return of the sectarian gaze. Once again, Al-Khalifa efforts to define the political field were shaped by regional politics. As a consequence of the mobilization of the Shi'a identity as a political tool in Iran's foreign policy arsenal, Shi'a groups in Bahrain – and across the Gulf – were quickly seen as fifth columnists and, increasingly, as security threats.[38] At this point, Shi'a groups had also become the 'hegemonic actors of the opposition'[39] deploying religious and cultural capital in an effort to transform the political field. Given the strong ties between Manama and Riyadh and shared fears about increased Iranian influence in Bahrain, work began on what would become the King Fahd Causeway, a 16-kilometre bridge linking the archipelago to the eastern coast of Saudi Arabia.[40] Moreover, the increase in oil prices helped facilitate the proselytizing of Wahhabism across the Islamic world in an effort to increase Saudi influence. As a consequence, Salafis with

---

[36] Louër, 'State and Sectarian Identities', p. 124.
[37] Ibid., p. 125.
[38] Justin Gengler, 'Understanding Sectarianism in the Persian Gulf', in Potter (ed.), *Sectarian Politics*.
[39] Louër, 'State and Sectarian Identities', p. 129.
[40] Mabon, 'End of the Battle of Bahrain'.

links to Saudi Arabia became more prominently involved in Bahraini politics during the 1980s.[41]

In response to unrest amongst Shi'a communities at this time, a large number of individuals were removed from the state's payroll and forced to find work in the private sector where they faced competition with foreign workers for low wages, prompting unrest.[42] As oil prices dropped in the 1990s, the clientelistic model preferred by the Al-Khalifa faced a number of serious challenges, leaving them increasingly reliant upon Saudi Arabia for economic and political support. In return, as the erstwhile British ambassador to Bahrain Francis Trew observed, Saudi Arabia 'calls the tune',[43] with concerns at developments in the transnational field shaping the melody.

A Decade (or Two) of Discontent

Across the 1990s, protesters took to the streets to express anger at the perceived corruption of the regime, a stagnant economy, the failure to enact political reforms, and perennial authoritarianism. The protests brought together a range of disparate factions including leftists, liberal, and Islamic groups, united in their hopes for political reform. In response, government forces undertook a dramatic crackdown against the protesters, once again drawing on a particular vision of domination to order society, predicated on creating schisms within the protesters and framing Shi'a actors as agents of Iran. In 1996, officials accused Iran of funding a group called Bahraini Hizbullah – allegedly responsible for conducting acts across the country in the previous year – prompting a widespread crackdown on political expression.[44]

During this period, relations between Saudi Arabia and Iran began to improve, yet unrest in Bahrain continued amidst ongoing allegations of Iranian meddling. Across Bahrain, the imposition of a vision of domination had created a habitus that viewed Shi'a groups with suspicion and, despite broader regional developments, the legacy of Iranian meddling remained. For Sa'ud al-Faysal, then foreign minister of Saudi Arabia, Iranian meddling was 'very serious', noting that while Iran had sent

---

[41] Sunni political movements in Bahrain are discussed in Baqir Salman al-Najjar, *al-Harakat al-Diniyyah fi al-Khalij al-Arabi* [*Religious Movements in the Arab Gulf*] (London: Dar al Saqi Press, 2007).

[42] Lawrence Louër, 'The Political Impact of Labor Migration in Bahrain', *City & Society* 20:1 (2008), pp. 32–53.

[43] Cited in Jones, *Political Repression*, p. 153.

[44] Graham E. Fuller and Rend Rahim Francke, *The Arab Shi'a: The Forgotten Muslims* (New York: St Martin's Press, 1999), p. 135.

messages to Bahrain and Saudi proclaiming a desire to 'do anything' to prove that it was not involved in Bahrain, these proclamations were not matched by actions.[45]

On 6 March 1999, Hamad bin Isa bin Salman Al-Khalifa succeeded his father as emir of the Kingdom of Bahrain after serving thirty-five years as crown prince. At this point, divisions within the Al-Khalifa re-appeared: the new king had to contend with his uncle, the powerful Prime Minister Sheikh Khalifa bin Salman Al-Khalifa, the de facto ruler of Bahrain under the erstwhile emir, and an individual who exerted a great deal of influence across the upper echelons of political, social, and economic life. The system of primogeniture placed Hamad's son, Salman, as crown prince – heir apparent – but also prompted a struggle for power resulting in the creation of a number of different factions vying for influence under the king, with different political outlooks and relationships with key figures in Bahrain and beyond, with tribal networks extending across the Gulf.[46]

Although beginning his rule as emir, Hamad changed the sovereign's title to king on 14 February 2002; the date would later have symbolic importance for those opposing the regime. Upon taking power, Hamad proclaimed a raft of political reforms that sought to address a growing dissatisfaction at the political climate across the island.[47] Additionally, Hamad released hundreds of prisoners, announced municipal elections, revised the *majlis al-shura* by increasing Shi'a representation and appointed a National Action Charter designed to facilitate political reform. Furthermore, Hamad allowed the return of over 100 dissidents who had been in exile, many of whom would later play a key role in Shi'a political leadership.[48] Unrest quickly followed Hamad's decision to unilaterally revise the constitution, which gave power to the executive branch over the legislature, rapidly prompting expressions of frustration from many. This left the new monarch on the horns of a dilemma: to address sectarian polarization by realigning with Shi'a groups and risking repercussions from the Al Khalifa's Saudi backers, or to continue advocating and privileging Sunni identities securing the continued backing of Saudi Arabia in the process, albeit at the cost of deepening societal divisions.

---

[45] 95RIYADH712_a, 'Iran: Meeting with Saudi Foreign Minister Saud Al-Faysal' (08.02.95), https://wikileaks.org/plusd/cables/95RIYADH712_a.html.

[46] See Justin Gengler, 'Royal Factionalism, the Khawalid, and the Securitization of "the Shi'a Problem" in Bah- rain', *Journal of Arabian Studies* 3:1 (June 2013), pp. 53–79.

[47] Frederic Wehrey, 'Bahrain's Decade of Discontent', *Journal of Democracy* 24:3 (2013), p. 118.

[48] Frederic Wehrey, *Sectarian Politics in the Gulf: From the Iraq War to the Arab Uprisings* (New York: Columbia University Press, 2013), p. 42.

One of the strategies of the new king was a process of controlled liberalization, capitalizing on a more accommodating regional economic environment and seeking to co-opt opposition figures, including members of al-Wifaq, into the structures of the state.[49] The reality, however, was very different, with no serious moves made to include Shi'a opposition figures at this time. Recalling a meeting with the king, one former MP stressed how the right tone was conveyed to members of al-Wifaq, yet few steps were taken to implement such remarks.[50]

Although the transition to a new monarch promised much, the power of the prime minister, Sheikh Khalifa, and his close relationship to Prince Nayef in Saudi Arabia demonstrated the salience of conservativism and an anti-Shi'a stance. Both Khalifa and Nayef were concerned about the threat from Iran, framing relations between Bahrain and Saudi Arabia in security terms.[51] Despite an apparent thaw in the transnational field the latent anxieties of Khalifa and Nayef – and with it, the habitus of Bahrain's political field – meant that security concerns remained prevalent in relations between the two Kingdoms, preventing political reform in the process.

Traditionally, the largest Shi'a party in Bahrain in terms of both its political wing and its popular support, al-Wifaq drew support from clerics, laypersons, and the country's middle class.[52] The group's leaflets refer to the State of Bahrain, demonstrating both the rejection of the Al-Khalifa – albeit with contrasting views about the form of this rejection – and large-scale support amongst *baharna* Shi'a. Other prominent groups include al-Amal, formed from the remnants of the IFLB, and Haq. Shi'a movements in Bahrain have historically been divided into a number of groups, shaped by class, ideology, religiosity, and contrasting views on electoral participation and the use of violence. These tensions became increasingly apparent following al-Wifaq's decision to engage in the 2006 elections. The shift came about following a number of Friday sermons from Sheikh 'Ali Salman, who encouraged democratic engagement in elections across the second half of the decade.[53] Differences also emerge over the use of violence, with prominent al-Wifaq

[49] J.E. Peterson, 'Bahrain: Reform, Promise, and Reality', in Joshua Teitelbaum (ed.), *Political Liberalization in the Persian Gulf* (New York: Columbia University Press, 2009), pp. 157–85.

[50] Interview with former Bahraini MP.

[51] Interview with Bahraini civil society activist.

[52] Katja Niethammer, *Voices in Parliamen: Debates in Majlis, and Banners on Streets: Avenues of Political Participation in Bahrain*, Mediterranean Programme Series, EUI RSCAS (2006/7), p. 17, https://cadmus.eui.eu/handle/1814/6224.

[53] Muhammad al-Ali, 'al-Wifaq to Vote on Political Societies Law Today', *Gulf Daily News* (6.10.2005).

MPs condemning violence from all sides. Jalal Fairouz, an al-Wifaq MP, declared violence to be haram, evoking ridicule amongst Haq supporters, yet prompting a sympathetic response for his actions – and those of al-Wifaq – from US officials.[54]

Beyond political and methodological differences, perceptions of Shi'a groups in Bahrain are also shaped by broader regional events, albeit conditioned by concerns about regime survival. Domestically, within the context of widespread frustration at the socio-economic and political environment in Bahrain, the Al-Khalifa sought to reduce the potential for dissent and insidious revolt by purging the security sector of Shi'a elements.[55] At this time, sect-based identities became increasingly common as the regime 'activated' Sunni identities as a means of creating distance from the Shi'a protesters, driven by developments across the region.

It was hardly surprising that such sectarian polarization shaped the wide spectrum of politics on the island. Beyond Shi'a organizations, Bahrain is also home to a number of Sunni Islamist societies who historically played a key role in aiding the Al-Khalifa, balancing against pan-Arabism, Communism and, more recently, in exploiting and regulating sect-based difference. Once again, the Iraq War played a key role in emboldening groups out of fear at rising Iranian influence and a sense of Sunni decline across Iraq. Yet much like Shi'a societies, their Sunni counterparts expressed a range of views on Bahraini politics, with some such as al-Minbar following the royal line while others such as the al-Asala bloc being more critical. Regional events conspired to bring Sunni groups together in support of the regime, putting an end to long-running disputes between the various groups and marginalizing the more moderate voices. At this time, Sunni societies took up increasingly vociferous anti-Shi'a stances in parliament, using antagonistic rhetoric and denigrating key figures such as 'Isa al-Qasim.

In the years that followed, parliamentary politics became increasingly polarized along sectarian lines as parliamentarians sought to articulate their identities rather than address constituent needs. The ensuing 2002 election boycott by Shi'a groups returned a vastly pro-regime parliament which then embarked on a series of anti-Shi'a policies, although a number of outlets were created for more liberal and Shi'a voices. In 2006, al-Wifaq participated in elections, winning seventeen out of forty seats

---

[54] 09MANAMA438_a, 'Bahrain's Shi'a Opposition: Managing Sectarian Pressures and Focusing on 2010 Parliamentary Elections' (22.07.09), https://wikileaks.org/plusd/cables/09MANAMA438_a.html.
[55] Khalaf, 'Contentious Politics in Bahrain'.

in spite of widespread allegations of gerrymandering, but the distribution of the other twenty-three created a parliament split along sect-based lines.[56] The performance of al-Wifaq at this time was driven by Shi'a issues but also sought to articulate national issues, working with Sunni parties to address corruption and questions about naturalization.

Parties such as al-Wifaq exerted a great deal of social capital not only through their engagement with local communities, but also through their relations with Bahrain's clerical establishment. Facing such levels of social capital – which translated into al-Wifaq winning over 60 per cent of the popular vote in 2006 – the Al-Khalifa's coercive mechanisms and efforts to impose symbolic violence over Bahrain's political field were fully operational. Further details of regime strategies were made public in the 2006 'Bandar Report' affair, the leaking of a 200-page report by Saleh al-Bandar who worked in the Royal Court Affairs Ministry entitled *Bahrain: The Democratic Option and Exclusion Mechanisms*.[57] The report articulated how sect-based identities had become a security threat in Bahrain, prompting the royal family to exploit these tensions ahead of upcoming parliamentary elections. The report also noted the impact of regional events on the archipelago's political and sectarian landscape:

the marginalization of Sunnis and the lessening of their role in Bahrain is part of a larger regional problem, whereas [our] sons of the Sunni sect in Iraq face the same problem, meaning there is a direct correlation between [the Iraqi situation and] the marginalization of the *Sunna* in the Gulf countries, and their marginalization in Bahrain in particular. There is a dangerous challenge facing Bahraini society in the increased role of the Shi'a [and] the retreat of the role of the *Sunna* in the Bahraini political system; namely, the problem concerns the country's [Bahrain's] national security, and the likelihood of political regime change in the long term by means of the current relationships between Bahrain's Shi'a and all the Shi'a in Iran, Iraq, Saudi Arabia's eastern region, and Kuwait.[58]

The report documented how the Al-Khalifa had cultivated myriad strategies including a network to reinforce Sunni identification with the ruling elite, while preventing the Shi'a from gaining prominent positions. According to the report, Ahmed bin Atiyatallah Al-Khalifa, the minister of state for cabinet affairs – and member of the royal family – was accused of distributing more than one million Bahraini dinar across a network of supporters as a means of manipulating the political system

---

[56] See Wehrey, *Sectarian Politics in the Gulf.*
[57] The report is available at https://drive.google.com/file/d/18MyshDHDSi0xI4bcJySRW WfxavOScMbPlYa2wPwBc1XYFLPswo0H_Kh_u_dX/view.
[58] Ibid.

in favour of Sunni causes and candidates. Funds were distributed for a number of different activities, including funding electoral campaigns, investigating political opponents and assisting the conversion of Shi'a Muslims to Sunni Islam.

The report had a seismic impact on relations between the different communities and the political landscape more broadly. For many Shi'a, the report confirmed long-standing fears about the regime's intent and documented the practice of recruiting Sunnis from across the region into the security services with the promise of citizenship in an attempt to address demographic imbalances between Sunni and Shi'a.[59] Essentially, the report confirmed Shi'a fears about their position in Bahraini society and the extent to which the Al-Khalifa sought to limit their political involvement through a range of different practices that challenged their very survival.

Unsurprisingly, communal tensions were exacerbated by regional developments in the formative years of Hamad's rule. The 2003 US-led invasion of Iraq had a dramatic impact on Bahrain, not only leaving it as the only case of a Sunni minority ruling over a Shi'a majority, but also exacerbating sect-based differences and increasing opposition criticisms of the regime. As Fred Wehrey asserts, conflict in Iraq became 'a filter' through which people in Bahrain viewed their own 'contentious politics', a form of 'political theatre' that encouraged citizens to participate and 're-enact' in a partisan manner.[60] Following the 2003 invasion of Iraq, fear about the loyalty of Shi'a groups across the Middle East dramatically increased, particularly as Iran gained greater influence in Iraq and Lebanon. King Abdullah's comments about the 'Shi'a crescent' served to support these concerns. Elections in Iraq reinforced al-Wifaq's call for electoral participation, with prominent members seeking to derive support from Grand Ayatollah 'Ali Sistani in Iraq for their engagement in the democratic process.[61] Such developments were viewed with suspicion by regime loyalists, who once again framed Shi'a politics in Bahrain as a product of regional developments, shaped by the Marja'iyyah. Once again, tensions between a Bahraini nationalism and loyalty to the transnational Shi'a movement were at the heart of regime perceptions of Shi'a groups in Bahrain.

Regional developments also affected Sunni groups in Bahrain, who expressed solidarity with their embattled sectarian kin in Iraq. Perhaps

[59] Habib Trabelsi, 'Bahrain's Shi'ite Muslims Cry Foul over Dual Nationality Plan', *Khaleej Times* (16.06.02), cited in Wehrey, *Sectarian Politics in the Gulf.*
[60] Wehrey, *Sectarian Politics in the Gulf*, p. 41.
[61] Ibid., p. 48.

more worryingly for regime officials, events in Iraq suggested an increase in Iranian influence, a view supported by developments in Lebanon and manifesting in the narrative of a 'Shi'a Crescent'. Increased influence of Iranian actors in Iraq and an empowered Shi'a population in the country suggested a return to the 1980s and fears of Iranian manipulation of Bahrain's own Shi'a population. These suspicions of transnational loyalties above Bahraini nationalism – products of Bahrain's political field and the evolution of the transnational field – shaped perceptions of Shi'a groups, helping create a habitus and principles of vision that were deeply anti-Shi'a. In such a climate, allegations of Iranian manipulation – either directly or through Hizbullah – easily found traction.

Although ties with Saudi Arabia had long been central to the survival of the Al-Khalifa – and stability across Bahrain more broadly – tensions between the two increased following the 2004 Saudi decision not to renew a grant of 50,000 barrels of oil per day from the Abu Sufah oil field, also halting the sale of sand.[62] The reduced number of barrels exacerbated a financial crisis which resulted in debt of around 16 per cent of GDP in 2004 and a drop in 14.6 per cent of government revenues.[63] Later that year, the signing of a free trade agreement between Bahrain and the United States exacerbated such concerns, prompting Saudi officials to threaten the imposition of tariffs amidst fears that the agreement could spell the end of the GCC.[64]

In conversation with US and British ambassadors, Crown Prince Salman articulated a broader concern about Saudi actions, declaring the response to be irrational. Although acknowledging that Saudi Arabia remained 'the most important country in the region', Salman stressed that Bahrain would 'stand firm' if the Saudis continued with this 'hissy fit'.[65] The Bahraini stance was later supported by officials from UAE, who declared that the free state agreement (FTA) was allowed by Article

[62] 05MANAMA1182_a, 'Bahrain Expects Continued Strong Relations with Saudi, Hopes for Resumption of Oil Grant' (16.08.05), https://wikileaks.org/plusd/cables/05MANAMA1182_a.html.

[63] 05MANAMA280_a, 'Bahrain Faces Budget Crunch Following Saudi Oil Grant Cutback' (01.03.05), https://wikileaks.org/plusd/cables/05MANAMA280_a.html.

[64] 05MANAMA38_a, 'Bahrain FTA: Full Speed Ahead Despite Protests from Saudi Arabia' (05.01.05), https://wikileaks.org/plusd/cables/05MANAMA38_a.html; 05MANAMA24_a, 'King Focuses on Relations with Saudi Arabia in Meeting with Ambassador' (04.01.05), https://wikileaks.org/plusd/cables/05MANAMA24_a.html; 05MANAMA176_a, 'Continuing Saudi Concerns about Bahrain FTA' (07.02.05), https://wikileaks.org/plusd/cables/05MANAMA176_a.html.

[65] 04MANAMA1814_a, 'Saudi Statement on GCC Bilateral Agreements Concerns Bahrain' (06.12.04), https://wikileaks.org/plusd/cables/04MANAMA1814_a.html.

31 of GCC law on economic cooperation.[66] In a speech at the concluding session of the International Institute for Strategic Studies (IISS)-sponsored Gulf Dialogue, Saudi foreign minister Prince Sa'ud al-Faysal – a late replacement for the King, reflecting a downgrading of Saudi involvement in the dialogue – expressed criticism of GCC countries who entered into bilateral agreements with international powers, articulating a regional security framework predicated on the interaction of subnational, regional, and international components.[67] The FTA had a dramatic impact on Saudi–Bahraini relations and wider GCC engagement, essentially curtailing economic integration. Resentment in Bahrain at Saudi actions began to rise, particularly after Bahrain spent $700 million on expanding the production of the Abu Safah oil field yet received less oil from the Kingdom than before.[68]

Discussions between Minister of Interior Shaikh Rashid and US Ambassador William T. Monroe in early 2005 reveal a Bahraini perception that tensions between Riyadh and Manama were a consequence of Saudi Arabia's 'apprehension about the pace of economic and political reform' in Bahrain and possible democratic repercussions in the Kingdom.[69] Although Saudi Arabia exerted vast influence in Bahrain's political field, the evolution of political life after King Hamad came to power points to an attempt to reassert Bahraini influence, albeit at a time when more conservative parts of royal families in both states continued to position security concerns as the driving force in bilateral relations.

A Shifting Transnational Field

Although tensions between Bahrain and Saudi Arabia increased, Riyadh and Manama shared concerns about developments in the transnational field which began to resonate domestically. On 27 February 2005 Mohammed Abd al-Ghaffar, minister of state for foreign affairs, summoned the Iranian ambassador to express 'deep concern' at Iranian activities and interference 'in Bahrain's internal affairs' which had reached a nadir during the year's Ashura celebrations. According to Ghaffar, camps had been established to provide training around Shi'a villages where images of Khomeini, Khamenei, and Hizbullah logos were prevalent. Ghaffar

---

[66] 05MANAMA38_a, 'Bahrain FTA'.
[67] 04MANAMA1814_a, 'Saudi Statement'.
[68] 05MANAMA24_a, 'King Focuses on Relations with Saudi Arabia'.
[69] 05MANAMA71_a, 'Minister of Interior Discusses CT, Saudi Arabia, Iran with Ambassador' (16.01.05), https://wikileaks.org/plusd/cables/05MANAMA71_a.html.

condemned al-Wifaq of supporting this, accusing Sheikh Isa Qassim of being 'a very dangerous man'. Regime officials argued that the opening up of civil society and increased freedom of speech created conditions for Iran to boost their influence. Reflecting on this, Ghaffar argued that 'when you give people more freedom, bad groups can exploit this freedom for their own sectarian purposes'.[70]

Adding to this were repeated claims from Iranian officials close to the supreme leader that Bahrain was a province of Iran. Hossein Shariatmadari, editor of *Kayhan* – a daily newspaper in Iran – claimed that Bahrain was the 14th province of Iran, a claim later reprinted in *al-Qabas*, a Kuwaiti newspaper. In the piece, Shariatmadari proclaimed that

Bahrain is a special case among GCC countries in the Persian Gulf because Bahrain is part of the Iranian territories and had been separated from Iran in light of an illegal settlement between the executed Shah and the governments of the United States and Britain. And the main demand for the Bahrain people is to return its province – which was separated from Iran – to the motherland which is Islamic Iran. It is self-evident that Iran and the people of this separated province must not give up this ultimate right.[71]

In conversations with their American counterparts, Bahraini officials declared the statement to be 'outrageous', reaffirming their suspicions about Iran and its aspirations in Bahrain.[72] In response to Shariatmadari's claims, over 500 Bahrainis – including al-Wifaq parliamentarians – protested outside the Iranian embassy,[73] while eighteen months later, al-Wifaq MPs vocally condemned a suggestion from Darious Ghanbari, an Iranian MP, that in the case of a referendum, Bahrainis would overwhelmingly vote in favour of joining Iran.[74]

In the months that followed, Bahraini officials regularly expressed concern about Iranian activity to their American counterparts. According to Foreign Minister Khalid bin Ahmed Al-Khalifa, Iran was playing a 'dirty role' in Iraq while concerns remained that 'Iran always starts

[70] 05MANAMA347_a, 'GOB Reacts to Outward Signs of Shi'a Activism during Ashura Observances' (09.03.05), https://wikileaks.org/plusd/cables/05MANAMA347_a.html.
[71] 07MANAMA650_a, 'Bahrain Reacts Angrily to Iranian Territorial Claim on Bahrain' (12.07.07), https://wikileaks.org/plusd/cables/07MANAMA650_a.html.
[72] Ibid.
[73] 'Bahrainis Protest against Iran Province Claim', *Reuters* (14.07.07), www.oneindia.com/2007/07/13/bahrainis-protest-against-iran-province-claim-1184337928.html.
[74] 'Bahraini Shi'ite Group Flays Iran Rhetoric', *Gulf News* (08.02.09), https://gulfnews.com/world/gulf/bahrain/bahraini-shiite-group-flays-iran-rhetoric-1.50686.

with Bahrain', and apprehension about 'every plan that lands from Iran. We don't know what they have up their sleeves.'[75]

The rising influence of Iran across the region – in Iraq and Lebanon in particular – helped to re-activate sect-based politics in Bahrain, albeit in an indirect manner, once more demonstrating the impact of the transnational field on domestic political fields. For the regime, the narrative of nefarious Iranian manipulation along with the perceived divided loyalties of Bahraini Shi'a was a powerful tool to discredit political opponents, particularly in elections. Such views resonated in a range of ways. Concerned by events in both Iraq and Bahrain, Saudi Arabia was increasingly reluctant to sanction political liberalization in Bahrain, fearing Shi'a gains through the ballot box. The Lebanese Shi'a cleric Mohammed Hussein Fadlallah gave an interview to *al-Wasat*, a Bahraini newspaper later closed by the regime for fostering dissent, urging Bahraini Shi'a to participate in elections.[76] Yet opposition groups were divided, particularly after al-Wifaq's decision to participate in the 2006 elections, prompting a move towards acts of civil disobedience by other movements.

Like other aspects of Bahraini politics, regional affairs had a marked impact on this decision, notably stemming from the December 2005 parliamentary elections in Iraq which returned a large Shi'a majority. A key architect of this result was the Iranian grand ayatollah 'Ali Sistani, a quietist Shi'a Marjah based in Najaf held by many to be responsible for mobilizing Shi'a voters in Iraq. As a consequence, key figures in the Bahraini Shi'a community vied for Sistani's approval.

US diplomatic cables released by Wikileaks document the ruling family's concerns. In one cable, an outgoing US ambassador reflected on the challenges facing the Al-Khalifa:

For the government and ruling family, the existential threat is Iran and its historical claims to Bahrain. Iran's increased aggressiveness under President Ahmadinejad, coupled with perceived Iranian inroads in Iraq, have only heightened Bahraini concerns. The government is only too happy to have us focus on potential threats from Iran and their alleged Shi'a allies in Bahrain. In contrast, Sunnis, even Sunni extremists, form the base of support against a potential Shi'a/Iranian threat. The government fully understands that any kind of terror attack by Sunni extremists in Bahrain – against U.S. or Bahraini interests – would be a disaster for the country and its economy, and it is ready to cooperate with us fully to make sure that doesn't happen. But our future cooperation will continue to

---

[75] 06MANAMA4_a, 'GCC Summit: Bahrain Focuses on Iran' (02.01.06), https://wikileaks.org/plusd/cables/06MANAMA4_a.html.
[76] أدعو قضاة لبنان للتعلّم من قضاة «إسرائيل», *Elaph* (05.05.07), https://elaph.com/ElaphWeb/NewsPapers/2007/5/231342.html.

be affected by two factors: Bahraini confidence that, in this small island country, the authorities can stay one step ahead of and deal with any extremists planning a local operation; and Bahraini reluctance to move against or alienate the Sunni Islamist community at a time of heightened concern about Iran and rising Shi'a influence in the region.[77]

Amid such instability and given the history of sectarian difference across Bahrain, it was hardly surprising that the Al-Khalifa viewed Shi'a unrest through the lens of a security challenge, as a threat to political stability.[78] Long-standing concerns about Iran are perhaps best articulated by King Hamad, who argued that 'as long as Khamenei has the title of Commander-in-Chief, Bahrain must worry about the loyalty of Shi'a who maintain ties and allegiance to Iran'.[79] At the same time, senior Bahraini officials, including Khalid bin Ahmed Al-Khalifa, drew parallels between the Iranian revolution and 'the export of terror'.[80]

In conversation with US general David Petraeus, the king expressed concern about Iranian activity across the Middle East and the potential impact of a nuclear Iran. For Hamad, the nuclear programme 'must be stopped', declaring that the 'danger of letting it go on is greater than the danger of stopping it'.[81] The narrative of the Shi'a crescent aggravated these fears, resulting in calls for the realignment of regional security in response to the perceived threat from Iran. In 2006, the King of Bahrain called for real peace with Israel. As a diplomatic cable from 2006 notes, the king declared that he was serious, 'pushing, meeting with Israelis', albeit in a clandestine manner, yet proclaimed that the region should make peace with Israel 'and then we can all face Iran'.[82]

These concerns about perfidious Iranian activity were also exacerbated by Saudi fears of increased Iranian behaviour and the long-standing perception that Tehran could manipulate Shi'a populations across the region. In spite of this, the Al-Khalifa were keen to stress that the 'disagreement between the Bahraini people and their government is strictly an internal affair'.[83]

---

[77] 07MANAMA669_a, 'Future of Bahrain: Ambassador's Parting Thoughts' (19.07.07), https://wikileaks.org/plusd/cables/07MANAMA669_a.html.

[78] Wehrey, 'Bahrain's Decade of Discontent', p. 118.

[79] 06MANAMA409_a, 'Luncheon with King Hamad' (15.03.06), https://wikileaks.org/plusd/cables/06MANAMA409_a.html.

[80] 06MANAMA595_a, 'U/S Joseph Discusses Iran and PSI with Bahraini FM' (12.04.06), https://wikileaks.org/plusd/cables/06MANAMA595_a.html.

[81] 09MANAMA642_a, 'General Petraeus with King Hamad: Iraq, Afghanistan, Iran Nato Awacs, Energy' (04.11.09), https://wikileaks.org/plusd/cables/09MANAMA642_a.html.

[82] 06MANAMA1849_a, 'King Hamad Supports Gulf Security Dialogue' (01.11.06), https://wikileaks.org/plusd/cables/06MANAMA1849_a.html.

[83] 07MANAMA662_a 'Iranian FM Assures Bahrain of Full Respect for Sovereignty' (17.07.07), https://wikileaks.org/plusd/cables/07MANAMA662_a.html.

Yet the stigma of foreign allegiances continued to plague Bahraini Shi'a, a fact that 'Ali Salman was all too aware of:

I have been involved in political activity since 1992 as a leader of the opposition. I can swear by God's book that from that time until now, we have not received a single dinar from Iran. If Iran supported Hizbullah with money and weapons, it has no foothold in Bahrain and has no influence on the *Shi'ite* position. We are extremely clear in Bahrain. Iran is a neighboring Muslim country, but it is a country, and we are a country. We are independent in our decisions and do not allow anyone to interfere in our internal affairs.'[84]

Similar remarks were made to me in a conversation with a senior Bahraini cleric, who vehemently rejected accusations of working with Iran, saying that 'it is deeply offensive'.[85] As Jalal Fairouz, a former Bahraini MP later recalled, 'in the 1970s, Shi'a groups were accused of being backed by Nasser and the pan-Arabists. In the 1980s, we were accused of being backed by the Soviet Union and the Communists. Now we are accused of being backed by Qatar.'[86] Despite these rejections, some Iranian officials continued to articulate the narrative that Bahrainis are 'originally Iranians' and that there is 'Iranian blood in the population'.[87]

In addition to events in Iraq, the 2006 war between Israel and Hizbullah had a marked impact on Bahraini political life, with the actions of Hassan Nasrallah and the Party of God inspiring Shi'a groups across the region. In Bahrain, Hizbullah flags quickly appeared across Shi'a communities and at al-Wifaq's headquarters, playing into Sunni and Al-Khalifa fears that Shi'a groups were foreign proxies. In the years that followed, regime officials would routinely accuse an organization by the name of Bahraini Hizbullah of committing violent acts across the state, comments that were echoed by international allies, yet there is little evidence of such a group existing.[88] Allegations were also made about members of al-Wifaq having met members of the nascent Houthi insurgency in 2009, prompting Bahrain's parliament to express solidarity with the Saudi struggle.[89]

Once again, Bahraini Shi'a were predictably accused of being Iranian agents. Shi'a groups on the archipelago continued to reach out to their counterparts in Iraq and Iran for advice on the political situation, while

---

[84] Salman al-Dawsiri, 'Interview with Ali Salman', *al-Sharq al-Awsat* (22.05.07).
[85] Interview with Bahraini Shi'a cleric, Vienna, 2014.
[86] Interview with former Bahraini politician, London, 2019.
[87] Interview with former Iranian official, 2020.
[88] Interviews with British and American officials.
[89] 'Bahrain: Yemen's Rebellion Adds to Sectarian Tensions', *Oxford Analytica Daily Brief* (12.01.10), www.oxan.com/display.aspx?ItemID=DB156920.

Nabil Rajab suggested that there was no guarantee that 'future frustration will not force people to adopt extremist views and seek help from foreign powers not liked by Bahrain, such as Iran'.[90] In response, the head of Bahrain's National Security Agency, Khalifa bin Abdullah bin Muhammad Al-Khalifa, warned the group that it would be banned if it continued to reach out to foreign actors.[91] At this point, a common principle of vision amongst Sunni Bahrainis was that Shi'a groups on the island were domestically marginalized, leaving them with little option but to seek help from Iran.[92]

These allegations had a serious impact on Bahrain's political sphere. While a new parliament was established in 2006, it was a consequence of broad manipulation as set out in the Bandar Report. This manipulation included electoral tampering and widespread gerrymandering designed to return a large number of Sunni politicians.[93] In spite of this, a number of Shi'a candidates were elected, in the face of nefarious conduct by Sunni candidates and their supporters, including one individual who burnt down his own house in an attempt to engender sympathy and popular support amongst his constituents albeit to no avail, losing both the election and his home.[94]

In June 2008, tensions between different sectarian groups escalated as the political crisis intensified. In his Friday sermon on 13 June, Sheikh Isa Qassim accused the Bahraini regime of torturing twenty-five Shi'a who were on trial. In the sermon, Qassim called on the Al-Khalifa to stop 'accusing [Shi'a] of terrorism and disloyalty to the nation'. Responding to Qassim's comments, Jassim al-Sa'idi, a Salafist member of parliament, criticized Qassim for his remarks in his own sermons and opinion pieces, while charging him with pursuing 'an Iranian agenda'.[95]

The criticism of Qassim prompted the leader of al-Wifaq, 'Ali Salman, to call on his followers to demonstrate their solidarity by taking to the streets. This appeal drew support from another Shi'a cleric, Ayatollah

---

[90] 'Nabil Rajab li, '*Aafaq*: al-Tabqa al-hakima bil Bahrayn tumaris al-t'athiir did al-Shi'a' ['Nabil Rajab to *Aafaq*: Bahrain's Ruling Class Practices Apartheid against Shi'ites'], *al-Aafaq* (26.10.08).

[91] 'Jami'ya al-tahdid al-Bahrayniya: Khitabna al-maraji'a al-fiqhiya fi al-Iyran al-'Iraq li dafa' al-durur 'n al-watan' ['BCR: We Talked to Religious Authorities in Iran, Iraq, to Avoid Problems in the Country], *Al-Aafaq* (22.09.08).

[92] Interview with Bahraini researcher.

[93] Lauren Frayer, 'al-Bander Ejection Exposes Bahrain Split', *Washington Post* (02.10.06), www.washingtonpost.com/wp-dyn/content/article/2006/10/02/AR2006100200868.html.

[94] Interview with former Bahraini politician.

[95] 08MANAMA420_a, Shi'a *and* Sunni Preachers Trade Insults, Government Steps In to Muzzle Sectarian Voices' (24.06.08)' https://wikileaks.org/plusd/cables/08MANAMA420_a.html.

Hussain Najati, and Hassan Mushaima, the leader of the Haq Movement. The following week, however, Friday sermons focused on unity and tolerance, taking the sting out of the burgeoning sect-based hostility, while newspaper columns condemned sectarianism. While this removed much of the immediate anger, structural grievances remained, bound up in the Al-Khalifa's principle of vision which positioned Shi'a groups as insidious Iranian agents, supported by the deployment of political, social, and economic capital in pursuit of its survival.

At the same time, the ruling family engaged in a series of performative acts, meeting with prominent Shi'a leaders from across the region, perhaps most notably Sayyid Ammar al-Hakim, chairman of the Islamic Supreme Council in Iraq. During the visit, Sayyid Ammar met with the king and prime minister, who sought to demonstrate Bahrain's commitment to all Iraqis, regardless of sect. According to reports, the king hoped that the meeting would help channel the political energy of Bahrain's Shi'a movements in a positive manner ahead of elections.[96] The meeting with al-Hakim demonstrated the influence of transnational Shi'a movements and the importance of regional currents, yet in doing so, the meeting reinforced perceptions about nefarious external influence.

Spring in Bahrain: Sectarianism as a Principles of Vision

Amidst decades of al-Khalifa symbolic violence and a habitus that sought to curtail pro-democracy demands and Shi'a activity, it was hardly surprising that people took to the streets of Manama in early 2011, inspired by the spate of protests that became known as the Arab Uprisings. Large crowds quickly occupied Pearl Roundabout in Manama, comprising people from all sectors of society, chanting 'No Sunni, No Shi'a, Just Bahraini', rejecting a discriminatory habitus in the process. The protests drew a huge crowd – some estimates place this at over a hundred thousand – with support from a trans-sectarian base. Indeed, in the early stages of the protests this was an *anti-sectarian* protest, demanding political reform. As Greg Gause observes, if 'Charles Kurzman's estimate that modern revolutions seldom involve more than 1 percent of the population is true, then what transpired was proportionally one of the greatest shows of "people power" in modern history'.[97]

---

[96] 09MANAMA651_a, 'Sayyid Ammar Al Hakim, Chairman of the Islamic Supreme Council in Iraq, Visits Bahrain' (12.11.09)' https://wikileaks.org/plusd/cables/09MANAMA651_a.html.

[97] F.G. Gause and S.L. Yom, 'Resilient Royals: How Arab Monarchies Hang on', *Journal of Democracy*, 23:74–88 (15.10.12), p. 118.

A facebook page run by the Bahrain Youth for Freedom articulated the protesters' main concerns:

> We have been suffering the ills of unmitigated corruption and brutal oppression for far too long, established under an irresponsible and unaccountable regime. The grievances may diverge but the cause is one. The regime has grown accustomed to creating crisis after crisis under the constructed banner of sectarianism, escaping accountability and suppressing the legitimate rights of the people. The plunder of the nation's wealth has reached unprecedented proportions, including the expropriation of public land and sea. They have used foreign security forces to humiliate and attack citizens, and endemic corruption has seeped throughout the state's institutions. Our thoughts and voices have been controlled through censorship and press control, while political naturalisation to change the population of the country has reached unprecedented levels. Anger and frustration is boiling amongst us all.[98]

Formal societies were generally surprised by the speed and intensity of the protest movements. Having watched events unfold across the region, Bahrainis took to the streets to express their own frustrations. Myriad Facebook pages emerged calling for protests against the regime on 14 February and while some called for the fall of the regime – *isqat al-nizam* – most of the protesters were peaceful, calling for political reform. Central to the protest movements was unabashed criticism of the Al-Khalifa's promises of reform and a rejection of the Al-Khalifa vision of political and social order.[99]

In the months leading up to the protests, a degree of cross-sectarian co-operation had occurred in an effort to investigate land appropriation by the royal family which was, unsurprisingly, met with a crackdown given that such co-operation was viewed as a security challenge by the Al-Khalifa. Prior to 14 February, negotiations took place between King Hamad and Ali Salman, who had been summoned to the royal palace, where the king urged Salman to call off the protests. In response, Salman pressed for political reform, namely the replacement of the prime minister, the staunchly anti-Shi'a Khalifa bin Salman Al-Khalifa, and the election of someone from beyond the royal family. In response, evoking a long-running argument, the king argued that such a move would not be countenanced by the prime minister's main external backer, Saudi Arabia, revealing the extent of Riyadh's capital in Bahrain's political field the process.

---

[98] 'A Statement by Bahraini Youth for Freedom', *CNN* (11.02.11), http://ireport.cnn.com/docs/DOC-55420 9.

[99] International Crisis Group (ICG), *Popular Protests in North Africa and the Middle East: Bahrain's Rocky Road to Reform*, Middle East/North Africa Report no. 111 (Brussels: ICG, 28 July 2011), pp. 1–2.

The morning of 14 February arrived with no declaration from the king. In response, Bahrainis took to the streets, occupying Pearl Roundabout – perhaps the most symbolic site in Manama – and other prominent sites. Like across much of the region, Bahrainis turned the street into sites of possibility, re-appropriating public space and transforming those spaces into revolutionary moments of radical emancipation.[100] Yet this moment was not to last as the Al-Khalifa's coercive machinery was deployed to prevent further unrest.

Three days later, on 17 February, a pre-dawn raid undertaken by government forces sought to clear the area of protesters. Using an array of riot control strategies including tear gas, birdshot, and rubber bullets, security forces embarked on a series of violent incursions seeking to disrupt the protests, resulting in the deaths of four along with hundreds of injuries in what would later become known as 'Bloody Thursday'. The following weeks were punctured by protest and counter protest, underpinned by violence made possible by the declaration of a 'state of emergency', which also allowed for the trial of civilians in military courts, arbitrary imprisonment, the denial of medical attention, and the prosecution of medical professionals for treating protestors.[101]

Alongside the clashes that took place across the streets of Manama, government officials and representatives from Shi'a societies engaged in talks designed to create space for future dialogue, perhaps best seen in the crown prince's 'seven principles' that would underpin dialogue moving forward. Yet with increasing pressure from the street and members of Shi'a societies, al-Wifaq representatives found themselves facing myriad often competing demands. As a consequence, the crown prince's initiative went without response. On 13 March, protesters blockaded the financial harbour in a move that would have serious repercussions. A day later, Saudi-led GCC forces entered Bahrain.

On 14 March, a month after the uprisings began, the GCC Peninsula Shield Force[102] crossed the King Fahd Causeway into Bahrain in support of the ruling family. The 'Saudi invasion', as one interviewee described it,[103] was followed by the establishment of martial law,

---

[100] See Hamid Dabashi, *The Arab Spring: The End of Postcolonialism* (New York: Zed Books, 2012); Charles Tripp, *The Power and the People: Paths of Resistance in the Middle East* (Cambridge: Cambridge University Press, 2013).

[101] *Report of the Bahrain Independent Commission of Inquiry* (23.11.11), www.bici.org.bh, p. 219.

[102] Dominated by Saudi and Emirati forces.

[103] Interview with former Bahraini politician.

supported by a network of security checkpoints and military courts.[104] The decision to send a Saudi-led military force into Bahrain was ultimately taken in Riyadh with the support of the Prime Minister of Bahrain, albeit supported by a 'collective agreement' across the wider GCC.[105]

The legacy of security concerns and strength of relations between Prince Nayef and Sheikh Khalifa – the two conservative princes – allowed the military incursion to take place at speed and ultimately, to shore up the House of Khalifa.[106] With the deployment of the Peninsula Shield Force, Bahrain's uprising was firmly located within broader regional concerns and, in an attempt to cultivate legitimacy, prompted key officials in Riyadh and Manama to frame the protesters as Iranian fifth columnists.[107] The commander of the GCC force, Mutlaq Bin Salem al-Azima, stated that the mission was to 'secure Bahrain's vital and strategically important military infrastructure from any foreign interference'.[108] In doing so, the intervention grounded unrest prominently within the transnational field, yet the decision was driven by Bahrain's hard-line prime minister, who put huge pressure on the king and crown prince to allow the Saudi-led intervention.[109]

The protesters were buoyed by actors across the region, including prominent clerics who supported the protests perhaps most notably Grand Ayatollah 'Ali Sistani, who stressed that Bahrainis have the right to peaceful protest.[110] According to one former Iranian official, the Iranian supreme leader sent a message to the king, declaring that Tehran 'doesn't want regime change' and offering to help keep the Al-Khalifa in power, but requiring moves towards power sharing in return.[111] While the veracity of such claims remains uncertain, the Bahraini response was clear.

[104] Amal Khalaf, 'Squaring the Circle: Bahrain's Pearl Roundabout', *Middle East Critique* 22:3 (2013), 265–80.
[105] Interview with former Bahraini politician.
[106] Interview with Bahraini civil society activist.
[107] This framing – a process of sectarianization – will be discussed in more detail later.
[108] 'Bin Salem al-Azima', *Asharq Al Awsat* (28.03.11), http://english.aawsat.com/2011/03/article55247010/a-talk-with-peninsula-shield-force-commander-mutlaq-bin-salem-al-azima.
[109] Interview with Bahraini civil society activist.
[110] 'Grand Ayatollah Sistani Condemns the Saudi and Bahrain's Crackdown on Bahrain's Shi'a While Kuwait Refuses to Send Troops', *JafriaNews* (17.03.11), http://jafrianews.com/2011/03/17/grand-ayatollah-sistani-condemns-the-saudi-and-bahrains-force-crackdown-on-bahrains-shi'a-while-kuwait-refuses-to-send-troops. See also 'Iraq's Sadr Calls for Protest against Bahrain Deaths', *World Bulletin* and 'Iraq's Zealous Sons', *al-Amarah News Network*.
[111] Interview with former Iranian official.

In the context of the Bahraini Uprising, 14 March was a seismic day, as a symbol of the growing geopolitical importance of Bahraini politics within the broader regional struggle between Saudi Arabia and Iran. Much like the events of the early 1980s, Bahrain's domestic political field intersected with developments in the transnational field. As a number of officials and military leaders have since acknowledged, the incursion was to ensure the survival of the Al-Khalifa against demonstrations that were alleged to have been incited and directed by Tehran. The Saudi-led intervention was part of a broader 'counter-revolutionary' effort, seeking simultaneously to curtail democratic aspirations and prevent increased Iranian influence. Moving to secure their ally in the face of rising instability, a GCC fund was established for Bahrain that provided $10 billion over ten years to facilitate infrastructural development, responding to a number of the challenges that had affected support for the Al-Khalifa in the previous decades.[112]

For the hard liners in the regime, particularly the prime minister, along with his backers in Riyadh, al-Wifaq's apparent intransigence and ongoing provocations from Shi'a societies left them with little option but to act, fearing the growing political, social, and religious capital of the protesters. The military intervention went alongside the deepening cultivation of sect-based divisions which helped to draw Sunni opposition movements to the Al-Khalifa. In pursuit of this, staunchly anti-Shi'a principles of vision were imposed across the political field, developing features previously cultivated across the habitus around Iranian manipulation and the penetration of Bahraini politics. While the incursion sought to prevent external manipulation, supporting this was an effort to impose symbolic capital on the social order, framing the protests as a consequence of external manipulation, requiring a firm response.

Fearing the power of the internet to mobilize and facilitate, a filtering policy was instituted, while a number of opposition websites were shut down and the software company Blackberry was ordered to close its service, reflecting efforts to define both the terms of the revolution and its narrative.[113] Despite this, social media outlets remained active

---

[112] 'KSA to Finance Morocco Projects Worth $1.25 bn', *Arab News* (18.10.12), www.arabnews.com/saudi-arabia/ksa-finance-morocco-projects-worth-125-bn; 'Saudi Arabia to Provide Jordan with $487 mln for Development Projects', *Jordan News Agency* (28.11.12), http://vista.sahafi.jo/art.php?id=3d37debd229104b267d5a3 1d8b628965c162b968.

[113] 'Drop Charges against Editor of Independent Daily', *Human Rights Watch* (04.11.11), www.hrw.org/news/2011/04/11/bahrain-drop-charges-against-editor-independent-daily.

and it was on the likes of Facebook, YouTube, and Twitter that political debate took place, also serving as an opportunity to organize and mobilize. Social media quickly became another site of conflict and contestation.[114] Regime officials urged Bahrainis to abstain from using social media between 10 am and 10 pm to facilitate national reconciliation.[115] All the while, key opposition political figures were being detained.

In May, a national dialogue was announced to take place between the government and the opposition, yet after only three weeks al-Wifaq withdrew, citing the government's non-negotiable preconditions and an apparent unwillingness to hold 'fair' and 'transparent' elections. A source present at the meetings suggested that the walkout was triggered by the use of defamatory language by the Salafi MP Jasim al-Sa'idi, who referred to the Shi'a as *rawafeda* (rejectionists).[116] Across 2012 amidst efforts to revive the moribund dialogue, similar issues re-emerged. On a cold autumn day in London, a discussion between the Bahraini ambassador to the United Kingdom, representing the regime, and representatives from al-Wifaq took place in a private meeting room in the Palace of Westminster. Despite beginning in a largely positive way with both sides acknowledging a desire to listen to the other and to resolve the situation in a favourable manner, the discussions proved futile. It quickly became apparent that the Bahraini ambassador was largely impotent and had little power to agree to further dialogue or, indeed, to acknowledge mistakes on the part of the regime. As a result, what appeared to be a positive initial step was ultimately in vain. In the following years, efforts to facilitate dialogue between the regime and opposition groups also proved futile.[117]

Developments across regional politics played a prominent role at this time, both with the spread of protest movements and rising fears about Iranian activity. Some, such as Fred Wehrey, suggest that the Al-Khalifa's actions were aimed at the United States, after Washington had turned its back on Husni Mubarak in Egypt.[118] Given that both Saudi Arabia and Bahrain heavily relied on US support in maintaining its security,

---

[114] See Sossie Kasbarian and Simon Mabon, 'Contested Spaces and Sectarian Narratives in Post-Uprisings Bahrain', *Global Discourse* 6:4 (2016), 677–66.

[115] 'Refrain from Using Social Networking Sites' Appeal', *Gulf Daily News* (20.02.11), www.gulf-daily-news.com/ArchiveNewsDetails.aspx?date=02/20/2011&storyid=300029.

[116] Quoted in Sadeep Singh Grewal, 'Former Intelligence Officer Eagerly Awaits Beginning of Negotiations', *Gulf Daily News* (29.06.11).

[117] I attended the initial meeting in 2012 and have been involved in trying to organize dialogue in the following years, albeit with no success. While opposition groups from across the spectrum are keen to engage in dialogue, there has been no response from government actors.

[118] Wehrey, *Sectarian Politics in the Gulf*, p. 82.

the very real concern that Washington might abandon its allies amidst what appeared to be the emergence of grassroots democratic movements was a source of much worry It was hardly surprising to see key political horse trading to maintain US support. As both Barack Obama and Hillary Clinton reveal in their memoirs, US policy towards the protests in Bahrain was beset by contradiction and inertia. The UAE threatened to withdraw from the Libya coalition if Washington responded harshly to events in Bahrain, while Saudi Arabia adopted a similar position, doubling down on their support for the Al-Khalifa.

The regime's response to protest movements was condemned by a range of international human rights organizations, prompting the establishment of the Bahraini Independent Commission of Inquiry, commonly known as BICI, to look into the government's conduct during the protests. Reporting back in November 2011, the report was highly critical of the regime's handling of events, citing the 'use of unnecessary and excessive force, terror-inspiring behavior, and unnecessary damage to property'. The report also criticized the systematic use of arbitrary detention, torture and the denial of medical care.[119] Largely well received, the report documented a culture of impunity across Bahrain's political system, suggesting that abuses could not have occurred without the knowledge of those in the upper echelons of the command structure.

Despite widespread allegations, the report found no evidence of links between the protesters and Iran – rejecting a key theme of the habitus created by the Al-Khalifa in the years after the revolution – instead, suggesting that unrest amongst Shi'a groups was a consequence of continued marginalization and a lack of political reform. The BICI set out a number of recommendations designed to facilitate reconciliation and bring Shi'a groups back into the political process, yet one year later, a report by the Project on Middle East Democracy found that only three of the twenty-six recommendations had been fully implemented, while fifteen had only been partially implemented. Of the six recommendations that were the most important for reconciliation, no meaningful progress had been made.[120] Ten years after the uprisings, recommended reforms are still to take place.

The years that followed continued along similar lines, shaped by efforts to dominate the political field with the hard-line faction within the royal family in the ascendancy, ably supported by their Saudi backers. Of

---

[119] Bahrain Independent Commission of Inquiry, *Report*, p. 416.
[120] *Report – One Year Later: Assessing Bahrain's Implementation of the BICI Report* (POMED, 2012), https://pomed.org/wp-content/uploads/2013/12/One-Year-Later-Assessing-Bahrains-Implementation-of-the-BICI-Report.pdf.

course, continued international support for the Al-Khalifa strengthened their position, with the United States and United Kingdom maintaining alliances with the ruling family. Arms deals with London and Washington demonstrate the extent of this support, in spite of condemnation from civil society and human rights organizations. While the United States viewed arms sales as a way of securing the position of the crown prince, Salman's authority had been dramatically eroded since the Saudi-led intervention, with some suggesting that he had been removed from public duties, although he has since taken on a more prominent role in political life.

The 'Sectarian Abyss'

A key part of regime efforts to consolidate power took place through the securitization of Shi'a groups across Bahrain, drawing on developments in the transnational field.[121] Events across the region in the previous decade had fuelled concerns amongst Sunni Arabs about nefarious Iranian activity, and revolutionary activity that drew support from Shi'a groups was seen as a consequence of pernicious activity from Tehran. This had a dramatic impact on public perceptions, with one Bahraini businessman declaring that 'the Persians are everywhere',[122] reflecting the cultivation of a habitus and dominant principles of vision which marginalized Shi'a groups from all aspects of daily life. Underpinning much of this were Saudi efforts to blame Iran for the unrest across the Arab world, a message that was presented to media outlets across Bahrain.[123]

A process of securitization took place that sought to frame Shi'a protesters as Iranian fifth columnists, doing the bidding of their 'Persian-speaking Iranian coreligionists across the Gulf'.[124] Writing in the British newspaper the *Daily Telegraph*, Fawaz bin Mohammad Al-Khalifa later noted the impact of the 'expansionist ambitions of the Persian Shi'a establishment', laying blame for unrest in Bahrain, Lebanon, Kuwait, and Yemen at the door of Iran.[125] To further consolidate their principle

---

[121] Mabon, 'The End of the Battle of Bahrain'; Toby Matthiessen, 'Sectarianization as Securitization: Identity Politics and Counter-Revolution in Bahrain', in Nader Hashemi and Danny Postel (eds.), *Sectarianization: Mapping the Politics of the New Middle East* (London: Hurst, 2017), pp. 199–214.
[122] Interview with Bahraini businessman.
[123] Doc105956, *The Saudi Cables*, https://wikileaks.org/saudi-cables/doc105956.html.
[124] Dalia Dassa Kaye and Frederic M. Wehrey, 'An Nuclear Iran: The Reactions of Neighbours', *Survival: Global Politics and Strategy* 49:2 (2007), 116.
[125] Fawaz bin Mohammad Al-Khalifa, 'The Gulf States Are Stuck between Isil and Iran', *The Telegraph* (21.01.16), www.telegraph.co.uk/news/worldnews/middleeast/bahrain/12113355/The-Gulf-states-are-stuck-between-Isil-and-Iran.html.

of vision and their symbolic capital, a number of prominent opposition figures such as Nabil Rajab were arrested. Later, emboldened by their successes, regime officials would arrest Sheikh Isa Qassim, who had long been targeted by the regime in an attempt to create tensions between Qassim and 'Ali Salman and al-Wifaq, most obviously seen in 2012 and diverging opinions about the use of violence.

As instability took hold across Bahrain, emergency legislation was put in place to ensure regime survival. This facilitated the establishment of a complex web of security checkpoints across major roads and on all entrances to Manama, ably supported by a special system of military courts. Article 36(B) of the Bahraini constitution declared a state of emergency which gave regime forces unlimited power to operate,[126] including systemic violence, torture, and discrimination, as documented by the BICI. The inquiry noted that there is 'evidence of a deliberate practice, which in some cases was aimed at extracting confessions and statements by duress, while in other cases was intended for the purpose of retribution and punishment'.[127]

To prevent protesters once again coalescing around symbols of resistance, the monument in Pearl Square was swiftly destroyed by bulldozers in a form of urbicide[128] while the 500 fils coin – which had a picture of the monument on one side – was withdrawn from circulation. Restrictions were placed on movement and the congregation of people, while travel restrictions operated across the island and beyond. What followed was a period of contestation across the social fabric of the Bahraini state, pitting family and friends against one another, both in person and across social media. This included the monitoring of students travelling abroad to study, often under the threat of having scholarships withdrawn if they became involved in any form of political activity. In the face of this, some displayed great levels of bravery, refusing to be pressured by state and rejecting the sectarianization of daily life. As one Bahraini student who was involved in the protests declared, 'I'm just a Bahraini.'[129] Many also refused to let external actors manipulate domestic affairs.[130]

Regime strategies after the uprisings included efforts to limit Shi'a participation and influence in political institutions, achieved through the mobilization of Sunni Islamists – including the Muslim Brotherhood – to

[126] 'Bahrain, Hundreds Stripped Citizenship', *HRW News* (27.07.18), www.hrw.org/news/2018/07/27/bahrain-hundreds-stripped-citizenship.
[127] Bahrain Independent Commission of Inquiry, *Report*, p. 417.
[128] Mabon, 'Sects and the City'.
[129] Interviews with Bahraini activist and student.
[130] Interview with Bahraini cleric.

balance against Shi'a groups, while prominent individuals from the military and security sector were recruited into politics to serve as independents in support of the Al-Khalifa.[131] While initially successful, pressure from Saudi Arabia in the years that followed meant that Sunni groups were no longer used to curtail Shi'a political activity, demonstrating the ongoing Saudi influence over Bahrain.[132]

Central to this was the perpetuation of a narrative of Iranian manipulation of communal difference. In spite of these allegations, the BICI found no evidence in the 2011 events, along with no Iranian role in Bahrain's political crisis.[133] Yet narratives of perfidious Iranian involvement in the protests resonated, reflecting the dominance of the Al Khalifa constructed habitus. Such views were not limited to Bahrainis, however; in conversations with American and British officials, there appeared to be a general belief that Iranian agents were behind the unrest, with the transnational field – and its habitus – playing a key role shaping the behaviour of Bahrain, Saudi Arabia, the United States, and United Kingdom.

This narrative was articulated by the king in an article for the *Washington Times*, in which he acknowledged that sectarian difference had

created a schism in our society that is a major challenge. As monarch of all Bahrainis, it pains me to see many harmed by the actions of a few. And yet I am optimistic and have faith in our people. We all realize that now is the time to strike a balance between stability and gradual reform ... In establishing democracy, we have to be sensitive to the regional and national context. Democracy also means to guarantee the rights of the minorities. That's my job as a king. We have for example a Jewish ambassador in the US and a Christian in the United Kingdom.[134]

The uprisings also fed into a broader effort to re-order regional politics and create an alliance against Iran. Speaking five years earlier, Hamad called for the cultivation of diplomatic relations with Israel to bring about a 'real peace' in order that 'we can all face Iran'.[135] Such views went against public opinion across the Arab world but reflected the general position of elites in Saudi Arabia and the UAE.

A secondary consequence of this was the international focus on Bahrain in the early months of the protests, with world leaders commenting

---

[131] Interview with Bahraini academic and activist.
[132] Interview with Bahraini academic.
[133] *Report of the Bahrain Independent Commission of Inquiry.*
[134] Hamad bin Isa bin Salman Al-Khalifa, 'Al-Khalifa: Stability Is Prerequisite for Progress', *Washington Times* (19.04.11), www.washingtontimes.com/news/2011/apr/19/stability-is-prerequisite-for-progress/.
[135] 06MANAMA1849_a, 'King Hamad Supports Gulf Security Dialogue'.

on events across the island. Leaders from the United States and United Kingdom spoke of the need for democratic reform and a peaceful resolution of the crisis. Ultimately these remarks fell on deaf ears as international actors reaffirmed their support for the Al-Khalifa in the face of broader geopolitical concerns, stifling demands for political reform in the process. Once again, the Al-Khalifa's symbolic capital – conditioned by coercive, social, and religious capital – shaped the habitus, principles of vision and of common sense, defining the protests as part of a broader Iranian plot to re-order regional politics.

This movement stemmed from a dual-pronged approach of simultaneously embarking on a PR strategy designed to improve the image of the state and, simultaneously, framing the protests as a consequence of nefarious Iranian activity. This strategy of framing Shi'a groups as a threat was designed to ensure the survival of the Al-Khalifa regime and to maintain support from Sunni groups across Bahrain. Moreover, it sought to position domestic unrest within the context of broader geopolitical turmoil amidst the escalation of tensions between Saudi Arabia and Iran.

Regime officials sought to justify the action of security forces at the Pearl Roundabout by invoking fears of what the foreign minister termed a 'sectarian abyss'.[136] In reality, however, regime officials sought to exacerbate these divisions as a means of dividing the protest movement along sect-based lines. In response to protests congregating at the roundabout, al-Wifaq withdrew its representatives from parliament while other Shi'a groups took on more extreme positions. On the street, chants quickly evolved from calls for reform to demands for the fall of the Al-Khalifa. In such precarious conditions religion served as a source of legitimacy – and 'the black turban' denoted religious capital – providing the means through which 'political and social alignments' were made across the state.[137]

As instability continued across 2011, the regime's strategy of securitizing the Shi'a threat became increasingly apparent. Key political societies were vocally attacked and framed as being agents of foreign powers. Claims about links between Hizbullah and Bahraini protesters had routinely been made by Bahraini officials in conversations with US officials, documented across diplomatic cables released by Wikileaks, albeit with little proof; the Syrian government was also alleged to be

---

[136] 'Bahrain Pulled Back from "Sectarian Abyss": Foreign Minister,' *Reuters* (17.02.11), www.reuters.com/article/us-bahrain-minister/bahrain-pulled-back-from-sectarian-abyss-foreign-minister-idUSTRE71G58F20110217.
[137] Interview with Bahraini cleric.

complicit.[138] During the 2011 uprisings, links between Hizbullah and Shi'a protesters were commonplace, while the Bahraini foreign minister even suggested that sectarian difference had been imported by Iran and Hizbullah.[139] The articulation of such claims – and their ability to find traction – reflects successes in defining principles of vision and the habitus across both Bahrain and the transnational field. Memories of the IFLB's efforts – supported by Iran – to topple the al-Khalifa, remain prominent and when coupled with Tehran's support for Hizbullah and militias in Iraq creates a fertile environment for sectarianizing moves to resonate. Claims about the presence of Hizbullah fighters in Bahrain – and the establishment of a 'Bahraini Hizbullah' – easily find traction, aided by the successes of Hizbullah and its potential as a 'franchise model'. Such narratives often refer to the presence of bomb-making factories across Bahrain and the training of young Bahrainis in the ways of violent insurgency. These narratives are regularly repeated by regime loyalists and key allies, albeit with little hard evidence in the public sphere to verify the claims.[140]

In support of these sectarianizing moves, media outlets were heavily regulated, meaning that domestic coverage of the protests came from Bahrain TV, the state-run channel. It was thus hardly surprising that the channel framed events through the prism of Iranian manipulation. To hear from opposition figures, one had to tune in to foreign channels such as Hizbullah's *al-Manar*, or channels in Iraq and Iran.[141] Of course, this fuelled suspicions about foreign involvement in the protest movements. Shortly after the roundabout was cleared, the king delivered a speech to the Peninsula Shield Force, later covered by the state-run media outlet Bahrain News Agency. In his remarks, the king proclaimed that 'An external plot has been fomented for twenty to thirty years for the ground to be right for subversive designs ... I here[by] announce the failure of the fomented subversive plot.'[142]

The regime was quick to play on Bahraini history and broader Iranian activity across the transnational field – in particular the actions of the

---

[138] 08MANAMA541_a, 'General Petraeus' Visit to Bahrain' (13.08.08), https://wikileaks.org/plusd/cables/08MANAMA541_a.html. In the cable, suspicion is expressed by US officials about Bahraini claims, given an inability to produce convincing evidence.

[139] 'Security and Stability Top Priorities Now, Foreign Minister Says', *Bahrain News Agency* (29.03.11).

[140] These claims have been regularly made in discussions with British and American officials over the past decade.

[141] ICG, *Popular Protests in North Africa and the Middle East*, p. 6.

[142] Quoted in Zoi Constantine, 'King of Bahrain Says Subversive "External Plot" Has Been Foiled,' *The National* (22.03.11), www.thenational.ae/world/mena/king-of-bahrain-says-sub-versive-external-plot-has-been-foiled-1.600506.

IFLB, support for Hizbullah and Iraqi groups – in an attempt to frame the protesters as Iranian agents. This anti-Shi'a – and anti-Iranian – habitus played a key role in shaping threat perceptions and the actions of the regime. Yet Shi'a actors vocally urged Iran not to 'meddle' in Bahraini affairs.[143] However, comments to *al-Akhbar*, a Lebanese newspaper, from Hassan Mushayma the leader of Haq in late February 2011, suggested that Shi'a groups could turn to Iran if Saudi Arabia intervened.[144] Comments such as this from Mushayma helped reinforce the narrative and perception of perfidious Iranian interference, built on historical foundations.

In these conditions, the ruling family was able to undertake a raft of measures designed to ensure their survival, beginning with the securitization of Shi'a groups which pervaded all facets of life across the archipelago. A crackdown on employees and students critical of the regime took place, resulting in the firing of around 4,500 people from the public and private sectors. Recipients of state scholarships who were studying abroad were placed under pressure to demonstrate loyalty to the regime or risk losing their funding, while also being subjected to monitoring.[145] Unsurprisingly, narratives of the uprisings were largely restricted, with a number of academics and human rights activists denied entry to Bahrain in the years after 2011. The conflation of sectarian difference with geopolitical agendas – driven by the regime's survival instinct and a desire to appease their Saudi backers – has ultimately proved detrimental to political reform and reconciliation across Bahrain, eroding demands for democracy and human rights in the process.

The impact on individuals across the state was devastating. Over time, all forms of dissent were vanquished with scope for civil society engagement reduced. While this initially began by focusing on Shi'a movements, this quickly evolved to focus on Salafists, human rights defenders, journalists, academics, and others critical of the Al-Khalifa regime. At this point, the two key features of Saudi Arabia's *nomos* – an anti-Iranian and anti-Islamist vision – began to diverge. Previously in Bahrain, Islamists groups including the Muslim Brotherhood and Salafi parties had played an integral role in countering the Shi'a groups, with the Muslim Brotherhood and other parties allying with the regime.

The cultivation of an exclusionary process of sectarianization rewarded regime loyalists and discouraged cross-sectarian expressions of political

---

[143] 'Stop Meddling' Call to Tehran,' *Gulf Daily News* (31.03.11), www.gulf-daily-news.com/Print.aspx?storyid=349823.
[144] *al-Akhbar*, interview with Hassan Mushayma, 28 February 2011.
[145] Interview with Bahraini student.

frustration. Although the conditions which led to the uprisings in 2011 affected large swathes of Bahrain's population members of the Muslim Brotherhood historically have had a close relationship with the Al-Khalifa. Largely conservative, the Brotherhood in Bahrain draws members from the Hawala tribe and the merchant elite, meaning that even when the Muslim Brotherhood established a political party – Jamiyyat al-Minbar al-Watani al-Islami, or al-Minbar, for short – the movement's political goals were ultimately pragmatic and conservative. Similarly, the largest Salafi organization, al-Asala, enjoyed a positive relationship with the Al-Khalifa, with. Although both al-Mibar and al-Asala voted with al-Wifaq, this was largely pragmatic and based on short term interests.[146] With the onset of protests in 2011, Sunni Islamists offered an important support base for the government, establishing an Islamist front to defend the stability of Bahrain – the National Unity Gathering – and reinforcing processes of sectarianization in the process. By 2014, however, the climate had dramatically changed.

Developments across the transnational field – in part driven by the emergence of Mohammad Morsi and the Freedom and Justice Party in Egypt – resulted in increased concerns about the spread of Islamism across the region, prompting Saudi Arabia and the UAE to proscribe the Muslim Brotherhood as a terrorist organization. This move posed challenges for the Al-Khalifa and Sunni Islamists in Bahrain, with the government declaring that the Brotherhood's Bahraini branch had 'special status', reflecting the prevalence of group members in parliament, the security services and judicial bodies.[147] Bahrain's Sunni Islamists have sought to demonstrate their loyalty to the regime given the financial stakes of further marginalization. At the same time, members of the Al-Khalifa sought to stress that the Brotherhood is not a global movement in an effort to circumvent Saudi moves against Sunni Islamist groups.[148] Once again, developments across the transnational field resonate within Bahrain's domestic political field, with Saudi principles of vision in the transnational field finding traction domestically. Ultimately, the nature

---

[146] See Courtney Freer, 'Challenges to *Sunni* Islamism in Bahrain Since 2011', *Carnegie Middle East Centre* (06.03.19), https://carnegie-mec.org/2019/03/06/challenges-to-sunni-islamism-in-bahrain-since-2011-pub-78510.

[147] 'Bahrain FM: Muslim Brotherhood Is a Terrorist Group', *Al Jazeera* (06.07.17), www.aljazeera.com/news/2017/7/6/bahrain-fm-muslim-brotherhood-is-a-terrorist-group.

[148] المؤتمر الصحفي المشترك لمعالي وزير الخارجية مع سعادة وزير المواصلات في جمهورية باكستان الإسلامية ('almutamar alsuhufiu almushtarak limaealay wazir alkharijiat mae saeadat wazir almuasalat fi jumhuriat bakistan al'iislamia' ['The Joint Press Conference of His Excellency the Minister of Foreign Affairs with His Excellency the Minister of Transportation of the Islamic Republic of Pakistan']), *Ministry of Foreign Affairs* (20.03.14), www.mofa.gov.bh/Default.aspx?tabid=8266&language=ar-BH&ItemId=4008.

of Bahrain's domestic political field meant that this attempt to impose principles of vision caused problems amongst a key Al-Khalifa support base, prompting the need for a creative response.

These developments also highlight an ongoing tension between Saudi Arabia and Bahrain in defining the habitus of Bahrain's political field. Following the death of Prime Minister Prince Khalifa, Crown Prince Salman took on an increasingly prominent role in Bahraini politics. Although Saudi officials had curtailed the influence of Salman after the uprisings of 2011, Salman's renaissance coincided with a shifting relationship with Saudi Arabia. By the start of 2022, Bahrain faced competition from a Saudi state that had embarked on a widespread economic liberalization which began to squeeze the Bahraini economy which had previously capitalized on the closed nature of Saudi society. As a consequence, Bahrain embraced a series of economic and human rights reforms as a means to strengthen its economic position. In addition, the crown prince sought to solidify control over the security forces, strengthening his capital in the process.[149] Crown princes in Bahrain and Saudi Arabia have sought to place economic goals as a strategic priority, with MbS declaring concerns about the economic situation on a visit to Manama in 2021.[150] While the transition to new crown princes in both states allowed for a shift from security to economic concerns, there were latent suspicions in Riyadh at the Bahraini crown prince's political acumen and his broader commitment to the Saudi vision of regional order. Such visions of order prevent political reform from taking place, yet amidst pressure from the United States to improve the human rights situation, a series of economic and human rights reforms have occurred. All the while, concerns about Bahrain's Shi'a community continue to linger. The presence of key Shi'a figures in Iran and Lebanon has exacerbated concerns about Iranian influence in Bahraini politics: Isa Qassim sought refuge in Iran and prominent leaders of al-Wifaq reside in Lebanon, while Houthi representatives are regularly invited to attend al-Wifaq events in Beirut.[151]

After the death of Sheikh Khalifa, Crown Prince Salman took on an increasingly important role in the political field, including dominating the security sector and embarking on a process of economic and human rights reform. Perhaps most significantly, this involved the normalization of relations with Israel under the banner of the Abraham Accords.

[149] Interview with former Bahraini MP.
[150] Interview with Bahraini civil society activist.
[151] Interview with former Bahraini MP.

The accords allowed the cultivation of political, economic, and security relations between Bahrain and Israel, particularly amidst shared security concerns emanating from the transnational field. As a result, increased intelligence sharing between the two took place, along with Israeli spying software being used by Bahrainis. Claims that Israel will provide a security guarantee to the Bahrainis against Iran are wide of the mark, although an increasing Mossad presence is already noticeable.[152]

Conclusions

Bahrain's geographical location and demographic makeup left it positioned prominently within competition between different *nomoi*. After independence, Bahrain's political field – and its social ordering – has been conditioned by the interplay between domestic actors and regional currents, oscillating between ideas of nationalism, demands for democracy, Shi'a grievances, anti-Shi'a sentiment, and the Al-Khalifa vision of order that typically precludes Shi'a and Islamist groups from operating. The ruling Al-Khalifa family's close relationship with the Al Sa'ud – predominantly through the relationship between Prince Nayef and Sheikh Khalifa – strengthened the Bahraini monarchy's claims to social and economic capital, albeit creating precarious conditions for the Bahraini state in the process, largely reliant upon the Kingdom for its economic survival. Much of this stems from concerns about the transnational field and the manipulation of Shi'a groups by Iran, a claim which has long featured in the habitus of individuals across Bahrain. In making such claims, and locating unrest within broader geopolitical dynamics, the Al-Khalifa secured the support of powerful regional allies while demanding the loyalty of Bahrain's Sunni community, albeit at the price of increased tensions with their Shi'a citizenry. Given concerns about the precarious demographic situation, the regime initially drew support from Sunni Islamists operating in the Kingdom before engaging in a process of repression as part of a broader Saudi process of restricting the space for Islamist groups to operate across the region.

Over time, principles of vision and division evolved: from pro-independence and nationalist claims, to demands for greater democratic representation for all, to the framing of events in the language of security, to the construction of a broader anti-Shi'a habitus dating back to the Iranian revolution of 1979 but taking on increased importance after the events of 2011 with the aim of ensuring regime survival. Despite

---

[152] This point has been made by a number of Bahrainis in conversations across 2022.

opposition groups laying claim to social and religious capital across the recent past, this capital was not able to challenge the Al-Khalifa's claims to symbolic capital and symbolic violence and, with it, the implementation of a principle of vision that shaped political life according to their vision.

Tracing the evolution of contestation within Bahrain's political field reveals the state's position within the transnational field, located prominently due to geopolitical and religious tensions. This centrality allows actors in Bahrain to derive support – both direct and indirect – from different actors in pursuit of their principles of vision. Understanding the nature of Bahrain's domestic political field offers important insight into the ways in which Saudi Arabia and Iran seek to impose principles of vision and, from this, to define the habitus.

For Saudi Arabia, reserves of economic, social, and cultural capital allowed them to play a central role in Bahrain's political field, reinforced through close relations with the Al-Khalifa. This is underpinned by the dominant principle of vision in the transnational field which was broadly anti-Shi'a and anti-Iranian. Of note, however, are the points of tension between Bahrain and Saudi Arabia, with the latter seemingly exerting greater capital in the former's political field, but Bahrain also finding ways to push back against Riyadh's principles of vision. In contrast, Iranian influence in Bahrain's political field is less prominent, typically reduced to religious linkages. Despite this, the development of an anti-Shi'a and anti-Iranian principle of vision is supported by the construction of a narrative of nefarious Iranian involvement across Bahrain (and the wider region) which dramatically overstresses Tehran's social, economic, and religious capital in Bahrain. As a result, Tehran's lack of capital in Bahrain appears secondary to the capital ascribed to it in an effort to justify the actions of the Al-Khalifa and their backers.

5   Lebanon

On the evening of 3 November 2017 a plane carrying Saad Hariri, a Saudi citizen and the Lebanese prime minister, landed in Riyadh. Hariri had been summoned to Riyadh to meet the crown prince of Saudi Arabia, Mohammed bin Salman, amidst increasing tensions in Lebanon and fears about the growing influence of Hizbullah, the Lebanese Party of God. Believing he was visiting the Kingdom to meet the king and go camping in the desert with the crown prince, Hariri's plane was immediately surrounded by security officials. Stripped of his phone and those of his bodyguards, Hariri was placed under house arrest before being forced him to resign as prime minister on 4 November. In a television address, Hariri expressed fears for his life in Lebanon, drawing parallels with the climate prior to his father's assassination, accusing Iran of creating an atmosphere of 'disorder and destruction' through support for its ally Hizbullah, the Party of God.[1] The interview was quickly a subject of extensive debate, with many suggesting that Hariri was speaking under duress. A week later, Michel Auon, the Lebanese president, told ambassadors that the country's prime minister had been 'kidnapped'.[2]

Less than a week later, a second diplomatic plane landed in Riyadh. On board was the French President Emmanuel Macron who had made a detour from the UAE out of concern at the situation in Lebanon. Eschewing diplomatic protocol, Macron did not receive a full royal welcome, nor did he leave the terminal building. Instead, Macron sat in a room in the airport with MbS and thrashed out a deal for the release of Saad Hariri, who returned home to Lebanon and rescinded his resignation less than a month after his appearance on television from Riyadh.

---

[1] 'Lebanese PM Hariri Resigns, Saying He Fears Assassination Plot', *BBC* (04.11.17), www.bbc.co.uk/news/world-middle-east-41870406.

[2] Ellen Francis, 'Lebanese President Presses Saudi to Say Why Hariri Has Not Been Returned', *Reuters* (11.11.17) www.reuters.com/article/us-lebanon-politics-aoun/lebanon-president-calls-on-riyadh-to-clarify-reasons-stopping-hariri-return-idUSKBN1DB0ET.

Central to the actions of the crown prince was an increasingly anti-Iranian agenda that meant events in Lebanon were viewed through the prism of Saudi Arabia's long-standing rivalry with the Islamic Republic of Iran. Much to the chagrin of Saudi Arabia, since 1982 Iran has exerted a great deal of influence across the Levant, achieved predominantly through the cultivation of relationships with the Assad regime in Syria and the establishment of Hizbullah in Lebanon. The formation of Hizbullah was a paradigmatic example of Iran's desire to export revolutionary goals across the Middle East, finding traction in the long-suffering Shi'a communities of Lebanon. Over the coming decades, Hizbullah's popularity across the region would increase dramatically, helping Iranian legitimacy in the process, much to the despair of Riyadh and others across the Arab world. Yet in the aftermath of the Arab Uprisings and the treatment of opposition groups in Syria, a great deal of this legitimacy was eroded as a consequence of Hizbullah's travails in support of their ally.

Yet to reduce Lebanese politics purely to geopolitical factors or sectarian politics misses a great deal of the nuance that has shaped political organization across the state. This nuance is seen when considering the different spatial contexts across the state, but perhaps are most obviously seen within Beirut. Although the confessional system gives prominence to sectarian identities – reinforcing this difference – space across Lebanon is (re)shaped through the interaction of myriad factors, creating a fluid state of possibility, albeit underpinned by the legacy of colonial rule and prominence of sect-based identity, re-enforced by external patrons. The establishment of a consociational power sharing system provided a range of opportunities for outside powers to exert influence through seeking to manipulate identity groups operating within the country's confessional system.

The following chapter traces the history of Lebanese politics, reflecting on the structural factors that facilitate the involvement of external powers. It suggests that the structural organization of the state allows local actors to cultivate external patronage in support of communal interests. Moreover, the geopolitical significance of Lebanon means that external actors also seek local allies as a means of countering rivals who already possess influence across the state, while local actors also seek to position themselves within broader regional currents. To understand the competition over Lebanon, we must trace the historical development of the Lebanese state which allows for identification of the structural factors conditioning – or limiting – the deployment of capital and foreign policy activities.

The Quest for Order and Lebanon
in the Transnational Field

While 'a small Mediterranean country', Lebanon has been viewed by many as 'a natural regional platform' for Middle Eastern states wishing to assert influence.[3] Although in part this is a consequence of its proximity to Israel, Lebanon's geostrategic importance and the presence of a range of different religious groups increased its importance as a site of contestation and competition, rather than as a prominent player in regional affairs. For Saudi Arabia, economic relations link Sunnis in the Kingdom with those in Lebanon, while the vibrancy of Lebanese politics provided the Al Sa'ud with opportunities to counter and outmanoeuvre their rivals; for example, in the 1950s and 1960s, Saudi support for Pierre Gemayyel and Kamil Sham'un was an attempt to erode the legitimacy of Nasser's pan-Arab vision. More recently, support for the Hariri family and their Future Movement has served to balance against Iranian-backed groups. For Iran, clerical links and close ties with Hizbullah have given Tehran a great deal of influence across Lebanese politics, particularly amongst Shi'a communities, while its support for the Party of God positions it on the frontline of resistance against Israel.

Lebanon offers a paradigmatic example of what Bassel Salloukh has termed the 'weak Arab State', where domestic instability plays out in the context of broader geopolitical dynamics, bringing together a Realist focus on security and state survival with transnational reverberations stemming from ideational permeability.[4] Indeed, the ability to speak to both national interest and broader regional *nomos* helps to demonstrate the ways in which local and regional groups interact across levels of analysis. As Waleed Hazbun argues, the fluidity of shifting patterns of alliances across domestic and regional arenas has fed into the construction of security politics and the 'complex geopolitics of insecurity',[5] which has serious repercussions for domestic and regional security.

Understanding the ways in which local politics is shaped by – and shapes – regional politics is fundamental for analysing the evolution of Lebanese politics after the end of the civil war. Over time, material and ideational capacities permitted the cultivation of relations between regional and local actors. Following the assassination of Rafiq Hariri in

---

[3] Mohammad Ataie, 'Revolutionary Iran's 1979 Endeavor in Lebanon', *Middle East Policy* 20:2 (2013), 140.

[4] Salloukh, 'Overlapping Contests', 660.

[5] Waleed Hazbun, 'The Politics of Insecurity in the Arab World: A View from Beirut', *Political Science & Politics* 50:3 (Special issue: Symposium: The Arab Uprisings and International Relations Theory) (2017), 658.

2005, however, sectarian identity markers took on increasing importance for patrons to cultivate relationships with clients and clients with patrons. In recent years, the cultivation of relationships between regional and local actors has begun to transcend sectarian affinity and to include cross-faith relationships along ideological lines, notably the Saudi support for Samir Geagea and the Lebanese Forces against Iran, suggesting that visions of order cut across communal lines.

While domestic groups position themselves within regional currents, relationships with external backers have also been used by local factions as a means of strengthening their positions and avoiding compromise, providing indirect influence for Riyadh, Tehran, and previously Damascus. These relationships are multi-directional, driven by both top-down and bottom-up processes that are determined by the complexities of time and space. They often result in complex sets of relationships that challenge the stunted narratives of patron–client relationships and proxy wars that have come to dominate understandings of Lebanese politics. Within these efforts, local actors have been able to exert influence, finding opportunities to push the boundaries of acceptable behaviour, conscious of the need to simultaneously speak to domestic and regional constituencies and audiences.

Although tensions between the various camps have been embedded into the social fabric, neither Saudi Arabia nor Iran has necessarily desired overt confrontation. This has resulted in periods of dialogue between the external powers, particularly after the Cedar Revolution when Saudi Arabia preferred Iran as a partner in negotiations over Syria. In the years that followed, in spite of broader regional tensions – notably in Iraq – the two rivals were able to collaborate to ensure the survival of the power-sharing agreement and, perhaps more impressively, to facilitate de-escalation after violence broke out between March 8 and March 14 factions in early 2007. Yet the rising influence of Hizbullah after the 2006 war, which saw the group move into West Beirut in May 2008, would ultimately upset the burgeoning equilibrium.

Saudi support to March 14 groups has been driven by efforts to erode Iranian power,[6] yet prior to the events of 2011, ideational balancing had been a key component of both Saudi and Iranian policy. Indeed, as Gause observes, the objective was not necessarily to defeat regional rivals on the battlefield but rather 'to promote the fortunes of their own clients in these weak-state domestic struggles and thus build up regional

---

[6] Salloukh, 'The Arab Uprisings', 41.

influence'.[7] Thus, providing support for Sunni groups across the state was designed to counter the gains made by Hizbullah, March 8, and Iran. Yet moments of pragmatism shape this approach, in both Lebanese politics and the transnational field, seen in efforts to bring Syria back into the Saudi camp.

Sectarianism and Permeability

Lebanon is typically – and often problematically – viewed as a state defined by the interaction of its sectarian parts. From the Orientalist framing of the state as a 'mosaic of identities', the nature of relations between the different groups shapes the essence of national politics. The modern Lebanese state is predicated upon the need to create a confessional political system that allows power to be shared, while political parties have been mapped onto religious difference, meaning that socioeconomic and political grievances are often reduced to religious aspects. Lebanese independence is born out of the National Pact, which created a confessional system designed to mitigate tensions between Sunni and Christian. This power-sharing agreement was built on existing divisions across Lebanese society which eventually erupted in civil war in 1975. The Tai'f Accords, which ended the civil war, reaffirmed the power-sharing aspect of the National Pact, albeit shaped by a different political context.

Scholars writing on Lebanon have spent a great deal of time engaging with the implications of sect-based tensions and the broader tension between loyalties to sect or nation, but a few points require repetition. While Ussama Makdisi is correct to assert that sectarianism is a neologism, born in the age of nationalism, serving as the antithesis of nationhood, the power of the sect as an identity signifier has long resonated across the Lebanese state, aiding in the ordering of all aspects of life.[8] Although there are certainly different identities in existence in the Lebanese state, one must place sectarian difference within the colonial context and questions about how to secure Christians within the Ottoman Empire and state-building efforts that followed.[9] In such a context, tensions between loyalty to the sect and to the national project has a dramatic impact on *wataniyya* ('patriotism'), meaning that events of

---

[7] Gause, *Beyond Sectarianism*, p. 8.
[8] See Melani Cammett, Sara Fregonese, Hiba Bou Akar, Bassel Salloukh, John Nagel, Mona Harb, Mona Fawaz. Joanna Rand Nucho and others.
[9] Ussama Makdisi, *The Culture of Sectarianism: Community, History and Violence in Nineteenth-Century Ottoman Lebanon* (Berkeley: University of California Press, 2000).

paramount importance for the national project are often viewed through the lens of sectarianism.

Historically, Lebanese politics was shaped by the rivalry between Sunni Muslims and Maronite Christians, marginalizing Shi'a groups in the process, but in the years after the civil war, intra-Muslim tensions became increasingly prominent. This growth in sectarian tensions in Lebanon reflects increasingly fractious relations in the transnational field, particularly in the aftermath of the US-led invasion of Iraq in 2003. As Imad Salamey articulates:

Lebanon's political track is dictated by a double-leveled power dynamic: domestic, which pits sectarian groups vying for political control against one another; and regional, which positions proxy sectarian groups at the ends of a polarized ideological spectrum. Therefore, as regional politics evolve, so do the dynamics of Lebanese sectarianism and its corresponding confessional power-sharing arrangements.[10]

Leaving aside claims about proxy sectarian groups, Salamey's comments evoke Massey's reflections on space where the interaction of global forces with domestic factors has an undeniable impact on Lebanese political life, leaving it in a continued process of (re)construction and site of possibility. When exploring domestic politics in Lebanon, it is imperative to contextualize events within broader regional affairs, given not only the geopolitical importance of the state but also the links between different sectarian, political, ideological, and economic communities. These factors are not independent and often coalesce, creating a complex set of interactions between actors within the Lebanese state and beyond, between political and transnational fields.

The salience of sectarian difference within and across Lebanese politics is widely accepted, ranging from the allocation of political portfolios and the distribution of resources and regulation of life according to sectarian membership. The political and religious makeup of the state has also created conditions that allow external actors to become involved in political life. The Lebanese political situation was allegedly described by Georges Corm, a former finance minister, as 'a state in the conditional, with sovereignty limited by the forbearance of its constituent' communities and their foreign protectors',[11] a point that reinforces Bassel Salloukh's observation about state weakness.

---

[10] Imad Salamey, 'The Double Movement & Post-Arab Spring Consociationalism', *Muslim World* 106:1 (2016), 202.
[11] Cited in Michael Young, *The Ghosts of Martyrs Square: An Eyewitness Account of Lebanon's Life Struggle* (New York: Simon & Schuster, 2010), p. 11.

State and Sect

The establishment of the Lebanese National Pact, *al-Methaq al-Watany*, in 1943 established 'corporate consociationalism' politics as the *de jure* form of power sharing amongst the various confessional groups.[12] As with other consociational projects, the distribution of power facilitates the capture of the state by sectarian elites operating predominantly out of self-interest. This feudalistic system – *al-Ikt'a al-Siyasii* – was supported by the implementation of a list-based majority system which undermined non-sectarian and independent challenges, leading to confessional elites becoming well versed at capitalizing on patronage networks to ensure survival. The National Pact embedded sectarian and confessional identities within the fabric of the Lebanese state, creating a stagnant form of politics without accountability and preventing movement towards the public good. Moreover, it created conditions that would allow networks of patronage to thrive, allowing those with distributionary power to trade alliance and allegiance in an attempt to maximize influence, at the cost of the rule of law and economic growth.[13]

The agreement gave Christian Maronites the presidency, Sunni Muslims the premiership, and Shi'a Muslims the speakership. Public offices were later distributed according to affiliation, along the principle of five Muslims to every six appointed Christians as reflected in a 1932 census. Similar ideas facilitated the distribution of elected seats for the National Assembly, cabinet ministers, heads of the armed forces, the Central Bank, and other prominent public positions. Each sect possessed veto power over public decisions, at the cost of a functioning governmental system, creating insecurity and instability, prompting people to turn elsewhere – including beyond Lebanon's borders – to meet their basic needs.[14]

Within this, it is hardly surprising that state politics is often neglected, meaning that communal groups have long been forced to rely on their social and security networks. Here, the state is immobile and unable to circumvent the increasingly intractable structures of communal difference which become self-perpetuating,[15] later resulting in what

[12] Imad Salamey, 'Failing Consociationalism in Lebanon and Integrative Options', *International Journal of Peace Studies* 14:2 (2009), p. 83.
[13] Imad Salamey and Rhys Payne, 'Parliamentary Consociationalism in Lebanon: Equal Citizenry vs. Quotated Confessionalism', *Journal of Legislative Studies* 14:4 (2008), 451–73.
[14] Michael Hudson, *The Precarious Republic: Political Modernization in Lebanon* (New York: Random House, 1968).
[15] Kerr, *The Arab Cold War*, p. 188.

John Nagle termed 'zombie power sharing'.[16] Lebanese politics has long been beset by such issues. With seemingly intractable communal difference preventing the emergence of a coherent state project, external actors have played a prominent role in Lebanese politics, reinforcing communal difference and securing elite interests in the process. The increased interconnectedness of communal groups with allies beyond the territorial borders of the state only serves to exacerbate these tensions, leaving the domestic political field open to the direct influence of external actors.

The development of a Lebanese political project has been shaped by regional factors since ideas of a 'Greater Lebanon' emerged. Initially regulated by French colonial actors, Lebanon was then affected by the creation of the state of Israel and the influx of Palestinians after the War of Independence in 1948.[17] Further Arab losses resulted in more Palestinian refugees, most notably after the 1967 Six-Day War, while Jordan's decision to expel the Palestinian Liberation Organization (PLO) in 1970 increased the presence of Palestinian militias on Lebanese soil. The signing of the Cairo Agreement in 1969 sought to curtail PLO activities in Lebanon, yet this served to legitimate the PLO, giving it a base from which to attack Israeli targets. With a large number of refugee camps existing for Palestinians across Lebanon, the PLO had a vast pool to draw from.[18] This had a dramatic influence on Lebanon, not only impacting upon the delicate demographic balance,[19] but also increasing tensions between the Lebanese state and its southern neighbour. Israeli retaliatory attacks had a profound impact on Lebanese institutions, further weakening the state's regulatory capacity, ultimately helping bring about civil war and, with it, Syrian involvement in Lebanon from 1976.[20]

Although all the major communities were allocated key governmental portfolios, Shi'a groups only occupied 3.2 per cent of the top civil service positions. Unsurprisingly, the influx of Palestinian refugees after the 1948 Israel further complicated demographics in the state, while also having a

---

[16] John Nagle, 'Consociationalism Is Dead! Long Live Zombie Power-Sharing', *Studies in Ethnicity and Nationalism* 20:2 (2020), 137–44.

[17] Itamar Rabinovich, *The War for Lebanon, 1970–1985* (New York: Cornell University Press, 1985), p. 40.

[18] A. El-Gemayel, 'Public International Law in Lebanon', in A. El-Gemayel (ed.), *The Lebanese Legal System* (Washington DC: International Law Institute, 1985), pp. 445.

[19] Walid Khalidi, *Conflict and Violence in Lebanon: Confrontation in the Middle East* (Cambridge, MA: Harvard University Press, 1979); Michael Hudson, 'The Breakdown of Democracy in Lebanon', *Journal of International Affairs* 38:2 (1985), 277–92.

[20] Hinnebusch articulates two possible reasons for Syrian involvement in Lebanon: 1) a Realist analysis designed to counter Israel and 2) on the basis of a common heritage of *Bilad al-Sham*. Raymond Hinnebusch, 'Pax-Syriana? The Origins, Causes and Consequences of Syria's Role in Lebanon', *Mediterranean Politics* 3:1 (1998), 137–60.

devastating impact on socio-economic factors, most notably amongst the Shi'a.[21]

This marginalization of Shi'a groups is a common feature of Lebanese history, often manifesting in spatial forms. According to Hasan Sharif, the south

has the fewest paved roads per person or per acre. Running water is still missing in all villages and towns although water pipes were extended to many areas in the early sixties. Electricity networks were erected at the same time, but they are inoperative most of the time. Sewage facilities are available only in large towns and cities. Outside the larger centres telephone service is completely absent except for a single manual cabin which is usually out of order. Doctors visit the villages once a week and sometimes only once a month.[22]

Despite a general economic boom that positioned Beirut as one of the most affluent places in the region during the 1960s, Shi'a communities continued to struggle. By 1974 the Shi'a comprised around 30 per cent of the population yet received less than 1 per cent of the state budget.[23] GDP per capita was around 2,000 Lebanese Lira lower than that of other confessional groups, while the community was under represented in the Lebanese parliament by ten seats.[24] Such factors were exacerbated by the weakness of the central government, which prompted each confessional group to develop its own welfare systems and institutions. Shi'a communities were hardest hit by political and economic changes, seen in the percentage share of the total workforce dropping from 38 per cent to 11 per cent with the move away from the agrarian sector. This prompted widespread migration from rural areas, particularly across the south, to urban centres, which had a dramatic impact on security, leaving local leaders unable to respond to the evolving security challenges and Shi'a groups caught in a 'double marginalization' from both city and village.[25] Such challenges made it difficult to transcend or indeed escape sectarian identities, which were expounded by civil war and the Israeli invasion, creating conditions that would engender ideational and material support from external patrons. While difficult, other forms of associations – around youth and labour – did initially offer some alternatives to

---

[21] Albert Hourani, *A History of the Arab Peoples* (London: Faber & Faber, 2005), p. 429.

[22] Hasan Sharif, 'South Lebanon: Its History and Geopolitics', in Elaine Hagopian and Sami Farsoun (eds.), *South Lebanon* (Detroit: Association of Arab-American University Graduates, 1978), pp. 10–11.

[23] Norton, *Amal and the* Shi'a, p. 18.

[24] Hassan Charif, 'Regional Development and Integration', in Deirdre Collings (ed.), *Peace for Lebanon?* (Boulder, CO: Lynne Reinner, 1993), pp. 151–2.

[25] Norton, *Amal and the* Shi'a, p. 28.

sectarian ordering, albeit becoming increasingly delicate in the descent to conflict.[26]

Repeated Israeli activity – incursion and invasion – across the south of Lebanon played a central role in Shi'a migration, creating new urban arrangements with socio-economic and political repercussions for the organization of life across Beirut. Amidst such mobilization, inter communal tensions increased, particularly when coupled with long-standing socio-economic challenges that typically – yet not exclusively – affected Shi'a groups. The rapid speed of growth across Beirut resulted in dramatic and often violent clashes as competing groups fought for control of strategic sites across the city. Efforts to control these sites led to allegations of demographic (re)engineering, with key officials on all sides being accused of conspiring to gain control of particular areas through either vast economic investment or building illegal housing.[27]

Although Shi'a groups often expressed sympathies with the Palestinian movements, the former found themselves caught in a precarious demographic, socio-economic position that was exacerbated by the Israeli invasion. Reflecting on the legacy of the Israeli invasion on Lebanese politics, former Israeli prime minister Ehud Barak – a special forces veteran of the war – suggested that 'when we entered Lebanon ... there was no Hezbollah. We were accepted with perfumed rice and flowers by the Shi'a in the south. It was our presence there that created Hezbollah.'[28]

In contrast, the Syrian presence in Lebanon began under the auspices of a peacekeeping force, yet at that time Syrian actors rejected the sovereignty of Lebanon due to their vision of broader Arab unity.[29] While the Syrian military presence was ostensibly an attempt to foster peace within the increasingly bloody civil war, many thought that the real goal was to crush the Palestinians.[30] In response, the Arab League agreed to send a symbolic Arab security force to facilitate the gradual withdrawal of Syrian troops. Ultimately unsuccessful, the fighting continued, prompting further discussions in Riyadh and Cairo in October 1976, resulting in

---

[26] See the work of Dylan Baum and Lea Bou Khater for more on this.
[27] Salamey, 'Failing Consociationalism', 90–1.
[28] Gilbert Achcar, *The 33-Day War: Israel's War on Hezbollah in Lebanon and Its Aftermath* (London: Saqi, 2007).
[29] Sandra M. Saseen, 'The Tai'f Accord and Lebanon's Struggle to Regain Its Sovereignty', *American University International Law Review* 6:1 (1990): 62 fn 29 where she sites Nader, *An Exclu.*
[30] W.B. Fisher, 'Lebanon', in *Middle East and North Africa, 1988* (London: Europa, 1987), p. 592.

the evolution of the security force into a 30,000-strong Arab Deterrent Force, albeit comprised primarily of Syrian troops.[31]

This action escalated tensions with Israel in a classic example of the spiralling moves of the security dilemma. The PLO and Israeli armed forces continued to trade reciprocal attacks, prompting an Israeli advancement into southern Lebanon in 1978, only to withdraw three months later. At this time the IDF supported a Christian Lebanese militia that would commit a number of atrocities across the civil war.[32] In spite of the withdrawal, tensions between the PLO and Israel remained, prompting a second invasion in 1982, in response to the attempted assassination of an Israeli ambassador.[33] While a peace agreement was reached between Lebanon and Israel, Syrian troops remained on Lebanese soil.

Civil War and the Party of God

Prior to the outbreak of war, Lebanon was viewed by many Western scholars as the 'most stable democracy' in the Arab world.[34] In contrast, scholars in the Arab world suggested that 'the system has always had plenty of freedom but suffered from a lack of democracy'.[35] Despite this apparent absence, the Lebanese economy enjoyed impressive growth, over 7 per cent in the 1950s and 5–6 per cent in the 1960s.[36] It was a space of interaction and possibility, where the Arab world met the international markets. Yet the economy was heavily reliant upon foreign capital, creating uneven regional and sectoral development, prompting migration from rural to urban centres and widespread unrest, exacerbated by the presence of a large number of Palestinian refugees.[37] The National Pact created a political space where sect-based identities were privileged above all others, with little space for alternative expressions of identity beyond sect-based markers. By 1975, even the Lebanese

---

[31] Rabinovich, *The War for Lebanon*, pp. 55–6; Brian L. Zimbler, 'Peacekeeping Without the U.N.: The Multinational Force in Lebanon', *Yale Journal of International Law* 10:1 (1984), 222, 223 n. 7.

[32] Rabinovich, *The War for Lebanon*, p. 108. Fisher, 'Lebanon', p. 592.

[33] Hudson, *Precarious Republic*, p. 287.

[34] E. Shils, 'The Prospect for Lebanese Civility', in L. Binder (ed.), *Politics in Lebanon* (New York: John Wiley and Sons, 1966), pp. 1–12.

[35] S. al-Hoss, *Lubnan ala al-Muftaraq* [*Lebanon at the Crossroads*] (Beirut: Beirut Arab Center, 1984), pp. 217–19.

[36] S. A. Makdisi, 'An Appraisal of Lebanon's Post-War Economic Development and a Look to the Future', *Middle East Journal* 31:3 (1977), 267–80.

[37] C. Dubar and S. Nasr, *al-Tabakat al-Ijtimaiyya Fi Lubnan* [*Social Classes in Lebanon*] (Beirut: Arab Research Institute, 1982).

army disintegrated along sect-based lines, with power dispersed across a range of militia-based networks whose fighting attached meaning to spatial arenas across Beirut.[38]

As a result, such identity markers had transnational resonance, which became increasingly important.

During the conflict, external powers began to play an important role, sponsoring local actors in pursuit of broader geopolitical agendas. As Fred H. Lawson suggests, this stems from structural factors within the regional system which created a number of different centres of power, notably a move towards a multi-polar system, shaping foreign policy processes as a consequence.[39] With the events of the 1979 revolution, Iran became a key player both in regional politics and in Lebanon, where it worked alongside Syria in supporting Shi'a movements. While Syria worked with the Amal Movement and the Progressive Socialist Party against Israel's collaboration with the Lebanese forces and the South Lebanese Army, Iran sought to develop a new movement based on a shared ideological vision.[40]

The establishment of Hizbullah was brought about through the provision of ideational and material support from Iran, who sent officials close to the supreme leader and prominent members of the elite IRGC to facilitate such developments. Central to much of this was Mohammad Montazeri, a founding member of the IRGC, who was responsible for extolling the virtues of *veleyat-e faqih* and, alongside 'Ali Akbar Mohtashamipour, for forging Hizbullah. The role of Montazeri and Mohtashamipour – key Khomeini allies – in establishing Hizbullah demonstrates the broader Iranian desire to export the revolution across the Middle East, providing support to the *mostaz'afin* ('the oppressed') in the process.[41]

Hizbullah articulated its ideological vision in a 1985 Open Letter, which set out its proximity to Iran:

We are often asked: Who are we, the Hizbullah, and what is our identity? We are the sons of the *umma* (Muslim community)—the party of God (Hizb Allah) the vanguard of which was made victorious by God in Iran. There the vanguard succeeded to lay down the bases of a Muslim state which plays a central role in the world. We obey the orders of one leader, wise and just, that of our tutor and *faqih*

[38] Sara Fregonese, 'The Urbicide of Beirut? Geopolitics and the Built Environment in the Lebanese Civil War (1975–1976)', *Political Geography* 38 (2009), 309–18.
[39] Fred H. Lawson, 'Syria's Intervention in the Lebanese Civil War, 1976: A Domestic Conflict Explanation', *International Organization* 38:3 (1984), 453.
[40] Brendan Sozer, 'Development of Proxy Relationships: A Case Study of the Lebanese Civil War', *Small Wars & Insurgencies* 27:4 (2016), 636–58.
[41] Husseini, 'Hezbollah and the Axis of Refusal'.

(jurist) who fulfills all the necessary conditions: Ruhollah Musawi Khomeini. God save him![42]

Hizbullah's Open Letter declared that 'we are an *umma* which fears God only and is by no means ready to tolerate injustice, aggression and humiliation'.[43] In accordance with its responsibility to protect the *umma*, the Party of God articulated a necessity to confront 'basic enemies: the US, France and Israel' and to stand 'against Westoxification', driven by a 'hatred of the US administration, not the US people'.[44] Underpinning ideas of resistance, Joseph Alagha suggests that Hizbullah's natural allies are 'the oppressed of the entire world, irrespective of their colour, race, or religion'.[45]

While the Open Letter speaks of membership of a broader collective shaped by fundamentally transnational ideals, we should not view its Shi'a identity as hegemonic, or in opposition to the Lebanese national identity. Instead, as Shaery-Eisenlohr correctly asserts, Shi'a practices historically sought to break hegemonic communal narratives in a process of re-imagining national politics and the self, placing different Shi'a identities more prominently within national politics.[46]

The formative stages of the group were aided by support from the IRGC, who provided widespread support from stipends to aid recruitment to the development of missile batteries. Training camps were quickly established in the Beqa with Syrian approval, which were run by 200 elite members of the IRGC. This material and logistical support was supplemented by theological training and the provision of financial resources which helped establish Hizbullah as one of the two main Shi'a militias, both of whom benefited from external patrons aiding their influence on the Lebanese political spectrum. Despite the contemporary strength of links between Iran and Hizbullah, serious political and ideological debate in Tehran at this time took place over which Shi'a

---

[42] An Open Letter, 'The Hizbullah Programme', *CNN* (11.12.11), www.cfr.org/terrorist-organizations-and-networks/open-letter-hizballah-program/p30967.

[43] Ibid.

[44] Ibid., p. 20.

[45] Joseph Alagha, *Hizbullah's Documents: From the 1985 Open Letter to the 2009 Manifesto* (Amsterdam: Pallas Publications, 2011), p. 16.

[46] Roschanack Shaery-Eisenlohr, *Shi'ite Lebanon: Transnational Religion and the Making of National Identities* (New York: Columbia University Press, 2011), p. 2. For a Bahraini parallel, see Justin Gengler, *Group Conflict and Political Mobilization in Bahrain and the Arab Gulf: Rethinking the Rentier State* (Bloomington: Indiana University Press, 2015), ch. 2. For Iraq, see Fanar Haddad, 'Shi'a-Centric State-Building and Sunni Rejection in Post-2003 Iraq', *Carnegie Endowment for International Peace*, 7 January 2016, https://carnegieendowment.org/2016/01/07/shia-centric-state-building-and-sunni-rejection-in-post-2003-iraq-pub-62408.

group should represent the Islamic Republic in Iran, with prominent officials in Iran such as Jalal el-Din Farsi, Ibrahim Yazdi, Mohammad Montazeri, and 'Ali Akbar Mohtashamipour supporting different warring factions in Lebanon.[47]

In the years that followed, Iranian support for Hizbullah – coupled with tacit Syrian approval – helped the Party of God position itself prominently in Lebanese politics and at the vanguard of resistance against Israel, securing regional support in the process. This articulation of resistance at the core of the Party of God's ideology reveals an additional component of both the group and Iranian foreign policy in an effort to circumvent communal difference along ethnic and sectarian lines. In particular, the presence of Islamic Culture and Relations Organization (ICRO) outlets across the south of Lebanon goes some way in supporting the narrative of resistance. As Edward Wastnidge argues, while religion plays a prominent part in Tehran's strategic vision, the deployment of cultural soft power helps cultivate Iranian influence amongst Shi'a communities through a range of different activities including art exhibitions.[48] ICROs serve as a base for cultural ambassadors to operate and although separate from the Ministry of Foreign Affairs, the ruling council of the ICRO report directly to the supreme leader, demonstrating their importance as a source of capital.

The civil war had a devastating impact on Lebanese politics, entrenching communal difference and resulting in the physical destruction of vast urban areas. Writing in 1984, Jim Muir paints a bleak picture of not only the conflict in Lebanon but also the country's future. Reflecting on the rapid escalation of fighting between different groups (Druze and Maronite, Shi'a and Lebanese Army) which created conditions of possibility for external powers to find local allies – and vice versa – Muir questioned if Lebanon's fate was to be dismembered by covetous neighbours, with the remainder, unable to overcome its internal contradictions, splitting up on sectarian lines or plunged into endless turmoil as local leaders and their outside allies struggled to tilt the balance of power one way or the other?[49] International actors capitalized on this domestic fragmentation, although the complexity of the conflict meant that it was not always easy to ascertain who was involved. In the same piece, highlighting the precarious position of Lebanon in regional affairs, Muir notes that the 'warplanes flashing through the sky over Beirut could be

[47] Ataie, 'Revolutionary Iran's 1979 Endeavor'.
[48] Edward Wastnidge, 'The Modalities of Iranian Soft Power: From Cultural Diplomacy to Soft War', *Politics* 35:3/4 (2015), 364–77.
[49] Jim Muir, 'Lebanon: Arena of Conflict, Crucible of Peace', *The Middle East Journal* 38:2 (1984), 206.

Americans off to bomb Syrians in the mountains, French on a mission against Iranians in the Bekaa, or Israelis attacking Palestinian guerrilla positions'.[50]

The competing agendas of international actors served to exacerbate and entrench local rivalries. The most successful of those was Iranian support for Hizbullah, but also included Saudi Arabia supporting the PLO, Sunni and Christian groups and Israel supporting Maronite Christian movements as the Arab–Israeli conflict began to be played out across the streets of Lebanon. Beyond supporting local actors, Saudi Arabia also sought to play a mediatory role, attempting to facilitate a ceasefire, although Syrian discontent and increased Israeli agitation ultimately put an end to the peace plan.

Many of those involved in the conflict took on service provider roles, embedding themselves within communities and increasing legitimacy through meeting communal needs. Towards the end of the war, factions within the military emerged, challenging the presence of Syrian forces in the Lebanese political arena. Two competing governments emerged from a political vacuum following the end of President Gemayel's term on 23 September 1988, led by Michel Aoun and Salim al-Hoss, creating a military and civilian government, respectively.

Tai'f and Reconstruction

After fifteen years of devastation, Lebanon's civil war was ended by the Tai'f Accords, negotiated by those surviving members of the 1972 parliament and facilitated by Prince Sa'ud al-Faysal of Saudi Arabia, – regularly known as the 'Dean of Arab Diplomats' – the United States, and Syria.[51] The agreement sought to end the conflict by reasserting Lebanese authority in southern Lebanon – then occupied by Israel – while repositioning Lebanon as a state with 'an Arab identity and belonging',[52] later supported by a range of states including Saudi Arabia, Syria, the United States, France and Iran.[53] A key component of this was the establishment of a power-sharing agreement that distributed the number of seats equally between Muslims and Christians, ending the 5–6 split that had been in operation since the National Convention and reflecting

[50] Ibid.

[51] Michael C. Hudson, 'Trying Again: Power-Sharing in Post-Civil War Lebanon', *International Negotiation* 2:1 (1997), 103–22. The collective approach was at odds with previous diplomatic efforts which had pitted geopolitical rivals against one another over mediatory plans.

[52] Bassel F. Salloukh, 'The Limits of Electoral Engineering in Divided Societies: Elections in Postwar Lebanon', *Canadian Journal of Political Science* 39:3 (2006), 635–55.

[53] Salamey, 'Failing Consociationalism'.

the demographic changes that had shaped Lebanese society. Parliamentary seats were to be subdivided along confessional lines, while most districts were home to a confessional mix. The agreement reaffirmed the National Pact and agreement to retain sovereign independence from a range of states, including Syria and France.

Yet full sovereignty – as much as such things are possible to claim – was impossible, given the continued presence of external forces, namely Syrian and Israeli forces, a position exacerbated by fragmenting political institutions. In the years that followed, socio-economic conditions created financial dependency on external powers – notably on Saudi Arabia – while the increased influence of Hizbullah facilitated Iranian involvement. Fundamentally, as Augustus R. Norton asserts, the Lebanese state had limited sovereignty – a point also made by Sara Fregonese, who speaks of 'hybrid sovereignty' – reflecting the regional factors affecting Lebanese politics.[54]

A great deal of work has been produced on the Tai'f agreement as a form of power sharing in a divided society that goes beyond the scope of this project. Yet what is important to stress is that the agreement was not a dramatic departure from earlier efforts to create a political system. Indeed, the accord agreed at Tai'f implicitly ratified the National Pact, and with it, emphasised confessional co-operation and inter communal compromise. The Maronites and the Shi'a were seen as the big losers from the Tai'f Accords, with Sunnis gained a de facto majority.[55] This processes of reinforcing communal divisions also created conditions for continued external involvement in Lebanese politics. While Tai'f sought to establish Lebanese sovereignty over the state, the involvement of external actors in domestic politics continued as Saudi Arabia, Syria, and Iran continued to exert influence over particular areas of political life, perhaps best seen in the Syrian-Iranian agreement to allow Hizbullah to maintain their presence in the south and Bekkaa.[56] Beyond Tai'f, Lebanon signed other treaties with Syria to institutionalize Damascus's influence across political affairs.[57]

Between 1991 and 2000, Lebanon transitioned from civil war to a negative peace brought about through the rejuvenation of political elites across governance institutions.[58] Former militia leaders became

---

[54] Augustus R. Norton, 'Lebanon after Tai'f: Is the Civil War Over?,' *Middle East Journal* 45:3 (1991), 466.

[55] Ibid., 464.

[56] Alan Cowell, 'Syria and Iran Agree Militias Can Remain in Parts of Lebanon', *New York Times* (30.04.91).

[57] Rola El-Husseini, 'Lebanon: Building Political Dynasties', in Volker Perthes (ed.), *Arab Elites: Negotiating the Politics of Change* (Boulder: Lynne Reinner, 2004), p. 242.

[58] Ibid., p. 239.

prominent *zu'ama*, figures within the political sphere, gaining legitimacy through their involvement in the conflict but also their ability to speak for particular communal groups. It is in this context that a number of powerful individuals began to exert influence over the political, social, and economic trajectory of Lebanon. The emergence of Rafik Hariri as a prominent player in the Sunni community is one such example. Born into a family of modest means in Sidon, Hariri rapidly built up a vast personal fortune working construction in Saudi Arabia, becoming a contractor of choice for the Kingdom and by 1983 was named as King Fahd's official envoy to Lebanon. Hariri exerted influence through the Islamic Institute for Culture and Higher Education – later the Hariri Foundation – while also using personal wealth to support precarious institutions across the state, including preventing desertions from the Lebanese army, and funding both American University of Beirut and the Lebanese American University.[59]

Hariri is viewed in deeply contrasting ways. For some he was 'Mr Lebanon', the billionaire tycoon responsible for helping Beirut transition out of the horrors of the civil war and to restore its position in the Middle East.[60] Yet for others, ties with the Bush White House were troubling. Serving as prime minister from 1992 to 1998 and again from 2000 to 2004, Hariri was seen by some as a hugely effective leader but maligned by critics as a result of allegations of corruption in the process of rebuilding Beirut. During his time out of office, an anti-crime organization was tasked by Selim Hoss, then prime minister, to prepare an anti-corruption strategy which was quickly frozen when Hariri returned to office.[61] Although Hariri had close ties with Saudi Arabia, he was initially appointed prime minister by Syria in 1992, after which he 'proved himself to be a loyal servant of Damascus'.[62] Yet over time, Hariri's relationship with Damascus became more complex.

Under his leadership, Lebanese politics took on a new dimension, balancing the interests of various groups and working towards reconstruction and socio-economic and political development. Through his company, Solidere, Hariri transformed large parts of Beirut which had

---

[59] See Melani Cammett, *Compassionate Communalism: Welfare and Sectarianism in Lebanon* (Ithaca, New York: Cornell University Press), pp. 65–7 and Hannes Baumann, *Citizen Hariri: Lebanon's Neo-Liberal Reconstruction* (London: Hurst, 2016).
[60] Baumann, *Citizen Harriri*.
[61] Richard Becherer, 'A Matter of Life and Debt: The Untold Costs of Rafiq Hariri's New Beirut', *Journal of Architecture* 10:1 (2005), 1–42.
[62] Gary C. Gambill and Daniel Nassif, 'Lebanon's Parliamentary Elections: Manufacturing Dissent', *Middle East Intelligence Bulletin* 2:8 (05.09.00), www.meforum.org/meib/articles/0009_11.htm.

been previously ravaged by war. In doing this, Hariri positioned himself as one of the most influential figures in Lebanese politics. Reflecting his influence on the state, on taking office, he was allegedly asked if he was not too big for a country like Lebanon.[63]

While the rebuilding process sought to return Beirut to the prominent regional position that it had occupied prior to the civil war, the process laid bare latent communal frustrations through archaeological work deemed central to the building works and, more fundamentally, the re-imagining of urban spaces and processes of exclusion that quickly emerged. Although in discussions between the state's eighteen different communal groups a desire to find a collective national heritage was articulated, finding consensus on what this meant proved impossible.

Debate over the nature of reconstruction featured prominently in elections, notably in 1996 where political parties positioned themselves in relation to Solidere and the actions of Hariri and Nabih Berri, the speaker of the parliament.[64] In this period of contestation, many viewed Solidere's plans as a form of spatial domination, shaping not only physical space but also collective memory. In response, opponents of Solidere's actions produced texts proposing alternate visions of Beirut, with some viewing the transformation as a form of Islamization, while others viewed it as the privileging of Sunni Islam or as a means of exploiting the poor.[65] While there was an undeniably neoliberal focus within Hariri's work, he remained a devout Muslim and rebuilt several mosques, perhaps best seen in the Mohammad al-Amin mosque at the periphery of Martyr's Square, which towers over nearby places of worship. The rebuilding process dramatically transformed over 1.2 million square metres of prime real estate, yet Solidere's approach was criticized for paying scant attention to history and culture, transforming space in a way that reinforced a particular – and exclusive – vision of order, along with widespread allegations of corruption. Close examination of elite politics in Lebanon reveals a complex web of networks of patronage that secure position through the distribution of resources and allocation of privileges, reinforcing a particular principle of vision in the process.

The emergence of a Hariri-led bloc of economic actors increased links with the Arab Gulf states while countering the interests of the militias and their foreign backers. The rise of Hariri coincided with an apparent

---

[63] Nicholas Blanford, *Killing Mr Lebanon: The Assassination of Rafik Hariri and Its Impact on the Middle East* (London: I. B. Tauris, 2006), p. 43.

[64] Aseel Sawalha, *Reconstructing Beirut: Memory and Space in a Postwar Arab City* (Austin: University of Texas Press, 2010), p. 43.

[65] Ibid., p. 38; Blanford, *Killing Mr Lebanon*, p. 45.

rapprochement in tensions across the Gulf, with leaders in Riyadh and Tehran appearing open to reconciliation. At this point, as Mehran Kamrava observes, Saudi Arabia played a mediatory role in Lebanon driven by pragmatic aims. At the heart of this were a number of concerns. First, Lebanon's precarious political system was at odds with the Saudi state's inherent conservativism. Second, close commercial and familial ties between the royal family and Sunni elites played an important role in Saudi decision making. Third, a concern about a concomitant rise of Shi'a and Iranian influence in Lebanon.[66]

This period also witnessed the gradual roll back of the Israeli presence from the south of the country. Following the complete Israeli withdrawal in 2000, questions began to emerge about the very nature of the Party of God, with some suggesting that it should focus on Lebanese politics, while others, including Iran's supreme leader 'Ali Khamenei, suggesting that its resistance and liberation obligations were incomplete.[67] Although the Israeli withdrawal was met with widespread jubilation across Lebanon, a number of tensions remained, notably the case of the Shebaa farms, a 25 kilometre square patch of land owned by the Lebanese yet found within the Golan Heights, occupied by Israel. Although international opinion views the Golan Heights as Syrian territory, Lebanese actors – supported by their Syrian counterparts – claim the farms as part of Lebanon, allowing Hizbullah to continue its resistance against Israel in spite of the 2000 withdrawal.[68]

In the following years, Hizbullah's focus turned to domestic politics, providing political representation to much maligned Shi'a voters who found the group's blend of Islamic, and non-religious themes (focusing on economic exploitation, inequality, security, and a lack of opportunities) appealing. Drawing on the theme of resistance, election slogans included 'they resist with their blood, resist with your vote', yet the ongoing manipulation of Lebanese politics by Syria would ultimately thwart the Party of God's ballot box successes.

The evolution of the Party of God was highlighted in 2009 by a new manifesto, once again driven by resistance, noting that its creation is 'a result of the priority of deeds and responsibility of sacrifice that we have experienced'.[69] The manifesto calls for the abrogation of sectarian

---

[66] See Mehran Kamrava, 'Mediation and Saudi Foreign Policy', *Orbis* 57:1 (2013), 159. See also: Thanassis Cambanis, 'A Father's Shadow Clouds His Son's Rise in Lebanon', *New York Times* (03.10.07), p. 6.

[67] See Norton, 'Lebanon after Tai'f', 479.

[68] Asher Kaufman, *Contested Frontiers in the Syria-Lebanon-Israel Region: Cartography, Sovereignty, and Conflict* (Baltimore: Johns Hopkins University Press, 2014).

[69] Section 6 Islam and Resistance, *The New Hezbollah Manifesto* (November 2009), www .lebanonrenaissance.org/assets/Uploads/15-The-New-Hezbollah-Manifesto-Nov09.pdf.

differences in the pursuit of democracy 'where an elected majority can rule and an elected minority can oppose, opening the door for a proper exchange of power between the loyalty and the opposition'.[70] It suggests that sectarian difference should be seen as a source of wealth and social vitality but in reality is 'exploited as factors of division and incitement as well as a means of social destruction'.[71] The discussion closes by stressing unity across the Muslim world: 'We also remind of the importance of cautiousness from sectarian sensitivities – especially between Sunnis and *Shi'ites*, as we wager on the conscience of the Muslims in facing the conspiracies and schemes on this level.'[72]

In spite of Hizbullah's apparent inward turn, the importance of relations with external patrons remained, notably with Syria and Iran. Although the Islamic Republic was integral in the formation of the Party of God, maintaining links with Syria was fundamental in solidifying its position, much to the chagrin of many across the international community.[73] In contrast, Hariri was viewed with a great deal of popularity amongst the international community, who saw his neo-liberal economic vision as something that matched the burgeoning global consensus. Moreover, close ties with Saudi Arabia helped support such perceptions, particularly in the context of the War on Terror, where US requests for Syrian co-operation had regularly been rebuffed. In this climate, Washington demanded that Damascus end its interference in Lebanon, also calling for the dismantling of Hizbullah and re-deployment of the Lebanese army across all of the state, including the south.[74]

Following Syria's refusal to comply with US demands, UN Security Council Resolution (UNSCR) 1559 was issued in early September 2004. The resolution expressed support for 'free and fair electoral process in Lebanon's upcoming presidential election conducted according to Lebanese constitutional rules and devised without foreign interference or influence'. In addition, it called for 'all remaining foreign forces to withdraw from Lebanon', along with mandating the 'disbanding and disarmament' of all militias across the state.[75] As Salloukh observes, this resolution 'became a tool against Damascus' within the context

---

[70] Ibid.
[71] Ibid.
[72] Ibid.
[73] See Amal Saad, 'Challenging the Sponsor-Proxy Model'; Adham Saouli, *Hezbollah: Socialisation and Its Tragic Ironies* (Edinburgh: Edinburgh University Press, 2018).
[74] See N. Nasif, 'Ma Taquluh Washington wa Dimashq 'an Muhadathat Burns', *al-Nahar* (14.09.04).
[75] UN Security Council, *Resolution 1559* (02.09.04), www.un.org/News/Press/docs/2004/sc8181.doc.htm.

of a broader geopolitical contest in the post-9/11 world.[76] Yet tensions between UNSCR 1559 and Tai'f continued to shape Lebanese politics, over both political reform and the extent of Syrian influence in Lebanon.[77]

US diplomatic cables from the time provide interesting insight, perhaps none more so than Saudi concerns that UNSCR 1559 should not target regime change in Damascus in spite of fluctuating relations between Saudi Arabia and Syria.[78] While the Saudi state desired a full Syrian withdrawal from Lebanon and the rapid establishment of a Lebanese government, there was concern about Syrian stability pertaining to a 'strategic void' vis-à-vis Israel that could emerge following a Syrian withdrawal and its possible impact on Hizbullah.

Despite these views, the post-Tai'f and pre-Cedar Revolution period was one of relative calm, with external actors consolidating their support bases through the deployment of financial, religious, and cultural capital, engaging with the structural arrangement of the political field in the process. Amidst a shifting transnational field, Syria's role in Lebanon became increasingly unstable as a consequence of Damascus's inability to assert capital in the transnational field, or to successfully navigate the structural constraints of the Lebanese political field. In contrast, Saudi economic support for Hariri ensured the Kingdom's influence in the Lebanese state. Additionally, although Hizbullah had begun an apparent inwards turn, Iranian influence remained strong, couched in ideational and material support for the Party of God.[79] Yet this period of relative tranquillity was not to last.

The 'Cedar Revolution'

On 14 February 2005, a remote-controlled bomb was detonated under Rafiq Hariri's motorcade as it passed the St George's Hotel on the corniche in Beirut. The attack left Hariri dead, along with eight of his bodyguards and a further thirteen bystanders. Unsurprisingly, given the manner of his death, Hariri's cult of personality increased after the

---

[76] Salloukh, 'The Arab Uprisings', 36.
[77] Karim Knio, 'Lebanon: Cedar Revolution or Neo-Sectarian Partition?', *Mediterranean Politics* 10:2 (2005), 225–31.
[78] 05PARIS2660_a, 'Saudi Crown Prince Visit Focuses on Lebanon, Close Ties with Chirac, but Concludes No New Contracts' (19.04.05), https://wikileaks.org/plusd/cables/05PARIS2660_a.html.
[79] Saouli, *Hezbollah*.

events of 14 February, with his family erecting a commemorative tomb, which evolved into a shrine, next to the Muhammad al-Amin mosque on Martyrs' Square.[80] The assassination had a devastating impact on Lebanon's fragile political balance, and the establishment of a tribunal investigating events loomed ominously over political life over the coming decade. In the months after Hariri's assassination, protests at his killing and the twenty-nine-year Syrian presence in Lebanon escalated, ultimately prompting the Syrian withdrawal in what became known as the Cedar Revolution. The event also solidified the political divisions that had been emerging across the state. Ultimately, the assassination opened up different national visions of Lebanese politics and their relationship with regional powers.

During Hariri's second term, he became an incredibly outspoken critic of Syria and Bashar al-Assad, leading to suggestions that the Syrian president later ordered his assassination. Walid Jumblatt, the Druze leader, alleged that al-Assad had threatened Hariri the August before, declaring that 'if you and Chirac want me out of Lebanon, I will destroy Lebanon',[81] a charge that was later repeated by Abdul Halim Khaddam, the former vice president of Syria. Others held Hizbullah responsible, yet Hariri and Nasrallah enjoyed close relations, and across some districts, Hariri's Future Movement and the Party of God were planning to run on joint parliamentary lists in the 2005 elections.

The events of 14 February had a profound impact on Lebanese politics. In the weeks that followed, people took to the streets to express their anger at the political situation, with Martyr's Square in Beirut – the site of Hariri's mausoleum – becoming the centre of calls for independence from Syria. A week after Hariri's assassination, Presidents George W. Bush and Jacques Chirac issued a joint statement calling for Syria to withdraw from Lebanon, and a further two days later, Walid Jumblatt, the Durze leader, revealed details of the threats that had been facing Hariri. On 5 March, Syrian president Bashar al-Assad announced that Syrian troops would be withdrawn from Lebanon. Three days later, in response to increasing tensions and as an expression of their own position, Hizbullah organized a demonstration on Riyad al-Suloh Square, close to Martyr's Square, where expressions of national unity were

---

[80] Ward Vloeberghs, 'Worshipping the Martyr President: The darîh of Rafiq al-Hariri in Beirut', in Baudouin Dupret, Thomas Pierret, Paulo G. Pinto, and Kathryn Spellman-Poots (eds.), *Ethnographies of Islam* (Edinburgh: Edinburgh University Press, 2008), pp. 80–92.

[81] Neil Macfarquahar, 'Behind Lebanon Upheaval, 2 Men's Fateful Clash', *New York Times* (20.03.05).

combined with portraits of al-Assad in an expression of gratitude. The date of 8 March was carefully chosen, commemorating the anniversary of the Ba'ath Party taking power in Syria.

Six days later, Lebanon witnessed the largest public rally in its history as an alleged one in four Lebanese participated in a gathering which left a profound mark on collective memory.[82] The cross-confessional protest was an expression of unity in response to the events of a week earlier, marked by changes of *hurrīya-siyāda-istiqlāl* ('Liberty, Sovereignty, Independence') or *haqīqa, hurrīya, wiḥda wataniya* ('Truth, Liberty, National Unity'). The protests were the manifestation and articulation of new schisms in Lebanese politics taking place along ideological, political, and sectarian lines, driven by competing visions of the national project.

These two protest movements helped political groups to coalesce around particular visions of political ordering. The mapping of multi-sectarian groupings onto a geopolitical rivalry added an additional layer of complexity to a precarious political environment. March 8, comprising Hizbullah, Amal – led by Nabih Berri – and the Maronite Free Patriotic Movement – representing a Christian majority under Michel Aoun – faced off against March 14, led by Hariri's Future Movement. Although both March 8 and March 14 groups coalesced around visions of who should control the post-Syrian Lebanese state, internally, both coalitions were replete with a range of tensions over security, alliance choices, and political priorities. In spite of these schisms cutting across a divided society, civil war did not erupt, to the surprise of many, perhaps reflecting Hizbullah's asymmetrical military power but also revealing the existence of a 'trans-sectarian politico-economic elite' which stood to lose most from a descent to war.[83]

Unsurprisingly, the two blocs created conditions wherein all aspects of political life took on a sectarian hue, with appointments, electoral laws, UNSCR 1559 and the disarmament of all militias, the Special Tribunal into the assassination of Hariri, Israel, and constitutional debate forming key arenas of consternation. The emergence of the two blocs was further complicated by the provision of support from regional and international camps, with the United States, Saudi Arabia, and its allies supporting the 14 March-led government under Prime Minister Fuad Siniora against the Hizbullah bloc, supported by Syria and Iran. Indeed, as Salloukh asserts, while Lebanon itself 'carried little merit', beyond

---

[82] 'Record Protest Held in Beirut', *BBC News* (14.03.05) http://news.bbc.co.uk/2/hi/middle_east/4346613.stm.

[83] Bassel F. Salloukh, 'The Syrian War: Spillover Effects on Lebanon', *Middle East Policy* 24:1 (2017), 64.

a symbolic importance, the organization of political life provided opportunities for Saudi Arabia and the United States to increase 'the sectarian ante' and not only to drown Hizbullah 'in a sectarian quagmire to contain the party's efforts to assume control over post-Syria Lebanon, but also to tarnish its appeal as a trans-Islamic and pan-Arab liberation movement'.[84]

Amidst rising pressure, the final Syrian troops stationed in Lebanon withdrew on 29 April, bringing an end to a twenty-nine-year military presence in the country. In the following months, a spate of explosions hit Beirut, deepening schisms across the country and increasing instability. In spite of the burgeoning rivalry between the two political blocs, neither Riyadh nor Tehran desired escalation. Moreover, in the immediate aftermath of the Harriri assassination, Saudi Arabia felt that Iran was a more desirable negotiating partner than Syria after the latter's perceived involvement in the killing of 'Mr Lebanon'.

Investigations into the Hariri assassination routinely allege that Hizbullah and their Syrian sponsors were responsible,[85] yet the UN investigators also believe that the inquiry was penetrated by the Party of God, leading to the death of a policeman.[86] The investigation was plagued by political consternation but in 2011, five men linked to Hizbullah were indicted on charges of terrorism and murder, and tried in abstention. One suspect, Mustafa Badreddine, was killed in Syria in 2016. Unsurprisingly, the legitimacy of the tribunal is rejected by Hizbullah, while Hassan Nasrallah asserted that no member of his party would be arrested.

After the death of his father, Saad Hariri took on the leadership of the Lebanese Sunni community. Speaking with *Time* magazine in 2007 shortly after two bombs exploded on buses in the town of Bikfaya, 20 miles north of Beirut, Hariri was vocal about Syrian actions in Lebanon:

There is a country and a regime that has been pounding at Lebanon with assassinations and explosions after explosions and killings after killings, which have been going on for over 30 years. It is important to punish those who commit these crimes, for them to understand they don't have a license to kill. And if this tribunal doesn't happen, then the international community will have given a license to kill to the regime of Bashar al-Assad and to Bashar al-Assad himself.[87]

---

[84] Salloukh, 'The Arab Uprisings', 37.

[85] UN Security Council, 'Security Council Unanimously Endorses Findings of Investigation into Murder of Rafik Hariri, Calls for Syria's Full Unconditional Cooperation', *United Nations* (31.10.05), www.un.org/press/en/2005/sc8543.doc.htm.

[86] Neil Macdonald, 'CBC Investigation: Who Killed Lebanon's Rafik Hariri', *CBC News* (21.09.10), www.cbc.ca/news/world/cbc-investigation-who-killed-lebanon-s-rafik-hariri-1.874820.

[87] Nicholas Blanford, 'A Martyr's Son Calls for Justice', *Time* (13.02.07), http://content.time.com/time/world/article/0,8599,1589446,00.html.

In the following years Saad Hariri took on an increasingly important role in Lebanon, not only as a leader for the Sunni community but also serving as a conduit for Saudi Arabia to distribute aid in an attempt to curtail Iranian influence in the state. As As'ad Abu Khalil articulates, Saudi action in Lebanon possesses a deeply symbolic resonance, tied to the very legitimacy of the House of Sa'ud as a consequence of Wahhabi views of Shi'a Islam and also the increasingly zero-sum competition with Iran for leadership of the Islamic world.[88] It was then hardly surprising that Saudi Arabia sought to distribute vast sums of money to the Lebanese army and Sunni clerics sympathetic to the Saudi cause, a great deal of which was channelled through Hariri, much like his father before him.[89]

The Summer War

It was in this context of domestic instability that war broke out between Hizbullah and Israel in summer 2006. The Summer War began after Hizbullah kidnapped two members of the Israeli Defence Force on the Israeli–Lebanese border. The thirty-four-day conflict laid bare the apparent bankruptcy of resistance against Israel amongst the Sunni Arab regimes. In the aftermath of the conflict, Hassan Nasrallah became one of the most popular figures across the region, followed by Iranian president Mahmoud Ahmadinejad.[90]

Resistance to Israel was a key feature of Hizbullah's essence. The Party of God had been forged out of the 1982 incursion, while the 2000 Israeli withdrawal from security zones in the south of Lebanon was a high point in the group's history. It provided a degree of prestige, allowing Hizbullah to position itself successfully in the Arab struggle against Israel and derive region-wide support. The outbreak of war in 2006 demonstrated the Party of God's popularity in the Middle East. The conflict also prompted a number of other questions concerning the extent of Iranian

---

[88] As'ad AbuKhalil, 'Determinants and Characteristics of the Saudi Role in Lebanon: The Post-Civil War Years', in Madawi al-Rasheed, *Kingdom without Borders* (London: Hurst, 2008), pp. 79–97.

[89] Some estimates put the amount of money channelled through Hariri in the aftermath of his father's death to be around $52 million, albeit not all of which was from Saudi Arabia. See https://carnegieendowment.org/2015/04/15/authoritarian-resurgence-saudi-arabia-s-anxious-autocrats-pub-59790.

[90] Morten Valbjørn and André Bank, 'The New Arab Cold War: Rediscovering the Arab Dimension of Middle East Regional Politics', *Review of International Studies* 38:1 (2012), 3–24.

control over their Lebanese ally and the extent to which Saudi Arabia was dependent upon an anti-Israeli position for its legitimacy.

Saudi responses to the summer's events laid bare a tension between Arab leadership aspirations and a fundamental aversion to Hizbullah, stemming from its Iranian backing.[91] While Saudi Arabia and its allies sought to frame events as an example of Iranian interference in 'Arab portfolios' through the manipulation of Shi'a communities, the attempt to add a sect-based dimension to regional politics at this time failed, largely as a consequence of resistance to Israel being seen as the main driver of regional politics.[92] Complicating matters for the Saudi leadership was the popularity of Hizbullah amongst the Kingdom's population – at a time when sectarian tensions were less salient regionally – coupled with the continued anti-Israeli sentiment which continued to find traction across the region.

In the aftermath of the 2006 war, Hizbullah proclaimed victory while Bashar al-Assad used the conflict as an opportunity to weaken his critics in Lebanon and beyond, portraying the March 14 bloc and Arab states who did not back Hizbullah as 'half-men', condemning their inaction.[93] In response, March 14 insisted that UNSCR 1701 – which brought an end to hostilities between Hizbullah and Israel – prohibited Hizbullah's military presence south of the Litani River, while Hizbullah interpreted the resolution as referring solely to visible weapons.

In spite of claims of victory, large parts of Beirut had been destroyed in an Israeli barrage. What quickly followed was the transformation of Lebanon from a site of conflict to a site of 'a development and reconstruction proxy war'.[94] In this context, the interests of regional powers can go some way in explaining the 'timing, publicity, sectoral prioritisation and the methods of aid disbursement'.[95] When the fighting stopped in August 2006, Nasrallah appeared on television and pledged support to rebuild homes and offered compensation for those whose homes were destroyed. Over $100 million was quickly distributed within three days

---

[91] Frederick Wehrey, et al., Op. Cit., p. 24. See also Mabon, 2013, pp. 64–5.

[92] Valbjørn and Bank, 'The New Arab Cold War'.

[93] Seth Wikas, 'The Damascus-Hizbullah Axis: Bashar al-Assad's Vision of a New Middle East', Washington Institute (29.08.06), www.washingtoninstitute.org/policy-analysis/view/the-damascus-hizballah-axis-bashar-al-asads-vision-of-a-new-middle-east.

[94] Emilie Combaz, 'International Aid to Lebanon', Governance, Social Development, Humanitarian, Conflict (02.08.13), http://gsdrc.org/docs/open/hdq979.pdf, p. 5.

[95] Roger Mac Ginty and C.S. Hamieh, 'Lebanon Case Study', in A. Harmer and E. Martin (eds.), Diversity in Donorship: Field Lessons (ODI, Humanitarian Policy Group, 2010), Report 30, p.40, www.odi.org.uk/sites/odi.org.uk/files/odi-assets/publications-opinion-files/5876.pdf.

of the end of the fighting, demonstrating the Party of God's power in the face of an apparently impotent Lebanese state.[96]

The weakness of the Lebanese economy – with debt servicing absorbing over 16 per cent of GDP in 2006 – meant that other actors were needed to provide financial support. In addition to the usual organizations involved in these processes, Arab states – predominantly from the Gulf – and Iran had a dramatic role to play in the reconstruction process. The process of neo-liberalization that had begun under Hariri left the Lebanese state playing a limited role, leaving reconstruction management to those directly affected and contractors[97] which, in turn, created space for sectarian divisions to emerge through clientelism, patronage, and urban planning.

A complex donor environment emerged, reflecting both the confessional organization of political life and the convoluted socio-economic processes that serve to reproduce this organization. As a result, external donors gave directly to a range of organizations. Saudi Arabia, responsible for the provision of around $1 billion support to the Central Bank during the war and budgetary support in its aftermath, gave aid directly to the government, funnelled through the office of the prime minister. In contrast, the Iranian Contributory Organization for Reconstructing Lebanon worked through municipalities and their relevant ministries.[98] Lebanese newspapers estimated that Iran ultimately gave around $1 billion and because of its strategy resulted in both immediacy and visibility in local communities, albeit subjected to delays waiting for approval from Beirut.

In the years that followed, Lebanese towns, cities, and villages were festooned with declarations of thanks to the various external sponsors, resulting in a form of symbolic competition, reflecting both the geopolitical rivalries at play and the spatial aspects of sect-based divisions. Unsurprisingly, pro-Saudi messages were more prominent in Sunni-dominated areas where their work had taken place and pro-Iranian messages were more prominent in Shi'a-dominated areas.

At this time, Iranian support for Hizbullah was reinforced through the manifestation of the shared *nomos* made real in the creation of commemorative sites of resistance. Perhaps the most important of these is the 'Iranian Garden', found outside the town of Maroun el Ras on the

---

[96] Christine Sylva Hamieh and Roger MacGinty, 'A Very Political Reconstruction: Governance and Reconstruction in Lebanon after the 2006 War', *Disasters* 34:1 (2010), 106.

[97] M. Fawaz, 'Beirut: The City as a Body Politic', *ISIM Review* 20 (Autumn 2007), 23, www.isim.nl/files/Review_20/Review_20–22.pdf.

[98] Hamieh and Mac Ginty, 'A Very Political Reconstruction', 108.

southern border with Israel. The garden, located just 400 metres from the border, was a site of prominent battles during the summer war and is an expression and articulation of resistance against Israel. Moreover, it serves to make Iran's *nomos real*, demonstrating the reach of Tehran's political and cultural capital across space (and later time). Built with the support of the Iranian Committee for Reconstruction of Southern Lebanon – with the support of erstwhile President Mahmoud Ahmadinejad – the garden is a site of resistance made real and a site to commemorate resistance through cultural displays of art.

Despite assertions of support from local Lebanese groups for their external allies – and vice versa – there was little appetite for an escalation in violence from either Riyadh or Tehran, even when such developments appeared likely, such as following clashes in early 2007. At a time of hostility across the transnational field and rampant anti-Shi'a sentiment, there was little appetite to open up a Lebanese front, perhaps as a result of the domestic challenges facing Mahmoud Ahmadinejad in Iran, or the Saudi desire to curtail Syria's regional influence. Instead, prominent Saudi and Iranian officials – Prince Bandar bin Sultan and 'Ali Larijani – engaged in face-to-face discussions, while senior Hizbullah officials travelled to Jeddah to meet King Abdullah.[99] Despite this, underlying suspicions about the others' manipulation and meddling in Lebanon remained with Iranian media coverage of developments in Lebanon continuing to be deeply critical of Riyadh's involvement, binding March 14 to the Saudi position.[100]

Saudi concerns were exacerbated in the early months of 2008, best seen in the controversy around Hizbullah's phone network, which was perceived as a means of eroding the sovereignty of the Lebanese government. By this point, Lebanese cabinet ministers questioned the legality of Hizbullah's private communications network, which ran in parallel to that of the Lebanese state.[101] For many in the Kingdom, the eruption of violence across West Beirut and Hizbullah's occupation of pro-Saudi media outlets – including those owned by Saad Hariri – revealed the limits of coordination with Tehran. This development points to the ability of domestic developments to shape regional currents. Amidst rising concerns about Hizbullah's influence in Lebanon, in conversation with US Ambassador David Satterfield, Prince Sa'ud al-Faysal called

[99] Leila Bassem, 'Hezbollah Fawaz with Saudi King', *Reuters* (21.01.07), www.reuters.com/article/us-lebanon-hezbollah-saudi-idUSL0313236420070103).

[100] 'Mavaze 14 Mars by mozoue Arabistan Saudi gereh khordeh' ['The Positions of March 14 Are Tied to the Saudi Position'], *Fars News Agency* (29.04.08).

[101] Lina Khatib, 'Hezbollah's Ascent and Descent', *Turkish Policy Quarterly* 14:1 (2015), 105–11.

for a 'security response' to counter Hizbullah's gains, proposing the establishment of an 'Arab force' to prevent the 'Iranian takeover' of Lebanon.[102]

By May 2008, tensions across Beirut had dramatically escalated. In response to government decisions, the Party of God stationed gunmen across the predominantly Sunni neighbourhoods of West Beirut, surrounding the residence of Saad Hariri and prompting him to turn to the army for protection. In doing this, Hizbullah turned its weapons inwards against Lebanese citizens, directly contradicting claims that the arsenal was solely to be aimed at Israel. Fearing the escalation of violence and the power of Shi'a militias, the Saudi ambassador fled Beirut on a private yacht. A standoff quickly followed between representatives from the two political blocs which was later resolved through Qatari mediation that ensured Hizbullah and its bloc veto power within a national unity government.[103] Ultimately, the events of 2008 demonstrated the impotence of opposition to Hizbullah and, as one Saudi analyst put it, 'the emperor was proven to have no clothes'.[104]

The years that followed saw Hizbullah consolidate its position in Lebanese politics, supported by Iran and a veto that allowed the group to keep its weapons. The veto helped ensure the weakness of opposition movements, blocking parliamentary elections and leaving the March 14 alliance increasingly reliant on external backers whose attentions were elsewhere. This position was reinforced by Iranian coverage of Lebanese politics. The Iranian newspaper *Fars News* argued that the political position of March 14 is 'bound to the Saudi position',[105] a point that was later also made by the reformist newspaper *Hambastagi*.[106]

Acknowledging the limitations of its capital and an inability to address Iranian power in Lebanon, Saudi Arabia reached out to Syria in 2010 in an attempt to erode Tehran's influence. In a meeting held at the presidential palace in Baabda, overlooking Beirut, King Abdullah and Bashar al-Assad sought to prevent Lebanon descending into a similar crisis to that of 2008, triggered by the impending Special Tribunal. Yet other considerations were also at play. In comments made at the end of the meeting, Bassim Shab, a representative of Hariri's Future Movement

---

[102] 08RIYAD768_a, Lebanon: SAG FM Says UN Peace Keeping Force Needed' (14.05.08), https://wikileaks.org/plusd/cables/08RIYADH768_a.html.

[103] Lina Khatib, Dina Matar, and Atef Alshaer, *The Hizbullah Phenomenon: Politics and Communication* (London: Hurst, 2014).

[104] Interview with Saudi analyst.

[105] 'Mavaze 14 Mars by mozoue Arabistan Saudi gereh khordeh'.

[106] 'Diplomasiye ashefte Arabistan dar Lobnan' ['Saudi Arabia's Messy Policy in Lebanon'],' *Hambastagi Online* (30.04.08).

suggested that 'the issue of the tribunal seems in a way to have been secondary to the support of stability, to the role of the state, with Saudi Arabia and Syria working together to prevent any sectarian flare-ups'.[107] In the meeting, privileging the Lebanese state over factions in an effort to ensure stability was paramount, with all parties – domestic and international – fearing the disintegration of the state.[108] Yet for many Saudis, Iran's influence was a key contributor to such concerns, with Tehran's support for Hizbullah and the advocacy of an alternative principle of vision – defined by resistance and anti-Israeli sentiment – at odds with the view from Riyadh.[109]

Sectarianism and Geopolitics

After the resignation of Egyptian president Hosni Mubarak on 11 February 2011, Lebanese message boards were full of people urging mobilization around the modified chant 'the people want the fall of the sectarian regime'. Frustration with the political, social, economic, and religious *zu'ama* was widespread, resulting in anger with the status quo, yet this burgeoning protest movement was unable to successfully navigate political structures. While political elites across the political spectrum had been condemned, Hassan Nasrallah remained untouched, standing alone as the central figure of resistance. The escalation of protests and ensuing deployment of survival strategies from regimes across the Middle East led to an increase in tensions along sectarian lines, reinforced by the deployment of capital across political fields, particularly in the context of the rivalry between Saudi Arabia and Iran.[110] The presence of a shared normative environment meant that these processes quickly resonated across the region, reflecting the permeability of political projects and, within this context, a number of states became sites of geopolitical competition, drawing in regional and international actors who were able to interact with local actors along a range of different lines.

As protesters took to the streets of the Syrian capital demanding political reform, Hizbullah faced an existential crisis, torn between protesters who represented 'the downtrodden' and a key ally, responsible for the oppression. The fall of the Assad regime would deprive the Party of God of weapons and access to logistical supply routes to Iran, leaving

---

[107] Jim Muir, 'Historic Saudi-Syrian Beirut Visit Shows Arab Concern', *BBC News* (31.07.10), www.bbc.co.uk/news/world-middle-east-10825228.
[108] Salloukh, 'The Syrian War'.
[109] This point was made in conversation with Saudis about Iranian influence in Lebanon.
[110] Mabon, *Houses Built on Sand.*

the group potentially caught between Israel and a possible pro-Saudi regime in Syria. With this in mind, Hizbullah embarked on a 'necessary war of choice in Syria', primarily designed to prevent the collapse of a key ally.[111] Yet the decision to become involved came at a heavy price, not only in terms of human and economic losses but also in damage to Hizbullah's legitimacy. Previously positioned at the vanguard of resistance against Israel, the Party of God was now complicit in the widespread repression of Syrian protesters. In response, key Hizbullah figures claimed that their involvement in the conflict was essential not only in preserving the Assad regime but also in protecting both Syria and Lebanon from the threat posed by Salafi-jihadi *takfiri* groups who had been attacking Shi'a towns across Lebanon's border with Syria.[112]

The emergence of Da'ish in summer 2014 strengthened such claims and posed a serious challenge to regional politics as the group positioned itself as the protectors of Sunni Muslims. For Hizbullah, Da'ish posed a threefold challenge: first, to Lebanon; second, to Shi'a Muslims and their holy sites across Iraq and Syria; and third, to the *umma* broadly.[113] In response to these fears, Hizbullah took the fight to Da'ish. According to Nasrallah, if the Party of God had not 'intervened in Syria the right way and at the right time, Da'ish would be in Beirut now'.[114]

Other officials supported this view. Sheikh Nabil Kaouk, deputy head of the Executive Council, argued that the 'terrorist threat on Lebanon is actual, real and continuous ... ISIS's decision has been announced. Their pretended slogan is to create the Islamic State in Iraq and Greater Syria, which includes Lebanon.'[115] The narrative of Karbala played a central role in efforts to justify Hizbullah's actions, providing support to the 'downtrodden' of the region, albeit prompting allegations of hypocrisy through their support to Assad and his regime. Moreover, in addition to supporting Shi'a Muslims, it was proclaimed that 'Hezbollah is willing to sacrifice for Iraq five times as much as we sacrificed in Syria for the significantly more important holy places.'[116] Yet Hizbullah also

[111] Aram Nerguizian, 'Assessing the Consequences of Hezbollah's Necessary War of Choice in Syria', *Centre for Strategic and International Studies* (17.06.13), http://csis.org/publication/assessing-consequences-hezbollahs-necessary-war-choice-syria.

[112] For more on this, see the text of Hassan Nasrallah's interview with Jean Aziz on OTV, reproduced in *al-Safir* (04.12.13).

[113] Mabon, 'The Circle of Bare Life', p. 17.

[114] 'Nasrallah: ISIS Would Be in Beirut If Not for Hezbollah Intervention in Syria', *Al Akhbar* (17.06.14), http://english.al-akhbar.com/node/20207.

[115] 'Hezbollah: ISIS Wants Lebanon', *Daily Star* (31.08.14), www.dailystar.com.lb/News/Lebanon-News/2014/Aug-31/269106-hezbollah-Daesh-wants-lebanon.ashx#axzz3CGYeUT5Y.

[116] Paula Asith, 'Lebanon's Hezbollah Ready to Fight ISIS in Iraq', *al-Sharq al-Awsat* (25.06.14), www.aawsat.net/2014/06/article55333611.

sought to downplay sectarian tensions, cautious at the potential for deepening Sunni-Shi'a divisions and the possible repercussions for domestic politics, caught between competing principles of vision and a divisive habitus.

While giving a speech marking the eighth anniversary of the 2006 war, Nasrallah warned of the dangers posed by Da'ish:

This danger does not recognize Sh'ias, Sunnis, Muslims, Christians, Druze, Yazidis, Arabs or Kurds. This monster is growing and getting bigger. I call on every Lebanese, Palestinian, Iraqi, Syrian and any Gulf national to leave sectarian intolerance behind and think that this phenomenon is not a threat against Shi'a only. No one should regard this battle as a sectarian one, it is a takfiri war against anyone who opposed it.[117]

In spite of his words, Hizbullah's actions in Syria were at odds with Nasrallah's aspirations to transcend sectarian divisions. Fearing a spill over of the Syrian conflict into Lebanon and an increased threat from Da'ish, the Interior Ministry, under Nohad Machnouk - a March 14 deputy - opened dialogue with the Party of God over security matters. This move brought Lebanese Sunni, Shi'a, and Christian together in the face of a serious security risk, but provoked serious concern amongst many in Saudi Arabia. This concern would grow in the years that followed, culminating in Saad Hariri's fateful trip to Riyadh in late 2017.

Domestically, the Lebanese political system remained in stasis as the two blocs prevented any institutional movement until 2016 when Michel Aoun was elected president. During this period of deadlock, the leaders of March 8 and March 14 sought to mobilize their followers as political expression moved from the parliament to urban spaces. Unsurprisingly, given the nature of the two blocs, March 8 was far better equipped to mobilize its followers, while the March 14 leadership lacked the cult of personality and gravitas that Nasrallah, Auon and others possessed. Although Hariri had worked to establish a political presence – as the scion of Rafiq he was the natural heir but lacked the political experience and charisma of his main rivals – he appeared ill equipped to balance the competing domestic and regional challenges. Moreover, his own position had become increasingly problematic in the years before his sojourn to Riyadh, driven by the erosion of political, social, and economic capital, resulting in diminishing support from the March 14 base, underpinned by doubts about his ability to counter Hizbullah.

In spite of this, Saudi Arabia continued to support the Lebanese government, offering around $3 billion to be distributed by Hariri across

---

[117] 'Nasrallah: ISIS Is a "Real Existential Danger" to the Whole Region', *Al Akhbar* (15.08.14), http://english.al-akhbar.com/node/21153.

military and security actors in Beirut.[118] Financial support was also pro-vided to Salafist clerics in an effort to influence local communities. In spite of this funding, the Salafism that emerged was not homogenous, but rather interacted with local context, meaning that the Salafism practised in Tripoli differs dramatically from that practised outside of Lebanon. Beyond support for Sunni groups, Saudi Arabia also sought to culti-vate relations with other members of the March 14 bloc, notably Samir Geagea, the leader of the Lebanese Forces and long time rival of Michel Aoun. Lebanese Christians such as Boutros Harb, a former presidential candidate, also began to reach out to Saudi Arabia for support, albeit independent of Saad Hariri.[119] Harb requested money from Saudi Ara-bia to establish a political party,[120] while Geagea sent a representative to Saudi Arabia asking for financial assistance in the midst of a deteriorat-ing financial situation, before saying 'I'm broke. I'm ready to do what the kingdom demands.' To strengthen this request, Geagea declared that he was central in efforts to deter Hizbullah and their principles of vision.[121]

Despite the provision of financial support, Saudi Arabia continued to receive criticism from many across Lebanon. During the Ashura festival of 2015, Nasrallah expressed anger at the political situation in Lebanon and Saudi Arabia's military actions in Yemen, eliciting chants of 'Death to the Al Sa'ud' from his supporters.[122] The Kingdom's decision to execute the prominent Shi'a cleric Nimr al-Nimr along with forty-seven others in early 2016 resonated across Lebanon, resulting in protests outside the Saudi embassy in Beirut. Hizbullah referred to the execution as an assassination while the Supreme Islamic Shi'a Council called it a 'grave mistake'.[123]

The failure of the Lebanese government to condemn the storming of the Saudi mission in Iran provoked more anger across the Kingdom, which revoked $4 billion of funding for the Lebanese army.[124] Speaking

[118] Hugh Naylor, 'Rivals Tehran, Riyadh Pledge Billions to Lebanon's Army', *Washington Post* (04.11.14), www.washingtonpost.com/world/middle_east/rivals-tehran-riyadh-pledge-billions-to-lebanons-army/2014/11/03/1505b9d4-9cb4-4f22-af4a-d5a9ab867e5c_story.html.
[119] Doc12139, *The Saudi Cables*, https://wikileaks.org/saudi-cables/doc12139.html.
[120] Doc32628, *The Saudi Cables*, www.wikileaks.org/saudi-cables/doc32628.html.
[121] Doc53032, *The Saudi Cables*, www.wikileaks.org/saudi-cables/doc53032.html.
[122] Michel Nasr, 'Hizbullah Implemented the Operation Professionally, Israel Is Floundering', *al-Diyyar* (Beirut) (06.01.15); and Nour Samaha, 'Hezbollah's Death Valley', *Foreign Policy* (03.03.16).
[123] Sam Wilkin, 'Shi'ites across the Middle East Decry Execution of Saudi Cleric', *Reuters* (03.01.16), www.reuters.com/article/saudi-security-shiites/shiites-across-the-middle-east-decry-execution-of-saudi-cleric-idINKBN0UG0CQ20160103.
[124] 'Saudis Cut Off Funding for Military Aid to Lebanon', *New York Times* (20.02.16), www.nytimes.com/2016/02/20/world/middleeast/saudis-cut-off-funding-for-military-aid-to-lebanon.html.

with reporters under conditions of anonymity, an official in the Saudi Foreign Ministry declared that this decision was a direct consequence of Hizbullah's influence across the state, its 'terrorist acts' across the region and its 'political and media campaigns' against the Kingdom.[125]

An opinion piece published in the *Khaleej Times* supported the Saudi decision:

Lebanon's failure to support Saudi Arabia was against the spirit of Pan-Arab consensus, and literally undermined the special relationship that both the countries have had all these years. Moreover, there are genuine concerns as far as the conduct of the Lebanese government is concerned, as it is seen acting as a proxy of Iran. While the Tehran-backed militia, Hezbollah, is part of the cabinet and the same is actively involved in Syria in supporting President Bashar Al Assad, it was more of a conflict of interest in the light of Saudi Arabia's stance over the dispute ... While extremist outfits, including Daesh, were knocking on the doors of Lebanon, Riyadh thought it appropriate to buck up Beirut's line of defense so that it could be in a better position to ward off the fallout from Syria. But Lebanon is unresponsive, and even refused to sign Saudi-drafted resolutions condemning the attacks. Lebanon's shift towards Iran and its over-reliance on Hezbollah are likely to act as a destabilizing factor, and harm its relations with the Arab fraternity.[126]

The remarks reflect a broader frustration amongst actors in the Gulf that many across March 14 had failed to do enough to counter Hizbullah's dominance across the state and in the government itself, perhaps emblematic of the contrasting levels of capital deployed by Hizbullah and March 14. Two days after the decision, Ashraf Rifi, the Lebanese justice minister, resigned from the cabinet and accused Hizbullah of fermenting the political crisis that had left the state paralyzed. Rifi's decision was commended by Samir Geagea, who expressed concern at the deterioration in relations with Saudi Arabia.

In Saudi documents released by Wikileaks, Geagea pleaded with Saudi Arabia for financial support in 2012 when his party faced serious financial challenges to the point that they were unable to afford protection for Geagea. In a letter sent by the Kingdom's ambassador to Lebanon, 'Ali Awad Asiri to Prince Sa'ud al-Faysal, then foreign minister, Geagea professed readiness 'to do what the kingdom asks him to do', particularly with regard to 'pushing back Hezballah and its allies in Lebanon'. Forwarding the letter to King Abdallah, Sa'ud advocated

---

[125] Josh Wood, 'Saudi Arabia Cancels $4bn Aid Package for Lebanon's Security Forces', *The National* (19.02.16).
[126] 'Saudi Arabia's Aid Halt to Lebanon is Justified', *Khaleej Times* (15.12.21), www .khaleejtimes.com/editorials-columns/saudi-arabias-aid-halt-to-lebanon-is-justified.

supporting Geagea as a means of countering the Kingdom's rivals in Lebanon.[127]

Speaking with Al Arabiya, Sami Gemayel, chief of the Phalange Party, warned that because of the failure to deal with Hizbullah's weapons, the Lebanese state had fallen hostage to the Party of God.[128] This decision to punish Hizbullah through the Lebanese state, leaving pro-Saudi allies in a state of limbo in the process, demonstrates how seriously the Saudi state views the challenge posed by Hizbullah, both in Lebanon and across the region.[129]

Regional events gave Lebanese figures the opportunity to score political points against the backers of domestic rivals. In an interview with a pro-regime Syrian TV channel later carried on Lebanese State TV, Hassan Nasrallah claimed that the 'Saudi defeat and Yemeni victory are very clear, which will be a relief for many of the region's governments.' He also stated that the Saudi defeat 'will be great and will reflect on the kingdom's internal affairs, its royal family and the entire region'. Nasrallah's remarks provoked concern amongst March 14 figures, prompting Ramzi Joreige, the information minister, to call Saudi Arabia's ambassador to Lebanon 'Ali Asiri to apologize, reaffirming 'that the Lebanese official media outlets are keen on appreciating Saudi Arabia'.[130]

Following these developments and the Party of God's ongoing activity in Syria, it was hardly surprising that the Saudi-led GCC took action directly against Hizbullah, declaring the group a 'terrorist organization'[131] amidst allegations of the group carrying out 'hostile acts' in the six member countries of the GCC. A week later, the Arab League also declared the group a terrorist organization, albeit with opposition from Lebanon and Iraq who expressed reservations. In response to these decisions, Bahrain expelled a number of Lebanese residents who

---

[127] '#SaudiCables: Ring-Wing Lebanese Chrstian Leader Asked Saudis for Money', *New Arab*, https://english.alaraby.co.uk/english/news/2015/6/22/saudicables-right-wing-lebanese-christian-leader-asked-saudis-for-money.

[128] 'Geagea warns of "more resignations" and Gemayel says Lebanon is a Hezbollah "Hostage"', *yalibnan* (21.02.16), http://yalibnan.com/2016/02/21/geagea-warns-of-more-resignations-and-gemayel-says-lebanon-is-a-hezbollah-hostage/.

[129] Matteo Legrenzi and Fred H. Lawson, 'Saudi Arabia Calls Out Hezbollah: Why Now?', *Middle East Policy* 23:2 (2016), 31–43.

[130] 'Lebanon Apologizes to Saudi over Nasrallah Speech', *World Bulletin* (08.11.15), www.worldbulletin.net/middle-east/lebanon-apologizes-to-saudi-over-nasrallah-speech-h157564.html.

[131] Reuters Staff, 'Lebanon's Hezbollah Condemns Gulf States for "Terrorist" Label', *Reuters* (03.03.16), www.reuters.com/article/us-mideast-crisis-lebanon-hezbollah-idUSKCN0W51RB.

were alleged to have proven links to or having expressed support for Hizbullah.[132]

Yet the inability of local allies to follow up on regional efforts to curtail Hizbullah's actions prompted frustration in Riyadh, demonstrating the capacity of local actors to exert agency against external patrons. In particular, Hariri's decision to continue dialogue with Hizbullah over security was a source of anger. The dialogue went against the strategic vision articulated by those in Riyadh who had taken steps to curtail Hizbullah's influence through the designation of the group as a terrorist group, ultimately prompting Hariri's trip to the Kingdom.

By 2018, elections returned Hariri as prime minister albeit with a dramatically reduced influence of March 14 in the political system. March 8 won more than 56 per cent of parliamentary seats, with March 14 taking slightly over 33 per cent. Yet the two blocs worked together to maintain the government, continuing a tacit acknowledgment of the need to collaborate to ensure the survival of the elite. Having resigned a second time in the summer of 2019 amidst rising pressure across the Lebanese political spectrum, confidence in Hariri began to plummet, prompting unrest within the Sunni community. Clashes broke out in Tariq el-Jedideh, a Sunni stronghold, as families shifted their allegiance from Saad to his half brother Bahaa. Yet as the following months would reveal, unrest was not limited to the Sunni community.

'All of them' means 'all of them'

As parabolic forces continued to shape Lebanese politics, it was hardly surprising that there would eventually be a form of resistance against the political status quo. On 27 October, the thirtieth anniversary of the Tai'f Accords, protesters took to the streets expressing anger at communal elites and what Rima Majed referred to as a system of 'sectarian neoliberalism', predicated on the fusion of power sharing with a fierce neo-liberal economics, financial capitalism, and deregulation.[133] Anger at the complex relationship between political and religious elites, embedded within the post-Tai'f agreement and the neo-patrimonial economic system – supported by *wasta* and clientelism – was widespread, cutting across communal groups. Chants of *thawra, thawra* ('revolution, revolution') rang across cities in Lebanon, supported by the refrain *kellon y'ani*

---

[132] 'Bahrain Expels Lebanese over "Hezbollah Links"', *Al Manar* (14.03.16), http://archive.almanar.com.lb/english/article.php?id=260434.

[133] Rima Majed, 'Lebanon and Iraq in 2019: Revolutionary Uprisings against "Sectarian Neoliberalism"', *TNI Longreads* (27.10.21), https://longreads.tni.org/lebanon-and-iraq-in-2019?fbclid=IwAR0o4MQi_a1BSYjYhe3BzKTKgSJSBvpodn2brxSfN frhM1miOHiOGfBbz8w.

kellon ('all of them means all of them') in a vocal rejection of sectarian politics, corruption, political elites, habitus and principles of vision.

In this tumultuous period, the ordering of life in Lebanon after the Tai'f agreement was called into question. Unlike other protest movements across the region, in Lebanon protesters were concerned with domestic issues rather than calls for an end to US or Iranian activity. Facing this challenge, Hizbullah doubled down on its sectarian identity, retreating, as Bassel Salloukh observes, to its 'sectarian citadel'.[134] This strategy is at odds with that of the protest movement broadly, which sought to cultivate a cross-sectarian and inclusive identity. Indeed, this tension between domestic anchoring and what Helle Malmvig and Tamirace Fakhoury have termed 'geopoliticization'[135] – discursive efforts to point to foreign manipulation of domestic affairs – results in a parabolic struggle for influence that was ultimately paused by the outbreak of Covid-19. The protests resumed once more in summer 2020 after the devastating Beirut port blast which exacerbated socio-economic challenges and further eroded the capital of communal elites.

Despite the devastating conditions facing many across the state, regional dynamics continued to impact on Lebanon. Following critical remarks about Saudi military actions in Yemen from Information Minister George Kordahi in October 2021, the Kingdom withdrew its ambassador 'for consultation' and ordered Lebanon's envoy to the Kingdom to leave. Kordahi, a former TV host, referred to the war in Yemen as 'absurd' and suggested that the Houthis have the right to defend themselves. Although recorded before Kordahi was named information minister in the government of Prime Minister Najib Mikati, the remarks were deemed 'offensive in Riyadh' and highlighted the inability of the Lebanese government to curtail the influence of Hizbullah in Lebanese politics and, by extension, beyond.[136] Speaking with Reuters, Prince Faysal bin Farhan Al Sa'ud, the Kingdom's foreign minister, stressed the importance of 'the government in Lebanon or the Lebanese establishment [forging] a path forward that frees Lebanon from the current

---

[134] Bassel F. Salloulkh, 'The Sectarian Image Reversed: The Role of Geopolitics in Hezbollah's Domestic Politics', *POMEPS Studies 38* (2020), https://pomeps.org/pomeps-studies-38-sectarianism-and-international-relations.

[135] Helle Malmvig and Tamirace Fakhour, 'Takes of the Unexpected: Will the Lebanese Uprising Stay Clear of Attempts at Geopolitization?', *POMEPS: Sectarianism and International Relations* (March 2020), https://pomeps.org/tales-of-the-unexpected-will-the-lebanese-uprising-stay-clear-of-attempts-at-geopolitization-1.

[136] Sarah El Deeb, 'Explainer: Why Saudi Arabia Is Upset, Lashing Out at Lebanon', *Associated Press* (02.11.21), https://apnews.com/article/entertainment-business-lebanon-saudi-arabia-beirut-787c1e342e3a46cdb11efc888f71f580.

political construct, which reinforces the dominance of Hezbollah'.[137]
Ultimately, the failure to establish a robust opposition to Hizbullah –
and by extension, Iran – either in the Sunni or Christian community,
coupled with the financial cost meant that Saudi Arabia ultimately took
the decision to 'give up' on Lebanon.[138]

Beyond this, the Saudi decision to suspend imports will have a devastating impact on the crippled economy while restrictions on flights will
dramatically lower remittances which have offered a small degree of hope
to those previously able to draw upon them.[139] In such conditions, actors
able to draw upon financial or political capital will become increasingly
influential across Lebanon's political field. Despite the widespread anger
of 2019, the crisis may well allow sectarian elites and their reserves of
social capital to reassert their position, rejecting the anti-sectarian protest movement in the process.

Conclusions

Lebanon has long been viewed as a key site in the rivalry between Saudi
Arabia and Iran, full of symbolic importance and strategic value. The
power-sharing arrangement of political life left Lebanon open to competition between different *nomoi*. From the formation of the modern
Lebanese state, the organization of political along sect-based lines has
contributed to the state's permeability, allowing regional powers to support local groups and giving domestic movements the opportunity to
position themselves within broader regional currents. In this climate,
the principles of vision and the Lebanese habitus have remained largely
static, until late 2019 being defined by sectarian power sharing, clientelism, and the capital of the *zu'ama*. Yet the onset of the October
Revolution was the articulation of a new principle of vision, opening up
competition between protesters and their social capital against the sectarian elite and their coercive capital.

The way in which Lebanon's divided society has been ordered created conditions that have routinely allowed for external penetration.
While initially top down, over time, groups across Lebanon, particularly
Hizbullah but to a lesser extent even Saad Hariri, were able to position
their aspirations clearly within the agendas of foreign powers. After the

[137] Aziz El Yaakoubi, 'Crisis with Lebanon Rooted Hezbollah Dominance – Saudi Minister',
Reuters (30.10.21), www.reuters.com/article/us-lebanon-crisis-saudi-minister-idAFKB
N2HK0HE.
[138] Interview with Saudi analyst.
[139] David Gardner, 'Rich Gulf Patrons Turn the Screws on a Bankrupt Lebanon', *Financial
Times* (03.11.21), www.ft.com/content/fc36ad5b-bbbb-4e3f-b2de-21cc5f19245e.

revolution, the nature of competition for influence in Lebanon dramatically shifted following improved clerical relations between the Shi'a of the south of the country and Iran provided Tehran with a great deal of influence and easy successes, seen in the ease of exporting the goals of *veleyat-e faqih* into Lebanon, much to the concern of Saudi Arabia.

The end of the civil war gave the key Saudi-ally Rafiq Hariri opportunities to re-imagine Beirut, yet through this process, neo-patrimonial relationships working within the contours of the sect-based ordering of life exacerbated divisions between communities and embedded corruption across the state. The Cedar Revolution triggered by Hariri's murder in 2005 brought about an end to Syrian influence but further deepened schisms within society, supported by – and shaped by – external backers.

Regional developments helped entrench domestic schisms, not just through the provision of material and ideational support by foreign powers, but through allowing local actors to position themselves in such a way as to facilitate this support. In part, groups across the Lebanese state sought to cultivate external patrons to secure their position internally, in part by positioning themselves against their patron's rivals. While initially occurring along sectarian lines, the entrenchment of the March 8 and March 14 camps added an additional layer of complexity to the cultivation of alliances and gave external patrons options to counter regional rivals.

While March 8 and March 14 actors have both sought to exert agency in the face of their regional patrons, Hizbullah has been more successful than Saad Hariri and the March 14 bloc in securing their goals, enforcing a dominant habitus based on their principles of vision, albeit not uncontested. This perhaps reflects the increasing importance of the Party of God to Iran and shared principles of vision within both the transnational field and domestic political field. In contrast, Saudi relations with a fragmented March 14 camp have typically been predicated on economic interests and a desire to counter Hizbullah and Iran, with limited scope for agency, as Saad Hariri experienced in 2017. There is little doubt that the transnational field has a dramatic impact on the Lebanese domestic political field, yet the complexities of local context mean that these interactions - through shared habitus and principles of vision - play out in contrasting and often surprising ways to other states in the region.

6   Syria

On 14 June 2018, the opening match of the 2018 football World Cup pitted hosts Russia against Saudi Arabia in front of a crowd of 78,011 at Moscow's Luzhniki Stadium. While hardly a heavyweight sporting contest, the fixture prompted a great deal of diplomatic curiosity as Russia's President Vladimir Putin came face to face with Saudi Arabia's Crown Prince Mohammed bin Salman. In what proved to be an awkward exchange for FIFA president Gianni Infantino, caught between Putin and MbS, the two statesmen spent the afternoon engaged in amicable discussions while around 1,500 miles away in Damascus, Syria's President Bashar al Assad continued to direct military forces supported by Russia and Iran in defence of his regime, against rebels who had previously received support from Saudi Arabia.

Syria has long been an integral player in the Middle East, positioning it central to shape – and be shaped by – regional currents. In *The Struggle for Syria*, published in 1965, Patrick Seale argued that Syria deserved special attention as 'a mirror of rival interests on an international scale'. Seale goes on to suggest that Syria's 'internal affairs are almost meaningless unless related to the wider context, first of her Arab neighbours and then other interested powers'.[1] Although made at the height of the pan-Arab movement, Seale's observations ring eerily true half a century later, where Syria remains a 'mirror of rival interests on an international scale'.

Building on Seale's premise, it was hardly surprising that after the Arab Uprisings, the nature of Syria's political landscape would be shaped by the interaction of local, regional, and international forces. The religious makeup of Syria's population coupled with the long-standing alliance between the Assad regime and the Islamic Republic meant that the rivalry between Saudi Arabia and Iran would play out across the state. The manifestation of conflict has drawn in an array of local, regional, and international powers seeking to further their own interests

---

[1] Patrick Seale, *The Struggle for Syria: A Study of Post-War Arab Politics, 1945–1958* (Oxford: Oxford University Press, 1965), pp. 1–2.

and capitalizing on the complexity of events on the ground. Described by Emile Hokayem as 'spill in', when a security vacuum attracts external intervention,[2] the importance of the Syrian conflict for a range of actors in the Middle East and beyond is easy to see.

Five decades later, Chris Phillips, in *The Battle for Syria*,[3] suggests that events in Syria are the greatest humanitarian crisis of the twenty-first century, a claim supported by data about the human cost of the conflict. The cover image of Phillips's powerful tome depicts hands bearing the flags of eight communities laying claim to parts of the Syrian state, yet the image – but not the monograph – is an oversimplification of the conflict. Conspicuous by their absence are representatives from Kurdish groups, Hizbullah, Iraqi PMFs, international organizations seeking to facilitate conflict reconciliation, and Syrians themselves all vying for influence. In spite of this complexity, the conflict is often reduced to a rivalry between Saudi Arabia and Iran, with other rivalries and relationships playing out within the context of a geo-sectarian rivalry that denies local agency to Syrian protesters – and the Assad regime – in the process.

The fragmentation that followed the emergence of pro-democracy protests in Syria in 2011 decimated the country, resulting in over 600,000 dead, two million wounded, five million forced out of the country, and a further seven million internally displaced, leading to serious schisms in an intractable conflict, while also deepening regional divisions.

In order to understand the ways in which the Saudi–Iranian rivalry plays out in Syria, it is essential to trace the evolution of the political field and its interaction with the transnational field. In doing so, the chapter critically reflects on the evolution of political life in Syria and the position of the state within broader regional currents, with a focus on Ba'athism, the Axis of Resistance, and the Arab Uprisings. Syria's importance within such movements meant that it became a state of interest for other regional powers, particularly seen in the aftermath of the Arab Uprisings.

The Quest for Order and Syria in the Transnational Field

Since 1970 Syria's political field has been dominated by the al-Assad family whose symbolic capital – supported by a coercive element – largely prevented the emergence of opposition groups. When such groups did propose alternative principles of vision, the regime's coercive machinery was largely able to decimate opposition movements, perhaps best seen in

---

[2] Emile Hokayem, 'Iran, the Gulf States and the Syrian Civil War', *Survival* 56:6 (2014), 59–86.

[3] Christopher Phillips, *The Battle for Syria: International Rivalry in the New Middle East* (New Haven: Yale University Press, 2016).

the Hama massacre in 1982. By 2011, however, alternative principles of vision emerging from the Arab Uprisings posed a serious challenge to the al-Assad regime. In what followed, the regime deployed coercive capital and its biopolitical mechanisms of control to ensure its survival.[4] When this failed to halt the progress of the opposition movements, Iran – Syria's key ally – and Hizbullah entered the fray, along with Russia, to support the embattled regime.

The centrality of Syria within the transnational field meant that what happened domestically would resonate internationally, and vice versa. The presence of elite Iranian troops in Syria prompted Saudi Arabia and other Arab Gulf states to provide support to opposition groups, leading to the rapid escalation of the conflict. For Iran, Syria occupies a central role in its vision of regional order – a part of the so-called 'Axis of Resistance' and gateway to Hizbullah – and the severity of the challenge to the al-Assad regime provoked serious concerns. Indeed, discourse positioned Syria as a 'vital cog' for Iran's regional aims,[5] along with Syria being the '35th province [of Iran] and a strategic province for us ... If we lose Syria, we cannot keep Tehran.'[6] The struggle to assert order and control across a state wilting under the pressure of an increasingly intractable conflict played a prominent part in entrenching regional and international actors in the fighting.

While often reduced to sectarian difference, the nature of the conflict and the contours of regional involvement are far more complex. For Genevieve Abdo, the Syrian conflict 'provided a mechanism for amplifying traditional sectarian conflict'.[7] Others such as Philippe Droz-Vincent hold a contrasting position, arguing that violent sectarianism is a consequence of the machinations of Bashar al-Assad and his father Hafez.[8] Writing in the inaugural SEPAD report, Chris Phillips suggests that cultivating sectarian difference in pursuit of foreign policy goals was not the desired strategy of Saudi Arabia or Iran, but rather reveals a 'degree of pragmatism' in their strategies to the conflict, with the funding of sectarian actors 'a plan B after backing other, more inclusive actors

[4] See Salwa Ismail, *The Rule of Violence: Subjectivity, Memory and Government in Syria* (Cambridge: Cambridge University Press, 2018) and Mabon, *Houses Built on Sand.*

[5] Edward Wastnidge, 'Iran and Syria: An Enduring Axis', *Middle East Policy* 24:2 (2017), 148–59.

[6] Cited in Eskandar Sadeghi-Boroujerdi, 'Head of Ammar Strategic Base: Syria Is Iran's 35th Province; If We Lose Syria We Cannot Keep Tehran', *Al Monitor – Iran Pulse* (14.02.14).

[7] Geneive Abdo, *The New Sectarianism: The Arab Uprisings and the Rebirth of the Shi'a-Sunni Divide* (Oxford: Oxford University Press, 2017), p. 2.

[8] Phillipe Droz-Vincent, 'State of Barbary' (Take Two): From the Arab Spring to the Return of Violence in Syria', *Middle East Journal* 68:1 (2014), 40.

failed'.[9] Instead, the construction and organization of Syria's political
field presented opportunities for actors – both local and regional – to
engage in competition for influence and to impose principles of vision.
The ensuing emergence of competing principles of vision and division
had a destructive impact on the state and although symbolic capital was
reasserted by the Assad regime, this came at a devastating price.

State Formation

Tracing the state building project in Syria, one sees the emergence of
the nation and minority groups in 1920 under the French mandate
(1920–46), which politicized both Syrian and sectarian identities.[10]
Much like in neighbouring Iraq, mandatory rulers and the considerable
violence that they exerted had a wide-ranging impact on life across the
state, brought about through rapid urbanization, education, and the
emergence of mass sympathy for independence from French rule and a
burgeoning Syrian nationalism.[11] In an effort to regulate their mandate,
the French Personal Status Law created the legal category of 'Syrian'
for the first time, while also defining people according to their religion,
creating majority and minority identities within the context of a broader
Syrian identity.[12]

The struggle between national and religious identities continued
after independence. In the years that followed, ideological movements
such as Ba'athism and pan-Arabism provided the means to circumvent this difference, yet beneath the surface religious, ethnic and tribal
identities remained. These cleavages also manifested in broader movements, including within Ba'ath politics, and in the spate of *coups d'etat*
that shaped Syrian politics in the decades after independence.[13] At this
point, aspiring elites were able to derive social capital from their sectarian identities, leading to allegations that the Ba'ath Party (in particular)
was propagating a sectarian agenda.

[9] Christopher Phillips, 'Sectarianism as Plan B', in Simon Mabon (ed.), *Saudi Arabia and Iran: The Struggle to Shape the Middle East* (SEPAD, 2018), www.sepad.org.uk/report/sectarianism-as-plan-b-saudi-iranian-identity-politics-in-the-syria-conflict.
[10] Benjamin Thomas White, *The Emergence of Minorities in the Middle East: The Politics of Community in French Mandate Syria* (Edinburgh: Edinburgh University Press, 2011), p. 1; J.L. Gelvin, *Divided Loyalties: Nationalism and Mass Politics in Syria at the Close of Empire* (Los Angeles: University of California Press, 1998), pp. 51–86.
[11] Daniel Neep, *Occupying Syria under the French Mandate: Insurgency, Space and State Formation* (Cambridge: Cambridge University Press, 2012), pp. 20–39.
[12] White, *The Emergence of Minorities*.
[13] Nikolaos Van Dam, *Destroying a Nation: The Civil War in Syria* (London: I.B. Tauris, 2017), pp. 29–30.

When Hafez al-Assad removed Saleh Jadid from power in November 1970, he embarked on a process of establishing his principle of vision for Syria, imposing symbolic capital and embedding key allies in prominent portfolios while populating the upper echelons of the military with members of the Alawi community. Assad also sought to woo Islamist circles, depicting himself as a pious Muslim and attaining a deeply contested *fatwa* from the Lebanese Shi'a cleric Musa al-Sadr that ruled that the Alawi should be considered as Shi'a Muslims.[14] Over the years that followed, this *fatwa* helped strengthen relations with Iran on the grounds of a shared religious identity.

When Hafez al-Assad became the country's first Alawi president on 22 February 1971, it ended the Syrian tradition of drawing a president from its Sunni majority. Although sectarian allegiance played a prominent role in securing his rule, this was not formally enshrined in the political fabric of the state and the Ba'ath Party was dismissive of the power and permanence of sectarianism; indeed, Nikolaos Van Dam goes as far to say that the Syrian Ba'athists wished to 'do away with primordial loyalties like sectarianism, regionalism and tribalism, which were considered to be despicable residues or illnesses of traditional society (*rawasib/amrad taqlidiyya*)'.[15]

Somewhat paradoxically, although deeply suspicious of sectarian identities, Ba'athist figures deployed traditional social channels for pragmatic purposes which, in turn, led to recruitment. Those from poor, rural backgrounds saw the military as an opportunity to climb the social ladder and escape a life of farming. Amongst the Alawi, this evoked charges of advocating sectarian difference, yet amidst the complexity of socio-economic factors this is perhaps better understood as the mobilization of networks of patronage in support of family members.[16] Under Hafez Assad, a malleable set of identities was constructed that was privileged in particular contexts and against specific threats, while the regime also continued communitarian practices started under the French, albeit while seeking to integrate Alawi experience within Sunni culture.[17]

Such strategies allowed the Syrian branch of the Muslim Brotherhood to capitalize on these conditions in an entrepreneurial manner,

[14] Yeuda U. Blanga, 'The Role of the Muslim Brotherhood in the Syrian Civil War', *Middle East Policy* 24:3 (2017), p. 49.
[15] Van Dam, *Destroying a Nation*, p. 47.
[16] Ibid., pp. 15–19. The dominance of Alawi in the military is documented in the same book, pp. 25–42.
[17] Christopher Phillips, 'Sectarianism and Conflict in Syria', *Third World Quarterly* 36:2 (2015), 365–6.

assassinating key Alawis and spreading anti-Alawi propaganda.[18] The anti-Assad campaign launched by the Brotherhood drew upon their prominent position within Syria, allowing them to derive a great deal of popular support from Sunnis across the state, which posed a serious threat to the Assad regime. After initial gains made by the Brotherhood, in the months and years that followed, the regime embarked on a systematic elimination of the group, deploying legal, political, and military strategies to eviscerate the Muslim Brotherhood. This process culminated in the artillery bombardment of Hama, a Brotherhood stronghold, which resulted in the deaths of between 20,000 and 30,000 and the destruction of the group as those who survived fled abroad.[19]

After power was transferred from Hafez to Bashar in June 2000, there were signs that sectarian importance might be loosened given that both he and his younger brother had married into Sunni families, resulting in the renaissance of the Muslim Brotherhood, albeit in different forms.[20] In spite of this, as Phillips notes, the political, social, and economic climate was deteriorating which 'laid the groundwork for the 2011 uprisings and increased the potential for sectarian resentment'.[21] Bashar quickly strengthened his position internally by removing stalwarts of his father's regime and surrounding himself with members of his extended family.[22] The new elite that quickly emerged under Bashar was driven by economic opportunism, perhaps best demonstrated by the president's cousin, Rami Makhlouf,[23] whose actions were emblematic of perceived regime excesses and the emergence of the *shahiba*, a violent pro-regime militia capitalizing on the conflict for self gain.[24]

Domestic hardships brought about by social instability and environmental degradation fed into rural–urban migration patterns, exacerbating urban tensions, adding to employment challenges and creating

---

[18] This was fuelled by the work of Ibn Taymiyya, an anti-Alawi thinker from the thirteenth century. See R. Lefevre, *Ashes of Hama: The Muslim Brotherhood in Syria* (London: Hurst, 2013).

[19] Ibid.

[20] Blanga, 'Role of the Muslim Brotherhood'; Hanna Batatu, 'Syria's Muslim Brethren', *Middle East Research and Information Project* 12 (1982); Thomas Pierret, *Religion and State in Syria: The* Sunni *'Ulama' from Coup to Revolution* (Cambridge: Cambridge University Press, 2013).

[21] Phillips, 'Sectarianism and Conflict', 366.

[22] R. Hinnebusch, 'Syria: From "Authoritarian Upgrading" to Revolution?', *International Affairs* 88:1 (2012), 95–113.

[23] Salwa Ismail, 'Changing Social Structure, Shifting Alliances and Authoritarianism in Syria', in Fred Lawson (ed.), *Demystifying Syria* (London: Sawi, 2009), pp. 13–28; Yassin Al Haj Saleh, *The Impossible Revolution: Making Sense of the Syrian Tragedy* (London: Hurst, 2017).

[24] Saleh, *The Impossible Revolution.*

large slums around key cities.[25] This migration aggravated existing socio-economic, political, and sectarian tensions, resulting in a serious challenge to a regime whose social reach was dramatically curtailed; as a result, the social contract holding regime and society together began to fray.[26] As Phillips notes, as state–society bonds were weakening amidst the strengthening of sect–society bonds, the social capital of sectarian entrepreneurs dramatically increased.[27] At this point, the regime's political capital had diminished, resulting in broad contestation across Syria's political field.

There is little doubt that the Assad regime was one of the key entrepreneurs responsible for exacerbating sectarian difference. In the formative stages of the 2011 uprisings, regime forces used excessive violence against protesters in an attempt to provoke retaliation against the much more powerful military presence. To facilitate this, regime figures revived fears of violent sectarianism, characterizing opposition figures as violent Islamists or jihadis targeting Alawi groups in the sectarianization of the conflict. The regime's actions exacerbated these fears, delivering sandbags to minority villages amidst suggestions that violent groups were close by, while also releasing Sunni extremists from state prisons to intensify these fears. In his role as British foreign secretary, Boris Johnson stressed that it was Assad's decision to free violent extremists from Syrian prisons, declaring him 'a recruiting sergeant for radicalism'.[28] Additionally, the regime also mobilized sectarian groups and symbols to shape the habitus and define principles of vision, drawing support from Hizbullah, Iran, and Iraqi Shi'a militia to ensure its survival.

Such developments exacerbated social and sectarian divisions within Syria's political and religious fields, with the added impact of currents in the transnational field becoming increasingly prominent in efforts to impose principles of vision on Syria. The increased salience of sect-based identities gave opportunities for regional actors to deploy religious and social capital in pursuit of their goals while also providing local actors with economic, social, and coercive capital in search of their own principles of vision, with devastating repercussions.

---

[25] Francesca De Chatal, 'The Role of Drought and Climate Change in the Syrian Uprising: Untangling the Triggers of the Revolution', *Middle Eastern Studies* 50:4 (2014), 521–35.

[26] Laura De Elvira and Tina Zintil, 'The End of the Ba'athist Social Contract in Bashar al-Assad's Syria: Reading Sociopolitical Transformations through Charities and Broader Benevolent Activism', *International Journal of Middle East Studies* 46:2 (2014), 329–49. See also Mabon, *Houses Built on Sand*.

[27] Phillips, 'Sectarianism and Conflict', 368.

[28] Boris Johnson, House of Lords testimony.

Syria's Regional Importance

Over time, the position of Syria within the context of Saudi–Iranian relations has fluctuated, its importance varies contingent on the complexities and currents of regional politics. All the while, however, Tehran's
relationship with Damascus provided Iran with an entry point into the
Arab world and the means through which to challenge accusations that
it operates solely as a *Persian* and Shi'a state, meaning that the survival of
the Assad regime was of paramount importance for Tehran.

A range of views has been presented seeking to understand the reasons for the alliance between Syria and Iran. In a study on the relationship, Anoushiravan Ehteshami and Raymond Hinnebusch assert that the
relationship between Syria and Iran is shaped by an external arena that
comprises both traditional security concerns and transnational forces.[29]
More recently, it has been suggested that relations between Iran and
Syria – and the axis of resistance broadly – comprise a form of deterrence.[30] Prior to the Iranian revolution of 1979, Hafez al-Assad was
deeply concerned about a possible Iranian–Israeli alliance, while also
disliking Iranian subservience to the United States under the Shah. As a
consequence, when the Phalavi regime was toppled, Syria was the first
Arab state to recognize the Islamic Republic, also offering substantial
military and political support in the formative years of the state.[31]

The roots of the relationship between Syria and Iran are found in the
sanctuary offered by Hafez al-Assad to members of the Iranian opposition who vehemently opposed the Shah's rule during the 1970s, including Khomeini who, with the support of Lebanon, was offered asylum
in 1978. Lebanon has occupied a central role in shaping relations
between Tehran and Damascus, largely facilitated by Musa al-Sadr,
an Iranian-born cleric who played a central role in the emergence of
the Lebanese Shi'a political consciousness. Al-Sadr was aware of the
importance of an external backer, developing close ties with the Assad
regime in the process. For Assad, al-Sadr played an important role

---

[29] Anoushiravan Ehteshami and Raymond A. Hinnebush, *Syria and Iran: Middle Powers in
a Penetrated Regional System* (London: Routeldge, 1997), p. 4.

[30] Hassan Ahmadian and Payam Mohseni, 'Iran's Syria Strategy: The Evolution of
Deterrence', in F. Osinga and T. Sweijs (eds.), *NL ARMS Netherlands Annual Review
of Military Studies 2020* (The Hague: Netherlands Annual Review of Military Studies,
2021).

[31] Shaul Bakhash, 'Iran's Relations with Israel, Syria and Lebanoin', in Miron Rezun
(ed.), *Iran at the Crossroads: Global Relations in a Turbulent Decade* (Boulder, CO:
Westview Press, 1990), pp. 116–17; Patrick Seale, *Assad: The Struggle for the Middle
East* (Berkley, CA: University of California Press, 1988), p. 353. Raymond Hinnebusch
and Anoushiravan Ehteshami (eds.), *The Foreign Policies of Middle East States* (Boulder,
CO, and London: Lynne Rienner, 2002), p. 297.

in developing relations with Shi'a groups in neighbouring Lebanon, which was central in exerting influence in Lebanon more broadly. In return, al-Sadr conferred religious legitimacy on Assad's own Alawite community[32] while also serving as a go between as links between Syria and Iran developed. After the revolution, Syria was the first Arab state to recognize the Islamic Republic – in spite of seemingly incongruent ideological outlooks[33] – and in the following years, the two shared a strategic vision, most notably concerning Saddam Hussein's Iraq.[34] In later years, the alliance between the two against Iraq, Israel, and the United States developed, but as Edward Wastnidge and others have argued, there is far more at play, stemming from the Islamic Republic's soft power strategies and efforts to project its influence through cultural practice in pursuit of its *nomos*.[35]

A strong strategic component is present in the relationship, emerging with the threat posed by Saddam Hussein during the 1980s. Shared concerns about Iraqi military activities strengthened the burgeoning relationship, prompting military co-operation best seen in the raid on the al-Walid airbase on 4 April 1981 which led to the destruction of around 20 per cent of Iraq's air force.[36] Systemic possibilities have created the conditions for an enduring alliance between Syria and Iran, predicated on efforts to balance power against the United States, Israel, and, more recently, the powerful Gulf monarchies. The organization of regional politics into conflicting blocs helped push Damascus and Tehran together, yet while subscribing to dramatically different forms of political organisation and ideological positions, the two have come to share security concerns.

In the years that followed, as Syria sided with Iran during the war with Iraq, it faced a great deal of pressure from other states across the region, many of whom accused Damascus of weakening Iraq's capability to launch a war against Israel. Amidst increased tensions between Syria and Iraq - and an abortive *coup d'état* against Saddam Hussein - Saddam forced all pro-Syria officials in Iraq to resign, severed diplomatic relations

[32] Martin Kramer, 'Syria's Alawis and Shiism', in Martin Kramer (ed.), *Shiism, Resistance, and Revolution* (Boulder, CO: Westview Press, 1987), pp. 237–54.

[33] Shireen Hunter, 'Syrian-Iranian Relations: An Alliance of Convenience or More?', *Middle East Insight* 4:2 (1985), 30–4.

[34] Jubin M. Goodarzi, *Syria and Iran: Diplomatic Alliance and Power Politics in the Middle East* (London: I. B. Tauris, 2009), pp. 16–18.

[35] On the alliance, see David Wallsh, 'Syrian Alliance Strategy in the Post-Cold War Era: The Impact of Unipolarity', *Fletcher Forum of World Affairs* 37:2 (2013), 107–23. On cultural practice, see Wastnidge, 'The Modalities of Iranian Soft Power' and Wastnidge, 'Iran and Syria'.

[36] Goodarzi, *Syria and Iran*, pp. 45–6.

with Damascus and provided financial resources to the Syrian Muslim Brotherhood in their struggle against the regime of Hafez al-Assad.[37] It was hardly surprising that these tensions pushed Syria closer to Iran, where actions in support of Tehran during the conflict included cutting an Iraqi oil pipeline, causing great financial expense to Baghdad.

Over the 1980s, Iran provided Syria with material, economic, and ideological support alongside the provision of oil at favourable rates. Tehran also spoke out when the international community condemned Syria as a terrorist supporter, declaring its intent to continue supporting the Assad administration.[38] In return, Syria provided Iran with a means of accessing the Arab world and circumventing allegations of conflict between Arabs and Persians. Discussing the Iran–Iraq War, a representative from the Office of the Supreme Leader argued that 'when some tried to portray the war as an Arab war against Persians, Syria contradicted this picture and stood side by side with Iran'.[39]

While a shared *nomos* and the organization of the transnational field created the conditions for collaboration, shared security concerns strengthened it. Both states felt isolated and threatened by imperialist forces, vulnerable amidst shifting geopolitical alliances.[40] Yet the alliance was shaped by a range of factors that created moments of possibility for both Damascus and Tehran, along with the shifting of power within the context of the relationship. While structural factors presented opportunities, tensions between Damascus and Tehran remained, particularly over the role of the secular state, Arab nationalism, and Iran's efforts to export the revolution. Yet after Khomeini's death, Iran's move towards a more pragmatic approach to foreign policy helped the relationship navigate these tensions.

As we have seen elsewhere, the establishment of the resistance axis brought together a range of groups united by shared visions of order, couched in anti-status quo aspirations. Comprising Iran, Syria, Hizbullah, and Hamas, the alliance brought together major Shi'a actors with the most vociferously anti-Israel Palestinian movement through common enemies, mainly Israel and the United States, and antagonism towards pro-Western status quo powers, notably Saudi Arabia, Jordan, and Egypt.[41] In spite of holding contrasting ideological positions and

---

[37] Ehteshami and Hinnebusch *Syria and Iran*, pp. 89–92.

[38] Chubin and Tripp, *Iran–Saudi*, p. 184.

[39] 'Iran's Security Is Due to the Wise Leadership of the Supreme Leader', Kayhan (12.09.14), http://kayhan.ir/fa/news/23898/.

[40] Ehteshami and Hinnebusch, *Syria and Iran*, p. 90.

[41] See Abbas William Samii, 'A Stable Structure on Shifting Sands: Assessing the Hezbollah–Iran–Syria Relationship', *Middle East Journal* 62:1 (2008), 32–53. Valbjørn and Bank, 'The New Arab Cold War', 15–21.

possessing independent interests and decision making channels, the resistance was loosely constructed around efforts to counter the transformation of regional politics towards the establishment of a pro-Western position. While relations within the axis are fluid, shaped by the contingency of local politics interacting with regional trends, links between Tehran, Damascus, and the Party of God increased in the years after the Arab Uprisings. This increase possessed strong military co-operation, much to the chagrin of Saudi Arabia, Israel, and the United States.[42] With this, as Shahram Akbarzadeh observes, Tehran views Syria as a 'lynchpin' of the Axis of Resistance. Relations between Damascus and Tehran have endured over 30 years and Syria remains the only Arab state to possess a security alliance with Iran.[43]

For Iran, Syria was a key ally in its outreach activities, in part because of its ability to support Hizbullah,[44] but also because its Arab identity helped circumvent the 'Arab vs Persian' narrative that had emerged after the revolution. It opened up new spaces of possibility, transcending claims of uniquely Shi'a and Persian interests.[45] Lebanon was such a space of possibility for both Tehran and Damascus, particularly amidst the Israeli occupation of the south and the presence of a pro-US government. As collaboration increased, spurred on by shared ideas of resistance, the two co-ordinated in an attempt to expel the United States and Israel, albeit leading to tensions amidst the rising influence of Hizbullah which limited the power of Amal, the traditional Syrian ally. Over the following years, Syria served as a conduit for Iran to pass arms to Hizbullah, while also supplying military hardware in its own right.[46] In return, Iran and Hizbullah officials became embedded within Syrian military decision-making structures, which would prove invaluable for the Assad regime in the years after the Uprisings.

In contrast, relations between Syria and Saudi Arabia oscillated between explicit rivalry and Riyadh's efforts to woo Damascus. In the years after Syrian independence, Saudi Arabia's stance towards the state was shaped by regional politics and competition, notably with the Hashemites in Jordan and the Arab nationalist movement whose successes

---

[42] International Crisis Group, 'Drums of War: Israel and the "Axis of Resistance"', *Crisis Group Middle East Report* 97 (2010), 6.

[43] Shahram Akbarzadeh, 'Why Does Iran Need Hezbollah?', *The Muslim World* 106 (2016), 134.

[44] Randa Slim, 'Hezbollah and Syria: From Regime Proxy to Regime Savior', *Insight Turkey* 16:2 (2014), 61–8; Phillips, *Battle for Syria*.

[45] Ibid., p. 58.

[46] Carl Anthony Wege, 'Hizbullah-Syrian Intelligence Affairs: A Marriage of Convenience', *Journal of Strategic Security* 3 (2011), 1–14; Yoel Guzansky, 'The Nature of the Radical Axis', *Military and Strategic Affairs* 2:2 (2010), 59–77.

resulted in the formation of the United Arab Republic. After the fall of the Egyptian–Syrian union, scope for an improvement in Syrian–Saudi ties increased, yet the Syrian regime's involvement in the Yemen conflict, supporting Leftist forces and propaganda calling for the fall of the House of Sa'ud, prevented this rapprochement.[47] The following years saw relations between the two deteriorate further under the Ba'athist regime of Jadid, which openly targeted monarchical regimes and provided support to Saudi opposition groups.[48]

Changes in the transnational field brought about by the death of Gamal Abdel Nasser and the coming to power of Hafez al-Assad created opportunities for the re-calibration of relations between Riyadh and Damascus. Nasser's death removed what the Saudis saw as their biggest regional challenge at this time and allowed the Kingdom to play a more proactive role across the region.[49] This was facilitated by the work of King Faisal, whose diplomatic skills and popularity in Arab politics had opened up relations with a number of states. The pragmatic position deployed by Assad allowed a Saudi aid package of $200 million to go to Damascus in 1972.[50] This economic assistance continued across the decade, providing much needed support to Damascus after the 1973 war with Israel. Following Sadat's peace deal with Israel, Syria took on a greater importance for Saudi Arabia, allowing the Kingdom to be on the 'front-line' in the struggle against Israel and to demonstrate its 'Arab credentials'.

While geopolitics clearly had a role to play in this thawing of relations under Assad, there was also a domestic dimension to this, with the president drawing on key social and tribal groups in an effort to ensure the survival of his regime. Indeed, Assad quickly surrounded himself with the tribes of Eastern Syria who possessed historical links to the Saudi state, along with Sunni bourgeoise groups in Syria who also possessed strong links with Saudi Arabia and under Assad found themselves occupying a key role within the state.[51]

Yet points of difference began to emerge once more as civil war broke out across Lebanon in 1975. Riyadh used its influence over Syria to bring about a temporary halt in the fighting. The establishment of an

---

[47] S. Sunayama, *Syria and Saudi Arabia. Collaboration and Conflict in the Oil Era* (London: I.B. Tauris, 2007), p. 30.

[48] Kerr, *The Arab Cold War*, p. 127.

[49] Sunayama, *Syria and Saudi Arabia*, p. 34.

[50] D. Holden and R. Johns, *The House of Saud* (London: Pan MacMillan, 1982).

[51] Madawi al-Rasheed, *Politics in an Arabian Oasis: Rashidis of Saudi Arabia* (London: I.B. Tauris, 1997); Torsten Schoel, 'The Hasna's Revenge: Syrian Tribes and Politics in their Shaykh's Story', *Nomadic People* 15:1 (2011), 96–113.

Arab Deterrence Force which formally recognized the Syrian role in Lebanon came out of the 'Riyadh Agreement' of 1976, yet with competing agendas and visions in Lebanon emerging, cracks in the relationship deepened. Yet there were also instances of success, perhaps best seen in the Tai'f Accord of 1989 which brought an end to the Lebanese civil war. Moreover, scholars have also identified a number of shared strategic interests that brought the two together, including Riyadh's support for Syria's position on the front line of Arab–Israeli conflict;[52] Syrian efforts to mobilize Arab resources against Israel which correspond with Saudi Arabia's desire to *appear* committed to the cause;[53] the trade-off between Syrian military power and Saudi economic might, leaving the former well placed to balance against Iraqi expansionism;[54] while others argue that the two countries share a long-standing social, cultural, and historical connection.[55]

Between 1978 and 1990, the two states were able to maintain a working relationship predicated on avoiding competition over Arabism and Islamism and instead drew from 'shared identities', which created space for diplomatic wrangling as each side sought to exert pressure on the other.[56] As Francesco Belcastro observes, a number of foreign policy principles can explain Saudi actions at this time: 1) working to prevent the emergence of a (hostile) hegemonic power; 2) creating an 'Arab consensus' but one that poses minimal threats to the Kingdom's domestic policy; and 3) forging an alliance with a superpower to offer protection from external threats.[57] As we have seen, Syria was central to the first two prongs of this policy, yet it was dramatically tested by events in Iran.

After the transition from Hafez to Bashar, Damascus's relationship with Riyadh improved, with both capitals seeking to strengthen the relationship. For Saudi Arabia, consolidating Bashar's rule was seen as an important step for regional stability[58] while for Assad, a strong relationship with Saudi Arabia was deemed important to balance the threat posed by Saddam Hussein and against any possible US antagonism

---

[52] Eberhard Kienle, *Ba'th v. Ba'th: The Conflict between Syria and Iraq 1968–1989* (London: I. B. Tauris, 1990), p. 93.

[53] A. Drysdale and R. Hinnebusch, *Syria and the Middle East Peace Process* (New York: Council on Foreign Relations, 1991), p. 85.

[54] Elie Chalala, 'Syria's Support of Iran in the Gulf War: The Role of Structural Change and the Emergence of a Relatively Strong State', *Journal of Arab Affairs* 7:2 (1988), 119.

[55] Sunayama, *Syria and Saudi Arabia*, p. 4.

[56] Ibid., pp. 9–10.

[57] Francesco Belcastro, 'An Odd "Foreign Policy Couple"? Syria and Saudi Arabia 1970–1989', *Journal of Balkan and Near Eastern Studies* 22:1 (2020), 39.

[58] Bruce Riedel, 'The Return of Prince Bandar: Saudi's New Spy Chief', Brookings Institution (07.23.12).

post-9/11.[59] Yet relations quickly soured over conflicting positions on both the Israeli–Palestinian peace process and the US-led invasion of Iraq. It was hardly surprising then that Riyadh gave Washington its blessing to isolate Damascus from regional and international politics.[60]

The assassination of Rafiq Hariri in 2005 led to charges from Saudi Arabia that Assad had ordered the hit, resulting in a spat between the two states playing out in local media outlets along with demands that Syria withdrew forces from Lebanon, and calls for an international investigation into the assassination.[61] In spite of this, Saudi Arabia sought to limit instability in Syria – and beyond – predicated upon a general conservativism on regional affairs. Within this strategy, Saudi officials expressed concern at the burgeoning importance of sectarian identities in regional politics, most obviously seen in the emergence of March 8 and March 14 camps in Lebanon. The dangers of such realignment was expressed by Abd al-Rahman Rashed, a prominent media official in Riyadh, who argued that dividing regional politics into 'a homogeneous Shi'a crescent and a Sunni rectangle and opposing sectarian or even ideological groupings is counter productive'. Rashed also rejected the prominence of sectarian identity as the basis of authority, arguing that a 'stable Syria is needed to guarantee the stability of the region'.[62]

This inherently conservative position revealed broader concerns about links between Syria and Iran. A US diplomatic cable documented conversations between the US ambassador to Iraq Zalmay Khalilzad and Sa'ud al-Faysal and Muqrin bin Abd al-Aziz – the Saudi foreign minister and head of the general intelligence directorate, respectively – in which Faysal warned 'the more Syria feels isolated, the more it will strengthen its ties with Iran'.[63] In discussions with the US ambassador, Deputy Minister for Multilateral Relations Prince Turki bin Mohamad bin Sa'ud al-Kabeer advocated that reaching out to Syria was essential for achieving stability across the region. He argued that 'Syria had been isolated for too long', and suggested that cultivating relations with Damascus had become 'a critical part of the Saudis' overall strategy of 'squeezing Iran'.[64]

---

[59] 'Interview with President Bashar al-Assad', *al-Bab* (08.02.01).

[60] Simon Jeffery, 'The Arab League Summit', The Guardian (28.03.02).

[61] Bassel Salloukh, 'Syria and Lebanon: A Brotherhood Transformed,' *Middle East Research and Information Project* 35 (Fall 2005).

[62] Abdul Rahman al-Rashed, 'Between *Sunni* and *Shi'a*', *al-Sharq al-Awsat* (04.09.05); Carla E. Humud, 'Lebanon', Congressional Research Service (25.07. 17).

[63] 06RIYADH9_a, 'Saudi Views on Iranian and Syrian Activities in Iraq and Elsewhere' (02.01.06), https://wikileaks.org/plusd/cables/06RIYADH9_a.html.

[64] 09RIYADH1684_a, 'Saudis Say Syria "Isolated for too Long"' (30.12.09), https://wikileaks.org/plusd/cables/09RIYADH1684_a.html.

As Yehuda U. Blanga argues, these fear goes some way in explaining the reasons why Saudi–Syrian relations began to thaw in 2006.[65] In spite of calls for an international investigation into the Hariri assassination, Saudi officials sought to prevent a further escalation in regional tensions and refrained from blaming Assad or regime supporters for the murder. Yet this burgeoning rapprochement was not to last. The 2006 war between Israel and Hizbullah caused a great deal of consternation across the region, exacerbated by Syrian support for the Party of God.

During the war, then US secretary of state Condoleezza Rice argued that the world was witnessing the 'birth pangs of a new Middle East'; although largely correct, it was not in the way she had hoped. In the years that followed, the Axis of Resistance gained a great deal of popularity across the Arab world through opposing Israel and the United States, while internal ties were strengthened following a well-publicized dinner between Bashar al-Assad, Mahmoud Ahmadinejad, and Hassan Nasrallah that took place in Damascus in February 2010.[66]

Fearing the empowerment of Hizbullah and, by extension Iran, a number of leaders condemned Assad's behaviour. In response, Assad referred to those leaders who had criticized him as 'half men'. The 2006 war and its aftermath demonstrated the failure of Saudi efforts to bring Damascus into its sphere of influence.[67] It was hardly surprising that Riyadh's frustration resulted in a shift in policy, seeking to exert influence amongst anti-Assad and anti-Syria elements across the state and beyond, with repercussions particularly felt in Lebanon and the entrenchment of March 8 and 14 blocs. One example of this saw Prince Bandar bin Sultan sent to Washington to co-ordinate Saudi–US support for democratic movements in Syria. Tensions were felt as officials crossed paths at regional and international diplomatic events and in Lebanon amidst efforts to find a successor to Emile Lahoud yet Saudi and Syrian support for different candidates had a marked impact on political manoeuvrings.

Although on the face of it relations between the two states had soured, though back channel diplomatic efforts remained open. In early 2009, the Saudi king's son, Abd al-Aziz, visited Damascus, which paved the way for official reciprocal visits from senior political and military officials.[68] From this, Assad visited Saudi Arabia in September, during

[65] Yehuda U. Blanga, 'Saudi Arabia's Motives in the Syrian Civil War', *Middle East Policy* 24:4 (2017), 45–62.
[66] 'Hezbollah Chief Nasrallah metts Ahmadinejad in Syria', *BBC News* (26.02.10).
[67] Syria Comment, 'Saudis and Syrians ... Brothers or Rivals?', *al-Hayat* (05.03.07).
[68] Bassel Qudat, 'Making up at Last', *Al-Ahram Weekly* (19–25.02.09); Syria Comment, 'Sanctions on the Table', *Al-Arabiya* (05.03.09); 'Saudi FM Urges Joint Arab Strategy on Iran', *Al-Arabiya* (03.03.09).

which time he held talks with the king who, the following month, visited Damascus.[69] While Syria hoped to avoid Arab isolation through working with Saudi Arabia, the Kingdom's ultimate goal of prising Syria from the Iranian orbit was ultimately unsuccessful, with Damascus playing a key role in supporting Iran's principle of vision in the transnational field.

The Uprisings and Regional Contestation

As protesters gathered across Syria's public spaces on 15 March 2011, few envisaged the horrors of what was to follow. Syrians had a new, seemingly pro-Western president and it was largely accepted that a few token reforms would be made to take the sting out of the protest movement. Instead, the Assad regime responded with seemingly unrestrained violence, resulting in a rapid escalation that led to the onset of a brutal conflict.[70] Through these events, Syria evolved from being a key player across the Middle East to an arena in which regional politics plays out.

Although initially viewed as a civil war, the conflict quickly took on regional and international importance, creating possibilities for external actors to work towards their own geopolitical goals and to impose their principles of vision on the transnational habitus.[71] Much like other states affected by the uprisings, regional powers cultivated relationships with local actors and vice versa. Here, in these multi-directional relationships, spatial and temporal factors were central in determining behaviour. As a number of scholars have documented, the eagerness of regional actors to send material and ideological support to groups fighting in Syria played a prominent role in the escalation of the conflict, quickly demonstrating the extent of external interest in events across the state.[72]

The uprisings challenged the power and legitimacy of states in the region, with repercussions felt beyond the borders of those directly affected. The mobilization of myth-symbol complexes reverberated across the region beyond the arenas in which they were initially deployed. As one Syria analyst noted, 'People in Syria started calling for their rights because they did not have any, and later when they picked up arms to defend themselves, that is when the regional powers had the ability basically to influence the agendas of locals along the lines of sectarian discourse.'[73]

---

[69] www.reuters.com/article/us-ba-syria-saudi/saudi-king-in-damascus-to-mend-fences-with-assad-idUSTRE59630I20091007.

[70] Ismail, *The Rule of Violence*.

[71] Phillips, *Battle for Syria*.

[72] Ibid., p. 82.

[73] Testimony, Haid Haid.

The conflict that quickly followed the protests was quickly framed along sect-based lines as a consequence of the sectarianization of local politics.[74] In the early stages of the protests, the Assad regime released violent Sunni Islamists from prisons in an attempt to support the narrative that the regime was fighting a war against groups such as al-Qaʿida. A survey by *The Day After* showed the devastating repercussions of such actions, with almost three-quarters of respondents noting that they had experienced discrimination along sect-based lines.[75] Yet this practice of the regime supporting violent Sunni Islamists was not new. Indeed, as Hayder Al Khoei argued, the Assad regime had long sought to manipulate the agendas of groups such as al-Qaʿida for their own ends, perhaps most notably in 2003 when Sunni Islamists were incited to fight in Iraq.[76] The use of sectarianism as the principle of vision resonated across Syria's recent past, shaped both by domestic divisions and by the nature of the transnational field.

Following the Assad regime's brutal response to the protests, Riyadh called for Syria's suspension from the Organization of Islamic Co-Operation, a symbolic yet strategic move that sought to drive a wedge in the organisation states between those supporting Saudi Arabia and those supporting Iran. As tensions increased, the OIC became an increasingly prominent arena of rhetorical competition, with Saudi Arabia appearing victorious following the organization's vocal condemnation of Iran as a consequence of 'its continued support for terrorism' and for interfering in the domestic affairs of states across the Middle East.[77] The deployment of religious capital by Saudi Arabia against the Syrian state resonated across the transnational field – where (geo)politically charged Islamism had become principles of vision and division shaping the field – but also in Syria's political field. As both Chris Phillips and Lina Khatib argue, the sectarian components of the conflict emerged after the failure of other strategies.[78] The sectarianization of the conflict thus took place within Syria's political field and as a product of the

---

[74] See 'Syrian Opinions and Attitudes towards Sectarianism in Syria –Survey Study', *The Day After* (22.02.16), http://tda-sy.org/en/publications/english-sectarianism-in-syria-survey-study.html. Yet One should be careful with claims such as this, which once again belie the complexity of events on the ground, where wealthy Sunni families, Sunni Kurds and Turkmen can support the Assad regime for a range of different reasons.

[75] Ibid.

[76] Testimony, Hayder Al Khoei.

[77] Yesim Dikmen and Melih Aslan, 'Muslim Nations Accuse Iran of Supporting Terrorism: Summit Communique', *Reuters* (15.04.16), www.reuters.com/article/us-turkey-summit/muslim-nations-accuse-iran-of-supporting-terrorism-summit-communique-idUSKCN0XC1LQ. See also Salloukh, 'The Arab Uprisings'.

[78] Phillips, 'Plan B'.

organization of the transnational field. The uprising in Syria and conflict that quickly followed challenged both the Saudi and the Iranian *nomoi*, presenting opportunities to reconfigure the ordering of the transnational field.

Iran's policy towards Syria in the aftermath of the 2011 protests was shaped by a need to preserve both the Assad regime and its narrative of resistance. According to one former Iranian official, the agreement between Iran and Syria was fundamentally to 'preserve security'.[79] While Tehran was initially reluctant to become directly involved in fighting in Syria as a means of circumventing Arab sensitivities regarding the involvement of non-Arabs in the conflict, as the threat to al-Assad's regime increased, it calculated that maintaining al-Assad's rule was imperative and increased its involvement. Rhetoric from prominent Iranian officials supports such a claim, with President Rouhani asserting that Tehran would stand by the Assad regime 'until the end of the road'. In the same speech, covered by the state news agency IRNA, Rouhani also suggested that Iran 'had not forgotten its moral obligations to Syria and will continue to provide help and support on its own terms to the government and nation of Syria'.[80]

As protesters took to the streets across Syria, political elites in Saudi Arabia sensed an opportunity to reconstruct regional politics and 'win Syria back to the Arab fold'.[81] In spite of this, the Saudi response to the onset of protests was restrained and the first condemnation of the regime's response came three months after people took to the streets. In part, this reflected the growing proximity of Riyadh and Damascus in previous months,[82] but it also demonstrates the complexity of events in Syria as the protests increasingly took place along sectarian lines, leaving Saudi Arabia with little option but to support opposition groups. Reflecting this strategy, Prince Bandar bin Sultan, then president of general intelligence and a senior member of the royal family, was tasked with 'winning' Syria, an assignment he sought to achieve through funding rebel groups.[83] The appointment of Bandar led officials inside the

[79] Interview with former Iranian official.
[80] 'Iran's Rouhani Vows to Back Syria "Until the End of the Road"', *Reuters* (02.06.15), https://uk.reuters.com/article/uk-mideast-crisis-syria-iran/irans-rouhani-vows-to-back-syria-until-the-end-of-the-road-idUKKBN0OI0UN20150602.
[81] Madawi al-Rasheed, 'The Saudi Response to the "Arab Spring": Containment and Co-option', *Open Democracy* (10.01.12), www.opendemocracy.net/5050/madawi-al-rasheed/saudi-response-to-%e2%80%98arab-spring%e2%80%99-containment-and-co-option.
[82] Hassan Hassan, 'Old Myths Perpetuate Poor Analysis of Saudi', *The National* (17.01.16), www.thenational.ae/opinion/comment/old-myths-perpetuate-poor-analysis-of-saudi.
[83] Mariam Karouny, 'Saudi Edges Qatar to Control Syrian Rebel Support', *Reuters* (31.05.13), www.reuters.com/article/us-syria-crisis-saudi-insight-idusBre94u0ZV20130531.

American Central Intelligence Agency to believe that Riyadh was serious about removing Assad from power. Speaking to the *Wall Street Journal*, one official suggested that the Saudis are 'indispensable partners on Syria', wielding considerable influence on Washington.[84]

Grassroots activity across Syria and the ensuing polarization of sect-based difference that emerged after the uprisings was amplified and reinforced through the intervention of regional powers. Support from Riyadh, Tehran, and Doha was given largely along sect-based lines in an effort to increase the social, economic, and coercive capital of local actors. In doing this, competition to dominate Syria's political field was conditioned by the nature of the transnational field whilst also operating as a prominent front in competition to shape the transnational field, allowing local actors to cultivate support from regional backers and vice versa.[85] Over the following years, a violent and seemingly intractable conflict consumed Syria as local tensions played out within the context of systemic geopolitical rivalries in the Middle East and globally.

Iranian officials sought to demonstrate the importance of the conflict for Iran's geopolitical aspirations and the survival of the resistance axis. Acknowledging the importance of Syria, Iranian supreme leader 'Ali Khamenei stressed that 'Syria is on the front lines today; it is our duty to defend the Syrian resistance'[86] while Mohammad Jawad Zarif justified Iranian activity in Syria in support of 'the legitimate government of Syria'.[87] In the formative stages of the conflict, the elite IRGC sought to establish the Syrian National Defence Forces, a local equivalent of the Iranian *Basij* militia created by Khomeini to protect the revolution. Over time, however, this level of involvement would dramatically increase; by March 2016, members of the IRGC unit were supported by ground forces who were also stationed in Syria. In an attempt to legitimize this presence, prominent figures in the Islamic Republic sought to demonstrate the religious importance of supporting Assad, which proved integral in embedding volunteers in the conflict, particularly in the defence of Shi'a shrines. While volunteers comprised Shi'a communities from Afghanistan, Iraq, Pakistan, and beyond, Iranian

---

[84] Adam Entoush, Nour Malas and Margaret Coker, 'A Veteran Saudi Power Player Works to Build Support to Topple Assad', *Wall Street Journal* (25.08.13), www.wsj.com/articles/a-veteran-saudi-power-player-works-to-build-support-to-topple-assad-1377473580?tesla=y.

[85] Interview with Syrian author, 2018.

[86] 'Khamenei Says Iran's Duty to Defend Syria's Assad', *New Arab* (02.03.18), www.alaraby.co.uk/english/news/2018/3/1/khamenei-says-irans-duty-to-defend-syrias-assad.

[87] 'Interview with Iranian Foreign Minister: We Will Have Differences with US No Matter What', *Der Speigel* (16.05.15), www.spiegel.de/international/world/interview-with-iranian-foreign-minister-mohammad-javad-zarif-a-1033966.html.

individuals were also active, in part as a consequence of rhetoric from the likes of IRGC Major General Rahim Nowi-Aghdam, who argued that 'If you do not volunteer to fight in Iraq and Syria, I will go myself, and I will martyr myself in the defence of Sayyida Zeynab or the Shi'a shrines in Iraq.'[88]

Iranian support for Assad was strengthened by the presence of Hizbullah fighters in Syria. Although the Party of God began by providing strategic advice to the Syrian regime, supported by the deployment of a number of elite units around the shrine of Sayida Zaynab in southern Damascus, this military engagement rapidly increased following attacks from members of the Free Syrian Army. With Syrian forces lacking military discipline and, as many have observed, elite units 'operating more like local militias controlled by warlords rather than professional military commanders',[89] Hizbullah quickly became a key player in defending the Assad regime, working alongside Iran.

Positioned centrally within a trans-Shi'a network of fighters from across the world, the decision to become heavily involved in the conflict demonstrates the importance of Syria to both Iran and Hizbullah.[90] It also resulted in the transformation of Hizbullah from a Lebanese actor to a regional player devoted to defending Shi'a interest across the Middle East. In a speech on 24 May 2013, over a year after Hizbullah entered the Syrian conflict, Hassan Nasrallah declared that the 'battle is ours'. As Genevie Abdo suggests, this speech signified a turning point in Hizbullah's operations, moving from a Lebanese resistance actor to a regional power.[91]

The Islamic Republic's support for the Assad regime led to its most substantive military activity since the Iraq War. While initially advising Assad on how best to deal with the protesters, as the conflict escalated, Iran sought to press Hizbullah to increase its involvement while also despatching key figures from the Revolutionary Guard's Quds force to serve in an advisory role including Qassem Suleimani, the senior figure who had cut his teeth in Iraq over the previous decade. Adding to Tehran's fears, prominent members of the Syrian National Council called into question relations with Iran if Assad were toppled. Speaking with the *Wall Street Journal*, Burhan Ghalioun suggested that the post-Assad government would not only reconsider ties with Iran but also work to

---

[88] Rayhab News, 'Iran: General Nowi-Aghdam Urges Recruites to Fight in Syria as Assad Stumbles', *Islam Media Analysis* (June 2015).

[89] Tobias Schneider, 'The Decay of the Syrian Regime Is Much Worse Than You Think', *War on the Rocks* (31.08.16), http://warontherocks.com/2016/08/the-decay-of-the-syrian-regime-is-much-worse-than-you-think/.

[90] Salloukh, 'The Syrian War'.

[91] Abdo, *New Sectarianism*, p. 93.

disrupt Iranian arms supplies to Hizbullah through Syria.[92] Ghalioun's comments provoked anxiety in Tehran, fearful about the loss of a key ally, prompting a doubling down of military engagement. Yet the ongoing violence against protesters was said to prompt serious concerns.[93]

The Kingdom's Response

Saudi Arabia's response to protests in Syria – and across the region broadly – were driven by the interaction of two concerns around domestic security and the rising influence of Iran. Initially many across the Kingdom believed that the best way curtail these concerns was to offer support to the Assad regime, a position aided by cosmetic reforms, and to this end King Abdullah sent his son to Damascus on three separate occasions to speak with Assad; each time he was rebuffed.[94]

Breaking the silence on events in Syria, King Abdullah declared that the violence was 'unacceptable' and recalled its ambassador to Syria in August 2011, followed shortly thereafter by Kuwait and Bahrain amidst a belief that the Assad regime was nigh.[95] Speaking to Al Arabiya, King Abdullah stressed that 'What is happening in Syria is not acceptable for Saudi Arabia ... There are only two options for Syria's future: either it chooses wisdom on its own, or it will be pulled down into the depths of chaos and loss.'[96] Abdullah also demanded 'an end to the killing-machine and bloodshed and calls for acts of wisdom before it is too late'.[97] In remarks that appeared paradoxical to many, Abdullah urged that Assad 'should think wisely before it is too late and issue and enact reforms that are not merely promises but actual reforms'.[98]

By November, the Arab League had suspended Syria's membership and began a process of economic sanctions. Qatar and Saudi Arabia then embarked on an Arab League monitoring plan to resolve the crisis, yet Assad's unwillingness to co-operate caused Riyadh to declare the efforts as a failure, prompting further Saudi and Qatari investment in Syria in

---

[92] 'Syrian Opposition Leader Interview Transcript', *Wall Street Journal* (02.12.11), http://online.wsj.com/article/SB10001424052970203833104577071960384240668.html.
[93] Interview with former Iranian official.
[94] Phillips, *Battle for Syria*, p. 68.
[95] 'Saudi Arabia Recalls Ambassador to Syria', *BBC* (08.08.11), www.bbc.co.uk/news/world-middle-east-14439303.
[96] 'Syrian army "resumes shelling Dier al-Zour"', *BBC* (08.08.11), www.bbc.co.uk/news/world-middle-east-14441323.
[97] Ibid.
[98] 'Saudi King Eyes End to Syrian Killing, Pulls Ambassador', *Reuters* (07.08.11), www.reuters.com/article/syria-saudi-idUSL6E7J70FP20110807.

an attempt to assert their own principles of vision.[99] Tensions between Riyadh and Doha quickly emerged regarding the type of group to support, with Qatar and Turkey favouring the Muslim Brotherhood and Saudi Arabia turning to anyone else. All, however, were unable to unite opposition groups. For Phillips, both Saudi Arabia and Qatar 'prioritized their own short-term interests over any chance of forming a united and effective political opposition, contributing to the failure of this body to form a realistic alternative to Assad that might have attracted undecided civilians and fighters'.[100]

Intervention went against traditional Saudi foreign policy which had been structured to avoid direct confrontation. Yet the perceived severity of events in Syria prompted Riyadh and Abu Dhabi to take action. Indeed, both Saudi Arabia and the UAE appeared to perceive events in Syria as a microcosm of wider regional politics and a threat to their own regimes. As Khatib articulates, this meant 'sending a clear message at the domestic level about the regimes' strength and ideological predilections, letting insiders know that autocratic status quo and its rulers are not to be defied and that structural violence would be used in their defence'.[101]

When intervention occurred, Riyadh initially took the decision to support the more secular parts of the opposition groups including Riad Hijab and Mustafa al-Assad, former Ba'athists, and Michael Kilo and Lu'ay Miqdad, a secular intellectual and secular representative of the Free Syrian Army, respectively.[102] Military support was initially sent to groups espousing nationalist, secular visions of political organization in an effort to circumvent the Islamist groups – both violent and non-violent – seeking to prevent a descent into the sectarian conflict that plagued Iraq. Additionally, this also reflects Saudi Arabia's actions in the transnational field where it has sought to curtail the influence of Islamists across the region. Yet as those groups struggled to make gains against the Syrian army, the plan B of supporting Islamist groups began to take shape, revealing the importance of a particular principle of vision over another.[103]

Although initially hesitant, the 2013 US decision to arm rebel groups fighting against Assad was facilitated by Saudi money, with some estimates suggesting that billions of dollars were provided. As one US official

---

[99] Christopher Phillips, 'Eyes Bigger than Stomachs: Turkey, Saudi Arabia and Qatar in Syria', *Middle East Policy* 24:1 (2017), p. 38.

[100] Ibid., p. 39.

[101] Lina Katib, 'Syria, Saudi Arabia, the U.A.E. and Qatar: The "Sectarianization" of the Syrian Conflict and Undermining of Democratization in the Region', *British Journal of Middle Eastern Studies* 46:3 (2019), 11.

[102] Thomas Pierret, 'The Reluctant Sectarianism of Foreign States in the Syrian Conflict', *USIP* (18.11.13), www.usip.org/sites/default/files/PB162.pdf.

[103] Phillips, 'Plan B'.

acknowledged, the US strategy was not possible without Saudi support, albeit alongside financial provision from other Gulf states.[104] Attempting to capitalize on the interest of Gulf Arab monarchies, some opposition groups framed themselves as Salafis in an attempt to secure money from Saudi Arabia, with members allegedly changing their names and growing beards to demonstrate piety and, ultimately, secure funding from wealthy Gulf donors.[105]

The escalation of the conflict meant existing schisms were entrenched. Gulf TV channels gave platforms to anti-Alawi clerics such as the Syrian Sheikh Adnan al-Arour and the Egyptian Yusuf al-Qaradawi, broadcasting messages of violent rejectionism. At a rally for Syrian solidarity in Doha in 2013, al-Qaradawi argued that 'Iran is pushing forward arms and men, so why do we stand idle?' He stressed that the 'leader of the party of the Satan [Hizbullah] comes to fight the Sunnis. Now we know what the Iranians want … continued massacres to kill Sunnis.'[106]

The Shifting Contours of the Conflict

The emergence of Da'ish in the summer of 2014 posed an existential challenge to the Westphalian ordering of political projects across the Middle East as the group seized large swathes of land across Iraq and Syria, symbolically breaking the border between the two and declaring an end to the 'Sykes Picot' Agreekejt. Rapid military successes were coupled with vociferously anti-Shi'a and anti-Saudi agendas, creating an environment where regional rivals found themselves with a common enemy.

Iran established a coalition known colloquially as the '4+1', comprising Iran, Iraq, Russia, the Syrian government, and Hizbullah. Central to the establishment of this coalition was Qassem Suleimani, who visited Moscow to lobby for Russian involvement in Syria, to go with his other work in Iraq.[107] In August 2016, two years after the coalition was formed,

---

[104] Mark Mazzetti and Matt Apuzzo, 'U.S. Relies Heavily on Saudi Money to Support Syrian Rebels', *New York Times* (23.01.16).

[105] Interview with Syrian author, albeit a view that some such as Valbjorn and Phillips call into question.

[106] 'Syria Conflict: Cleric Qaradawi Urges Sunnis to Join Rebels', *BBC News* (01.06.13), www.bbc.co.uk/news/world-middle-east-22741588. Qatar's involvement in regional affairs at this time has been well documented by others such as Kristian Ulrichsen and is beyond the scope of our inquiry, yet it is worth stressing that Doha's behavior at this point offered a challenge to Saudi efforts to impose order under a Sunni, Arab, monarchical vision.

[107] Laila Bassam and Tom Perry, 'How Iranian General Plotted out Syrian Assault in Moscow', *Reuters* (06.10.15), www.reuters.com/article/us-mideast-crisis-syria-soleimani-insight-idUSKCN0S02BV20151006.

Iran allowed Russia to use its Hamedan airbase to launch attacks against opposition groups in Syria under the guise of a fighting violent Islamist movements, the first time that the Islamic Republic had allowed a foreign power to use its airbase since the revolution.[108]

In response, Saudi Arabia formed the Islamic Military Counter Terrorism Coalition (IMCTC) in late 2015. The brainchild of Mohammed bin Salman, the IMCTCT was an anti-terror coalition operating in line with the OIC provision on terrorism and predicated upon the unity of the *umma*.[109] The formation of the IMCTC reflects broad geopolitical currents, initially driven by concern at erstwhile US president Barack Obama's frosty relationship with the Saudi state. Moreover, the IMCTC was formed entirely of Sunni-dominated states, with Iran, Iraq, and Syria conspicuous by their absence, leading to the obvious charge that the organization was driven by an anti-Shi'a – read Iranian – agenda. Thus, while the fight against Da'ish was a key part of the IMCTC's remit, so too was countering gains made by Iran and its allies across the region.

While it later transpired that the Assad regime had played a prominent role in facilitating the emergence of Da'ish through the sectarianization of protests, achieved through the release of violent Islamist prisoners, in Tehran and amongst Shi'a held areas of Lebanon, Da'ish posed a serious threat to regional order. Yet beyond the group's vociferously anti-Shi'a rhetoric, many believed Da'ish – and other rebel groups – to be direct or indirect products of US security policy designed to improve Israel's security.[110]

Mohammad Reza Naqdi, the commander of the *Basij*, alleged that Da'ish was 'part of Israel's plan',[111] a point reinforced by Israeli airstrikes against Hizbullah forces in Syria which killed a senior member of the IRGC.[112] In addition to remarks made by Naqdi, the supreme leader set out the reasons for Iran's continued involvement in Syria:

Our presence in Syria, in opposition to US-supported terrorism, is not in vain … We got involved in the West-Asian region—in Syria—because there was, and there is, resistance against oppression. Thus, you witness, with God's grace,

[108] Andrew Osborn, 'Russia Uses Iran as Base to Bomb Syrian Militants for First Time', *Reuters* (16.08.16).

[109] 'Joint Statement on the Formation of the Islamic Military Alliance', *Embassy of the Kingdom of Saudi Arabia in the United States of America* (15.12.15), http://embassies .mofa.gov.sa/sites/usa/EN/PublicAffairs/Statements/Pages/Joint-Statement-on-the-Formation-of-the-Islamic-Military-Alliance.aspx.

[110] Akbarzadeh, 'Why Does Iran Need Hizbullah', 135. Conversations with Israeli academics held a different view, believing that the uprisings across Syria were bad for Israel and that they would rather stick with Assad, who was viewed as 'the devil we know'.

[111] Cited in ibid., 135.

[112] 'Iran General Died in Israeli Strike in Syrian Golan', *BBC News* (19.01.15), www.bbc .com/news/world-middle-east-30882935.

thanks to the aid provided and thanks to the bravery of warriors, the Syrian forces have managed to defeat the US-supported terrorists—which were created by the West and their allies in our region, like the Saudis.[113]

Stressing the importance of Iran's involvement in Syria, Khamenei declared that if Da'ish was not stopped 'we would have to fight them in Kermanshah and Hamedan'.[114] Similar points were also made by Jawad Zarif, who argued that 'If we had not provided that support, you would have had Daesh sitting in Damascus now.'[115] This rhetoric was echoed by key Hizbullah officials, equally concerned at the possible impact of Da'ish in Lebanon.

After years of fighting, the emergence of Da'ish and its subsequent defeat took a devastating toll on the Syrian state, its people, and its economy. In addition to ongoing military and ideological aid, Iran provided material support through trade agreements that helped sustain the Syrian economy through war, while Tehran also helped Syrian oil exports circumvent Western embargoes. Additionally, Iran offered three sizeable loans to help stabilize the Syrian economy, coming to a total of almost $6 billion.[116] Iranian activity in Syria also resulted in widespread loss of life, with thousands of elite troops estimated to have died, along with several senior commanders.

The framing of those Iranians who died in Syria as selfless individuals also sought to demonstrate the importance of the Syrian arena, a point stressed by the head of the IRGC, Mohammad Al Jafari, who argued that 'the formation of Daesh and Takfiri groups, and the events that occurred in the past years are paving the ground for the emergence of Imam Mahdi, and you can now see the positive results in the readiness of nearly 200,000 armed youth in Syria, Iraq, Afghanistan, Pakistan and Yemen' who were trained to support the resistance.[117]

The Russian Question

There is little doubt that Russian involvement in the Syrian conflict was essential in ensuring the survival of the Assad regime, while then UK foreign secretary, Boris Johnson accused Russia of engaging in 'nefarious

---

[113] 'The U.S's Claims about Fighting Terrorism Are Really Ludicrous: Ayatollah Khamenei', *Khamenei.ir* (26.09.18), http://english.khamenei.ir/news/5967/The-U-S-s-claims-about-fighting-terrorism-are-really-ludicrous.

[114] Golnaz Esfandiari, 'Iran Promotes Its New "Martyrs", Cementing Role in Syria Fighting', *Radio Free Europe* (12.07.16).

[115] 'Interview with Iranian Foreign Minister', *Der Speigel*.

[116] Wastnidge, 'Iran and Syria', pp. 154–5.

[117] 'Iran's Revolutionary Guards: We Have Armed 200,000 Fighters in the Region', *Middle East Monitor* (15.01.16).

activities' across the Middle East.[118] In contrast, Saudi Arabia viewed Russian activities with much trepidation. Diplomatic cables released by Wikileaks reveal the existence of a directive from Saudi officials to media outlets in the Kingdom 'not to oppose Russian figures and to avoid insulting them'.[119] The cable articulates the need to be resolute in its position given the potential repercussions of an Assad victory:

The fact must be stressed that in the case where the Syrian regime is able to pass through its current crisis in any shape or form, the primary goal that it will pursue is taking revenge on the countries that stood against it, with the Kingdom and some of the countries of the Gulf coming at the top of the list. If we take into account the extent of this regime's brutality and viciousness and its lack of hesitancy to resort to any means to realize its aims, then the situation will reach a high degree of danger for the Kingdom, which must seek by all means available and all possible ways to overthrow the current regime in Syria.[120]

Officials in Riyadh also sought to influence Russian policy towards Syria. To this end, Bandar is alleged to have met senior Russian officials in an attempt to break the deadlock at a clandestine meeting at Putin's dacha outside Moscow in 2013, details of which were later leaked to the Russian press. At the meeting, Bandar purportedly offered cheaper oil in return for dropping Assad, along with guarantees 'to protect the Winter Olympics next year. The Chechen groups that threaten the security of the games are controlled by us.' Despite this offer, Putin appeared unmoved proclaiming knowledge of Saudi support for 'Chechen terrorist groups for a decade. And that support, which you have frankly talked about just now, is completely incompatible with the common objectives of fighting global terrorism that you mentioned.' As the conversation moved to Syria, Bandar articulated Saudi Arabia's position:

The Syrian regime is finished as far as we and the majority of the Syrian people are concerned. [The Syrian people] will not allow President Bashar al-Assad to remain at the helm. The key to the relations between our two countries starts by understanding our approach to the Syrian issue. So you have to stop giving political support, especially at the UN Security Council, as well as military and economic support. And we guarantee you that Russia's interests in Syria and on the Mediterranean coast will not be affected one bit. In the future, Syria will be ruled by a moderate and democratic regime that will be directly sponsored by us and that will have an interest in understanding Russia's interests and role in the region.[121]

---

[118] Boris Johnson, House of Lords testimony.

[119] Doc 110212, *The Saudi Cables*, www.wikileaks.org/saudi-cables/doc110212.html.

[120] Ibid.

[121] 'No Changes in Border with Yemen, Says Prince Khaled', *Arab News* (07.03.10), www.al-monitor.com/pulse/politics/2013/08/saudi-russia-putin-bandar-meeting-syria-egypt.html#ixzz2d5UVLSNv.

Putin's response to Bandar was equally firm:

Our stance on Assad will never change. We believe that the Syrian regime is
the best speaker on behalf of the Syrian people, and not those liver eaters.
During the Geneva I Conference, we agreed with the Americans on a package
of understandings, and they agreed that the Syrian regime will be part of any
settlement. Later on, they decided to renege on Geneva I. In all meetings of
Russian and American experts, we reiterated our position. In his upcoming
meeting with his American counterpart John Kerry, Russian Foreign Minister
Sergey Lavrov will stress the importance of making every possible effort to
rapidly reach a political settlement to the Syrian crisis so as to prevent further
bloodshed.[122]

Tensions between Russia and Saudi Arabia would remain as Moscow continued to provide a range of support for Assad both within
the conflict and at diplomatic events designed to end the conflict. In
the midst of all this, Assad, his supporters, and local actors continued to struggle to impose principles of vision over a political field that
was increasingly penetrated by transnational elements whose coercive,
economic, religious, and social power appeared far greater than that
exerted by Syrians. In the following years, the situation would deteriorate dramatically.

In early 2019, Assad travelled to Iran on the first excursion outside
Syria to anywhere other than Russia in eight years. On arrival, he was
met with a glorious welcome and proclaimed by Supreme Leader 'Ali
Khamenei as 'the hero of the Arab world, and the resistance in the
region'. Khamenei remarked that

The Islamic Republic of Iran considers supporting the Syrian government and
people as helping the resistance movement and current and takes pride in it
from the bottom of its heart ... Iran and Syria are each other's strategic depth
and the identity and power of the resistance front depends on this continued
and strategic relationship. This will prevent enemies from making their plans
operational.[123]

In response, Assad stressed that the Islamic Republic 'was faithful to us
and it is necessary to celebrate the success with all Iranians', seeking to
deepen relations between the two states.[124]

During the visit, Assad met the supreme leader and Syrian state TV
reported that he 'thanked the Islamic Republic's leadership and people

---

[122] Ibid.

[123] www.presstv.com/Detail/2019/02/25/589535/Khamenei-Leader-Bashar-alAssad-
Tehran-resistance-US.

[124] 'Khamenei Declares Assad "Hero of the Arab world" during Syrian Dictator's
Surprise Iran Visit', *New Arab* (25.02.19), www.alaraby.co.uk/english/news/2019/2/25/
khamenei-declares-syrian-dictator-hero-of-the-arab-world.

for what they have given to Syria during the war'. Assad's office also stated that 'both sides expressed their satisfaction with the strategic levels reached between the two countries in all fields'.[125] Beyond this vocal expression of support, Iran was rewarded with vast contracts as Syria entered into a phase of reconstruction, albeit as conflict continued.[126]

Yet the complexity of events on the ground posed challenges for Iranian attempts to impose principles of vision on the Syrian political field. In particular, Turkey's increased involvement in the conflict stemming from security concerns about Kurdish groups meant that there were routine breaches of Syrian sovereignty. Russia, caught in the middle of this burgeoning hostility, helped resolve concerns, announcing a deal in late October in an effort to halt further Turkish engagement, predicated on the 1998 Adana Agreement that recognized Syrian territorial integrity and called for cooperation in combatting terrorism.[127] While the agreement appeared to bring an end to Kurdish demands for autonomy in Syria, the absence of Iran from Turkish–Russian discussions highlights the complex relationship between Russia and Iran.

While Iran and Russia worked together in support of the Assad regime, their goals did not always coalesce. As one Russian analyst noted:

Iran has a set of goals in Syria that go way beyond Russia's goals … Iran's goals in the Middle East are not supported by Russia, so there is more of a tactical alignment of interest between Moscow and Tehran on Syria. Yet the two parties depend on each other to an equal degree, which makes them partners for the time being.[128]

By late 2021, Russian officials were largely of the opinion that the conflict in Syria was over and that the scars of the conflict would be healed by economic investment and post-conflict reconstruction.[129] With the survival of the Assad regime, Russia and Iran's main strategic goal had been achieved and, with it, Iran's efforts to create a resistance driven *nomos* across the Middle East remained, albeit damaged by the legacy of the war.

[125] 'Syria's Assad Visits Iran, Meets Khamenei', *Radio Free Europe* (25.02.19), www.rferl .org/a/syria-s-assad-visits-iran-meets-khamenei/29790299.html.
[126] 'Syria Regime Repays War Debt by Awarding Iran Huge Construction Contract', *New Arab* (25.02.19), www.alaraby.co.uk/english/news/2019/2/25/syria-regime-repays-ally-iran-with-huge-construction-project.
[127] Hamidreza Azizi, 'How Iran Sees Russia-Turkey Deal on Northeastern Syria', *al-Monitor* (24.10.19), www.al-monitor.com/pulse/originals/2019/10/iran-deal-russia-turkey-northeast-syria.html.
[128] Testimony by Dmitri Trenin.
[129] Private discussion with Russian official, October 2021.

Conclusions

While Syria's political field has largely been dominated by the Assad dynasty, its strategic importance within the transnational field meant that periods of regional contestation resonated in the domestic political field. Domestically, however, the principles of vision are firmly articulated by the Assad regime, whose coercive and economic capital erodes what any remaining social or religious capital that opposition groups may possess. While the immediate aftermath of the Arab Uprisings pointed to an alternative principle of vision – and, in the years that followed, alternative principles of vision as the opposition fractured – the ability of the Assad regime to deploy different forms of capital and count on support from regional allies ensured its continued dominance of the political field.

The case of Syria demonstrates the extent to which regional politics can play out within domestic arenas and vice versa. Here, identity, ideology, and material forces are all deployed across a complex political arena underpinned by regional and international rivalries. Yet a decade after the conflict began, states who had previously been involved in efforts to topple the regime began to re-engage with the Assad regime.

The UAE and Bahrain took steps to re-open diplomatic missions in Syria in an attempt to normalize relations with the Assad regime and to curb regional interference in 'Arab, Syrian affairs'.[130] In early January 2019, the UAE, Bahrain, and Oman resumed flights to Damascus hinting at greater engagement with Syria.[131] Before this thaw in relations could continue, assurances were sought – and given – from Russia that Moscow was serious in curbing Tehran's influence across Syria. Russia announced plans to support Syrian reconstruction efforts amid rumours of a $500 million development of the Tartus seaport,[132] coupled with the development of commercial and relief projects across the state.[133] Investors from Russia pledged financial aid for an international terminal

---

[130] 'UAE Reopens Syria Embassy in Boost for Assad', *Reuters* (27.10.18), www.reuters .com/article/us-mideast-crisis-syria-emirates-idUSKCN1OQ0QV.

[131] 'UAE, Oman and Bahrain to Resume Flights to Syria', *Middle East Monitor* (14.01.19), www.middleeastmonitor.com/20190114-uae-oman-and-bahrain-to-resume-flights-to-syria/.

[132] '5 Russian-Syrian Projects Announced This Week', *Moscow Times* (18.12.19), www .themoscowtimes.com/2019/12/18/5-russian-syrian-projects-announced-this-week-a68655.

[133] Mohammed Shokair, 'Russia Assures Arab Capitals of Curbing Iran Influence in Syria Before Normalization', *al-Sharq al-Awsat* (23.01.19), https://aawsat.com/english/ home/article/1558211/russia-assures-arab-capitals-curbing-iran-influence-syria-normalization?utm_source=dlvr.it&utm_medium=facebook&fbclid=IwAR29MCNw YHSt1-yHmpMH7FKuOHDMwqkFLbevwu8QGm-6beYwGPeWa3DQaA8.

at Damascus airport[134] while other international funders took interest in the process until the Covid-19 crisis of early 2020, which brought efforts to a standstill.

While there were calls for international support for the reconstruction process, ongoing sanctions on members of the Assad regime continued to pose problems for those wishing to secure lucrative contracts in Syria, which would require close cooperation with the Assad regime. The appeal of such contracts is obvious to smaller GCC states, yet the risks of falling foul of US sanctions are real.[135] In spite of this, Saudi Arabia declared that it was too early to restore full diplomatic ties with the Syrian government. Rather, as Adel al-Jubeir argued, the re-opening of the embassy 'is related to the progress of the political process' based on UNSCR 2254.[136] Yet if Emirati overtures to Syria go well, it would not be surprising to see Saudi Arabia also become involved in Syria – as continued rumours suggest – adding a new chapter to a complex relationship. Despite being largely reluctant to deal with Assad, GCC states have accepted that it is necessary to do so in order to exercise any degree of influence in Syria, and with it, to counter Iran.[137] Here, we see Syria occupying a central role in the struggle to define the principles of vision in the transnational field, a battleground once more in overlapping *nomoi*.

---

[134] Russian investors to participate in rebuilding of Damascus Airport', Damascus international airport (20.01.19) https://www.damascus-airport.com/en/informations_airport.php?idnew=1049.

[135] 'GCC States Boxed in by US Sanctions on Syria', *al-Monitor* (01.02.19), www.al-monitor.com/pulse/originals/2019/02/gcc-us-dilemma-assad-arabs-qatar-lebanon-netanyahu.html.

[136] 'Saudi's Jubeir: "Too Early" to Reopen Syria Embassy', *Al Jazeera* (04.03.19), www.aljazeera.com/news/2019/03/saudi-foreign-minister-early-reopen-syria-embassy-190304184023059.html.

[137] Giorgio Cafiero, 'Gulf States Slowly Warm to Damascus', *al-Monitor* (09.01.19), www.al-monitor.com/pulse/originals/2019/01/gulf-states-accept-syria-damascus-conflict.html.

7 Yemen

Anecdotally, while on his death bed, Ibn Sa'ud, the founder of the modern Saudi state, urged the Kingdom to 'keep Yemen weak', fearing the establishment of a strong state to the south. The proximity of Yemen has traditionally meant that events in the south of the Arabian Peninsula have a serious impact on threat perceptions in Riyadh. From the tribal groups, militias, Sunni Islamists, and Shi'a insurgents of the north to the multifarious federalists, secessionists, militias, AQAP, and Da'ish franchises in the south, coupled with the presence of a number of external, politics in Yemen is a consequence of the interaction of these groups underpinned by the existence of patronage networks that historically served as a means of ensuring the survival of the long-standing president, 'Ali Abdullah Saleh. Unsurprisingly, the fragmentation of the Republic of Yemen in the years after the Arab Uprisings, particularly after the Houthi takeover of Sanaa in 2014, was viewed as a serious challenge by Saudi Arabia.

To understand the way in which Saudi Arabia, Iran, and other groups have become involved in the conflict in Yemen, we must understand the complexities of both political life and the conflict itself. The existence of myriad groups with competing agendas reveals the parabolic pressures working broadly within the context of the Yemeni state. Although largely reduced to either a 'proxy struggle' between Saudi Arabia and Iran, or a conflict between the Houthi insurgents and the regime of President Hadi, events on the ground are far more complex. While there are aspects of both narratives that ring true, both require contextualization and must be located within the struggle to shape Yemen's political field.

The Quest for Order and Yemen in the Transnational Field

The struggle to dominate Yemen's political field since the Arab Uprisings is shaped by the interaction of domestic contestation – notably the arrangement of political life after unification – and a transnational field conditioned by the rivalry between Saudi Arabia and Iran. Post-2011, contestation in the political field is a consequence of competing principles of vision and division, and the complex interplay of local and regional actors, resulting in widespread violence. Yet the inability of any one actor to impose symbolic capital and a particular principle of vision over the entirety of the state has created a seemingly intractable conflict playing out in parabolic ways with devastating repercussions.

While events in Yemen are often lazily reduced to the manifestation of sectarian tensions mapped onto a broader conflict between Saudi Arabia and Iran, the reality is far more complex amidst the centrifugal interplay of a range of a number of issues. These include competing claims to political and religious legitimacy, governance failings, the failure of the National Dialogue process, tribal competition, environmental crises, secessionist movements, and a violent Sunni Islamist presence. As such, to reduce the conflict to a proxy war, or indeed a sectarian struggle, ignores much of the underlying sources of anger driving the behaviour of actors across the state.

Political instability and violence in Yemen stems from the interplay of these issues but also has historical roots, pre-dating the establishment of North Yemen in 1962 and the People's Republic of South Yemen in 1967.[1] The interaction of such forces has facilitated the fragmentation of the national political project and created conditions through which more localized politics have emerged, in a number of cases supported by regional powers. Yemeni history is replete with instances of regional actors becoming involved in domestic issues, perhaps best seen in the case of the 1962 civil war and more recently the 2014 civil war. The outbreak of violence in the aftermath of the Arab Uprisings combines regional concerns with what Asher Orkaby has termed the 'shadow of the past',[2] the legacy of discrimination, marginalization, and persecution of a number of groups across Yemen as political and economic elites sought to exert influence across networks of patronage.

While there are myriad forces at play in shaping the conflict, there is little doubt that contestation in the transnational field plays a prominent role, interacting with the precarious makeup of life across the state. Yet relations between Saudi Arabia and Yemen are themselves complex and often fraught, seen in the conflict of 1934, ended by the Treaty of Tai'f

---

[1] Charles Dunbar, 'The Unification of Yemen: Process, Politics, and Prospects', *Middle East Journal* 46:3 (1992), 456–76.

[2] Asher Orkaby, 'Yemen's Humanitarian Nightmare: The Real Roots of the Conflict', *Foreign Affairs* 96:6 (2017), 93–101.

that ceded the provinces of Asir, Najran, and Jizan to Saudi Arabia, and set in motion a process of peaceful coexistence underpinned by Riyadh's efforts to maintain a 'precarious stability' in Yemen.[3] The importance of Yemen to Saudi Arabia prompted the establishment of a Special Office for Yemen Affairs, long overseen by Prince Sultan, responsible for the distribution of stipends across networks of patronage to politicians, religious leaders, tribal sheikhs, and military officers in support of Saudi Arabia's vision. This support typically required a balancing act of maintaining the 'status quo' in their southern neighbour while preventing Yemen from growing too strong. Beyond this, Saudi–Yemeni relations have been plagued by antagonism, conflict, and border disputes,[4] with Riyadh routinely interfering in the domestic politics of Yemen as a form of containment.

As Madawi al-Rasheed suggests, events in Yemen should not be seen as 'an inevitable war' predicated on claims of self-defence stemming from concerns about Houthi expansionism; rather, it should be seen as 'a pre-emptive strike to inaugurate an aggressive Saudi regional foreign policy'.[5] This was driven by a desire not only to eradicate threats to the Saudi state from Yemen, but also to prevent Iran gaining a foothold on the Arabian Peninsula. In what followed, Riyadh embarked on an 'aggressive military interventionist policy' designed to counter perceived Iranian gains and to establish Saudi Arabia as the 'policing agency of the Arabian Peninsula'.[6]

Ascertaining the character of direct Iranian involvement in Yemen is far harder.[7] In spite of allegations of long-standing involvement from Tehran in support of Shi'a groups, it is generally accepted that Iranian support for the Houthis and secessionist groups dates to 2009, at which point it provided weapons, training, finances, and PR strategies. While the Houthis are a Shi'a group, they follow the Zaydi strand of Shi'a Islam which has its roots in North Yemen and differs greatly from the Twelver

---

[3] May Darwich, 'The Saudi Intervention in Yemen: Struggling for Status', *Insight Turkey* 20:2 (Special issue: The Gulf on the Verge: Global Challenges and Regional Dynamics) (Spring 2018), 125–42.

[4] Madawi Al-Rasheed and R. Vitalis, *Counter-Narratives: History, Contemporary Society, and Politics in Saudi Arabia and Yemen* (New York: Palgrave Macmillan, 2004), p. 2.

[5] Madawi Al-Rasheed, 'Saudi War in Yemen Impossible to Win', *al-Monitor* (02.10.15), www.al-monitor.com/pulse/originals/2015/10/saudi-arabia-lose-protracted-war-yemen .html.

[6] Madawi Al-Rasheed, 'Riyadh's War on Yemen Stokes Saudi Nationalism', *al-Monitor* (27.03.15), www.al-monitor.com/pulse/originals/2015/03/saudi-yemen-houthi-gcc-military-islamist.html.

[7] A recent report by the UN Panel of Experts looking at the threats to peace, security and stability in Yemen goes some way in doing this, https://reliefweb.int/report/yemen/ final-report-panel-experts-yemen-s202179-enar.

strand of Shi'a thought followed in both Iran and Iraq. Since then, and increasingly after Houthi gains, Iran has exerted a great deal more influence across Yemen yet this remains limited, reflecting the complexity of events in Yemen and a number of strategic considerations in Iran.

The existence of parallel conflicts in Yemen reveals the complexity of the political field and its importance to the transnational field, allowing regional actors to deploy capital in pursuit of their principles of vision. The fragmentation of the Yemeni state exacerbated contestation within the political field, resulting in the deployment of forms of capital and the emergence of competing principles of vision and division which resonated across the state. Tracing the interplay of these factors requires, like the preceding chapters, engaging with the evolution of the Yemeni state over time.

State Formation

The demise of the Ottoman Empire in 1922 caused reverberations that were felt across the Middle East. In the south of Arabia, the end of the Ottoman era created space for a new form of political organization under the rule of a Zaydi monarch, later known as the Mutawakkilite Kingdom. While internationally recognized as the legitimate government of North Yemen, the Mutawakkilite Kingdom lost a border war with their northern neighbours in 1934, and dispute over the border would plague relations between the two states until a final border agreement was reached in 2000. The 1934 agreement resulted in Saudi Arabia annexing three border provinces from Yemen as Riyadh sought to create a buffer between the new Kingdom and its Yemeni counterpart to the south.

In 1962 the Mutawakkilite Kingdom was overthrown by an Egyptian-backed revolutionary cabal which established an Arab nationalist regime based in Sanaa. The *coup d'état* provoked a civil war which pitted the Imamate-supporting royalists against Arab nationalists. Geopolitical currents across the region meant that Egypt's involvement in the conflict would prompt the involvement of other states across the region, notably Saudi Arabia and Israel, with backing from Britain and Iran who supported the Zaydi monarchy, as a means of preserving the status quo and reducing the influence of Gamal Abd Al Nasser.[8]

There is little doubt that Egypt's involvement in Yemen stemmed from a perceived humiliation at the Syrian secession from the United Arab Republic, which was later described by Nasser as 'my Vietnam',

---

[8] Clive Jones, 'Among Ministers, Mavericks and Mandarins': Britain, Covert Action and the Yemen Civil War, 1962–64', *Middle Eastern Studies* 40:1 (2004), 99–126.

and efforts to reassert authority across the Arab world.[9] The conflict contributed to the creation of the Federation of South Arabia in 1962, albeit taking place within the context of the British withdrawal from the world stage.

Direct Saudi involvement in the south of the Arabian Peninsula can be traced back to the late 1970s and the establishment of economic and theological networks of patronage in support of its political goals. This involvement included the provision of financial support to the Yemeni government to allow them to buy wheat on global markets, although this financial support came at a price. In response to the threat posed by Nasser and Arab Nationalism broadly, Saudi Arabia's foreign policy took on an increasingly Islamic dimension at this time, with religious proselytizing a key aspect of the Kingdom's foreign policy in the 1970s and 1980s.[10] The funding of religious institutions in Yemen was an effort to erode the membership of the Zaydi community through converting its members to Salafism. During this period, the influence of traditional schools of Islamic thought in Yemen began to be eroded. The Zaydi, Shafi'i, and al-Shawkani schools of thought in particular were marginalized in a religious field that was increasingly dominated by Salafi and Muslim Brotherhood groups.[11] These groups used education as a tool of recruitment, shaping the habitus of local areas in the process and, as a consequence, creating opposition from liberals, leftists, and Zaydis. Although Iran provided support to the Zaydi Imam during the 1962–7 civil war alongside Saudi Arabia, this was limited, reflecting Tehran's cautious regional aspirations at this time.[12] Following the Iranian revolution, small numbers of Zaydis travelled to Iran to study in Qom, gradually increasing Iran's influence through the proliferation of religious belief.

Unification and the Political Field

The history of modern Yemen begins in 1990 with the unification of the Yemen Arab Republic in the north and the People's Democratic Republic of Yemen in the south as the Republic of Yemen. Under the leadership of 'Ali Abdullah Saleh, the leader of the northern state, the

[9] See Jesse Ferris, *Nasser's Gamble: How Intervention in Yemen Caused the Six-Day War and the Decline of Egyptian Power* (Princeton: Princeton University Press, 2012); Fawaz A. Gerges, 'The Kennedy Administration and the Egyptian-Saudi Conflict in Yemen: Co-Opting Arab Nationalism', *Middle East Journal* 49:2 (1995), 292–311.

[10] Farquar, *Circuits of Faith*.

[11] Maysaa Shuja al-Din, 'Yemen's War-torn Rivalries for Religious Education', in Frederic Wehrey (ed.), *Islamic Institutions in Arab States: Mapping the Dynamics of Control, Co-option and Contention* (Carnegie Endowment for International Peace, 2021).

[12] Ehteshami, 'The Foreign Policy of Iran'.

new state established Sanaa as its capital, much to the chagrin of southerners. Although unification was broadly popular, the legal agreement
bringing north and south together was a mere one and a half pages long.
The agreement was a product of global currents interacting with local
events, as the fall of the Soviet Union allowed political elites to transcend
Cold War rivalries, while infighting in the Yemen Socialist Party weakened the state. Yet fissures between north and south remained amidst
rampant poverty.

After the unification of north and south, the new government faced
an almost existential struggle to meet basic needs, exacerbated by the
weakness of national infrastructure and the strength of local, non-state
governance. Across the 333 districts that constitute the Yemeni state,
individuals in rural areas have little awareness of the state as a political
presence, where life is regulated by competition between tribal sheikhs
and recourse to *turath* ('heritage and tradition'), which plays an important role in shaping life.[13] In such uncertainty, strikes, protests, riots,
and violence became commonplace. Economic conditions were made
worse by the expulsion of Yemeni migrant workers from Saudi Arabia
in 1990, increasing the number of unemployed and politically restless.
An additional challenge was a dramatic fall in the amount generated
from remittances, which was an invaluable source of income for the local
development associations responsible for decentralized governance and
infrastructural development.

Unification surprised many and with a wide range of challenges to the
very survival of the state, particularly in peripheral areas, Saleh's authority was quickly contested. Drawing on experience from his time ruling
the north, Saleh was able to cultivate a complex network of patronage
that ensured the survival of his rule. Tribes occupied a key role in these
patronage networks, allowing Saleh to wield a form of authority across
the state in spite of bureaucratic weakness. As Nadwa al-Dawsari suggests, tribal norms played a prominent role in regulating life across the
newly formed republic, albeit occupying a complex relationship with the
state.[14] For some tribes, engaging with the state brought wealth, reinforced through co-option in Saleh's patronage networks. Yet others who
did not receive this financial support sought to push back against the

---

[13] Interview with Yemen analyst.
[14] Nadwa al-Dawsari, 'Tribal Governance and Stability in Yemen', *Carnegie Endowment
for International Peace* (03.12.15), http://carnegieendowment.org/2012/04/24/tribal-
governance-and-stability-in-yemen#, p. 8. See also Marieke Brandt, *Tribes and Politics
in Yemen: A History of the Houthi Conflict* (Oxford: Oxford University Press, 2017).

state, notably tribal groups in the north and south who were ostracized by Saleh's governance processes.

Yet the fluid nature of tribal groups and the need to maintain networks of patronage left Saleh in a precarious position, relying on tribal leaders to exert influence across peripheral areas, but with the Yemeni economy facing serious challenges, the ability to maintain this influence became increasingly perilous. At this point Saleh remained largely reliant upon external sponsors for survival, most notably on Saudi Arabia.[15] Through close links with tribal groups in Yemen, Saudi Arabia was able to exert influence on the Yemen Arab Republic, cultivating their own networks of patronage along tribal lines across the border. This reliance on Saudi support made his decision to support Iraq after the invasion of Kuwait in 1990 all the more surprising. In response to Saleh's decision, Saudi Arabia cut funding to Yemen and expelled around one million Yemenis from the Kingdom, exacerbating economic challenges in the process.[16]

Although a swift development, the concept of a unified Yemen had existed long in the memory of many across the south of Arabia, dating back to the 1920s and the development of poetry, songs, and stories imagining its existence.[17] These dreams were developed with the 1934 Treaty of Mutual Bordering, yet political wrangling served to prevent their realization. Unification made such aspirations real, albeit the first stage in a complicated process of state – and nation – building. Divisions between the erstwhile ruling elites in the north and south continued to plague the early years of unification, with figures from both sides expressing concern at the plight of their constituents. These tensions erupted in 1994 as civil war broke out.

In the coming years, many in the south expressed frustration that unification favoured the north. Parliamentary elections in 1993 returned a majority of northern groups in what was the first instance of multi-party elections on the Arabian Peninsula. Amidst such conditions, it was hardly surprising that widespread feelings of frustration, suspicion, and persecution amongst southerners would once again raise the spectre of a secessionist movement. By 1994, this movement had gathered enough capital to challenge Saleh's authority, resulting in the out-break of civil war. In an attempt to secure his rule, Saleh had positioned close relatives

---

[15] F. Gregory Gause, *Saudi-Yemeni Relations: Domestic Structures and Foreign Influence* (New York: Columbia University Press, 1990).

[16] Robert Burrowes, 'The Republic of Yemen,' in Michael Hudson (ed.), *The Middle East Dilemma* (New York: Columbia University Press, 1991), p. 192. See also Sheila Carapico, 'Yemen: Unification and the Gulf War', *Middle East Report* 170 (May/June 1991).

[17] Al-Rasheed and Vitalis, *Counter-Narratives*, p. 250.

across key institutional portfolios and continued to exert influence across networks of patronage, hidden under the language of democracy and political reform. In this vein, a programme of decentralization was set out that sought to grant peripheral regions greater democratic and fiscal autonomy, albeit too little too late. By May 1994, Saleh declared a state of emergency and dismissed political figures who had been critical of him before launching a military campaign against the south, which ultimately defeated the secessionist forces within three months.[18]

Contestation and Religious Capital

Since unification, Yemenis have been the victims of elite efforts to exert capital across networks of patronage, exploiting all facets of life in an attempt to maintain power. In a number of cases these networks transcend domestic politics and are embedded within regional affairs, resulting in devastating consequences for Yemenis across the state. Although unification was successful in bringing north and south together, the process of building institutions to regulate life across the entire territory of the new Yemeni state was far from smooth. Instead, issues arising from competing principles of vision and understandings of republicanism opened deep fissures in the political landscape that allowed for the emergence of groups that challenged the future of the state and fed into the conflict that began almost a quarter of a century after unification.

Saleh's nod to decentralization in the run up to the 1994 civil war was quickly shelved after the north was victorious. Instead, Saleh embarked on a process of consolidating his power through patronage networks, which had implications for relations with peripheral groups across the state. Indeed, the failure to cultivate inclusive forms of political organization prompted groups located across the state and its political spectrum to push back against the central government in pursuit of greater political engagement. This contestation plays a prominent role in shaping the current conflict, driven by a continuous dispute within – and across – the Yemeni political elite which, in turn, created an environment rife for foreign intervention.[19]

Perhaps the most powerful of these groups was the Houthi movement, whose formation is closely linked to the birth of the Yemeni republic in 1962. Amidst the development of a post-revolutionary elite, the role of Zaydi Imams in political life diminished, with few *sayyids* included in an

---

[18] Brandt, *Tribes and Politics in Yemen*.
[19] Observation made by Yemeni researcher during private workshop.

elite alongside 'Ali Abdullah Saleh. Across the following decades, Zaydis faced widespread discrimination in both North Yemen and the Republic of Yemen. In spite of this, prominent Zaydi clerics derived a great deal of social capital from their religious capital, aiding the formation of the Houthi movement in the 1990s out of *Shabab al-Mu'mineen* ('Believing Youth'), a group that was formed to peacefully re-assert the Zaydi identity in the face of Saudi proselytizing efforts. While a branch of Shi'a Islam, some in the Gulf – both Arab and Iranian – do not see Zaydis as Shi'a due to their rejection of certain Shi'a beliefs that are fundamental to Twelver *Shi'ism*.

Initially viewed with a great deal of trepidation by other Zaydi scholars, Believing Youth gained a great deal of popularity through its activities, notably a cultural education programme that held religious camps before splitting amidst debates about the group's future direction. One of the protagonists in such debates was Hussein Badr al Deen al-Houthi, the son of a prominent Zaydi cleric who joined Believing Youth in the early 2000s and quickly took on a prominent role through vocal criticism of the regime and its ties to the West. Al-Houthi's political position was shaped by his experience serving in the Yemeni parliament as a member of the Haqq Party but driven by a sense that Khomeini's vision offered salvation for the Muslim world.[20] In 1986 Hussein al-Houthi travelled to Tehran with his father, consolidating a relationship with Iran on the grounds of a shared *nomos*.[21]

Much like other groups across the region, 2003 was an important year for the Houthis, serving as a catalyst for a more active campaign against the Saleh regime and prompting them to adopt the slogan 'God is great, death to the US, death to Israel, curse the Jews and victory for Islam'. Having witnessed the successes of Hizbullah in Lebanon, the Houthis modelled themselves on the Party of God, yet quickly faced a challenge from the Saleh government, which launched a military campaign to defeat the group. A year into this campaign, Hussein al-Houthi was killed, prompting the Houthis to launch an insurgency against the central government led by Hussein's brother, Abdul-Malik Badr al Deen al-Houthi. In spite of Hussein's death, the group was able to defy the Yemeni army, which embarked on an aerial bombing campaign, later supported by the Saudis. The death of the group's leader marked the end

[20] 'الموت لأمريكا، الموت لإسرائيل، النصر للإسلام...' أنصار الله، ['Death to America, Death to Israel, Victory to Islam'], *Ansr Allah*, http://archive.almanar.com.lb/article.php?id=1134274.
[21] Baraa Shiban, 'Brothers in Arms – Dissecting Iran-Houthi Ties', *The Brief* (02.11.18), https://the-brief.co/brothers-in-arms-dissecting-iran-houthi-ties/?fbclid=IwAR3p8Ymp-NQKa37mY5b-5k89ETpYCfWLy0CspCll_MRHtxD9-dJGy2bcZg0.

of the first of the so-called Sadaa wars, yet a further five were to follow. Nine years after his death, thousands of Zaydi mourners attended Hussein al-Houthi's funeral in the northern city of Saada. Originally buried in a prison in Sanaa to prevent the grave becoming a shrine, al-Houthi's remains were later returned to the group by the Yemeni government in an ultimately unsuccessful conciliatory move that sought to reduce tensions.

Between 2004 and 2010, the Houthis engaged in a largely successful guerrilla warfare campaign which aided their evolution from a cadre of fighters comprising those close to their former leader into a group that would ultimately help bring down the regime of 'Ali Abdullah Saleh. The emergence of a political wing, Ansar Allah ('The Partisans of God') in 2011 demonstrated the reserves of capital that the Houthis exerted across Yemeni politics at this point. Increasingly emboldened, the Houthis articulated an increasingly intolerant stance towards the other groups across Yemen, most notably with Islah, a group combining tribal elements with the influence of the Yemeni Muslim Brotherhood and more radical Salafi groups. Houthi gains at this point owe more to the cultivation of relationships with tribal groups rather than support from regional states.[22]

Houthi successes reflect an ability to respond to political challenges in Yemen, at this time largely operating independently of external sponsors.[23] This deftness at navigating Yemen's political and social terrain resulted in a willingness to adopt transient alliances with former rivals in pursuit of goals, Between 2004 and 2010, six wars took place in and around Saada, in the north of Yemen.[24] The causes of these conflicts are multifaceted, ranging from claims about Zaydi revivalism, economic neglect, elite rivalry, regional interference, core-periphery relations and other localised issues. The ferocity and complexity of the conflicts left thousands dead, although as Ginny Hill acknowledges, there are no formal or informal body counts.[25]

The resumption of fighting in 2008 – after the failure of a Qatari negotiated ceasefire – was the most ferocious yet. Direct Saudi military intervention against the Houthis added a new dimension to the conflict,

---

[22] Marieke Brandt, 'Sufyan's "Hybrid" War: Tribal Politics during the Huthi Conflict', *Journal of Arabian Studies: Arabia, the Gulf, and the Red Sea* 3:1 (2013), 120–38.

[23] Michael Knights, *The Houthi War Machine: From Guerrilla War to State Capture* (CTC Sentinel, Washington Institute, September 2018), p. 17.

[24] Samy Dorlian, 'The Saada War in Yemen: Between Politics and Sectarianism,' *The Muslim World* 101:2 (2011), 182–201.

[25] Ginny Hill, *Yemen Endures: Civil War, Saudi Adventurism and the Future of Arabia* (London: Hurst, 2017), p. 176.

occurring after rebels crossed into the Kingdom, killing border guards and seizing control of a number of villages. This was later alleged to be in response to Saudi Arabia allowing Saleh to use their territory to strike against the Houthis.[26] Operation Scorched Earth was the largest Saudi combat operation since the Gulf War, lasting a year before a ceasefire came into operation and Riyadh was able to reassert control over border areas.[27] At this time the conflict spread beyond Saada, closing in on the outskirts of the city but a ceasefire was once again agreed in 2008, albeit with a number of ambiguities. The conflicts left over one hundred thousand displaced and created conditions of future uncertainty and instability, ultimately, sowing the seeds of protests in 2011.

Although the war ended, grievances remained and Houthi capital across the north of Yemen increased. As a result, other groups with external sponsors sought to curtail the influence of the Zaydis and the members of *ahl bayt* – the *sayyid* movement – more generally. Increased Saudi proselytizing was seen by tribal leaders as a way of circumventing the legacy and influence of the *sayyid* ('descendants of the prophet'), simultaneously fracturing the Shi'a body politic and increasing their own capital.[28]

In particular, the presence of a well-funded Salafi movement exacerbated sectarian divisions around Saada. Partially funded by the Saudis from the 1980s onwards, albeit with tacit approval from Saleh, the Salafist movement had a dramatic impact on the local political balance, becoming a 'significant local force'.[29] Unsurprisingly, many viewed the spread of Salafi madrassas as an attempt to erode the Zaydi political and social capital.[30] As one Houthi spokesperson declared, the Salafi narrative brought 'evil to Yemen'.[31] For others, the Salafi presence provided Saudi Arabia with 'an opportunity to manipulate the Yemeni political scene'.[32] Supporting the deployment of religious capital was the distribution of economic capital that created an environment where many Saudis believed 'they had a right to

---

[26] 'Saudis Held Briefly by Yemeni Rebels', *Arab News* (25.04.10).
[27] 'No Changes in Border with Yemen, says Prince Khaled', *Arab News* (07.03.10).
[28] Stacey Philbrick Yadav, 'Sectarianization, Islamist Republicanism, and International Misrecognition in Yemen', Hashemi and Postel (eds.), *Sectarianization*, p. 188.
[29] Laurent Bonnefoy, *Salafism in Yemen: Transnationalism and Religious Identity* (London: Hurst, 2012), p. 147.
[30] Laurent Bonnefoy, 'Salafism in Yemen: A "Saudisation"?', in al-Rasheed (ed.), *Kingdom without Borders*, pp. 245–62.
[31] Observation made in private workshop, December 2020.
[32] Observations made by a Yemeni researcher in private workshop, December 2020.

have a say in the government of Yemen and that it should at least not be in opposition to Riyadh'.[33]

During the 2000s, Saudi officials were suspicious of Yemeni attempts to frame the Houthis as an Iranian client, believing that this was a case of the Saleh regime seeking to secure further funding and support in his struggle against the insurgency. US officials were equally suspicious of such claims. Investigations into arms in Yemen revealed that many were sold by Yemeni army officials or purchased on the black market.[34] US diplomatic cables released by Wikileaks document Washington's awareness of the source of the Houthis weapons. A US diplomatic cable from 2009 sheds some light on Iranian support for the Houthis and their involvement in Yemen more broadly: although 'Tehran's shadow looms large' over events in the state, 'its footprint is small'. At the time, the cable suggests that 'the only visible Iranian involvement remains the Iranian media's proxy battle with Saudi and Yemeni outlets over support for the Houthis'.[35] Others suggest that the footprint, while small, was quickly growing. During the late 2000s, as Iran sensed opportunities to increase its influence across the region it sought to establish a larger network in Yemen, comprising military professionals, development experts, spies, informers, PR experts, and media consultants, many of whom were 'fired up with the zeal of change or religion'.[36]

Another US diplomatic cable reports an allegation made by Radio Tehran that in a telephone conversation between King Abdullah and President Saleh, the former offered to 'cover the cost of the offensive, to provide weapons and ammunition and to put an end to the Houthi movement no matter the cost'.[37] As the Yemeni information minister Hassan al-Lawzi suggests, there was a widespread belief that Iran was responsible for financing the Houthis. Media outlets controlled by the state were vocal in their condemnation of the role played by their Iranian counterparts.

the treachery of the Persian media ... (which) reveals the ugly face of the trumpets of sabotage outside Yemen's borders, imposing upon the Yemeni media the patriotic duty of confronting the Iranian misinformation machine and its support for subversive elements in Saada.[38]

[33] Interview with Yemeni analyst.
[34] 09SANAA2186_a, 'Who Are the Houthis, Part Two: How Are They Fighting?' (09.12.09), https://wikileaks.org/plusd/cables/09SANAA2186_a.html.
[35] 09SANAA1662_a, 'Iran in Yemen: Tehran's Shadow Looms Large, but Footprint Is Small' (12.09.09), https://wikileaks.org/plusd/cables/09SANAA1662_a.html.
[36] Interview with Yemen analyst, 2018.
[37] 09SANAA1628_a, 'Saada Conflict: A Proxy War of Words between Iran, Saudi Arabia' (02.09.09), https://wikileaks.org/plusd/cables/09SANAA1628_a.html
[38] Ibid.

In the years that followed, a number of incidents supported the claim that Tehran had provided the Houthis with weapons, resulting in shifting perceptions in both Riyadh and Washington. In September 2015, Saudi officials announced that they had seized an arms shipment destined for the Houthis, dispatched by Iran.[39]

Uprisings, Dialogue, and War

Much like across other states that experienced popular protests in early 2011, events in Yemen saw a disparate collection of people take to the streets with a range of often competing demands. Formal opposition parties remained largely off the streets, but after regime soldiers killed over fifty unarmed protesters and injured many more, the opposition to Saleh's rule swelled, with key military officials and tribal leaders abandoning their patron.[40] The most significant of these was General 'Ali Muhsin, an influential military figure whose defection split the Yemeni army, who redeployed units under his command to protect the protesters, in direct opposition to regime military forces. Conditions of instability across Yemen were hardly surprising, with the state in a precarious situation, caught between two fractious blocs underpinned by complex tribal–religious alliances and supported by regional and international powers.

Exacerbating events was widespread corruption, nepotism, and elite infighting, resulting in the marginalization of groups across the state. By this point, the Yemeni state was in disarray, after years of systematic dismantling by the Saleh regime. By 2011, legal structures barely existed and, when they did, they were there to 'reinforce the authority of the state', meaning the Saleh regime.[41] These challenges were made worse by the actions of judges who were appointed by the state and were 'free to be corrupt and draw payment from both sides of a case'. Ultimately, the Yemeni state was a shell, governed by a constitution that was mere 'ink on paper', disregarded by people.[42] While the state was visible, it was symbolically visible, with little substance.

In the north of the country, Abdul-Malik al-Houthi sought to capitalize on the uncertainty and declared his support for the protesters.

---

[39] Ahmed al-Omran and Asa Fitch, 'Saudi Coalition Seizes Iranian Boat Carrying Weapons to Yemen', *Wall Street Journal* (30.09.15), www.wsj.com/articles/saudi-coalition-seizes-iranian-boat-carrying-weapons-to-rebels-in-yemen-1443606304.

[40] Khaled Fattah, 'Yemen: A Social Intifada in a Republic of Sheiks', *Middle East Policy* 18:3 (2011), 79–85.

[41] Interview with Yemen analyst, 2018.

[42] Ibid.

Thousands of his followers were sent to join rallies in Sanaa, resulting in powerful images of tribesmen and women from rural areas joining their urban kin in a widespread rejection of the Saleh regime. Similar grievances were felt across the state amongst groups who had been marginalized by the Saleh regime.

Fearing the consequences of increased instability, notably fragmentation, violence, and a potential rise in Iranian influence, the GCC – led by Saudi Arabia – proposed a settlement designed to bring about an end to instability by transferring power from Saleh to his vice-president Abd Rabbu Mansur Hadi within 30 days and, in return, offering Saleh immunity. After the transfer of power, a power-sharing government was to be implemented, followed by the drafting of a new constitution. The agreement, however, was 'ridden with loopholes' allowing Saleh to renege on promises three times in the months that followed.[43] Tensions between the Saleh regime and protesters increased at this time, breaking out in fighting and leaving over 100 dead and a further 400 wounded. On 3 June, an explosion at a mosque in the presidential compound killed a number of senior officials and injured a great number more, including the president, who was flown to Saudi Arabia for treatment.

The summer was plagued with fighting between groups competing for control of Sanaa and, ultimately, the very survival of the Saleh regime. On 23 September Saleh returned from Saudi Arabia, vocally expressing support for the GCC deal yet doing very little to implement it. As the situation across the country became more precarious, and with increasing pressure from his two main backers, Saudi Arabia and the United States, Saleh conceded and agreed to the deal, bringing an end to his domination of Yemen's political field. On 23 November 2011, Saleh signed a deal that transferred power to Abd Rabbu Mansour Hadi who formed a government of national unity.[44]

The (Failure of the) National Dialogue Conference

In addition to the unity government, Hadi also established a National Dialogue Conference, which was seen as a positive move by many. Created as a transitional process, designed to bring a divided state together and give groups the opportunity to articulate grievances alongside a

---

[43] Sheila Carapico, 'No Exit: Yemen's Existential Crisis', *Middle East Research and Information Project* (03.05.11).

[44] Vincent Durac, 'Yemen's Arab Spring – Democratic Opening or Regime Maintenance?', *Mediterranean Politics* 17:2 (2012), 161–78.

chance to have a say in the future organization of the country, it was described by the UN special envoy to Yemen Jamal Ben Umar as a source of inspiration for other Arab countries.[45] Yet in spite of the achievements of the conference, it ended without a final agreement, prompting the perception that the dialogue was little more than a 'reshuffling of elites'.[46]

The dialogue brought together all aspects of Yemeni society in an effort to address the issues that had plagued the state since unification. While progress was made in a number of areas, the fundamental question about the structure of the state as a federal or unitary structure was avoided until the end of the conference. While the conference recommended the establishment of a federation made up of six self-governing regions and two autonomous cities, the day-to-day needs of Yemenis were not addressed and, ultimately, federalism became a distraction from more pressing basic needs.[47]

Although the dialogue allowed previously marginalized communities to articulate their grievances, it was, broadly speaking, a conservative process that favoured the interests of the Hadi government and its external sponsors, Saudi Arabia and the United States, who saw it as the preservation of the status quo. Critics of the agreement argued that it amounted to little more than an agreement between the regime and 'loyal' opposition figures from *Mushtarak*, the Joint Meeting Parties Alliance dominated by Islah, the 'old guard' of Sanaa, and the tribal Hashid confederation. This lack of substantive change reaffirmed perceptions that the dialogue was little more than an 'elite pact' made between those in power as a means of repackaging the *ancien regime* amidst attempts to demobilize the events of 2011.[48]

Unsurprisingly, the agreement exacerbated latent anger across the state. In the south, the Hirak al-Janoubi ('The Southern Movement'), staged demonstrations, while the Houthis marched on Sanaa. By 21 September 2014, Houthi forces were able to take control of the capital with support from forces loyal to the former president, signing the Peace and National Partnership Agreement with Hadi that called for the implementation of the National Dialogue Conference plan and the formation

[45] 'US Intercepts Multiple Shipments of Iranian Weapons Going to Houthis in Yemen', *CNN* (28.10.16), www.sabanews.net/en/news339378.htm.

[46] Maria-Louise Clausen, 'Understanding the Crisis in Yemen: Evaluating Competing Narratives', *The International Spectator* 50:3 (2015), 19.

[47] Peter Salisbury, 'Federalism, Conflict and Fragmentation in Yemen', *Saferworld* (October 2015), p. 12.

[48] Sheila Carapico and Stacey Philbrick Yadav, 'The Breakdown of the GCC Initiative', *Middle East Report* 273 (Winter 2014).

of an *inclusive* government.[49] In response, both president and cabinet resigned in protest.

The conflict in 2014 was precipitated by a *coup d'état* that took place over a number of months between September 2014 and March 2015, during which time the Houthis seized control of Sanaa and placed President Hadi under house arrest. On 21 February 2015, Hadi escaped and quickly fled to the south, setting up office in Aden where he rescinded his resignation. By March 2015, the situation facing Hadi was perilous, prompting a retreat to Saudi Arabia after he had formally requested assistance from Gulf leaders.

The 2014 takeover of Sanaa prompted Iran to increase its involvement in Yemen, sensing an opportunity to exert greater influence at a limited cost. One aspect of this was the development of training programmes for Houthi fighters, delivered by members of the Quds force. In spite of the relationship between Houthis and Iran and the presence of a great number of Iranian individuals in Yemen to undertake the training,[50] this ultimately proved unpopular as many Yemenis were suspicious of their Persian trainers with language issues posing an additional problem. To circumvent this issue, the Houthis later received training and support from Arab Hizbullah fighters from Lebanon.[51]

The precarious and fluid nature of the conflict created a number of unusual and ultimately transient alliances who lay claim to different reserves of capital. The Hadi regime was supported by a number of groups who had violently rejected the authority of centralized rule across Yemen, most notably the secessionist groups of the south, including Hirak and the Southern Transitional Council. In the conflict against the Houthis, the Hadi government was also supported by a number of militias who shared disdain for the insurgents. Moreover, rival elites struggled to exert influence even within what were typically assumed to be coherent blocs. For example, militias affiliated with the Islah Party under the leadership of Vice-President General 'Ali Muhsin – former commander of the 1st Armoured Division in the Yemeni Army – shared the strategic aims of the Hadi government concerning the Houthis yet little else.

---

[49] 'Yemen: The Peace and National Partnership Agreement', *Jadaliyya* (23.09.14), www.jadaliyya.com/Details/31248/Yemen-The-Peace-and-National-Partnership-Agreement.

[50] Some reports note this figure to be dozens while others suggest a less realistic figure of hundreds. See Yara Bayoumy and Mohammed Ghobari, 'Confirmed: Iran's Foreign Military Arm is Backing Yemeni Rebels Who Took Control of the Country', *Reuters* (15.12.14).

[51] Alexander Corbeil and Amarnath Amarasingam, 'The Houthi Hezbollah: Iran's Train-and-Equip Program in Sanaa', *Foreign Affairs* (31.03.16).

Escalating violence across Yemen was a source of concern to many across the international community, prompting United Nations Security Council Resolution 2201 on 15 February 2015, which 'strongly deplore[d] actions taken by the Houthis to dissolve parliament and take over Yemen's government institutions, including acts of violence'.[52] Two months later, the Security Council adopted resolution 2216 which ultimately allowed the coalition to begin its military campaign.[53]

Escalation and Intervention

Yemen's recent history offers a timely reminder of the importance of looking beyond easily accepted narratives to explore the complexity and messiness of political fragmentation. Accepting such a reminder allows one to reflect on the ways in which the intimately tiny aspects of local politics across Yemen interact with the broader geopolitical currents to devastating effect; put another way, from 2015 onwards, Yemeni politics took on increased importance in the transnational field, with competing *nomoi* shaping the actions of local and regional actors. The increasing influence of the Houthis and the perception of ties between the group and Iran was a source of great concern to many in Saudi Arabia. In an attempt to counter gains made by the group, a military coalition was formed along with the UAE, Qatar, Bahrain, and Egypt, which attempted to eradicate the group. Unsurprisingly, the coalition's bombardment of Yemen exacerbated domestic issues, resulting in catastrophic humanitarian disasters, allegations of war crimes, and further fragmentation of political life.[54]

In 2014, Rouhani declared the Houthi takeover of Sanaa as a 'brilliant and resounding victory'.[55] Others, such as the country's deputy foreign minister, pledged support for the Houthis, describing their actions as essential for restoring 'domestic peace and stability'.[56] Yet it was a deputy in the Iranian Majlis, 'Ali Reza Zakani, whose comments caused the most concern. Speaking to Iranian press, Zakani suggested that the

---

[52] United Nations Security Council, *Resolution 2201* (2015), http://unscr.com/en/resolutions/doc/2201.

[53] Ibid.

[54] Josh Halliday and Anushka Asthana, 'Met Police Look at Allegations of Saudi war Crimes in Yemen', *The Guardian* (02.04.17), www.theguardian.com/world/2017/apr/02/met-police-examine-allegations-saudi-arabia-war-crimes-yemen.

[55] 'Iranian President: Recent Events in Yemen Are Part of the brilliant and Resounding Victory', *Aden al-Ghad* (25.09.14), http://adenghad.net/news/124484/#.VZ6SA_3bKM-.

[56] 'Iran Reiterates Support for Restoration of Political Tranquillity to Yemen', *Fars News* (23.02.15), http://english.farsnews.com//newstext.aspx?nn=13931204000524.

Houthi seizure of Sanaa was a 'victory for the regime in Tehran', later adding that Iran now controlled four Arab capitals – Baghdad, Beirut, Damascus, and Sanaa – in what would provoke existential concern in Riyadh.[57]

On 25 March 2015, Operation Decisive Storm was launched, comprised of a Saudi-led coalition seeking to crush the Houthi rebellion and re-assert the authority of the internationally recognized Hadi government. Justified as an attempt to 'defend the legitimate government of President Hadi from the takeover attempts by the Houthi militia in Yemen',[58] the action was requested by Hadi in accordance with Article 51 of the UN Charter. All the while, a broader campaign of securitization took place, framing both Iran and the Houthis as an existential threat to Yemen and the wider region. The intervention took place at a time when Riyadh saw its position in regional affairs as increasingly precarious due to the recent US diplomatic successes with Tehran culminating in the signing of the JCPOA between Iran and the permanent five members of the UN Security Council plus Germany. At a time when many in the Kingdom and elsewhere feared that the nuclear deal would result in an emboldened Iran, the price the United States paid for Saudi acquiescence was to tacitly support military intervention in Yemen.[59]

Speaking at the twenty-sixth meeting of the Arab League in March 2015, King Salman vowed to continue the military campaign until 'it achieves its goals for the Yemeni people to enjoy security'.[60] Yet the conflict quickly became an arena of much criticism. UNSCR2216 was an attempt to uphold Yemeni sovereignty in accordance with the UN charter, meaning that the coalition's actions in Yemen were initially in accordance with international law, helping the Hadi government to survive in the face of a powerful insurgent movement whose reserves of capital were increasing. At the same time, Saudi capital on the streets of Yemen had dramatically decreased, in part as a consequence of the deaths of Prince Sultan (2011) and Grand Sheikh Abdallah al-Ahmar (2007), the most powerful tribal leader in Yemen and a 'Saudi man'. While Saudi largesse continued after their deaths, the loss of two figures with knowledge and influence of Yemeni politics had a devastating impact on their

---

[57] 'Sanaa Is the Fourth Arab Capital', *Middle East Monitor*.
[58] 'Saudi Ambassador in U.S. Speaks on Military Campaign in Yemen', *Al Arabiya* (26.03.15), http://english.alarabiya.net/en/webtv/reports/2015/03/26/Video-Saudi-ambassador-in-U-S-speaks-on-military-campaign-in-Yemen.html.
[59] Farea al-Muslimi, 'Analysis', *Sanaa Centre* (18.11.18), https://sanaacenter.org/publications/analysis/6665.
[60] 'King Salman Vows to Continue Yemen Campaign', *Al Arabiya* (28.03.15), https://english.alarabiya.net/en/News/middle-east/2015/03/28/King-Salman-arrives-in-Egypt-for-Arab-summit-.

ability to assert capital socially or culturally. While MbS took on responsibility for Saudi's Yemen policy, his lack of knowledge of the intricacies of Yemeni politics and limited social capital left the Kingdom reliant on force to pursue its goals.

From March 2015, the conflict became internationalized, adding additional layers of complexity to a war already composed of a number of moving parts and beset by increasingly intractable differences. The internationalization of the conflict created a precarious situation from which resolution appeared difficult. At the start of the month, Iran Air operated a flight between Tehran and Sanaa, the first of its kind in twenty-five years[61] before hosting a Houthi delegation that resulted in thirteen agreements being signed between the two. On 14 March, Saudi Arabia placed the Houthis on its terrorism list, demonstrating the level of animosity in the Kingdom.

Recognizing the complexity of the challenge ahead, Saudi and Emirati forces engaged in a de facto demarcation of zones of responsibility across the state, leaving Saudi Arabia addressing challenges in the north and the UAE working in the south. Yet while the coalition was united in its desire to defeat the Houthis, a number of tensions emerged over strategic aims, particularly seen in Emirati activity in the south of the state. In the south, the UAE deployed special forces, hired Latin American mercenaries, financed local militias, and empowered local strong men, all reinforced by air support from Emirati bases in the Horn of Africa.[62]

The coalition initially made quick progress, helping forces loyal to Hadi to retake Aden and other parts of the south, yet as the fighting moved closer to Houthi heartland in the north, progress slowed, despite Saudi Arabia allegedly spending billions of dollars each month to finance the bombing missions which destroyed much of Yemen's infrastructure. The fragmentation of the state and opening up of Yemen's political field created opportunities for local groups to find external sponsors who deployed social, economic, and religious capital in pursuit of greater influence, further devastating the state in the process.[63] Here, existing religious linkages between members of the Houthis and Iran – both its clerical establishment and members of the IRGC – facilitated the development of relations over time.[64]

---

[61] الحوثيون يفتحون أبواب صنعاء لإيرا, *Al Jazeera* (01.03.15), http://mubasher.aljazeera.net/news/
الحوثيون-يفتحون-أبواب-صنعاء-لإيران.
[62] Emily B. Hager and Mark Mzzetti, 'Emirates Secretly Sends Colombian Mercenaries to Yemen to Fight', *New York Times* (25.11.15).
[63] Interview with Yemen analyst.
[64] Interview with Iranian scholar and foreign policy analyst.

There is little doubt that geopolitical concerns were central to the Saudi–Emirati decision to go to war. Reflecting on the decision to embark on military action, a Saudi analyst suggested that Yemenis 'can't burn our backyards and harm neighbours ... and expect neighbours to stay still'.[65] One Emirati-Yemeni woman told me that 'we went to war in Yemen because we are next', documenting widespread fears about Iranian expansionism that had spread across Emirati society. Speaking on local TV, the mother of an Emirati soldier killed in Yemen declared 'we have to stop them there', once again referring to Iran. Remembering a conversation with the late foreign minister of Saudi Arabia Prince Sa'ud al-Faysal, the Saudi analyst recalled the prince saying, 'you can't feast and leave your neighbour hungry', with a clear sense of normative responsibility over Yemen.[66] Similar ideas of normative responsibility were identified by an Iranian scholar and foreign policy analyst, who pointed to a growing anger at the situation in Yemen amidst questions about Tehran's perceived failure to meet its responsibilities to the *mostaz'afin*.[67]

While members of the GCC have largely been supportive of the coalition, many in Oman were critical of the 'Yemen adventure', most notably Sultan Qaboos, who expressed concerns about the impact of the conflict upon regional politics, along with the devastating humanitarian consequences.[68] Members of the coalition sought to keep Oman on side, expressing concern about the flow of Iranian weapons from Oman into Yemen[69] yet recognising that the Omani government maintained a relationship with the Houthis; this relationship was later used in diplomatic efforts aimed at ending the war.

After the erstwhile President 'Ali Abdullah Saleh was forced to step down, he joined forces with the Houthis, against whom he had fought a series of wars in the decade previously. The alliance between Saleh – and forces loyal to him – and the Houthis proved too much for the Hadi government, whose forces were quickly overrun. The complexity and confusion of events increased as front lines became increasingly fluid, while the Houthi–Saleh successes were not always a product of rapid expansion but of units joining the alliance. Saleh's relationship with the Houthis became increasingly essential for the Houthis, who sought to

[65] Interview with Saudi journalist, 2017.
[66] Interview with Saudi analyst.
[67] Interview with Iranian scholar and foreign policy analyst.
[68] Giorgio Cafiero and Theodore Karasik, 'Yemen War and Qatar Crisis Challenge Oman's Neutrality', *Middle East Institute* (06.07.17), www.mei.edu/content/article/oman-s-high-stakes-yemen.
[69] 'Exclusive: Iran Steps up Weapons Supply to Yemen's Houthis via Oman – Officials', *Reuters* (20.10.16).

deploy Saleh's neo-patrimonial patronage networks in pursuit of their military and political ambitions. The ability to convince key military allies to support the group's aims through acquiescence or direct support proved essential in helping the Houthis take Sanaa in September 2014. Moreover, Saleh allies served to enforce security across the capital after the Houthi takeover, comprising a 'significant proportion' of the informal security mechanisms operating across Sanaa.[70] After pledging to rejoin the coalition, Saleh called for peace: 'We will open a new page for them, a new dialogue. What is happening in Yemen is enough. We vow to our brothers and neighbours that, after a ceasefire is in place and the blockade is lifted ... we will hold dialogue directly through the legitimate authority represented by our parliament.'[71] Unsurprisingly, his former allies were less than pleased, with a Houthi spokesperson stating that this was 'a coup against our alliance and partnership ... and exposed the deception of those who claim to stand against aggression'.[72]

The presence of US military personnel in the region added to the internationalization of the conflict. After an attack on US warships in the Bab al-Mandab, the head of US naval forces central command Kevin Donegan suggested that 'Iran is connected to this.'[73] Donegan also acknowledged that five Iranian shipments of weapons to the Houthis had been intercepted since April 2015.[74] A number of other reports document similar incidents of maritime smuggling, including a fishing boat that was delivering key munitions and supplies.[75] Such narratives found traction as a consequence of the broader sectarianization of regional politics and efforts to impose certain principles of vision within the transnational field.

Of course, there are good reasons to believe that Iran has sought to capitalize on opportunities that emerged within the context of a fragmenting Yemeni body politic, rather than seeing Yemen as a strategic priority. As Thomas Juneau suggests, Tehran's involvement in Yemen has produced a 'limited return on a modest investment', yet it is also accepted that Iran has little desire to increase this investment, given the perceived

---

[70] Thomas Juneau, 'Iran's Policy towards the Houthis in Yemen: A Limited Return on a Modest Investment', *International Affairs* 92:3 (2016), 647–63.

[71] 'Yemen: From Civil War to Ali Abdullah Saleh's Death', *Al Jazeera* (05.12.17), www.aljazeera.com/programmes/aljazeeraworld/2017/11/yemen-north-south-divide-171129152948234.html.

[72] Ibid.

[73] 'U.S. Officials: Iran Supplying Weapons to Yemen's Houthi Rebels', *NBC News* (27.10.16).

[74] 'US Intercepts Multiple Shipments of Iranian Weapons Going to Houthis in Yemen', *CNN* (28.10.16).

[75] 'Weapons Bound for Yemen Seized on Iran Boat: Coalition', *Reuters* (30.09.15).

cost of achieving significantly greater influence and risking overstretch.[76] Despite this, the conflict continued to offer Iran relatively easy results at a low cost, achieved in part through pledges of increased support to the Houthis from prominent Iranian officials at times of need.[77] With the onset of conflict, as one former Iranian official observed, it was easy for the Houthis 'to get Iranian support'.[78]

For Iran, the cultivation of relations with the Houthis was 'in line' with its usual approach to providing support to non-state actors across the Middle East; it was an attempt to build trust and create a long-term relationship that could be upgraded in the future.[79] Here, the desire to provide support to the *mostaz'afin* of the Muslim world neatly coalesced with a broader effort to assert Iranian influence across the Middle East. In the case of Yemen, this desire came at a limited cost, in the form of weapons and financial aid before the Houthi entrance to Sanaa.[80]

Narratives emerging from Yemen have great strategic value to Iran: a much-maligned Shi'a group standing up against a more powerful dominant group evokes the memory of the Karbala narrative. Parallels with the establishment of Hizbullah in Lebanon were also evident, yet the Houthi emergence is far more a consequence of local activity. Moreover, there is no evidence to suggest that the Houthis are either *dependent* on Iranian assistance or indeed *subservient* to Tehran. Although some suggest that the Houthis are reliant upon Iran for weapons, the reality is more complex. A report from the UN Security Council Committee Meeting on Panel of Experts concluded that while there was evidence of small-scale weapons transfer between Iran and the Houthis, there was insufficient evidence of a direct, large-scale supply from Iran. In spite of this, the panel did note that 'there are indicators that anti-tank guided weapons being supplied to the Houthi or Saleh forces are of Iranian manufacture'.[81]

Over the following years, the conflict endured ebbs and flows, with acts of devastating violence committed by actors on all sides of a war punctured by intermittent ceasefires. It also spilled out beyond the

[76] Juneau, 'Iran's Policy', 658–9.
[77] 'Iran Steps up Support for Houthis in Yemen's War – Sources', *Reuters* (21.03.17).
[78] Interview with former Iranian official, 2020.
[79] Juneau, 'Iran's Policy', 657.
[80] Yara Bayoumy and Mohammed Ghobari, 'Iranian Support Seen Crucial for Yemen's Houthis', *Reuters* (15.12.14), www.reuters.com/article/us-yemen-houthis-iran-insight/iranian-support-seen-crucial-for-yemens-houthis-idUSKBN0JT17A20141215.
[81] Letter dated 27 January 2017 from the Panel of Experts on Yemen addressed to the President of the Security Council, 31 January 2017.

borders of the Yemeni state, with missiles regularly fired at Saudi Arabia. On one occasion in March 2018, Saudi forces intercepted seven missiles fired from Yemen, while in another incident later that year, a missile bearing 'all the hallmarks of previous attacks using Iranian-provided weapons' was shot down by the Saudi military.[82] US ambassador to the UN Nikki Haley proclaimed that Iranian actions posed a serious threat to regional security, arguing that the international community 'must act co-operatively to expose the crimes of the Tehran regime and do whatever is needed to make sure they get the message. If we do not, then Iran will bring the world deeper into a broadening regional conflict.'[83] In a similar vein, a statement from the Arab Coalition articulated allegations of Iranian involvement as a 'hostile act by the Iran-backed Houthi militia proves that the Iranian regime continues to provide the Houthi militia with qualitative capabilities'.[84]

By late 2018, conflict centred on the Red Sea port of Hodeida, a strategically important port held by the Houthis that was the source of 70 per cent of all goods entering Yemen. In the months previously, Emirati-led forces had pushed up from the south and viewed retaking Hodeida as a means of forcing the Houthis to compromise, much to the chagrin of humanitarian groups who warned of the potential devastation that could occur if fighting affected the port city. Martin Griffiths, the newly appointed UN envoy, embarked on an intensive period of shuttle diplomacy seeking to bring about a ceasefire, albeit to no avail.

The death of Jamal Khashoggi, the Saudi dissident and an outspoken critic of the Saudi bombing of Yemen, would have a marked impact on the conflict, prompting members of the US Congress to draw links between Khashoggi's assassination and the war. Calls for de-escalation from the United States, United Kingdom, and others helped bring about the Stockholm Agreement, which sought to facilitate trust building through a series of prisoner exchanges, demilitarization, and talks. After a short ceasefire, the fighting continued. Despite huge investment in their military campaign, Saudi Arabia's actions were described as 'extremely incompetent and short sighted'.[85]

---

[82] 'Yemen Rebel Missile Fired at Riyadh "Bears Hallmarks" of Iran', *BBC News* (20.12.17), www.bbc.co.uk/news/world-middle-east-42421289.

[83] Michelle Nichols, 'Latest Houthi Missile "Bears Hallmarks" of Iran Arms Attacks: U.S.', *Reuters* (19.12.17), www.reuters.com/article/us-yemen-security-saudi-usa/latest-houthi-missile-bears-hallmarks-of-iran-arms-attacks-u-s-idUSKBN1ED2PC.

[84] 'Saudi Arabia Intercepts Missiles from Yemen Heading over Riyadh', *Financial Times* (09.05.18), www.ft.com/content/6fe57680-536c-11e8-b24e-cad6aa67e23e.

[85] Interview with Yemeni researcher.

Sectarianism: A Principle of Vision?

In the immediate aftermath of the Houthi occupation of Sanaa in September 2014, narratives of Iranian manipulation of sectarian divisions and a desire to export Khomeini's revolutionary ideas were heard across the Gulf and in Western capitals. Developments in the transnational field had allowed an anti-Iranian habitus to take hold, supported by the articulation of principles of vision that framed Iran as the architect of instability and violence across the region. Much like in Bahrain, Lebanon, Iraq, and Syria, Riyadh feared the cultivation and manipulation of Shi'a groups by Iran, exacerbating tensions and ultimately, helping to establish a Shi'a 'crescent' of influence across the Middle East. In response, the Saudis, followed closely by the Emiratis, Bahrainis, and others, embarked on a process of securitizing and sectarianizing the conflict in Yemen. Yet such processes of sectarianization were not solely imposed by external actors; indeed, Saleh stressed that the group, operating with the support of Iran, sought to return the state to 'the dark ages of the imamate'.[86]

While the narratives of sectarian animosity gained traction after the outbreak of war, the roots of sectarianization are found far earlier, dating back to the emergence of Salafist movements in Yemen in the 1980s, notably around the figure of Muqbil al-Wadi'i. Stemming from a tribal and Zaydi background, al-Wadi'i spent time in Saudi Arabia during the 1950s at which point he rejected his Zaydi identity and developed a strong anti-Shi'a bias.[87] After being expelled from Saudi Arabia al-Wadi'i returned to Yemen and in 1979 established a Salafi institute called Dar al-Hadith, in Saada Province, the heartland of Zaydism. At this point, the movement had an anti-Saudi current, despite receiving funding from Saudi clerics seeking to spread the Wahhabi message. After the death of al-Wadi'i in 2001 the movement began a process of realignment with the Saudi government, abandoning criticism and increasing their funding in the process. As Laurent Bonnefoy correctly observes, the case of Saudi funding of Salafis in Yemen not only demonstrates the ways in which capital plays out across the transnational field but also the ways in which funding and theological proximity do not necessarily result in the desired outcomes of those wielding this capital.[88]

In the early years of the twenty-first century, Salafist groups in Yemen began to side with the Saleh government against the Houthi movement,

[86] Brandt, *Tribes and Politics in Yemen*, p. 148.
[87] See Laurent Bonnefoy, 'The Salafis and the War in Yemen', forthcoming.
[88] Laurent Bonnefoy, 'Saudi Arabia and the Expansion of Salafism', *NOREF: Norwegian Peacebuilding Resource Centre*, Policy Brief (September 2013), p. 2.

becoming involved in fighting and the discursive stigmatization of the Zaydi identity, contributing to the equivocation of Zaydism with Iran.[89] The increasingly prominent role of religion within conflict across Yemen had a marked impact on the way in which groups framed themselves. Houthis named a fighting brigade after Hossein, a prominent figure within Shi'a thought whose death is commemorated in the festival of Karbala. In addition to being the son of 'Ali, Hossein is celebrated for contesting the rule of the Sunni caliph Yazid bin Muawiya. In contrast, militias fighting against the Houthis embraced anti-Shi'a figures, including Abdurraqeeb Abdulwahhab, a Sunni military figure who played a prominent role in intra-republican conflict, fighting against the Zaydis during the Yemeni civil war.

Deeper reflections and discussions with Yemenis suggest that the role of sectarianism in shaping tensions across the state is less important than socio-economic grievances and a broader struggle for power.[90] The Houthis drew upon widespread anger at the presence of regional actors in Yemeni politics, positioning themselves at the vanguard of the fight against external interference. As a consequence, not all those who support the Houthis share their ideological vision; moreover, despite the repressive nature of Houthi rule, they are still able to retain support.[91]

In spite of this, the salience of sectarian identities resonates through processes of sectarianization that take place domestically and regionally, cutting across the meanderings of tribal and geographical allegiance in the process. Over time, sectarian difference predominantly occurring along regional–tribal lines became the dominant principle of vision shaping Yemen's political field, positioning conflicts within the transnational field in the process.[92] They also serve as a way of creating social cohesion and a shield against other hierarchical social structures. In this vein, sectarian difference serves as a mechanism of control, enforced through the act of closing off a group against an external enemy.[93]

While many are quick to reduce conflict in Yemen to a 'proxy war' between Saudi Arabia and Iran within the context of 'ancient hatreds'

---

[89] See 'al-Judhur al-Fikriyya lil-Fitna al-Huthiyya', *al-Muntada* (April 2005), or Muhammad bin Muhammad al-Mahdi, 'al-Zaydiyya fi al-Yaman: Hiwar Maftuh', *Sana'a: Markaz al-Kalima al-Tayiba* (2008), p. 98.

[90] Interviews with Yemeni researcher, Yemeni scholar, Yemeni civil society activist, and Yemen security analyst all point to this conclusion, as do discussions during a private workshop on the future of Yemen held in December 2020.

[91] Observations made during private workshop on the future of Yemen, held in December 2020.

[92] al-Din, 'Yemen's War-torn Rivalries for Religious Education'.

[93] Observations made during private workshop on the future of Yemen, held in December 2020.

between Sunni and Shi'a, such a view is infelicitous and distorts analysis of events.[94] Before the events of 2014, sectarian difference was of little consequence for politics, which was shaped by tribal, political and ideological difference, yet in the aftermath of the *coup d'état* against Abd Rabbu Mansour Hadi, sectarian entrepreneurs sought to capitalize on communal divisions in an attempt to increase their own influence through processes of sectarianization, deepening divisions within Yemen and amongst those who travel to fight there. Indeed, Saudi soldiers who fight in Yemen are told by loyalist clerics that they are fighting against Shi'a heretics.

The process of framing the Houthis as Shi'a agents of Iran – conditioned by developments in the transnational field – creates a narrative of nefarious interference, an insidious presence and activity amongst a non-indigenous group that was cultivated by Iran to undermine the Yemeni project.[95] It also reinforces the narrative that Iran's *nomos* runs contrary to that of Saudi Arabia's *nomos*, resulting in competition across the transnational field, with Yemen framed as another front in this broader struggle.

Developments in Yemen provoked a furious spate of accusations from Riyadh and the Kingdom's allies. Speaking to Reuters in April 2015, a month after the coalition began its military action in Yemen, Prince Mohammed bin Nawaf said that

Iran should not have any say in Yemeni affairs. They are not part of the Arab world. Their interference has ignited instability, they have created havoc in our part of the world and we've seen the events that took place because of their malignant policies. Hence you have the coalition and a new foreign policy for all of us. We want an Arab world free of any outside interference. We can deal with our own problems.[96]

Such remarks echo those made by Saudi officials in the decade previously who were of the view that Yemeni politics should, at least, not oppose Riyadh.

In response to perceived Iranian support for the Houthis, MbS (architect of the Kingdom's military strategy in Yemen) accused Tehran of

---

[94] See interviews with Yemen security analyst, Yemeni scholar, and Yemeni researcher; Thomas E. Ricks, 'What Would a Saudi-Iran War Look Like? Don't Look Now, but It Is Already Here', *Foreign Policy* (28.12.17), http://foreignpolicy.com/2016/12/28/what-would-a-saudi-iran-war-look-like-dont-look-now-but-it-is-already-here-3/.

[95] See Dina Esfandiary and A. Tabatabai, 'Yemen: An Opportunity for Iran-Saudi Dialogue?' *Washington Quarterly* 39:2 (2016), 159.

[96] Richard Mably and Dominic Evans, 'Interview – Saudi Says Yemen Strikes Show Arab Resolve to Act Alone', *Reuters* (22.04.15), https://in.reuters.com/article/yemen-security-saudi/interview-saudi-says-yemen-strikes-show-arab-resolve-to-act-alone-idINL5N0XJ2JZ20150422.

'direct military aggression'. He also stressed that Tehran's actions 'may be considered an act of war against the Kingdom'.[97] For Adel al-Jubeir, 'Iranian interventions in the region are detrimental to the security of neighbouring countries and affect international peace and security. We will not allow any infringement of our national security.'[98] Beyond this, 'Iran's role and its direct command of its Houthi proxy in this matter constitute a clear act of aggression that targets neighbouring countries, and threatens peace and security in the region and globally'.[99] On 7 May 2018, al-Jubeir tweeted that 'The Iranian-planned Houthi attacks, which are strongly denounced by the international community, reveal their terrorism and never affects our stability and development.'[100] The tweet also had the hashtag #Houthi_Iranian_Terrorism.

Such remarks are not solely the remit of 'high' politics. Indeed, as Maria Louise Clausen acknowledges, Salafis in Yemen played a key role in framing the Houthis as a threat, locating the Zaydi movement 'as part of a global *Shi'ite*, Iranian conspiracy that seeks to divert the Muslim world'.[101] Here, once more, developments in Yemen were situated within an increasingly fractious transnational field. Supporting these efforts while also reflecting the Saudi-dominance of the organization, the OIC issued a statement condemning 'Iran's interference in the internal affairs of the States of the region and other Member States (including Bahrain, Yemen and Syria and Somalia) and its continued support for terrorism.'[102]

Despite claims to the contrary, Iranian involvement in Yemen has developed in response to the Arab Uprisings and Houthi successes, rather than existing independent of such events. While Saudi officials sought to frame Iran as playing a key role in the development of the Houthis in the 2000s, this has largely been rejected. While there has been a marked increase in Iranian support for the Houthis since 2014, this remains at relatively low levels, revealing a great deal not only about

[97] Saeed Kamali Dehghan, 'Saudi Arabia Accuses Iran of "Direct Aggression" over Yemen Missile', *The Guardian* (07.11.17), www.theguardian.com/world/2017/nov/07/saudi-arabia-accuses-iran-of-supplying-missile-to-houthi-rebels-in-yemen.

[98] Siraj Wahab, 'Missile Attack on Riyadh "An Act of War" by Iran', *Arab News* (07.11.17), www.arabnews.com/node/1189476/saudi-arabia.

[99] Ibid.

[100] Adel Aljubeir (07.05.18, 21:53), https://twitter.com/AdelAljubeir/status/993594737704751105.

[101] Clausen, 'Understanding the Crisis in Yemen', 21.

[102] 'Final Communiqué of the Extraordinary Meeting of the Council of Foreign Ministers of the Organization Of Islamic Cooperation on Aggressions on the Embassy of the Kingdom of Saudi Arabia in Tehran and Its Consulate General in Mashhad', *Organisation of Islamic Cooperation* (22.01.16), www.oic-oci.org/oicv2/topic/?t_id=10837&t_ref=4262&lan=en.

both Iran's strategic goals in Yemen but also about the relationship between Tehran and the Houthi movement. Although Iran exerts influence in Yemen, the Houthis continue to exert agency, rejecting calls from Tehran not to capture Sanaa.[103] Despite this intransigence, there is little doubt that Yemen is an appealing arena for Iran. The Houthis serve as a cost-effective ally with a shared vision of regional order – predicated on the fusion of resistance and Shi'a values – who provide access to a geographical area from which Iran can project its influence onto the Arabian Peninsula, confronting Saudi Arabia on the Kingdom's southern border. Beyond this, for some, Yemen also possesses apocalyptic importance, with fighting in the state a necessary event before the coming of the Mahdi. This view, according to one Iranian foreign policy analyst, is important in understanding Tehran's support for the Houthis, albeit also prompting some in Iran to question why more support had not been provided to Yemenis.[104]

Although there are theological differences between the two, a shared *nomos* couched in a narrative of resistance and anti-imperialism has brought the two together against the United States, Israel, and Saudi Arabia. Gains made by the Houthis result in gains made by Iran, which also benefits from military activities which demonstrate Saudi vulnerability. Here, links between the two have been made following an attack on Saudi Aramco, which was claimed by the Houthis, albeit allegedly with technical support provided by Iran.[105]

When the coalition's military campaign began in Yemen, social media users quickly expressed support for MbS and efforts to thwart Shi'a and Iranian expansionism.[106] The war was framed as a *duty*, with those dissenting from this narrative framed as traitors to both nation and religion. While some viewed the war as an attempt to defeat the Safavids and the Shi'a broadly, others framed the conflict in terms of defending the Arab identity of Yemen. A statement from the Embassy of Saudi Arabia suggested that the devastation of the Yemeni state was a 'direct result of Iran's blatant intrusion into internal Yemeni affairs. It seems that Tehran is aiming to undermine Yemen's security and stability, stoke sectarian divisions and thwart international efforts seeking to achieve

---

[103] Ryan Grim, 'Iran Tried to Stop Houthi Rebels in Yemen Obama Says', *Huffington Post* (06.08.15), www.huffingtonpost.co.uk/entry/iran-tried-to-stop-houthi-rebels-in-yemen_n_55c3ba1be4b0d9b743db627c.

[104] Interview with Iranian scholar and foreign policy analyst.

[105] Fatima Abo al-Asrar, 'The Houthis Cover Up for Iran. Here Is Why', *al-Arabiya* (29.09.19), https://english.alarabiya.net/en/views/news/middle-east/2019/09/29/The-Houthis-cover-up-for-Iran-Here-is-why-.

[106] Al Rasheed, 'Riyadh's War on Yemen'.

a peaceful settlement of the Yemeni crisis in accordance with the UN Security Council's Decision 2216.'[107]

For Adel al-Jubeir, Tehran's regional activity was further evidence that 'Iran remains the single main sponsor of terrorism in the world. It is determined to suspend the order in the Middle East', and that 'Iran is the problem, not the solution, in Syria and Yemen.'[108] This increased regional hostility over events in Yemen had a dramatic impact on the conflict in a number of ways. Not only did the rivalry shape regional politics, but it also created an increasingly sectarianized context within which groups in Yemen were forced to operate, highlighting the interplay of transnational and domestic political fields. Drawing on both the group's religious identity and support from Iran, Hadi referred to the Houthis as Twelver Shi'a, with clear implications of supporting Iran.[109] Hadi was not alone in this remark. Speaking with al-Jazeera, Hamoud al-Mikhlafi – the leader of a group fighting against the Houthis – referred to the group as Persians.[110]

This message was reinforced by clerics in Saudi Arabia. In a speech one week after the Saudi bombing campaign in Yemen began, Abd al-Rahman al-Sudais, a preacher of the Grand Mosque in Mecca, declared 'let us be clear, our war in Yemen is one between Sunnis and *Shi'ites* ... We must turn it into a sectarian war.'[111] Prominent figures in the transnational Salafi movement echoed such remarks, including the Saudi cleric Rabi'a al-Madkhali, who urged all Yemenis to 'prevent Yemen from becoming worse than Iran'.[112] In doing this, contestation across Yemen's political field became shaped by the interplay of local and regional voices, many of whom were reinforcing the sectarianization process.

---

[107] 'Saudi Arabia Condemns Ongoing Iranian Regional Interference and Aggression', *Embassy of the Kingdom of Saudi Arabia, Brussels* (09.11.16), http://ksaembassy.be/en/saudi-arabia-condemns-ongoing-iranian-regional-interference-aggression/.

[108] 'Iran Is World's 'Main Sponsor of Terrorism', Says Saudi Arabia', *Middle East Eye* (20.02.17), www.middleeasteye.net/news/iran-worlds-main-sponsor-terrorism-says-saudi-arabia.

[109] اول خطاب للرئيس عبدربة منصور هادي من عدن 21 مارس ('Awal Khitab llRais Abed Rabbu Mansour Hadi min Aden' ['The First Speech of President Abd Rabbo Mansour Hadi from Aden']), *YouTube* (21.03.15), www.youtube.com/watch?v=AQ9PDlftIJc.

[110] لقاء اليوم- المخلافي :من يصدق صالح والحوثي 'واهم ('Liqa alyoum – al-Mikhlafi: mun yosadeq Saleh u al-Houthi Wahem' [Today's Meeting – al'Mikhlafi: Who Believes Saleh and al-Houth are "the Most Important"']), *YouTube* (20.11.15), www.youtube.com/watch?v=p4xcrxJDGhI.

[111] الشيخ عبد الرحمن السديس كلمته عن الحرب في اليمن ('lShaykh Abdul Rahman al-Sudais Kalimathu 'an Alharab fi Alyaman' ['Sheikh Abdul Rahman al-Sudais, His Speech on the War in Yemen']), *YouTube* (28.11.15), https://youtu.be/yBKF7eYXusk.

[112] نصيحة لأهل اليمن في مواجهة الحوثيين - ربيع بن هادي المدخلى ('Nasiha lahl Alyaman fi Mwajhet al-Houthiyyn-Rab'i Hadi al-Madkhali' ['Advice to the People of Yemen in the Face of the Houthis – Rabie bin Hadi al-Madkhali']), *YouTube* (08.11.14), https://youtu.be/b4r3ecxN7l8.

Iranian officials were equally vocal in their comments. Speaking to participants of the Ahlu al-Bayt World Assembly in 2015, the supreme leader stressed that

The war in Yemen is a political war, not a religious one. They falsely claim that the issue is about Shi'a and Sunni while this is not the case. Some of those people who are losing their children, women, infants and their hospitals and schools in Yemen under the bombardment of the Saudis are Shafi'i and some of them are Zaidi. So, the issue is not about Shi'a and Sunni. The conflict is a political conflict, the conflict between policies. Today, they are creating such a situation in the region. It was they who created discord.[113]

Khamenei was similarly robust about Saudi airstrikes, calling on Riyadh to 'stop their criminal actions in Yemen immediately'.[114] In contrast, Rouhani was more diplomatic in his remarks, calling for a return to the negotiating table and an acceptance that 'the future of Yemen will be in the hands of the people of Yemen, not anyone else'.[115]

An article in the *Tehran Times* reported comments from Ramin Mehmanparast, an official in the Iranian foreign ministry, who stressed that 'the current course of events show that people's demands have not been responded to properly and unfortunately (the Yemeni government) has taken violent actions against the people'.[116] The same newspaper later carried comments from Hossein Amir-Abdullahian, the deputy foreign minister, who accused Saudi Arabia of intervening to prevent medical aid from reaching injured Yemenis.[117]

In spite of the widespread securitization of the Iranian threat across the transnational field and in global politics, there were some in the Obama administration – including the president – who doubted conventional narratives about the relationship between the Houthis and Iran. Contrary to general assumptions, Obama suggested that Tehran had 'advised the Houthis against taking the capital' in September 2014. In a talk at

---

[113] 'Leader's Speech to Members of Ahlul Bayt World Assembly and Islamic Radio and TV Union', *Khamenei.ir* (17.08.15), http://english.khamenei.ir/news/2109/Leader-s-speech-to-members-of-Ahlul-Bayt-World-Assembly-and-Islamic.

[114] Ali Hashem, 'Khamenei Criticizes Saudi Airstrikes, Nuclear Agreement', *al-Monitor* (09.04.15), www.al-monitor.com/pulse/originals/2015/04/iran-khamenei-saudi-airstrikes-yemen.html#ixzz4KF3HE4dc.

[115] 'Iranian President Calls for Halt to Yemen Air Strikes', *Reuters* (09.04.15), https://af.reuters.com/article/worldNews/idAFKBN0N00IA20150409.

[116] 'Yemenis Will Not Allow Interference in Internal Affairs: Iran', *Tehran Times* (08.06.11), www.tehrantimes.com/news/242067/Yemenis-will-not-allow-interference-in-internal-affairs-Iran.

[117] 'Iran Says Saudi Arabia Prevents Sending Aid to Yemenis', *Tehran Times* (25.04.15), www.tehrantimes.com/news/246312/Iran-says-Saudi-Arabia-prevents-sending-aid-to-Yemenis.

the American University that was later distributed by the White House, Obama elaborated on these points:

When the Houthis started moving, that wasn't on orders from Suleimani, that wasn't on an order from the IRGC. That was an expression of the traditional Houthi antagonism towards Sanaa, and some of the machinations of the former president, who was making common cause out of expediency with the Houthis.[118]

He later acknowledged that 'there were moments where Iran was actually urging potential restraint'.[119] Bernadette Meehan, spokeswoman for the National Security Council, echoed such concerns, acknowledging that it 'remains our assessment that Iran does not exert command and control over the Houthis in Yemen'.[120] Despite such calls, however, sectarianization processes found traction across the transnational field and, much like elsewhere in the region, Iran was framed as threat to the existing habitus and principles of vision in Yemen.

Future Challenges: Fragmentation and Secessionism

Aside from the Saudi-led bombing campaign, a number of other issues shape Yemeni politics. In the south, secessionist movements continue to threaten the territorial integrity of the state. The demarcation of zones of influence gave the UAE control of the south where Abu Dhabi was able to shape political currents, helping establish the Southern Transitional Council under the leadership of Aidorous al-Zoubaidi.

While the Emirates have largely supported Saudi efforts to curtail the Houthi influence and, by extension, to counter any Iranian gains, Abu Dhabi has been active in supporting the cause of secessionist groups in the south as a means of cultivating a group that can support its cause, most evident in the 2017 Qatar crisis where the Southern Transitional Council (STC) broke off all ties with Doha after the blockade. Anecdotally, al-Zoubaidi is said to wear a Manchester City tracksuit at home in the south of Yemen, representing another strand of Emirati influence on the state. Paradoxically, al-Zoubaidi argued for the legitimacy of the Hadi regime in order to justify the presence of the Saudi and Emirati-led

---

[118] Ryan Grim, 'This Is the Kind of President Donald Trump Is Replacing', *Huffington Post* (01.12.16), www.huffingtonpost.co.uk/entry/barack-obama-foreign-policy-trump_us_5824ce48e4b034e3899091ed.

[119] Grim, 'Iran Tried to Stop'.

[120] Cited in Ali Watkins, Ryan Grim, and Akbar Shahid Ahmed, 'Iran Warned Houthis against Yemen Takeover', *Huffington Post* (20.04.15), www.huffingtonpost.co.uk/entry/iran-houthis-yemen_n_7101456.

coalition, yet simultaneously framed the Hadi government as illegitimate as a consequence of their treatment of the south.

Emirati engagement in Yemen reveals trends about the nature of modern warfare, with private militaries comprising a global pool of mercenaries deployed in pursuit of strategic goals set by Abu Dhabi. In Yemen, Emirati strategy, articulated by Mohammed Dahlan, included the targeting of leaders of Islah by a group of mercenaries belonging to the Spear Operations Group, including Abraham Gold, a Hungarian-Israeli 'security contractor', who recounted his involvement in an interview to *Buzzfeed News*.[121] This strategy, which took place under the banner of the Saudi–Emirati coalition, was to disrupt the Muslim Brotherhood influence in Yemen, damaging a key local ally in the process, with Islah proving to be one of the most important Hadi allies in the fight against the STC.[122] Ultimately, however, the Emirati decision to withdraw from the conflict represented broader concerns at both the financial and the humanitarian cost of the conflict amidst an effort to position itself as a leading humanitarian actor on the world stage.

In light of the changing dynamics of the conflict in Yemen, an agreement between the Hadi government and the STC was reached in late 2020 in an effort to present a united front in the fight against the Houthis. Overseen by Saudi Arabia's Crown Prince, the agreement brought together two staunch rivals, united in the face of a common enemy, albeit without addressing long-standing questions regarding the future of Yemen.

Political and institutional fragmentation created opportunities for groups to function, often in competition, largely within the territorial boundaries of the state. Underpinning political life is a complex, malleable, and often transient set of tribal networks that are driven by the needs of local sheikhs. Local context is key in understanding the action of these groups, with a number of 'mini-states' emerging, facing their own challenges yet held together by internal logic, economies, and political ecosystems.[123]

By the turn of 2021, five cantons had been forged out of the Yemeni conflict, reflecting the power of different groups across the state. With

[121] Aram Roston, 'A Middle East Monarchy Hired American Ex-Soldiers to Kill Its Political Enemies. This Could Be the Future of War', *BuzzFeed News* (16.10.18), www.buzzfeednews.com/article/aramroston/mercenaries-assassination-us-yemen-uae-spear-golan-dahlan.
[122] Ammar al-Ashwal, 'UAE, Yemen's Islah Party Try to Tolerate Each Other', *al-Monitor* (06.12.18), www.al-monitor.com/pulse/originals/2018/12/yemen-islah-party-uae-relations-brotherhood-saudi-arabia.html.
[123] Peter Salisbury, 'Yemen: National Chaos, Local Order', *Chatham House* (20.12.17).

the Hadi government holding Marib, north Hadramawt and Taizz city, the Houthis occupying the north, STC in the south, Joint Resistance Forces in the Red Sea coast area, and local authorities regulating life in coastal Hadramawt, the Yemeni state had been hollowed out to a shell. In spite of this, the international community's peace-building efforts, either through the United Nations or the donor community, focus on regulating life through the state, an entity which is incapable of meeting the needs of people through its institutions even if peace could be achieved. Fighting across the state exacerbated challenges facing Yemenis seeking to meet their basic needs. Serious environmental challenges, mismanagement and ongoing drug problems have led to severe water scarcity, with 18.8 million people in need of humanitarian assistance and 17 million defined as food insecure.[124]

On 1 April 2022, a UN-brokered truce was signed, giving an degree of respite to those involved in the conflict. On 7 April, President Hadi – under pressure from Riyadh and Abu Dhabi – transferred power to a presidential council with the aim of facilitating negotiations. Since the start of the year, Yemenis had endured further destruction across Marib and Sabwa as coalition forces sought to prevent Houthi advances, with devastating repercussions; January alone saw 650 civilian casualties.[125] Humanitarian infrastructure has been devastated, with half of Yemen's hospitals out of commission, leading to the rapid spread of disease.[126] War in Ukraine has left Yemen desperately short of wheat imports, with 30–40 per cent of the country's wheat coming from Ukraine and Russia; Yemen imports 95 per cent of its overall needs.

Much of Yemen's suffering is a consequence of external manipulation, which shows little sign of diminishing, while Yemenis themselves seek to exert agency in the face of myriad – often competing – centrifugal forces that threaten to tear the state into a number of distinct parts. Yemen's

---

[124] 'Statement to the Security Council on Missions to Yemen, South Sudan, Somalia and Kenya and an update on the Oslo Conference on Nigeria and the Lake Chad Region', *United Nations Office for the Coordination of Humanitarian Affairs* (10.03.17), https://reliefweb.int/sites/reliefweb.int/files/resources/ERC_USG%20Stephen%20O%27Brien%20Statement%20to%20the%20SecCo%20on%20Missions%20to%20Yemen%2C%20South%20Sudan%2C%20Somalia%20and%20Kenya%2C%20and%20update%20on%20Oslo%20Conference%20-%2010%20March%202017.pdf.

[125] 'Despite Military Escalation, Increased Humanitarian Crisis in Yemen, 'A Way Out of This War' Still Exists, Special Envoy Tells Security Council', *UNSC 14793* (15.02.22), www.un.org/press/en/2022/sc14793.doc.htm.

[126] 'Humanitarian Crisis in Yemen: Seven Years on, WHO is Strengthening the Health System, Responding to Vital Health Needs, and Saving Lives', *Reliefweb* (27.03.22), https://reliefweb.int/report/yemen/humanitarian-crisis-yemen-seven-years-who-strengthening-health-system-responding-vital.

position within the transnational field and the organization of its domestic political field have left the state at the vanguard of competing visions of order and, thus, open to the actions of others.

The destructive cost of these factors will continue to be felt until both military and political solutions to the crisis are found. Then, and only then, can the fundamental aspects of everyday life such as water, agriculture, and human security be addressed. In such conditions, with centrifugal forces pulling at the fabric of the state, the unity of the Yemen Republic is at risk, increasingly as separatists in the south declared a state of emergency, rejecting the legitimacy of the government and its Saudi backers.[127]

Conclusions

The competition to shape Yemen's political field in the years after the Arab Uprisings has had devastating repercussions for Yemenis across the state. The absence of a dominant principle of vision has manifested in violent conflict cutting across the contours of geographically charged identity markers, deepening divisions in the process and contributing to the fragmentation of the state. In such conditions there is scope for a range of different actors (internal and external) to deploy capital in pursuit of their goals, albeit often with catastrophic consequences. The fragmentation of the state and emergence of communal schisms has allowed regional powers to provide support for particular groups, deepening divisions and firmly positioning Yemen within competition between different *nomoi* to define the principles of vision in the transnational field.

Building a lasting peace in Yemen requires addressing a range of challenges and resolving both military and political conflicts. While the former has evolved into an all-encompassing, intractable struggle, resolving political conflicts in a way that is acceptable to all parties may prove to be the more difficult challenge. Further challenging efforts to build peace, UNSCR 2216 – a Security Council Resolution designed to create a ceasefire and begin moves towards power sharing – has failed to reflect facts on the ground, calling for a Houthi disengagement and does not recognize the role played by key groups such as the STC and civil society organizations in the conflict.

---

[127] Interview with Yemeni-Emirati student. See also Mohammed Mukhashaf, 'Southern Yemen Separatists Want Saudi-Backed Government Overthrown', *Reuters* (21.01.18), https://uk.reuters.com/article/uk-yemen-security-southerners/southern-yemen-separatists-want-saudi-backed-government-overthrown-idUKKBN1FA0WT.

Yet regional powers continue to play a central role in the conflict, deploying different forms of capital in pursuit of their *nomos*. The continuation of the conflict, at great cost to the Saudis, is a source of much frustration. In emails leaked in 2017, MbS allegedly told US officials of a desire to leave the Yemen conflict[128] and while the Kingdom apparently demonstrated a willingness to deal with the Houthis, this was contingent upon the group ending their relationship with Iran.[129] In spite of this, efforts to facilitate a lasting ceasefire between local and regional actors has been difficult to achieve, reflecting the increasingly intractable and localized nature of a conflict that also occupies a prominent role in shaping the transnational field.

The levels of permeability stemming from state fragmentation, failed efforts at decentralization, and increasingly sectarianized identities have provided ample opportunities for the penetration of Yemeni politics from external actors, dating back to the middle of the twentieth century. Recent instances of external involvement have seen Saudi Arabia and Iran become embroiled in conflict in pursuit of respective *nomoi*. Yet in the case of Saudi Arabia, an additional goal of preventing the emergence of a strong state on its southern border – following the apocryphal saying of Ibn Sa'ud – has proved to be an additional consequence. Competition in Yemen's political field is clearly conditioned by developments in the transnational field, with efforts to impose principles of vision resonating across both fields, to the detriment of Yemenis.

---

[128] Clayton Swisher and David Hearst, 'Exclusive: Saudi Crown Prince Wants out of Yemen War, Email Leak Reveals', *Middle East Eye* (16.08.17), www.middleeasteye .net/news/exclusive-saudi-crown-prince-wants-out-yemen-war-email-leak-reveals).
[129] Colum Lynch, Lara Seligman, and Robbie Gramer, 'Can a Young Saudi Prince End the War in Yemen?' *Foreign Policy* (20.11.19), https://foreignpolicy.com/2019/11/20/ can-khalid-bin-salman-young-saudi-prince-end-yemen-war-mohammed-mbs/.

Conclusions

Across 2021, while the world was navigating the challenges of the Covid-19 pandemic, Saudi Arabia and Iran sought to resolve their own crisis, engaging in a process of track II dialogue aimed at improving relations between the two long-time rivals. By October Saudi Arabia was considering a request from Tehran to re-open a consulate in Jeddah, but while the Kingdom was 'serious' about dialogue, there had not been, in their view, sufficient progress to fully restore diplomatic relations which had been cut in 2016.[1]

In addition to bilateral talks between Riyadh and Tehran, there were also efforts to improve relations between regional powers including Egypt, Qatar, Jordan, Turkey, Saudi Arabia, and Iran. Despite narrowly avoiding a diplomatic incident as the Iranian foreign minister sat in the wrong seat, the talks were viewed as a success by those closely involved. To outsiders, they represented a positive step in a broader effort to improve relations between Saudi Arabia and Iran. Yet ongoing violence in Yemen, dialogue in Vienna over the JCPOA, war in Ukraine and stagnant talks in Amman at the end of 2021 highlight the challenges of improving relations. There is little doubt that improving relations between Riyadh and Tehran is a necessary step in addressing conflict across the region; after all, as we have seen, the rivalry has had a devastating impact on people across the Middle East, exacerbating existing divisions and contributing to increasing violence across the region.

While surprising to some, there are sound pragmatic reasons for Saudi Arabia and Iran to engage with one another, most notably concerning future aspirations. Indeed, with both states facing economic challenges, the desire to engage in a costly rivalry – or war – appears limited.[2] As

---

[1] Andrew England, 'Saudi Arabia 'Serious' about Talks with Iran', *Financial Times* (15.10.21), www.ft.com/content/8665b1d2-b0ca-4dd0-8a18-837e3ad5b110.

[2] Simon Mabon, Samira Nasirzadeh, and Eyad Al Refai, 'De-Securitisation and Pragmatism in the Persian Gulf: The Future of Saudi-Iranian Relations', *The International Spectator* 56:4 (2021), 66–83.

several Saudi analysts observed, the Kingdom would be happy to work with Iran if Tehran was keen to work within the framework of regional politics.[3] Yet serious challenges remain which require resolution, notably conflict in Yemen and questions about the nuclear deal, while there are also possible spoilers found across both states. Talks aimed at improving relations between the two states requires resolution not only of the grievances and concerns held by Riyadh and Tehran, but also of conflicts in which the Saudis and the Iranians are involved.

Saudi Arabia's engagement with Iran points to a marked shift in its policy towards the Islamic Republic under MbS. While economic factors are undeniably important, the changing dynamics of domestic and international politics also played a key role, notably the position of the United States. The Biden administration's adoption of an increasingly critical stance towards Saudi Arabia left many in the Kingdom concerned about the organization of security in the Gulf. Historically Saudi Arabia had been reliant upon the United States as a security guarantor in the face of threats from Iraq or Iran – providing a constant supply of oil in return – yet changing US strategic priorities pointed to a recalibration of its relationship with Riyadh. This process manifested in a number of ways, from vocal criticism of human rights in the Kingdom (and its allies), a lawsuit in the United States against the Saudi state for its involvement in the 9/11 attacks, and condemnation of the killing of Jamal Khashoggi. The Saudi decision to cut oil production in 2022 in the face of strong US pressure (as part of a global campaign against Russia's invasion of Ukraine) highlights the level of friction between Riyadh and Washington.

As we have seen, understanding the rivalry and its impact on the region is multifaceted. While the rivalry has produced a great deal of sensationalist literature which frames events in terms of a 'Cold War' or a 'proxy war', little has been written on the impact of the rivalry across the Middle East. Tracing the impact of the rivalry on states across the region requires an understanding not only of the nature of relations between Saudi Arabia and Iran, but also of the states in which Riyadh and Tehran compete for influence. The nature of competition between Riyadh and Tehran is conditioned by context, meaning that developments in the transnational field do not always resonate within the domestic field in the same way and vice versa. As a result, to understand the manifestation of tensions within states, it is necessary to look at not only the position of that state within the transnational field but also the organization of power within the domestic political field.

---

[3] Interviews with Saudi analysts between 2018 and 2022.

While there are broader visions of order – *nomoi* – that condition the foreign policies of Saudi Arabia and Iran, these visions are themselves conditioned by developments within and between political and transnational fields, perhaps best seen in processes of sectarianization. Although the Saudi-led process of sectarianization (and by extension, securitization) of Iran took place in the transnational field, it resonated across societies divided along sectarian lines, allowing the move from transnational to domestic political field. As a consequence, understanding the nature of the political field is of paramount importance in gaining a more nuanced awareness of the impact of the rivalry between Saudi Arabia and Iran. Put another way, to understand the nature of the rivalry and its peculiarities, it is imperative to look at the manifestation of competition within political fields – where contrasting strategies can be found – alongside the transnational field.

It is often assumed that Saudi Arabia derives support from Sunni communities while Iran derives support from Shi'a communities, yet as Iranian support for Hamas and Saudi support for Lebanese Christians and Iraqi Shi'a demonstrates, this is overly simplistic. Other assumptions suggest that material or ideational support are central components of relationship building. While ideational and material support is undeniably important, as I have sought to demonstrate, the existence of a shared *nomos* – a fundamental vision of order – underpins the strongest transnational relationships. In deploying the concept of *nomos* we are better equipped to see how transnational relationships develop without resorting to lazy stereotypes about 'proxy wars' or sectarian networks. Instead, shared visions of regional order can unite actors from different backgrounds in a way that does not essentialize or homogenize. While there are clear hierarchies of power at play within a *nomos*, the ability to exert agency within a shared vision far easier to see than in the problematic proxy wars thesis.

Competition between different *nomoi* followed by domestic and regional powers determines the nature of a political field (domestic or transnational) and its principles of vision. *Nomoi* articulated by Saudi Arabia and Iran find traction in states across the region, resulting in the cultivation of strong transnational relationships between actors driven by a shared vision of order. These relationships are supplemented by more transient relationships typically based on the provision of material support, but all conditioned by the complexities of time and space.

Saudi Arabia's *nomos* is largely conservative, predicated on maintaining the status quo, supporting monarchical regimes and preventing both the rising influence of Iran and the spread of Islamist movements. While largely driven by a desire to preserve the status quo, this *nomos* also involves what some might view as revolutionary activity such as in

Syria, where support was given to key opposition groups in an attempt to topple Bashar al-Assad. In contrast, Iran's *nomos* is largely driven by concepts of resistance and an anti-status quo position. Yet much like Saudi Arabia, its *nomos* also has somewhat contradictory moments, best seen in its counter-revolutionary stance in Syria.

Understanding these *nomoi* reveals a great deal about the pragmatic nature of foreign policies, rejecting much of the ideological or sectarian framing of Saudi and Iranian activities across the region. Indeed, by looking at actions across different states we are better placed to understand the ways in which Riyadh and Tehran have sought to counter each other and to enact their respective *nomoi*. Such analysis also reveals much about the ways in which domestic politics shapes foreign policy. While we are constrained by access to knowledge at the highest level – WikiLeaks offers a degree of understanding – changes in approach can reveal important insights about the inner workings of both states. In Iran, for example, tensions between the broad factions and competing visions of the Iranian *nomos* have seen a dramatic evolution from the early years of the Islamic Republic, which were driven by a desire to export revolutionary goals. More recently, however, a more pragmatic *nomos* has seen Iran become more restrained in regional politics, albeit continuing to support groups such as Hizbullah and the Houthis.

In Iraq, the rivalry found traction most prominently after the toppling of Saddam Hussein in 2003 and the fragmentation of the state. At this point, opportunities actors engaged in competition to define principles of vision of Iraq's political field. Here, the demographic makeup of Iraq's political field meant that Iran was well placed to deploy religious capital grounded in Shi'a experience and theology, a process aided by the return of Iraqi political figures who had sought refuge in Iran during the rule of Saddam Hussein. In the years that followed, Iran supplemented its religious capital with economic and coercive capital to consolidate its position of dominance in the political field, yet widespread unrest amongst the Iraqi population eroded this capital, resulting in the *Tishreen* protests of 2019. After the military defeat of Da'ish, financial pressures emerging from processes of post-conflict reconstruction and general anger at widespread corruption created opportunities for Saudi Arabia to deploy economic capital in Iraq's political field, supplemented by a form of cultural capital along the lines of shared 'Arabness'. Though other Saudi leaders had previously failed to gain ground in Iraq's political field, MbS was able to engage in a competition to define the principles of vision, although it remains to be seen how receptive Iraqis will be to such moves in the long term.

In Bahrain, the habitus and principles of vision have been dominated by the Al-Khalifa and, by extension, by Saudi Arabia. Riyadh's influence is achieved through economic and coercive capital to ensure the survival of their allies in the face of decades of political unrest, often defining the ordering principles in accordance with concerns shaped by developments in the Saudi and transnational fields. While Iran has historically made claims to ownership over Bahrain – perhaps partially out of a mischievous desire to cause unrest – these claims do not always resonate well across the archipelago, with Shi'a Bahrainis asserting autonomy in the face of such claims. The evolution of the habitus and the dominant principles of vision reflects developments across the political field. While opposition groups were able to lay claim to religious and social capital, Saudi involvement in Bahrain's political field ultimately prevented a shift in the habitus and principles of vision which allowed for political reform. This Saudi presence demonstrates the position of Bahrain in the transnational field as a site of strategic importance for Saudi Arabia, shaped by its anti-Shi'a and anti-democracy principle of vision.

In Lebanon, the Tai'f Accords and power-sharing agreement enshrined communal difference within political life, allowing external powers to provide support to local groups and Lebanese groups to secure support from regional powers. Here, economic capital played a key role in increasing Saudi influence a cross t he s tate, while I ranian i nfluence was initially achieved through social and religious capital in pursuit of a *nomos* defined by resistance, but over time its political capital also grew. Despite the disparity in provision of financial support, Tehran's *nomos* found greater traction, reflecting both the importance of its vision and the weakness of the March 14 bloc. Ultimately, however, the emergence of protests in late 2019 served as a widespread rejection of the dominant principles of vision – of power sharing along communal lines and supported by external powers – prompting a struggle to shape the Lebanese political field that continues to this day. Although sectarian elites continue to receive support from their regional allies amidst the presence of shared *nomoi*, their survival is contingent upon working with each other in the face of a shifting habitus.

In Syria, the perpetuation of conflict reflects Assad's ongoing attempts to define principles of vision and the broader habitus. In pursuit of this, with support from Hizbullah, Iran, and Russia, Assad has deployed coercive capital, supported by social and economic capital in such a way that prevents the emergence of pro-democracy movements. While this was typically mapped onto sectarian lines, Assad has sought to capture the mainstream Sunni *'ulama'* in an effort to circumvent such divisions. Although Iran is unlikely to abandon Assad, having sacrificed religious and cultural capital in supporting the Syrian president in his counterrevolutionary campaign, Saudi Arabia and other Arab states have begun to normalize relations with Syria, in the coming together of competing *nomoi*. There is little doubt that Syria occupies an important position in the transnational field, providing Iran with the means to circumvent the Persian–Arab dichotomy and providing Tehran with access to the Arab world. These relations are reinforced by a shared resistance *nomos*, albeit one that has not prevented Saudi Arabia and other Arab states from trying to woo Damascus, seemingly ignoring Assad's crimes.

In Yemen, the fragmentation of the state after the onset of conflict created opportunities for a range of actors to deploy capital in pursuit of defining the principles of vision. Processes of sectarianization exacerbated latent socio-economic divisions cutting across the state, shaping a new habitus characterized by division. This division emerged from political, socio-economic, tribal, and geographical tensions, but the sectarianization process added a religious component to these differences, increasing Yemen's strategic importance within the transnational field in the process. As a consequence, competing *nomoi* once again found traction in the domestic political field. While Saudi Arabia has long been concerned about instability in Yemen spilling into the Kingdom, Houthi gains and Iranian support prompted direct military involvement; in contrast, Iranian involvement in Yemen reflects a low cost-high return strategy emerging from a shared *nomos*, albeit complicated slightly by Arab–Persian tensions. The Saudi bombing campaign that followed was condoned by the United States in return for acquiescence over the JCPOA and supported by Washington, London, and others. As a result, Saudi coercive capital exacerbated the destruction of the Yemeni state, resulting in the fracturing of Yemen's political field, with devastating repercussions for Yemenis.

Developments across the transnational field create possibilities for figures seeking to shape domestic political fields to define principles of vision and ultimately the habitus. Historical events are important in this regard, providing context and, in some cases, reserves of capital to those seeking to define principles of vision. The organization of capital within domestic political fields has a key role to play here. Principles of vision and division, the habitus, and the forms of capital in operation determine the ability of external powers to exert influence within political fields. Understanding the distribution of power within political fields and the type of actor defining the principles of vision, conditions the capacity of external actors to compete for influence. When competition over defining the principles of vision is rife, there is often scope for external actors to become embroiled in the domestic political field. Moreover, when actors seek to derive capital from the transnational political field – either by recourse to claims of religious legitimacy or resistance – the justification for external actors to become involved increases. Yet when political fields are dominated by actors shaping the habitus, deploying capital and defining principles of vision, there is limited scope for competition to take place, as the case of Lebanon post-2006 shows.

The rivalry between Saudi Arabia and Iran also has indirect consequences. Much like competition in the transnational field shapes domestic fields and vice versa, there is also a horizontal dimension, with developments within domestic fields resonating across other domestic political fields. For example, a political event in Beirut in December 2021 that hosted members of the Bahraini al-Wifaq organization prompted a furious response in Manama, with the regime angry that individuals deemed 'terrorists' had been hosted.[4] Undeniably shaped by currents in its own political field and the transnational field, the response from the Bahraini state reveals the extent to which capital – and its perceived possible impact – may have on principles of vision and division.

Across these developments, little has changed in the construction of *nomoi*. Iran's *nomos* – as initially articulated by the architect of the Islamic Republic Ruhollah Khomeini – remains firm, defined by a vision that is anti-monarchical, anti-Israel, anti-oppressor, and anti-imperialist. Unlike Iran, Saudi Arabia's *nomos* has evolved slightly in recent years. While previously the Kingdom's *nomos* was defined by an anti-Iranian, anti-Shi'a, anti-Islamism, and anti-democracy fusion, in recent years the anti-Shi'a component within the Kingdom's domestic political field has been quietly removed through a process of desectarianization taking place within the Kingdom.

To understand foreign engagement within a political field it is imperative to understand not only the position of the state within the transnational field but also the structural organization of the political field. In understanding the structural organization of the political field, we are better placed to understand the ways in which Riyadh and Tehran engage with people and groups across the state and, conversely, the conditions that prompt local groups to engage with external backers.

From reflecting on five different arenas, it is clear to see that there are particular structural factors that condition the ability of Saudi Arabia and Iran to engage across the region. The nature of these structural factors determines the form of engagement, ranging from direct military or political engagement to ideational support. The Iranian strategy of supporting groups reflects a broader *nomos* driven by a broadly anti-status quo agenda, cutting across state borders, albeit with pragmatically

---

[4] Ismaeel Naar, 'Bahrain conDemns Beirut Hosting Press Conference for 'Hostile Personnel', *Al Arabiya* (12.12.21), https://english.alarabiya.net/News/gulf/2021/12/12/Bahrain-condemns-Beirut-hosting-press-conference-for-hostile-personnel-.

counter-revolutionary moments. Conversely, the Saudi *nomos* points to a largely status-quo driven agenda, albeit with pragmatically revolutionary components. These apparent contradictions in foreign policy agendas in Saudi Arabia and Iran point to a broader desire to order politics in accordance with *nomoi* that require different forms of actions which may appear incongruent with other strategies. Here the use of *nomos* helps to better understand foreign policy agendas which may appear contradictory.

What is also clear is that the transnational field matters in determining the nature of domestic politics and vice versa. While scholars have embraced the interplay between regional and domestic developments in the Middle East, this interplay requires more detailed theorization, in terms of both Bourdieu's work and empirically. Indeed, as we have seen, developments in the transnational field can resonate within domestic political fields in different ways, contingent upon the distribution of capital within such political fields. For example, the deployment of capital is contingent upon the nature of fields and habitus, meaning that principles of vision find traction in different ways across time and space. Sectarianism is an obvious example of something that resonates in different ways, contingent upon the nature of the habitus and the position of a state within the transnational field. Yet sectarian difference – and sectarianization – alone does not serve to achieve this goal. For example, in Lebanon, sectarian difference transcends the impotence of the rule of law, while in Iraq, where structural factors are largely similar, sectarian difference serves to restrict action, existing as a form of ordering principle. The political economy of sectarianism serves to reinforce this position.

Theoretical Ruminations

In addition to contributing to debates on the nature of the rivalry between Saudi Arabia and Iran, sectarianism, and regional politics, I have also endeavoured to contribute to a burgeoning body of literature that uses the ideas of Pierre Bourdieu in the Middle East. Bourdieu's concepts of capital, fields, habitus, and principles of vision have offered rich conceptual tools through which to look at the construction of political fields across the region. For Bourdieu, the field is a space of social relations or configurations defined by a struggle over (different forms of) capital. Although typically associated with the state, there is nothing analytically binding the field to the state. Instead, much like actors can pursue different forms of capital, competition can cut across different fields which are defined by actors operating in relation to one another.

While fields are relatively autonomous – by which he means they follow their own inherent logics – they are connected with other fields.

This is particularly evident in our study, seen in the case of a political field's location within a transnational field. Much like Paul Noble spoke of a regional sound chamber in which developments across the region reverberate, competition within the transnational field resonates within (and across) political fields, helping determine the habitus and principles of vision in the process. The autonomy of a particular field evolves over time, contingent upon the interplay between competing forms of capital and the ability to define the principles of vision. The fundamentally relational component of the field means that the interplay between domestic and regional actors and capital is central in shaping the nature of the field.

The transnational field, much like its domestic counterparts, is produced by the relational interplay between different actors. Contestation and efforts to impose principles of vision over the transnational field have reverberated in the domestic fields of states across the region both through the cultivation of a habitus and through the deployment of capital. The deployment of this capital is conditioned by the habitus of a field, allowing certain forms (and arrangements) of capital to define principles of vision at particular times but not at others. From this, questions emerge as to the ways in which capital translates from the transnational field into domestic political fields. While a prevailing assumption holds that sectarian affinity will determine the construction of transnational relationships, this assumption fails to consider the ways in which capital is deployed by actors seeking to increase their influence. The deployment of capital by regional powers in the domestic political field of another state demonstrates several things. First, that competition within the transnational field resonates across the region, manifesting in different forms contingent upon the organization of the transnational field and the domestic political field. While capital can be deployed by an actor in the same way in two fields, the relational organisation of those fields may be such that different results emerge. Similarly, questions also emerge as to the ways in which developments in domestic political fields resonate in other political fields, as seen in the case of the December 2021 event in Beirut.

As has been illustrated, there are multiple forms of capital that have been deployed by actors, defined by the rules of the game and the context within which actors are operating. This is particularly evident moving from the transnational field to domestic fields, and also across political fields covered in this book. At times, economic capital is valorized over cultural or religious capital, yet at others, cultural, religious, or political capital are more valuable. These forms of capital may also feed into each other, reinforcing symbolic capital and the principles of vision, or contesting such articulations. Competition over capital – both its accumulation and its deployment – shapes the nature of the political field and, with it, the habitus. The dominance of particular actors and their ability to impose principles of vision on a society determines the rules of the game and the parameters through which existing rules operate.

Moving forward, there is more work to be done exploring the ways in which Bourdieu's ideas can aid our exploration of Middle Eastern politics, both within and between states. There is clear benefit to using such approaches but there is also a need for more rigorous interrogation of the ways in which concepts of *fields*, *capital*, and habitus operate in the Middle East. Similarly, the concept of *nomos* offers prescient analytical insight in understanding the ordering of life, yet aside from passing mention in other works, there is very little by way of detailed theoretical exploration. Despite this, there is a new generation of scholars working with Bourdieu's ideas and applied political theory in the Middle East, which will offer valuable and fascinating insight.

The Future of the Struggle and Regional Order

As diplomatic talks between the Saudis and the Iranians continue, it remains to be seen if a lasting breakthrough can be made. Talks in Baghdad, Vienna, Amman, and backchannel conversations across the world have all sought to improve relations between the long-time rivals. Yet as we have seen, it is increasingly difficult to untangle the rivalry from developments in domestic political fields. Moreover, although the book has focused upon five states in the Middle East, this is not an exhaustive exploration of arenas of rivalry between the Saudis and the Iranians. Indeed, it is possible to also see competition play out in Libya, India, Pakistan, Indonesia, Malaysia, and other states with sizeable Muslim populations that are divided along communal lines, albeit also shaped by the presence of other regional actors such as Turkey, Qatar, and the UAE.

Furthermore, the future of the struggle between Saudi Arabia and Iran will be shaped by developments in the transnational field and the manifestation of these developments in domestic political fields across the region. Additionally – and certainly beyond the scope of this book – are a number of domestic factors which will determine the capacity of Riyadh and Tehran to operate. Both states face serious economic pressures, stemming from a 'maximum pressure' sanctions regime in Iran and a desire to move to a 'post-oil' economy in Saudi Arabia. These economic challenges are exacerbated by impending political transition, as Iran prepares to anoint a new supreme leader, and Saudi Arabia prepares itself to move beyond the sons of Ibn Sa'ud to the grandsons of the founding father of the Kingdom. Neither will be free from problems, meaning that addressing perilous domestic conditions may be a serious concern for the next generation of rulers. As history has shown us, it is often useful to have an external enemy in precarious times. Saudi Arabia and Iran have long fulfilled that role for each other, albeit to differing degrees. The international community should work to ensure that some form of diplomatic agreement is in place to ameliorate any tensions that may emerge during such processes of transition.

Even if diplomatic mechanisms are in place, however, and a lasting agreement is found, the legacy of the rivalry between Riyadh and Tehran will continue to be felt for decades to come. With close to one million people killed in the conflicts following the Arab Uprisings and tens of millions displaced from their homes – suffering all manner of physical and mental health problems, facing devastating economic conditions, and a generation of children missing out on school – the fallout from conflicts featuring Riyadh and Tehran on opposing sides is devastating. The human cost of the struggle for supremacy and the clash of competing *nomoi* is immeasurable.

Bibliography

Academic Sources

Abdo, G. *The New Sectarianism: The Arab Uprisings and the Rebirth of the Shi'a-Sunni Divide* (Oxford: Oxford University Press, 2017).

Abrahamian, E. *Khomeinism: Essays on the Islamic Republic* (Berkley: University of California Press, 1993).

AbuKhalil, A. 'Determinants and Characteristics of the Saudi Role in Lebanon: The Post-Civil War Years', in Madawi al-Rasheed (ed.), *Kingdom without Borders* (London: Hurst, 2008), 79–97.

Achcar, G. *The 33-Day War: Israel's War on Hezbollah in Lebanon and Its Aftermath* (London: Saqi, 2007).

Agnew, J. and S. Corbridge. *Mastering Space: Hegemony, Territory and International Political Economy* (London: Routledge, 1995).

Ahmadian, H. and P. Mohseni. 'Iran's Syria Strategy: The Evolution of Deterrence', in F. Osinga and T. Sweijs (eds.), *NL ARMS Netherlands Annual Review of Military Studies 2020* (The Hague: Netherlands Annual Review of Military Studies, 2021), 341–64.

Ajami, F. 'The End of Pan-Arabism', *Foreign Affairs* Winter (1978/79), 355–73.

Akbarzadeh, S. 'Why Does Iran Need Hizbollah?', *The Muslim World* 106:1 (2016), 127–40.

Akbarzadeh, S. and Z. S. Ahmed. 'Impacts of Saudi Hegemony on the Organization of Islamic Cooperation (OIC)', *International Journal of Politics, Culture and Society* 31:3 (2018), 297–311.

Akbarzadeh, S. and K. Connor. 'The Organization of the Islamic Conference: Sharing an Illusion', *Middle East Policy* 12:2 (2005), 79–92.

Akbarzadeh, S., W. Gourlay, and A. Ehteshami. 'Iranian Proxies in the Syrian Conflict: Tehran's "Forward-defence" in Action', *Journal of Strategic Studies* (2022), 1–24.

Alagha, J. *Hizbullah's Documents: From the 1985 Open Letter to the 2009 Manifesto* (Amsterdam: Pallas Publications, 2011).

Algar, H. *Wahhabism: A Critical Essay* (New York: Islamic Publications International, 2002).

Al Haj Saleh, Y. *The Impossible Revolution: Making Sense of the Syrian Tragedy* (London: Hurst, 2017)

Alhasan, H. 'The Role of Iran in the Failed Coup of 1981: The IFLB in Bahrain', *Middle East Journal* 65:4 (2011), 603–17.

al-Hoss, S. *Lubnan ala al-Muftaraq* [*Lebanon at the Crossroads*] (Beirut: Beirut Arab Center, 1984).

al-Kadhem, N. *Isti'malat al-dhakira fi mujtama 'ta 'taduddi mubtala bi al-tarikh* [*Uses of Memory in a Multicultural Society Burdened with History*] (Manama Bahrain: Maktaba Fakhrawi, 2008).

al-Najjar, B. S. *al-Harakat al-Diniyyah fi al-Khalij al-Arabi* [*Religious Movements in the Arab Gulf*] (London: Dar al Saqi Press, 2007).

Al-Rasheed, M. *Politics in an Arabian Oasis: Rashidis of Saudi Arabia* (London: I. B. Tauris, 1997).

Al-Rasheed, M. (ed.). *Salman's Legacy. The Dilemmas of a New Era in Saudi Arabia* (London: Hurst, 2018).

Al-Rasheed, M. and R. Vitalis. *Counter-narratives: History, Contemporary Society, and Politics in Saudi Arabia and Yemen* (New York: Palgrave Macmillan, 2004).

Allinson, J. *The Struggle for the State in Jordan: The Social Origins of Alliances in the Middle East* (London: I. B. Tauris, 2016).

AlShehabi, O. H. *Contested Modernity: Sectarianism, Nationalism and Colonialism in Bahrain* (London: Oneworld, 2019).

Alvandi, R. 'Muhammad Reza Pahlavi and the Bahrain Question, 1968–1970', *British Journal of Middle East Studies* 37:2 (2010), 159–77.

Aras, B. and E. Yorulmazlar. 'Mideast Geopolitics: The Struggle for a New Order', *Middle East Policy* 24:2 (2017), 57–69.

Ataie, M. 'Revolutionary Iran's 1979 Endeavor in Lebanon', *Middle East Policy* 20:2 (2013), 137–57.

Ayubi, N. N. *Political Islam: Religion and Politics in the Arab World* (London: Routledge, 1991).

Babakhan, A. 'The Deportation of Shi'a during the Iran–Iraq War: Causes and Consequences', in Faleh Abdul-Jabar (ed.), *Ayatollahs, Sufis, and Ideologues: State, Religion, and Social Movements in Iraq* (London: Saqi Books, 2002), 192–200.

Badie, D. *After Saddam: American Foreign Policy and the Destruction of Secularism in the Middle East* (New York/London: Lexington Books, 2017).

Bakhash, S. 'Iran's Relations with Israel, Syria and Lebanoin', in Miron Rezun (ed.), *Iran at the Crossroads: Global Relations in a Turbulent Decade* (Boulder, CO: Westview Press, 1990), 116–17.

Batatu, H. 'Iraq's Underground Shi'a Movements', MER102 (1981), www .merip.org/mer/mer102/iraqs-underground-shii-movements.

Batatu, H. *The Old Social Classes and the Revolutionary Movements in Iraq* (Princeton: Princeton University Press, 1978).

Batatu, H. *The Old Social Classes and the Revolutionary Movements of Iraq: A Study of Iraq's Old Landed and Commercial Classes and of Its Communits, Ba'athists and Free Officers* (Princeton: Princeton University Press, 1978).

Baumann, H. *Citizen Hariri: Lebanon's Neo-Liberal Reconstruction* (London: Hurst, 2016).

Becherer, R. 'A Matter of Life and Debt: The Untold Costs of Rafiq Hariri's New Beirut', *Journal of Architecture* 10:1 (2005), 1–42.

Belcastro, F. 'An Odd 'Foreign Policy Couple'? Syria and Saudi Arabia 1970–1989', *Journal of Balkan and Near Eastern Studies* 22:1 (2020), 29–46.

Bell, G. *A Woman in Arabia: The Writings of the Queen of the Desert* (New York: Penguin, 2015).

Berger, P. *The Sacred Canopy* (New York: Doubleday, 1967).

Berti, B. and Y. Guzansky. 'Saudi Arabia's Foreign Policy on Iran and the Proxy War in Syria: Toward a New Chapter?', *Israel Journal of Foreign Affairs* 8:3 (2014), 25–34.

Blanford, N. *Killing Mr Lebanon: The Assassination of Rafik Hariri and Its Impact on the Middle East* (London: I.B. Tauris, 2006).

Blanga, Y. U. 'The Role of the Muslim Brotherhood in the Syrian Civil War', *Middle East Policy* 24:3 (2017), 45–62.

Blanga, Y. U. 'Saudi Arabia's Motives in the Syrian Civil War', *Middle East Policy* 24:4 (2017), 45–62.

Bonnefoy, L. 'The Salafis and the War in Yemen', forthcoming.

Bonnefoy, L. 'Salafism in Yemen: A "Saudisation"?', in Madawi al-Rasheed (ed.), *Kingdom without Borders* (London: Hurst, 2008), 245–62.

Bonnefoy, L. *Salafism in Yemen: Transnationalism and Religious Identity* (London: Hurst, 2012).

Bourdieu, P. 'The Forms of Capital', in J. Richardson (ed.), *Handbook of Theory and Research for the Sociology of Education* (New York: Greenwood, 1986), 241–58.

Bourdieu, P. *Language and Symbolic Power* (Cambridge: Polity, 1991).

Bourdieu, P. *The Logic of Practice* (Stanford: Stanford University Press, 1980).

Bourdieu, P. *In Other Words: Essays Towards a Reflexive Sociology* (Cambridge: Polity Press, 1990).

Bourdieu, P. *Pascalian Meditations* (Cambridge: Polity Press, 1997).

Bourdieu, P. 'Postface', in Erwin Panofsky, *Architecture gothique et pensée scolastique* (Paris: Editions de Minuit, 1967), 133–67.

Bourdieu, P. 'Rethinking the State: Genesis and Structure of the Bureaucratic Field', *Sociological Theory* 12:1 (1994), 1–18.

Bourdieu, P. and L. J. D. Wacquant. *An Invitation to Reflexive Sociology* (Cambridge: Polity Press, 1992).

Brandt, M. 'Sufyan's "Hybrid" War: Tribal Politics during the Huthi Conflict', *Journal of Arabian Studies: Arabia, the Gulf, and the Red Sea* 3:1 (2013), 120–38.

Brandt, M. *Tribes and Politics in Yemen: A History of the Houthi Conflict* (Oxford: Oxford University Press, 2017).

Bronson, R. 'Understanding US-Saudi Relations', in Paul Aarts and Gerd Nonneman (eds.), *Saudi Arabia in the Balance: Political Economy, Society, Foreign Affairs* (London: Hurst, 2005), 372–98.

Brubaker, R. 'Religious Dimensions of Political Conflict and Violence', *Sociological Theory* 33:1 (2015), 1–19.

Burrowes, R. 'The Republic of Yemen', in Michael Hudson (ed.), *The Middle East Dilemma* (New York: Columbia University Press, 1991) 187–214.

Buzan, B. and G. Lawson. 'Capitalism and the Emergent World Order', *International Affairs* 90:1 (2014), 71–91.

Buzan, B. and O. Wæver. *Regions and Powers* (Cambridge: Cambridge University Press, 2003).

Buzan, B., O. Wæver, and J. de Wilde. *Security: A New Framework for Analysis* (Boulder, CO: Lynne Rienner, 1998).

Cammett, M. *Compassionate Communalism: Welfare and Sectarianism in Lebanon* (Ithaca, NY: Cornell University Press).

Caporaso, J. A. 'Across the Great Divide: Integrating Comparative and International Politics', *International Studies Quarterly* 41:4 (1997), 563–92.

Chalala, E. 'Syria's Support of Iran in the Gulf War: The Role of Structural Change and the Emergence of a Relatively Strong State', *Journal of Arab Affairs* 7:2 (1988), 119.

Charif, H. 'Regional Development and Integration', in Deirdre Collings (ed.), *Peace for Lebanon?* (Boulder, CO: Lynne Rienner, 1993), 151–2.

Chilcot, J. *The Report of the Iraq Inquiry: Report of a Committee of Privy Counsellors*, Vol. 8 (London: Crown Copyright, 2016).

Chubin, S. and C. Tripp, *Iran-Saudi Arabia Relations and Regional Order* (London: Oxford University Press for IISS, 1996).

Clausen, M. L. 'Understanding the Crisis in Yemen: Evaluating Competing Narratives', *The International Spectator* 50:3 (2015), 16–29.

Commins, D. D. *The Wahhabi Mission and Saudi Arabia* (London: I. B. Tauris, 2006).

Coughlin, C. *Khomeini's Ghost* (London: Macmillan, 2009).

Dabashi, H. *The Arab Spring: The End of Postcolonialism* (New York: Zed Books, 2012).

Dalby, S. 'Crossing Disciplinary Boundaries: Political Geography and International Relations after the Cold War', in Eleonore Kofman and Gillian Youngs (eds.), *Globalization: Theory and Practice* (London and New York: Pinter, 1996), 29–42.

Darwich, M. 'The Saudi Intervention in Yemen: Struggling for Status', *Insight Turkey* 20:2 (2018), 125–42.

David, S. R. 'Explaining Third World Alignments', *World Politics* 43:2 (1991), 233–56.

Dawisha, A. *Iraq: A Political History from Independence to Occupation* (Princeton: Princeton University Press, 2013).

Dazi-Héni, F. 'The New Saudi Leadership and Its Impact on Regional Policy', *The International Spectator* 56:4 (2021), 49–65.

De Chatal, F. 'The Role of Drought and Climate Change in the Syrian Uprising: Untangling the Triggers of the Revolution', *Middle Eastern Studies* 50:4 (2014), 521–35.

De Elvira, L. and T. Zintil. 'The End of the Ba'athist Social Contract in Bashar al-Asad's Syria: Reading Sociopolitical Transformations through Charities and Broader Benevolent Activism', *International Journal of Middle East Studies* 46:2 (2014), 329–49.

Dezalay, Y. and B. G. Garth. 'Hegemonic Battles, Professional Rivalries, and the International Division of Labor in the Market for the Import and Export of State-Governing Expertise', *International Political Sociology* 5 (2011), 276–93.

Diwan Smith, K. 'Sectarian Politics in the Persian Gulf', in Lawrence Potter (ed.), *Sectarian Politics in the Persian Gulf* (London: Hurst, 2013), 143–78.

Dodds, K. *Global Geopolitics: A Critical Introduction* (Harlow: Pearson Education, 2005).

Dodge, T. 'Beyond Structure and Agency: Rethinking Political Identities in Iraq After 2003', *Nations and Nationalism* 26:1 (2020), 108–22.

Dodge, T. '"Bourdieu Goes to Baghdad": Explaining Hybrid Political Identities in Iraq', *Journal of Historical Sociology* 31:1 (2018), 25–38.

Dodge, T. 'The Failure of Peacebuilding in Iraq: The Role of Consociationalism and Political Settlements', *Journal of Intervention and Statebuilding*, 15:4 (2021), 459–75.

Dodge, T. 'Iraq and Muhassasa Tai'fiyya; The External Imposition of Sectarian Politics', in Simon Mabon (ed.), *Saudi Arabia and Iran: The Struggle to Shape the Middle East* (London: Foreign Policy Centre, 2018), 13–14

Dodge, T. and R. Mansour. 'Sectarianization and De-sectarianization in the Struggle for Iraq's Political Field', *The Review of Faith & International Affairs*, 18:1 (2020), 58–69.

Dorlian, S. 'The Saada War in Yemen: Between Politics and Sectarianism', *The Muslim World* 101:2 (2011), 182–201.

Droz-Vincent, P. '"State of Barbary" (Take Two): From the Arab Spring to the Return of Violence in Syria', *Middle East Journal* 68:1 (2014), 33–58.

Dunbar, C. 'The Unification of Yemen: Process, Politics, and Prospects', *Middle East Journal* 46:3 (1992), 456–76.

Dubar, C. and S. Nasr. *al-Tabakat al-Ijtimaiyya Fi Lubnan* [Social Classes in Lebanon] (Beirut: Arab Research Institute, 1982).

Durac, V. 'Yemen's Arab Spring – Democratic Opening or Regime Maintenance?', *Mediterranean Politics*, 17:2 (2012), 161–78.

Ehteshami, A. 'The Foreign Policy of Iran', in Raymond Hinnebusch and Anoushiravan Ehteshami (eds.), *The Middle East in the International System* (London: Lynne Reiner, 2002), 283–309.

Ehteshami, A. and R. A. Hinnebush. *Syria and Iran: Middle Powers in a Penetrated Regional System* (London: Routledge, 1997).

El-Gemayel, A. 'Public International Law in Lebanon', in A. El-Gemayel (ed.), *The Lebanese Legal System* (Washington, DC: International Law Institute, 1985), 445.

El-Husseini, R. 'Hezbollah and the Axis of Refusal: Hamas, Iran and Syria', *Third World Quarterly* 31:5 (2010), 803–15.

El-Husseini, R. 'Lebanon: Building Political Dynasties', in Volker Perthes (ed.), *Arab Elites: Negotiating the Politics of Change* (Boulder, CO: Lynne Reinner, 2004), 242.

Emirbayer, M. and V. Johnson. 'Bourdieu and Organizational Analysis', *Theoretical Sociology* 37 (2008), 1–44.

Esfandiary, D. and A. Tabatabai. 'Yemen: An Opportunity for Iran-Saudi Dialogue?' *Washington Quarterly* 39:2 (2016).

Farhi, F. 'Creating a National Identity amidst Contentious Politics in Contemporary Iran', in Homa Katouzian and Hossein Shahidi (eds.), *Iran in the 21st Century, Politics, Economics and Conflict* (Oxon: Routledge, 2008), 13–27.

Farquar, M. *Circuits of Faith: Migration, Education, and the Wahhabi Mission* (Stanford: Stanford University Press, 2016).

Farquhar, M. 'Saudi Petrodollars, Spiritual Capital, and the Islamic University of Medina: A Wahhabi Missionary Project in Transnational Perspective', *International Journal of Middle East Studies* 47:4 (2015), 701–21.

Fattah, K. 'Yemen: A Social Intifada in a Republic of Sheiks', *Middle East Policy* 18:3 (2011), 79–85.

Ferris, J. *Nasser's Gamble: How Intervention in Yemen Caused the Six-Day War and the Decline of Egyptian Power* (Princeton: Princeton University Press, 2012).

Fisher, W. B. 'Lebanon', in *Middle East and North Africa, 1988* (London: Europa, 1987), 554–82.

Fregonese, S. 'The Urbicide of Beirut? Geopolitics and the Built Environment in the Lebanese Civil War (1975–1976)', *Political Geography* 38 (2009), 309–18.

Fuccaro, N. *Histories of City and State in the Persian Gulf: Manama since 1800* (Cambridge: Cambridge University Press, 2009).

Fuller, G. E. and R. R. Francke, *The Arab Shi'a: The Forgotten Muslims* (New York: St Martin's Press, 1999).

Fraihat, I. *Iran and Saudi Arabia: Taming a Chaotic Conflict* (Edinburgh: Edinburgh University Press, 2020).

Furtig, H. *Iran's Rivalry with Saudi Arabia Between the Gulf Wars* (Reading: Ithaca Press, 2006).

Gambill, G. C. and D. Nassif. 'Lebanon's Parliamentary Elections: Manufacturing Dissent', *Middle East Intelligence Bulletin* 2:8 (2000), www.meforum.org/meib/articles/0009_11.htm.

Gause, F. G. 'Balancing What? Threat Perceptions and Alliance Choice in the Gulf', *Security Studies* 13:2 (2003/4), 273–305.

Gause, F. G. *Beyond Sectarianism: The New Middle East Cold War* (Brookings: Brookings Doha Centre, 2014).

Gause, F. G. 'Ideologies, Alliances, and Underbalancing in the New Middle East Cold War', *International Relations Theory and a Changing Middle East*, 16 (2015), 16–20.

Gause, F. G. 'Ideologies, Alignments, and Underbalancing in the New Middle East Cold War', *PS: Political Science & Politics* 50:3 (2017), 672–5.

Gause, F. G. *Saudi Arabia and Regional Leadership: The Impossibility of Hegemony* (Singapore: Middle East Institute, 2020).

Gause, F. G. *Saudi-Yemeni Relations: Domestic Structures and Foreign Influence* (New York: Columbia University Press, 1990).

Gause, F. G. 'Sovereignty, Statecraft, and Stability in the Middle East', *Journal of International Affairs* 45 (1992), 441–67.

Gause, F. G. and S. L. Yom. 'Resilient Royals: How Arab Monarchies Hang On', *Journal of Democracy* 23:4 (2012), 74–88.

Gelvin, J. L. *Divided Loyalties: Nationalism and Mass Politics in Syria at the Close of Empire* (Los Angeles: University of California Press, 1998).

Gengler, J. 'Understanding Sectarianism in the Persian Gulf', in Lawrence Potter (ed.), *Sectarian Politics in the Persian Gulf* (London: Hurst, 2013), 31–66.

Gengler, J. 'Royal Factionalism, the Khawalid, and the Securitization of "the Shi'a Problem" in Bah-rain', *Journal of Arabian Studies* 3:1 (2013), 53–79.

Gengler, J. *Group Conflict and Political Mobilization in Bahrain and the Arab Gulf: Rethinking the Rentier State* (Bloomington: Indiana University Press, 2015).

Gerges, F. A. 'The Kennedy Administration and the Egyptian-Saudi Conflict in Yemen: Co-Opting Arab Nationalism', *Middle East Journal* 49:2 (1995), 292–311.

Goetze, C. *The Distinction of Peace: A Social Analysis of Peacebuilding* (Michigan: University of Michigan Press).

Goldberg, J. 'The Saudi Arabian Kingdom', in Itovar Rabinovich and Haim Shaked (eds.), *Middle East Contemporary Survey*,vol. XI:*1987* (Boulder : Westview Press, 1987), 589.

Goodarzi, J. M. *Syria and Iran: Diplomatic Alliance and Power Politics in the Middle East* (London: I.B. Tauris, 2009).

Guzansky, Y. 'The Nature of the Radical Axis', *Military and Strategic Affairs* 2:2 (2010), 59–77.

Haas, M. L. 'Ideological Polarity and Balancing in Great Power Politics', *Security Studies* 23:4 (2014), 715–53.

Haddad, F. 'From Existential Struggle to Political Banality: The Politics of Sect in Post-2003 Iraq', *The Review of Faith & International Affairs* 18:1 (2020), 70–86.

Haddad, F. *Sectarianism in Iraq: Antagonistic Views of Reality* (New York : Columbia University Press, 2011).

Haddad, F. 'Sectarian Relations in Arab Iraq: Contextualising the Civil War of 2006–2007', *British Journal of Middle Eastern Studies* 40:2 (2013), 115–38.

Halliday, F. *Nation and Religion in the Middle East* (London: Saqi Books, 2000).

Halliday, F. *The Middle East in International Relations: Power, Politics and Ideology* (Cambridge: Cambridge University Press, 2005).

Hamieh C. S. and R. Mac Ginty. 'A Very Political Reconstruction: Governance and Reconstruction in Lebanon after the 2006 War', *Disasters* 34:1 (2010), 103–23.

Harknett, R. and J. Vandenberg. 'Alignment Theory and Interrelated Threats: Jordan and the Persian Gulf Crisis', *Security Studies* 6:3 (1997), 112–53.

Harvey, K. *A Self Fulfilling Prophecy: The Saudi Struggle for Iraq* (London: Hurst, 2021).

Hashim, A. S. 'Military Power and State Formation in Modern Iraq', *Middle East Policy* x/4 (2003), 29–47.

Hashemi, N. and D. Postel. 'Sectarianization: Mapping the New Politics of the Middle East', *The Review of Faith & International Affairs* 15:3 (2017), 1–13.

Hashmi, S. H. 'International Society and Its Islamic Malcontents', *The Fletcher Forum of World Affairs* 13 (1996), 13–29.

Hazbun, W. 'The Politics of Insecurity in the Arab World: A View from Beirut', *Political Science &Politics* 50:3 (2017), 656–9.

Heydemann, S. 'The Syrian Conflict: Proxy War, Pyrrhic Victory, and Power-Sharing Agreements', *Studies in Ethnicity and Nationalism* 20:2 (2020), 153–60.

Hill, G. *Yemen Endures: Civil War, Saudi Adventurism and the Future of Arabia* (London: Hurst, 2017).

Hinnebusch, R. *The International Politics of the Middle East* (Manchester: Manchester University Press, 2003).

Hinnebusch, R. Pax-Syriana? The Origins, Causes and Consequences of Syria's Role in Lebanon, *Mediterranean Politics* 3:1 (1998), 137–60.

Hinnebusch, R. 'Syria: From "Authoritarian Upgrading" to Revolution?', *International Affairs* 88:1 (2012), 95–113.

Hinnebusch, R., and Ehteshami, A. (eds.) *The Foreign Policies of Middle East States* (Boulder and London: Lynne Rienner, 2002).

Hiro, D. *Cold War in the Islamic World: Saudi Arabia, Iran and the Struggle for Supremacy* (London: Hurst, 2019).

Hokayem, E. 'Iran, the Gulf States and the Syrian Civil War', *Survival* 56:6 (2014), 59–86.

Holden, D. and R. Johns. *The House of Saud* (London: Pan Macmillan, 1982).

Hooshang, A. and N. Entessar (eds.) *Iran and the Arab World* (Basingstoke: Macmillan, 1993).

Hourani, A. *A History of the Arab Peoples* (London: Faber & Faber, 2005).

Hudson, M. 'The Breakdown of Democracy in Lebanon', *Journal of International Affairs* 38:2 (1985), 277–92.

Hudson, M. *The Precarious Republic: Political Modernization in Lebanon* (New York: Random House, 1968).

Hudson, M. C. 'Trying Again: Power-Sharing in Post-Civil War Lebanon', *International Negotiation* 2:1 (1997), 103–22.

Hunter, S. 'Syrian-Iranian Relations: An Alliance of Convenience or More?', *Middle East Insight* 4:2 (1985), 30–4.

Ismail, S. 'Changing Social Structure, Shifting Alliances and Authoritarianism in Syria', in Fred Lawson (ed.), *Demystifying Syria* (London: Sawi, 2009), 13–28.

Ismail, S. *The Rule of Violence: Subjectivity, Memory and Government in Syria* (Cambridge: Cambridge University Press, 2018).

Jones, C. 'Among Ministers, Mavericks and Mandarins': Britain, Covert Action and the Yemen Civil War, 1962–64', *Middle Eastern Studies* 40:1 (2004), 99–126.

Jones, C. and Y. Guzansky. *Fraternal Enemies* (London: Hurst, 2020).

Jones, M. O. *Political Repression in Bahrain* (Cambridge: Cambridge University Press, 2020).

Juneau, T. 'Iran's Policy towards the Houthis in Yemen: A Limited Return on a Modest Investment', *International Affairs* 92:3 (2016), 647–63.

Kadercan, B. 'Triangulating Territory: A Case for Pragmatic Interaction between Political Science, Political Geography and Critical IR', *International Theory* 17:1 (2015), 125–61.

Karam, J. *The Middle East in 1958: Reimaging a Revolutionary Year* (London: I. B. Tauris, 2021).

Kasbarian, S. and S. Mabon. 'Contested Spaces and Sectarian Narratives in Post-Uprisings Bahrain', *Global Discourse* 6:4 (2016), 677–96.

Katib, L. 'Syria, Saudi Arabia, the U.A.E. and Qatar: The "Sectarianization" of the Syrian Conflict and Undermining of Democratization in the Region', *British Journal of Middle Eastern Studies* 46:3 (2019), 1–19.

Kaufman, A. *Contested Frontiers in the Syria-Lebanon-Israel Region: Cartography, Sovereignty, and Conflict* (Baltimore: Johns Hopkins University Press, 2014).

Kaye, D. D. and F. M. Wehrey. 'An Nuclear Iran: The Reactions of Neighbours', *Survival: Global Politics and Strategy* 49:2 (2007), 111–28.

Keddie, N. R. (ed.) *Religion and Politics in Iran: Shi'ism from Quietism to Revolution* (New Haven: Yale University Press, 1983).

Kerr, M. *The Arab Cold War 1958–1964: A Study of Ideology in Politics* (London: Royal Institute of International Affairs/Oxford University Press, 1965).

Keynoush, B. *Saudi Arabia and Iran: Friends or Foes?* (London: Palgrave, 2016).

Khalaf, A. 'Contentious Politics in Bahrain: From Ethnic to National and Vice Versa', *Fourth Nordic Conference on Middle Eastern Studies* (1998), https://org.uib.no/smi/pao/khalaf.html.

Khalaf, A. 'Squaring the Circle: Bahrain's Pearl Roundabout', *Middle East Critique* 22:3 (2013), 265–80.

Khalidi, W. *Conflict and Violence in Lebanon: Confrontation in the Middle East* (Cambridge, MA: Harvard University Press, 1979).

Khatib, L., D. Matar, and A. Alshaer. *The Hizbullah Phenomenon: Politics and Communication* (London: Hurst, 2014).

Khomeini, R. *Islam and Revolution: Writing and Declarations of Imam Khomeini*, translated and annotated by H. Algar (Berkely: Mizan Press, 1981).

Khuri, F. I. *Tribe and State in Bahrain: The Transformation of Social and Political Authority in an Arab State* (Chicago: University of Chicago Press, 1980).

Kienle, E. *Ba 'th v. Ba 'th: The Conflict between Syria and Iraq 1968–1989* (London: I. B. Tauris, 1990).

Knio, K. 'Lebanon: Cedar Revolution or Neo-Sectarian Partition?' *Mediterranean Politics* 10:2 (2005), 225–31.

Kostiner, J. 'On Instruments and Their Designers: The Ikhwan of Najd and the Emergence of the Saudi State', *Middle East Studies* 21:3 (1985), 298–323.

Kostiner, J. 'State, Islam and Opposition in Saudi Arabia, The Post-Desert Storm Phase', *Middle East Review of International Affairs* 1:2 (1997), 75–89.

Kostiner, J. (ed.) *Middle East Monarchies: The Challenge of Modernity* (London: Lynne Rienner, 2000).

Kramer, M. 'Muslim Congresses', in John L. Esperito (ed.), *The Oxford Encyclopedia of the Modern Islamic World* (Oxford: Oxford University Press, 1995), 309.

Kramer, M. 'Syria's Alawis and Shiism', in Martin Kramer (ed.), *Shiism, Resistance, and Revolution* (Boulder: Westview Press, 1987), 237–54.

Krause, M. 'How transnational fields vary', paper delivered at the IR Theory Seminar, International Relations Department, London School of Economics and Political Science, 12 March 2018, p. 4.

Lawson, F. H. 'Syria's Intervention in the Lebanese Civil War, 1976: A Domestic Conflict Explanation', *International Organization* 38:3 (1984), 451–80.

Lefebvre, H. *The Production of Space* (Oxford: Blackwell, 1991).

Lefevre, R. *Ashes of Hama: The Muslim Brotherhood in Syria* (London: Hurst, 2013).

Legrenzi, M. and F. H. Lawson. 'Saudi Arabia Calls Out Hezbollah: Why Now?' *Middle East Policy* 23:2 (2016), 31–43.

Louër, L. 'The Political Impact of Labor Migration in Bahrain', *City & Society* 20:1 (2008), 32–53.

Louër, L. 'The State and Sectarian Identities in the Persian Gulf Monarchies: Bahrain, Saudi Arabia and Kuwait in Comparative Perspective', in Lawrence

Potter (ed.), *Sectarian Politics in the Persian Gulf* (London: Hurst, 2013), 117–42.

Louër, L. *Transnational Shi'a Politics: Religious and Political Networks in the Gulf* (New York: Columbia University Press, 2008).

Mabon, S. 'The Apocalyptic and The Sectarian', in Tim Clack and Rob Johnson (eds.), *Upstream Operations* (Palgrave Macmillan, 2019), 165–90.

Mabon, S. 'The Battle for Bahrain', *Middle East Policy* 19:2 (2012), 84–97.

Mabon, S. *Houses Built on Sand: Violence, Sectarianism and Revolution in the Middle East* (Manchester: Manchester University Press, 2020).

Mabon, S. 'Muting the Trumpets of Sabotage: Saudi Arabia, the US and the Quest to Securitize Iran', *British Journal of Middle Eastern Studies* 45:5 (2018), 742–59.

Mabon, S. *Saudi Arabia and Iran: Soft Power Rivalry in the Middle East* (London: I. B. Tauris, 2013).

Mabon, S. 'The World Is a Garden: Nomos, Sovereignty and the (Contested) Ordering of Life', *Review of International studies* 45:5 (2019), 870–90.

Mabon, S. (ed.), *Saudi Arabia and Iran: The Struggle to Shape the Middle East* (London: Foreign Policy Centre, 2018).

Mabon, S. and L. Ardovini. 'The Politics of Pilgrimage: Exploring the Hajj as a Site for Dialogue between Saudi Arabia and Iran', in Luigi Narbone and Abdolrasool Divsallar (eds.), *Stepping Away from the Abyss: A Gradual Approach towards a New Security System in the Persian Gulf* (San Domenico di Fiesole: MEI, 2021), https://cadmus.eui.eu/handle/1814/71221.

Mabon, S. and A. M. Kuramasamy. 'Da'ish, *stasis* and bare life in Iraq', in Jacob Erikson and Ahmed Khaleel (eds.), *Iraq after ISIS* (Cham: Palgrave Macmillan, 2018), 9–28.

Mabon, S. and J. Nagle (eds.) *Urban Spaces and Sectarian Contestation* (Lancaster: SEPAD, 2020).

Mabon, S., S. Nasirzadeh, and E. Al Refai. 'De-securitisation and Pragmatism in the Persian Gulf: The Future of Saudi-Iranian Relations', *The International Spectator* 56:4 (2021), 66–83.

Makdisi, S. A. 'An Appraisal of Lebanon's Post-War Economic Development and a Look to the Future', *Middle East Journal* 31:3 (1977) 267–280.

Makdisi, U. *The Culture of Sectarianism: Community, History and Violence in Nineteenth-Century Ottoman Lebanon* (Berkeley: University of California Press, 2000).

Mamadouh, V. and G. Dijkink. 'Geopolitics, International Relations and Political Geography: The Politics of Geopolitical Discourse', *Geopolitics* 11:3 (2006) 349–366.

Mandaville, P. *Global Political Islam* (Oxon: Routledge, 2007), 287.

Mansour, R. *Networks of Power: The Popular Mobilization Forces and the State in Iraq* (London: Chatham House, 2021).

Marschall, C. *Iran's Persian Gulf Policy: From Khomeini to Khatami* (London: Routledge, 2003).

Mason, R. *Foreign Policy in Iran and Saudi Arabia: Economics and Diplomacy in the Middle East* (London: I.B. Tauris, 2014).

Massey, D. *For Space* (London: Sage, 2005).

Matthiesen, T. 'Hizbullah al-Hijaz: A History of the Most Radical Saudi Shi'a Opposition Group', *The Middle East Journal* 64:2 (2010), 179–97.

Matthiessen, T. *The Other Saudis: Shiism, Dissent and Sectarianism* (Cambridge: Cambridge University Press, 2014).

Matthiessen, T. *Sectarian Gulf: Bahrain, Saudi Arabia and the Arab Spring that Wasn't* (Stanford, CA: Stanford University Press, 2013).

Matthiessen, T. 'Sectarianization as Securitization: Identity Politics and Counter-Revolution in Bahrain', in N. Hashemi and D. Postel (eds.), *Sectarianization: Mapping the Politics of the New Middle East* (London: Hurst, 2017), 199–214.

Moin, B. *Khomeini: Life of the Ayatollah* (London: I. B. Tauris, 1999).

Muir, J. 'Lebanon: Arena of Conflict, Crucible of Peace', *The Middle East Journal* 38:2 (1984), 204–19.

Mumford, A. 'Proxy Warfare and the Future of Conflict', *The RUSI Journal* 158:2 (2013), 40–6.

Nagle, J. 'Consociationalism Is Dead! Long Live Zombie Power-Sharing', *Studies in Ethnicity and Nationalism* 20:2 (2020), 137–44.

Nakash, Y. *Reaching for Power: The Shi'a in the Modern Arab World* (Princeton: Princeton University Press, 2006).

Nasr, V. *The Shi'a Revival: How Conflicts within Islam Will Shape the Future* (New York: W. W. Norton, 2007).

Neep, D. *Occupying Syria under the French Mandate: Insurgency, Space and State Formation* (Cambridge: Cambridge University Press, 2012).

Neep, D. 'State-Space beyond Territory: Wormholes, Gravitational Fields, and Entanglement', *Journal of Historical Sociology* 30:3 (2017), 466–95.

Noble, P. C. 'The Arab System: Pressures, Constraints, and Opportunities', in Bahgat Korany and Ali E. Hillal Dessouki (eds.), *The Foreign Policies of Arab States* (Boulder: Westview Press, 1991), 55–7.

Norton, A. R. *Amal and the Shi'a: Struggle for the Soul of Lebanon* (Austin, TX: University of Texas Press, 1987).

Norton, A. R. *Hezbollah* (Princeton: Princeton University Press, 2007).

Norton, A. R. 'Lebanon after Tai'f Is the Civil War Over?', *Middle East Journal* 45:3 (1991), 466.

O'Loughlin, J. 'Geography as Space and Geography as Place: The Divide Between Political Science and Political Geography Continues', *Geopolitics* 5:3 (2000) 126–37.

O'Loughlin, J. 'Responses: Geography as Space and Geography as Place: The Divide between Political Science and Political Geography Continues', *Geopolitics* 5:3 (2000), 126–37.

Pandya, S. 'Women's Shi'a Ma'atim in Bahrain', *Journal of Middle East Women's Studies* 6:2 (2010), 31–58.

Partrick, N. *Saudi Arabian Foreign Policy: Conflict and Cooperation* (London: I. B. Tauris, 2016).

Peterson, J. E. 'Bahrain: Reform, Promise, and Reality', in Joshua Teitelbaum (ed.), *Political Liberalization in the Persian Gulf* (New York: Columbia University Press, 2009), 157–85.

Phillips, C. *The Battle for Syria: International Rivalry in the New Middle East* (New Haven: Yale University Press, 2016).

Phillips, C. 'Eyes Bigger than Stomachs: Turkey, Saudi Arabia and Qatar in Syria', *Middle East Policy* 24:1 (2017), 36–47.

Phillips, C. 'Sectarianism and Conflict in Syria', *Third World Quarterly* 36:2 (2015), 365–6.

Phillips, C. and M. Valbjørn. 'What Is in a Name?': The Role of (Different) Identities in the Multiple Proxy Wars in Syria', *Small Wars & Insurgencies* 29:3 (2018), 414–33.

Pierret, T. *Religion and State in Syria: The Sunni 'Ulama' from Coup to Revolution* (Cambridge: Cambridge University Press, 2013).

Rabinovich, I. *The War for Lebanon, 1970–1985* (New York: Cornell University Press, 1985).

Rauta, V. 'Proxy Warfare and the Future of Conflict: Take Two', *The Rusi Journal* 165:2 (2020), 1–10.

Ricotta, I. The Arab Shi'a Nexus: Understanding Iran's Influence in the Arab World, *The Washington Quarterly* 39:2 (2016), 144.

Rosenberg, J. 'International Relations in the Prison of Political Science', *International Relations* 30:2 (2016), 127–53.

Roshandel, J. 'Iran's Foreign and Security Policies: How the Decisionmaking Process Evolved', *Security Dialogue* 31:1 (2000), 105–17.

Rubin, B. 'The Gulf States and the Iran-Iraq War', in E. Karsh (ed.) *The Iran-Iraq War* (New York: Palgrave Macmillan, 1989), 13–26.

Rubin, L. *Islam in the Balance: Ideational Threats in Arab Politics* (Stanford: Stanford Security Studies, 2014).

Ryan, C. 'Shifting Alliances and Shifting Theories in the Middle East', in Marc Lynch (ed.), *Shifting Global Politics and the Middle East* (POMEPS Studies 34, 2009), 7–13.

Ryan, C. *Inter-Arab Alliances: Regime Security and Jordanian Foreign Policy* (Gainesville: University Press of Florida, 2009).

Ryan, C. 'Inter-Arab Relations and the Regional System', in Marc Lynch (ed.), *The Arab Uprisings Explained: New Contentious Politics in the Middle East* (New York: Columbia University Press, 2014), 110–23.

Saad, A. 'Challenging the Sponsor-Proxy Model: The Iran-Hizbullah Relationship', *Global Discourse* 9:4 (2019), 627–50.

Salamey, I. 'The Double Movement & Post-Arab Spring Consociationalism', *Muslim World* 106:1 (2016), 187–204.

Salamey, I. 'Failing Consociationalism in Lebanon and Integrative Options', *International Journal of Peace Studies* 14:2 (2009), 90–1.

Salamey, I. and R. Payne. 'Parliamentary Consociationalism in Lebanon: Equal Citizenry vs. Quotated Confessionalism', *Journal of Legislative Studies* 14:4 (2008), 451–73.

Salloukh, B. F. 'The Arab Uprisings and the Geopolitics of the Middle East', *The International Spectator* 48:2 (2013), 32–46.

Salloukh, B. F. 'The Limits of Electoral Engineering in Divided Societies: Elections in Postwar Lebanon', *Canadian Journal of Political Science* 39:3 (2006), 635–55.

Salloukh, B. F. 'Overlapping Contests and Middle East International Relations: The Return of the Weak Arab State', *PS: Political Science & Politics* 50:3 (2017), 660–3.

Salloukh, B. F. 'The Syrian War: Spillover Effects on Lebanon', *Middle East Policy* 24:1 (2017), 62–78.

Samii, A. W. 'A Stable Structure on Shifting Sands: Assessing the Hezbollah Iran Syria Relationship', *Middle East Journal* 62:1 (2008), 32–53.

Saouli, A. *Hezbollah: Socialisation and Its Tragic Ironies* (Edinburgh: Edinburgh University Press, 2018).

Saouli, A. (ed.) *Unfulfilled Aspirations* (London: Hurst, 2020).

Saseen, S. M. 'The Tai'f Accord and Lebanon's Struggle to Regain Its Sovereignty', *American University International Law Review* 6:1 (1990), 57–75.

Schmidt, S. 'The Role of Religion in Politics. The Case of Shi'a-Islamism in Iraq', *Nordic Journal of Religion and Society* xxii/2 (2009), 129.

Schoel, T. 'The Hasna's Revenge: Syrian Tribes and Politics in their Shaykh's Story', *Nomadic People* 15:1 (2011), 96–113.

Schweller, R. 'Unanswered Threats: A Neoclassical Realist Theory of Underbalancing', *International Security* 29:2 (2004), 159–201.

Seale, P. *Assad: The Struggle for the Middle East* (Berkley: University of California Press, 1988).

Seale, P. *The Struggle for Syria: A Study of Post-War Arab Politics, 1945–1958* (Oxford: Oxford University Press, 1965).

Sharif, H. 'South Lebanon: Its History and Geopolitics', in Elaine Hagopian and Sami Farsoun (eds.), *South Lebanon* (Detroit: Association of Arab-American University Graduates, 1978), 10–11.

Shils, E. 'The Prospect for Lebanese Civility', in L. Binder (ed.), *Politics in Lebanon* (New York: John Wiley and Sons, 1966), 1–12.

Shuja al-Din, M. 'Yemen's War-torn Rivalries for Religious Education', in Frederic Wehrey (ed.), *Islamic Institutions in Arab States: Mapping the Dynamics of Control, Co-option and Contention* (Washington, DC: Carnegie Endowment for International Peace, 2021), 33–52.

Slim, R. 'Hezbollah and Syria: From Regime Proxy to Regime Savior', *Insight Turkey* 16:2 (2014), 61–8.

Sunayama, S. *Syria and Saudi Arabia. Collaboration and Conflict in the Oil Era* (London: I.B. Tauris, 2007).

Soja, E. W. *Postmodern Geographies: The Reassertion of Space in Critical Theory* (London: Verso: 1980).

Soja, E. W. 'Regions in Context: Spatiality, Periodicity, and the Historical Geography of the Regional Question', *Environment and Planning D: Society and Space* 3 (1985) 175–90.

Soja, E. W. 'The Socio-Spatial Dialectic', *Annals of the Association of American Geographers* 70 (1980), 207–25.

Sozer, B. 'Development of Proxy Relationships: A Case Study of the Lebanese Civil War', *Small Wars & Insurgencies* 27:4 (2016), 636–58.

Starr, H. 'On Geopolitics: Spaces and Places', *International Studies Quarterly* 57:3 (2013), 433–9.

Stein, E. *International Relations in the Middle East* (Cambridge: Cambridge University Press, 2020).

Strobl, S. *Sectarian Order in Bahrain: The Social and Colonial Origins of Criminal Justice* (London: Lexington Books, 2018).

Tibi, B. *Arab Nationalism: Between Islam and the Nation State* (New York: St Martin's Press, 1997).

Tripp, C. *A History of Iraq* (Cambridge: Cambridge University Press, 2007).

Tripp, C. *The Power and the People: Paths of Resistance in the Middle East* (Cambridge: Cambridge University Press, 2013).

Valbjørn, M. 'Beyond the beyond(s): On the (Many) Third Way(s) beyond Primordialism and Instrumentalism in the Study of Sectarianism', *Nations and Nationalism* 26:1 (2020), 91–107.

Valbjørn, M. and A. Bank. 'The New Arab Cold War: Rediscovering the Arab Dimension of Middle East Regional Politics', *Review of International Studies* 38:1 (2012) 3–24.

Van Dam, N. *Destroying a Nation: The Civil War in Syria* (London: I. B. Tauris, 2017).

Vloeberghs, W. 'Worshipping the Martyr President: The darîh of Rafiq al-Hariri in Beirut' in Th. Pierret, P. Pinto et al. (eds.), *Ethnographies of Islam* (Edinburgh: Edinburgh University Press, 2008), 80–92.

Wallsh, D. 'Syrian Alliance Strategy in the Post-Cold War Era: The Impact of Unipolarity', *Fletcher Forum of World Affairs* 37:2 (2013), 107–23.

Walt, S. M. *The Origins of Alliances* (Ithaca: Cornell University Press, 1987).

Walt, S. M. *Revolution and War* (Cambridge: Cambridge University Press, 1992).

Wastnidge, E. 'Iran and Syria: An Enduring Axis', *Middle East Policy* 24:2 (2017), 148–59.

Wastnidge, E. 'Iran's Own "War on Terror": Iranian Foreign Policy towards Syria and Iraq during the Rouhani Era', in Luciano Zaccara (ed.), *Foreign Policy of Iran under President Hassan Rouhani's First Term (2013–2017)* (Singapore: Palgrave Macmillan, 2020), 107–29.

Wastnidge, E. 'The Modalities of Iranian Soft Power: From Cultural Diplomacy to Soft War', *Politics* 35:3/4 (2015), 364–77.

Wege, C. A. 'Hizbullah-Syrian Intelligence Affairs: A Marriage of Convenience', *Journal of Strategic Security* 3 (2011), 1–14.

Wehrey, F. 'Bahrain's Decade of Discontent', *Journal of Democracy* 24:3 (2013), 116–26.

Wehrey, F. *Sectarian Politics in the Gulf: From the Iraq War to the Arab Uprisings* (New York: Columbia University Press, 2013).

Wehrey, F., T. W. Karasik, A. Nader, J. Ghez, L. Hansell, and R. A. Guffrey. *Saudi-Iranian Relations since the Fall of Saddam: Rivalry, Cooperation, and Implications for U.S. Policy* (Santa Monica, CA: RAND Corporation, 2009).

White, B. T. *The Emergence of Minorities in the Middle East: The Politics of Community in French Mandate Syria* (Edinburgh: Edinburgh University Press, 2011).

Wimmer, A. and N. G. Schiller. 'Methodological Nationalism, the Social Sciences, and the Study of Migration: An Essay in Historical Epistemology', *The International Migration Review* 37:3 (2003), 576–610.

Young, M. *The Ghosts of Martyrs Square: An Eyewitness Account of Lebanon's Life Struggle* (New York: Simon & Schuster, 2010).

Young, R. 'Equitable Solutions for Offshore Boundaries: The 1968 Saudi-Iran Agreement', *The American Journal of International Law* 64:1 (1970).

Zimbler, B. L. 'Peacekeeping without the U.N.: The Multinational Force in Lebanon and International Law', *Yale Journal of International Law* 10 (1984), 222–51.

Reports, Briefings and Statements

والحوثيون يفتحون أبواب صنعاء لإيرا, *Al Jazeera* (01.03.15), http://mubasher.aljazeera.net/news/
الحوثيون-يفتحون-أبواب-صنعاء-لإيران
www.alhayat.com/article/536275/السعودية-تعتبر-الاخوان-و-الحوثي-و-حزب-الله-في-الداخل-منظمات-ارهابية.
www.almasdarnews.com/article/russian-investors-to-participate-in-rebuilding-of-damascus-airport/.
www.presstv.com/Detail/2019/02/25/589535/Khamenei-Leader-Bashar-alAssad-Tehran-resistance-US.
www.reuters.com/article/us-ba-syria-saudi/saudi-king-in-damascus-to-mend-fences-with-assad-idUSTRE59630I20091007.

AA. 'Reduction of Iranian Exports to Iraq due to Increase in Customs Tariffs' (08.06.16), www.aa.com.tr/fa/586400/ایران/کاهش-صادرات-ایران-به-عراق-به-دلیل-افزایش-تعرفه-های-گمرکی.
Agence France Presse. 'Bahrain Jails Three for Spying for Iran: Report', *Gulf News* (06.07.11), https://gulfnews.com/world/gulf/bahrain-jails-three-for-spying-for-iran-report-1.833932.
Agence France Presse and *NOW Lebanon*. 'Thousands across Iraq Protest Bahrain Crackdown' (18.03.11).
Alaaldin, R. 'Proxy War in Iraq', *PWP Conflict Studies* (2019).
al-Ali, M. 'al-Wifaq to Vote on Political Societies Law Today', *Gulf Daily News* (06.10. 05).
al-Ashwal, A. 'UAE, Yemen's Islah Party Try to Tolerate Each Other', *al-Monitor* (06.12.18), www.al-monitor.com/pulse/originals/2018/12/yemen-islah-party-uae-relations-brotherhood-saudi-arabia.html.
al-Asrar, F. A. 'The Houthis Cover Up for Iran. Here Is Why', *al-Arabiya* (29.09.19), https://english.alarabiya.net/en/views/news/middle-east/2019/09/29/The-Houthis-cover-up-for-Iran-Here-is-why-.
Al Bandar Report: Demographic engineering in Bahrain and mechanisms of exclusion, www.bahrainrights.org/en/node/528.
al-Chazli, Y. 'Adviser to Bahrain King: GCC Basis of Balance in Region', *al-Monitor* (04.11.13), http://almon.co/2olf.
al-Dawsari, N. 'Tribal Governance and Stability in Yemen', *Carnegie Endowment for International Peace* (03.12.15), http://carnegieendowment.org/2012/04/24/tribal-governance-and-stability-in-yemen#.
al-Dawsiri, S. 'Interview with Ali Salman', *al-Sharq al-Awsat* (22.02.07).
al-Faysal, T. 'Mr. Obama, We Are Not "Free Riders"', *Arab News* (14.03.16), www.arabnews.com/columns/news/894826.
Al-Jamal, M. M. and S. Farid. 'Is Iran "Sectarianizing" Bahrain Conflict?' al-'Arabiya (20.04.11), http://english.alarabiya.net/articles/2011/04/20/146144.html.
al-Jubeir, Bin Ahmed, A. 'Can Iran Change?', *New York Times* (19.01.16), www.nytimes.com/2016/01/19/opinion/saudi-arabia-can-iran-change.html?_r=2.

Aljubeir, A. 'The Iranian-Planned Houthi Attacks' (07.05.18 21:53), https://
    twitter.com/AdelAljubeir/status/993594737704751105.
'al-Judhur al-Fikriyya lil-Fitna al-Huthiyya', *al-Muntada* (04.05).
Al Khalifa, Hamad bin Isa bin Salman, 'Al Khalifa: Stability is Prerequisite
    for Progress', *Washington Times* (19.04.11), www.washingtontimes.com/
    news/2011/apr/19/stability-is-prerequisite-for-progress/.
Allam, H., Landay, J. S., and Strobel, W. P. 'Iranian Outmaneuvers U.S. in Iraq',
    McClatchy Newspapers (28.04.08), www.mcclatchydc.com/2008/04/28/35146/
    iranian-outmaneuvers-us-in- iraq.htm.
Al Khalifa, Fawaz bin Mohammad. 'The Gulf States are Stuck between Isil and
    Iran', *The Telegraph* (21.01.16), www.telegraph.co.uk/news/worldnews/middle
    east/bahrain/12113355/The-Gulf-states-are-stuck-between-Isil-and-Iran
    .html.
al-Mahdi, Muhammad bin Muhammad. 'al-Zaydiyya fi al-Yaman: Hiwar
    Maftuh', *Sana'a: Markaz al-Kalima al-Tayiba* (2008), p. 98.
المؤتمر الصحفي المشترك لمعالي وزير الخارجية مع سعادة وزير المواصلات في جمهورية باكستان الإسلامية (almutamar alsuhu-
    fiu almushtarak limaealay wazir alkharijiat mae saeadat wazir almuasalat fi jum-
    huriat bakistan al'iislamia [The Joint Press Conference of His Excellency the
    Minister of Foreign Affairs with His Excellency the Minister of Transportation of
    the Islamic Republic of Pakistan]), Ministry of Foreign Affairs (20.03.14), www
    .mofa.gov.bh/Default.aspx?tabid=8266&language=ar-BH&ItemId=4008.
al-Muslimi, Farea. 'Analysis', *Sanaa Centre* (18.11.18), https://sanaacenter.org/
    publications/analysis/6665.
Al-Qabas (23 March 1980), in *FBIS* (25 March 1980).
al-Omran, Ahmed, and Asa Fitch. 'Saudi Coalition Seizes Iranian Boat
    Carrying Weapons to Yemen', *Wall Street Journal* (30.09.15), www.wsj.com/
    articles/saudi-coalition-seizes-iranian-boat-carrying-weapons-to-rebels-in-
    yemen-1443606304.
Al-Ra'i al-Amm (13 February and 4 June 1974), in *FBIS* (16 February and 6
    June 1979).
al-Rashed, Abdul Rahman. 'Between *Sunni* and S*hi'a*', *al-Sharq al-Awsat*
    (04.09.05).
al-Rasheed, M. 'Riyadh's War on Yemen Stokes Saudi Nationalism', *al-Monitor*
    (27.03.15),   www.al-monitor.com/pulse/originals/2015/03/saudi-yemen-
    houthi-gcc-military-islamist.html.
al-Rasheed, M. 'The Saudi Response to the 'Arab Spring': Containment and
    Co-option', *Open Democracy* (10.01.12), www.opendemocracy.net/5050/
    madawi-al-rasheed/saudi-response-to-%e2%80%98arab-spring%e2%80%99-
    containment-and-co-option.
al-Rasheed, M. 'Saudi War in Yemen Impossible to Win', *al-Monitor* (02.10.15),
    www.al-monitor.com/pulse/originals/2015/10/saudi-arabia-lose-protracted-
    war-yemen.html.
Amwaj. 'Exclusive: Despite Baghdad Photo Blunder, Iran-Saudi Talks Set to
    Resume' (08.09.21), https://amwaj.media/article/exclusive-despite-baghdad-
    photo-blunder-iran-saudi-talks-set-to-resume.
Asith, P. 'Lebanon's Hezbollah Ready to Fight ISIS in Iraq', *al-Sharq al-Awsat*
    (25.06.14), www.aawsat.net/2014/06/article55333611.

(Awal Khitab llRais Abed Rabbu Mansour اول خطاب للرئيس عبدربة منصور هادي من عدن 21 مارس
Hadi min Aden [The First Speech of President Abd Rabbo Mansour Hadi
from Aden]) (21.03.15), www.youtube.com/watch?v=AQ9PDlftIJc.

Badawi, T. 'Iran's Iraqi Market', *Carnegie Endowment for International Peace*
(27.07.16), https://carnegieendowment.org/sada/64187.

'Bahrain Accuses Foreign Media of Exaggeration', *Al Jazeera* (02.05.12), www
.aljazeera.com/news/middleeast/2012/05/20125220628139601.html.

'Bahrain Expels Lebanese over "Hezbollah Links"', *Al Manar* (14.03.16), http://
archive.almanar.com.lb/english/article.php?id=260434

'Bahrain FM: Muslim Brotherhood is a Terrorist Group', *Al Jazeera* (06.07.17),
www.aljazeera.com/news/2017/7/6/bahrain-fm-muslim-brotherhood-
is-a-terrorist-group.

'Bahrain, Hundreds Stripped Citizenship', *HRW news* (27.07.18), www.hrw
.org/news/2018/07/27/bahrain-hundreds-stripped-citizenship.

Bahrain Independent Commission of Inquiry, *Report of the Bahrain Independent
Commission of Inquiry* (2011), www.bici.org.bh/BICIreportEN.pdf.

'Bahrain Jails 19 *Shi'a* Accused of Spying for Iran,' *New Arab* (30.10.17),
www.alaraby.co.uk/english/news/2017/10/30/bahrain-jails-19-shias-accused-
of-spying-for-iran.

'Bahrain Pulled Back from "Sectarian Abyss"—Foreign Minister,' *Reuters*
(17.02.11).

'Bahrain Sentences 12 People for Life for Spying, Iran Links', *Reuters* (22.04.14),
https://reut.rs/2Wandkp.

'Bahrain: Yemen's Rebellion Adds to Sectarian Tensions', *Oxford Analytica
Daily Brief* (12,01.10), www.oxan.com/display.aspx?ItemID= DB156920.

'Bahraini Shi'ite Group Flays Iran Rhetoric', *Gulf News* (08.02.09), https://
gulfnews.com/world/gulf/bahrain/bahraini-shiite-group-flays-iran-
rhetoric-1.50686.

Goods', *Mehr News Agency* (n.d.), www.mehrnews.com/news/2350491/
شلمچه-دروازه-طلایی-تجارت-عزم-عراق-برای-جایگزینی-کالای-ایرانی

Bassem, L. 'Hezbollah Holds Talks with Saudi King', *Reuters* (2007), www
.reuters.com/article/us-lebanon-hezbollah-saudi-idUSL0313236420070103).

Batatu, H. 'Syria's Muslim Brethren', *Middle East Research and Information
Project 12* (1982).

Bayoumy, Y. and Ghobari, M. 'Confirmed: Iran's Foreign Military Arm is
Backing Yemeni Rebels Who Took Control of the Country', *Reuters* (15.12.14).

Bayoumy Y. and Ghobari, M. 'Iranian Support Seen Crucial for Yemen's
Houthis', *Reuters* (15.12.14), www.reuters.com/article/us-yemen-houthis-
iran-insight/iranian-support-seen-crucial-for-yemens-houthis-id
USKBN0JT17A20141215.

'Bin Salem al-Azima', *Asharq Al Awsat* (28.03.11), http://english.aawsat
.com/2011/03/article55247010/a-talk-with-peninsula-shield-force-commander-
mutlaq-bin-salem-al-azima.

Black, I. 'Fear of a *Shi'a* full moon', *The Guardian* (26.01.07), www.theguardian
.com/world/2007/jan/26/worlddispatch.ianblack.

Blanford, N. 'A Martyr's Son Calls for Justice', *Time* (13.02.07), http://content
.time.com/time/world/article/0,8599,1589446,00.html.

Bonnefoy, L. 'Saudi Arabia and the Expansion of Salafism', NOREF: Norwegian Peacebuilding Resource Centre, Policy Brief (September 2013), p. 2.

Bronner, E. and M. Slackman. 'Saudi Troops Enter Bahrain to Help Put Down Unrest', *New York Times* (14.03.11), https://nyti.ms/2Kr5UWt.

Brzezinkski, Y. 'The Cold War and Its Aftermath', *Foreign Affairs* 81 (1991–93).

Cafiero, G. 'Gulf States Slowly Warm to Damascus', *al-Monitor* (09.01.19), www.al-monitor.com/pulse/originals/2019/01/gulf-states-accept-syria-damas cus-conflict.html.

Cafiero, G. and T. Karasik. 'Yemen War and Qatar Crisis Challenge Oman's Neutrality', *Middle East Institute* (06.07.17), www.mei.edu/content/article/ oman-s-high-stakes-yemen.

Cambanis, T. 'A Father's Shadow Clouds His Son's Rise in Lebanon', *New York Times* (03.10.07), p. 6.

Carapico, S. 'No Exit: Yemen's Existential Crisis', *Middle East Research and Information Project* (03.05.11).

Carapico, S. and S. P. Yadav. 'The Breakdown of the GCC Initiative', *Middle East Report* 273 (2014).

Cliffe, J. 'Iran and Saudi Arabia Are Locked in a Cold War-style Stand-Off – but the Situation Is Even More Volatile', *New Statesman* (08.01.20), www.newstatesman.com/world/2020/01/iran-and-saudi-arabia-are-locked-cold-war-style-stand-situation-even-more-volatile.

Combaz, E. 'International Aid to Lebanon', *Governance, Social Development, Humanitarian, Conflict* (02.08.13), http://gsdrc.org/docs/open/hdq979.pdf.

Constantine, Z. 'King of Bahrain Says Subversive "External Plot" Has Been Foiled', *The National* (22.02.11), www.thenational.ae/world/mena/ king-of-bahrain-says-sub- versive-external-plot-has-been-foiled-1.600506.

Corbeil, A. and A. Amarasingam. 'The Houthi Hezbollah: Iran's Train-and-Equip Program in Sanaa', *Foreign Affairs* (31.03.16).

Cowell, A. 'Syria and Iran Agree Militias Can Remain in Parts of Lebanon', *New York Times* (04.30.91).

الموت لأمريكا، الموت لإسرائيل، النصر للإسلام'... أنصار الله (Death to America, Death to Israel, Victory to Islam'), *Ansr Allah* (n.d.), http://archive.almanar.com.lb/article .php?id=1134274.

Dehghan, S. K. 'Saudi Arabia Accuses Iran of "Direct Aggression' Over Yemen Missile", *The Guardian* (07.11.17), www.theguardian.com/world/2017/ nov/07/saudi-arabia-accuses- iran-of-supplying-missile-to-houthi-rebels-in-yemen.

'Despite Military Escalation, Increased Humanitarian Crisis in Yemen, 'a Way Out of This War' Still Exists, Special Envoy Tells Security Council', UNSC 14793 (15.02.22), www.un.org/press/en/2022/sc14793.doc.htm.

Dikmen, Yesim, Melih Aslan, 'Muslim Nations Accuse Iran of Supporting Terrorism: Summit Communique', *Reuters* (15.04.16), www.reuters.com/article/ us-turkey-summit/muslim-nations-accuse-iran-of-supporting-terrorism-summit-communique-idUSKCN0XC1LQ.

'Diplomasiye ashefte Arabistan dar Lobnan [Saudi Arabia's Messy Policy In Lebanon]', *Hambastagi Online* (30.04.08).

'Drop Charges against Editor of Independent Daily', *Human Rights Watch* (04.11.11), www.hrw.org/news/2011/04/11/bahrain-drop-charges-against-editor-independent-daily.

Drysdale, A. and R. Hinnebusch. *Syria and the Middle East Peace Process* (New York: Council on Foreign Relations, 1991).

Eisenstadt, M., M. Knights, and A. Ali. *Iran's Influence in Iraq: Countering Tehran's Whole-of-Government Approach* (Washington, DC: Washington Institute for Near East Policy, 2011).

إسرائيل, إسرائيل دعو قضاة لبنان للتعلّم من قضاة «إسرائيل», *Elaph* (05.05.07), https://elaph.com/ElaphWeb/NewsPapers/2007/5/231342.html.

El Dahan, M. and W. Maclean. 'Bahrain Says Foils Arms Smuggling Bid, Recalls Iran Envoy', *Reuters* (25.07.11), https://reut.rs/2Fe3MR1.

El Deeb, S. 'Explainer: Why Saudi Arabia is Upset, Lashing out at Lebanon', *Associated Press* (02.11.21), https://apnews.com/article/entertainment-business-lebanon-saudi-arabia-beirut-787c1e342e3a46cdb11efc888f71f580.

El Yaakoubi, A. 'Crisis with Lebanon Rooted Hezbollah Dominance – Saudi Minister', *Reuters* (30.10.21), www.reuters.com/article/us-lebanon-crisis-saudi-minister-idAFKBN2HK0HE.

England, A. 'Saudi Arabia "serious" about Talks with Iran', *Financial Times* (15.10.21), www.ft.com/content/8665b1d2-b0ca-4dd0-8a18-837e3ad5b110.

Entoush, A., N. Malas, and M. Coker. 'A Veteran Saudi Power Player Works to Build Support to Topple Assad', *Wall Street Journal* (25.08.13), www.wsj.com/articles/a-veteran-saudi-power-player-works-to-build-support-to-topple-assad-1377473580?tesla=y.

Esfandiari, Golnaz. 'Iran Promotes Its New "Martyrs", Cementing Role in Syria Fighting', *Radio Free Europe* (12.07.16).

'Excerpts from Khomeini Speeches', *New York Times* (04.08.87), www.nytimes.com/1987/08/04/world/excerpts-from-khomeini-speeches.html.

'Exclusive: Iran steps up Weapons Supply to Yemen's Houthis via Oman—Officials', *Reuters* (20.10.16).

Fam, M. 'Militias Growing in Power in Iraq', *Associated Press* (07.10.05), www.washingtonpost.com/wp-dyn/content/article/2005/11/07/AR2005110700977_pf.html.

Fawaz, M. 'Beirut: The City as a Body Politic', *ISIM Review* 20 (2007), 22–3. www.isim.nl/files/Review_20/Review_2022.pdf. P23.

Felter, J. and Fishman, B. *Iranian Strategy in Iraq: Politics and 'Other Means'* (West Point, NY: Combatting Terrorism Center, 2008).

Filkins, D. 'A Saudi Prince's Quest to Remake the Middle East', *New Yorker* 02.04.18), www.newyorker.com/magazine/2018/04/09/a-saudi-princes-quest-to-remake-the-middle-east.

'Final Communiqué of The Extraordinary Meeting of The Council of Foreign Ministers of The Organization of Islamic Cooperation on Aggressions on the Embassy of the Kingdom of Saudi Arabia in Tehran and Its Consulate General in Mashhad', *Organisation of Islamic Cooperation* (22.01.16) www.oic-oci.org/oicv2/topic/?t_id=10837&t_ref=4262&lan=en.

'5 Russian-Syrian Projects Announced This Week', *Moscow Times* (18.12.19), www.themoscowtimes.com/2019/12/18/5-russian-syrian-projects-announced-this-week-a68655.

Francis, E. Lebanese President Presses Saudi to Say Why Hariri Has Not Been Returned', *Reuters* (11.11.17), www.reuters.com/article/us-lebanon-politics-aoun/lebanon-president-calls-on-riyadh-to-clarify-reasons-stopping-hariri-return-idUSKBN1DB0ET.

Frayer, L. 'al-Bander Ejection Exposes Bahrain Split', *Washington Post* (02.10.06), www.washingtonpost.com/wp-dyn/content/article/2006/10/02/AR2006100200868.html.

Freer, C. 'Challenges to *Sunni* Islamism in Bahrain Since 2011', *Carnegie Middle East Centre* (06.03.19), https://carnegie-mec.org/2019/03/06/challenges-to-sunni-islamism-in-bahrain-since-2011-pub-78510.

Gambil, G. G. and D. Nassif. 'Lebanon's Parliamentary Elections: Manufacturing Dissent', *Middle East Intelligence Bulletin* 2:8 (05.09.00), https://www.meforum.org/meib/articles/0009_l1.htm.

Gardner, D. 'Rich Gulf Patrons Turn the Screws on a Bankrupt Lebanon', *Financial Times* (03.11.21), www.ft.com/content/fc36ad5b-bbbb-4e3f-b2de-21cc5f19245e.

Gause, F. G. 'Fresh Prince: The Schemes and Dreams of Saudi Arabia's Next King', *Foreign Affairs* (05/06.18), www.foreignaffairs.com/articles/middle-east/2018-03-19/fresh-prince.'

'GCC States Boxed in by US Sanctions on Syria', *al-Monitor* (01.02.19), www.al-monitor.com/pulse/originals/2019/02/gcc-us-dilemma-assad-arabs-qatar-lebanon-netanyahu.html.

'Geagea Warns of "More Resignations" and Gemayel Says Lebanon is a Hezbollah "Hostage"', *yalibnan*(21.02.16), http://yalibnan.com/2016/02/21/geagea-warns-of-more-resignations-and-gemayel-says-lebanon-is-a-hezbollah-hostage/.

Goldberg, J. 'The Obama Doctrine', *The Atlantic* (2016), www.theatlantic.com/magazine/archive/2016/04/the-obama-doctrine/471525/#5.

Goldberg, J. 'Saudi Crown Prince: Iran's Supreme Leader "Makes Hitler Look Good"', *The Atlantic* (02.04.18), www.theatlantic.com/international/archive/2018/04/mohammed-bin-salman-iran-israel/557036/.

Gordon, M. R. and Schmitt, E. 'Iran Secretly Sending Drones and Supplies Into Iraq, U.S. Officials Say', *NY Times* (26.06.14), www.nytimes.com/2014/06/26/world/middleeast/iran-iraq.html.

'Grand Ayatollah Sistani Condemns the Saudi and Bahrain's Crackdown on Bahrain's Shi'a While Kuwait Refuses to Send Troops', *JafriaNews* (17.03.11), http://jafrianews.com/2011/03/17/grand-ayatollah-sistani-condemns-the-saudi-and-bahrains-force-crackdown-on-bahrains-shi'a-while-kuwait-refuses-to-send-troops.

Grim, R. 'Iran Tried to Stop Houthi Rebels in Yemen Obama Says', *Huffington Post* (06.08.15), www.huffingtonpost.co.uk/entry/iran-tried-to-stop-houthi-rebels-in-yemen_n_55c3ba1be4b0d9b743db627c.

Grim, R. 'This is the Kind of President Donald Trump is Replacing', *Huffington Post* (01.12.16), www.huffingtonpost.co.uk/entry/barack-obama-foreign-policy-trump_us_5824ce48e4b034e3899091ed.

Haddad, F. 'The Language of Anti-Shi'ism', *Foreign Policy* (09.08.13), https://foreignpolicy.com/2013/08/09/the-language-of-anti-shiism/.

Grewal, S. S. 'Former Intelligence Officer Eagerly Awaits Beginning of Negotiations', *Gulf Daily News* (29.06.11).

Haddad, F. 'Shi'a-Centric State-Building and Sunni Rejection in Post-2003 Iraq', *Carnegie Endowment for International Peace* (07.01.16), https://

carnegieendowment.org/2016/01/07/shia-centric-state-building-and-sunni-rejection-in-post-2003-iraq-pub-62408.

Hager, E. B. and M. Mzzetti, Emirates Secretly Sends Colombian Mercenaries to Yemen to Fight', *New York Times* (25.11.15).

Halliday, F. 'Arabs and Persians beyond the Geopolitics of the Gulf', *Cahiers d'etudes sur la Mediterranee orientale et le monde turo-iranien* [En ligne] 22 (1996), https://journals.openedition.org/cemoti/143?lang=fr#quotation.

'Hajj hijacked by Oppressors, Muslims Should Reconsider Management of Hajj: Ayatollah Khamenei', *Tehran Times* (05.09.16), www.tehrantimes.com/news/406107/Hajj-hijacked-by-oppressors-Muslims-should-reconsider-management.

Halliday, J. and A. Asthana. 'Met Police Look at Allegations of Saudi War Crimes in Yemen', *The Guardian* (02.04.17), www.theguardian.com/world/2017/apr/02/met-police-examine-allegations-saudi-arabia-war-crimes-yemen.

Hamidreza, A. 'How Iran Sees Russia-Turkey Deal on Northeastern Syria', *al-Monitor* (24.10.19), www.al-monitor.com/pulse/originals/2019/10/iran-deal-russia-turkey-northeast-syria.html.

'Hardball with Chris Matthews: King Abdullah II of Jordan', *NBC News* (07.12.08.), event occurs at 02:06.

Hashem, A. 'Khamenei Criticizes Saudi Airstrikes, Nuclear Agreement', *al-Monitor* (09.04.15), www.al-monitor.com/pulse/originals/2015/04/iran-khamenei-saudi-airstrikes-yemen.html#ixzz4KF3HE4dc.

Hassan, H. 'Old Myths Perpetuate Poor Analysis of Saudi', *The National* (17.01.16), www.thenational.ae/ opinion/comment/old-myths-perpetuate-poor-analysis-of-saudi.

'Hezbollah Chief Nasrallah Mets Ahmadinejad in Syria', *BBC News* (26.02.10).

'Hezbollah: ISIS Wants Lebanon', *Daily Star* (31.08.14), www.dailystar.com.lb/News/Lebanon-News/2014/Aug-31/269106-hezbollah-Daesh-wants-lebanon.ashx#axzz3CGYeUT5Y.

'Humanitarian Crisis in Yemen: Seven Years on, WHO is Strengthening the Health System, Responding to Vital Health Needs, and Saving Lives', *Reliefweb* (27.03.22), https://reliefweb.int/report/yemen/humanitarian-crisis-yemen-seven-years-who-strengthening-health-system-responding-vital.

Humud, C. E. 'Lebanon', *Congressional Research Service* (25.07.17).

International Crisis Group, 'Drums of War: Israel and the "Axis of Resistance"', *Crisis Group Middle East Report*, 97 (2010), 6.

International Crisis Group, 'Make or Break: Iraq's Sunnis and the State', *Middle East Report* No. 144 (2013), www.crisisgroup.org/~/media/Files/Middle%20East%20North%20Africa/Iraq%20Syria%20Lebanon/Iraq/144-make-or-break-iraq-s-sunnis-and-the-state.pdf.

International Crisis Group, 'Popular Protests in North Africa and the Middle East: Bahrain's Rocky Road to Reform' (28.07.11).

International Crisis Group, 'Saudi Arabia: Back to Baghdad' (22.05.18), https://d2071andvip0wj.cloudfront.net/186-saudi-arabia-back-to-baghdad%20(1).pdf p5.

International Crisis Group, '10 Conflicts to Watch in 2018' (02.01.18), www.crisisgroup.org/global/10-conflicts-watch-2018.

'Interview with Hassan Mushayma', *al-Akhbar* (28,02.11.).

'Interview with Iranian Foreign Minister: We Will Have Differences with US No Matter What', *Der Speigel* (16.05.15), www.spiegel.de/international/ world/interview-with-iranian-foreign-minister-mohammad-javad-zarif-a-1033 966.html.

'Interview with President Bashar al-Asad', *al-Bab* (08.02.01).

'Iran Backed Militia Behind Attack, Iraqi PM', *Reuters* (08.11.21), www .reuters.com/world/middle-east/iran-backed-militia-behind-attack-iraqi-pm-sources-2021-11-08/.

'Iran Calls for Violent Shi'ite Reaction against Saudi Arabia', *Memri* (12.02.14), www.memri.org/reports/iran-calls-violent-shiite-reaction-against-saudi-arabia.

'Iran's Deadly Puppet Master', *Foreign Policy Magazine* (2019), https:// foreignpolicy.com/gt-essay/irans-deadly-puppet-master-qassem-suleimani/.

'Iran FM: Sectarian Strife is Worst Threat in World', *BBC News* (11.11.13), www.bbc.co.uk/news/world-middle-east-24893808.

'Iran's FM Voices Concern about Bahrain in Letters to UN, OIC, Arab League', *Fars News Agency* (17.03.11).

'Iran Furious over Saudi Arabia's Execution of Shi'ite Sheikh Nimr al-Nimr', *Memri* (04.01.16), www.memri.org/reports/iran-furious-over-saudi-arabias-execution-shiite-sheikh-nimr-al-nimr.

'Iran General Died in Israeli Strike in Syrian Golan', *BBC News* (19.01.15), www.bbc.com/news/world-middle-east-30882935.

'Iran Gets Negative Reviews in Iraq Even from Shi'ites', *Washington Institute* (04.05.10), www.washingtoninstitute.org/policy-analysis/view/iran-gets-negative-reviews-in-iraq-even-from-shi'ites.

'Iran is World's "Main Sponsor of Terrorism," Says Saudi Arabia, *Middle East Eye* (20.02.17), www.middleeasteye.net/news/iran-worlds-main-sponsor-terrorism-says-saudi-arabia.

Iranian Constitution, www.constituteproject.org/constitution/Iran_1989.pdf? lang=en.

Iranian Constitution, Article3.16, www.alaviandassociates.com/documents/ constitution.pdf.

'Iranian President Calls for Halt to Yemen Air Strikes', *Reuters* (09.04.15), https://af.reuters.com/article/worldNews/idAFKBN0N00IA20150409.

'Iranian President: Recent Events in Yemen Are Part of the Brilliant and Resounding Victory', *Aden al-Ghad* (25.09.14), http://adenghad.net/ news/124484/#.VZ6SA_3bKM-.

'Iran Provide Weapons to Iraq's Kurds: Barzani', *Middle East Eye* (12.02.15), www.middleeasteye.net/news/iran-provided-weapons-iraqs-kurds-barzani.

'Iran Reiterates Support for Restoration of Political Tranquility to Yemen', *Fars News* (23.02.15), http://english.farsnews.com//newstext.aspx?nn=1393 1204000524.

'Iran's Revolutionary Guards: We Have Armed 200,000 Fighters in the Region', *Middle East Monitor* (15.01.16).

'Iran's Rouhani Urges Muslim Countries to Unite', *EuroNews* (27.12.15), www .euronews.com/2015/12/27/iran-s-rouhani-urges-muslim-countries-to-unite.

'Iran's Rouhani Vows to Back Syria "Until the End of the Road"', *Reuters* (02.06.15), https://uk.reuters.com/article/uk-mideast-crisis-syria-iran/irans-rouhani-vows-to-back-syria-until-the-end-of-the-road-idUKKBN0OI0UN201 50602.

'Iran Says Saudi Arabia Prevents Sending Aid to Yemenis', *Tehran Times* (25.04.15), www.tehrantimes.com/news/246312/Iran-says-Saudi-Arabia-prevents-sending-aid-to-Yemenis.

'Iran's Security Is due to the Wise Leadership of the Supreme Leader', *Kayhan* (12.09.14), http://kayhan.ir/fa/news/23898/.

'Iran Steps up Support for Houthis in Yemen's War – Sources', *Reuters* (21.03.17).

'Iraq's Zealous Sons March in Support of Downtrodden Bahraini People', *al-Amarah News Network* (16.03.11), http://al3marh.net/news.

'I. R. Iran's Main Export Destinations in 2013', Iran Trade Statistics in Brief', *Iranian Trade Planning Office* (2013), http://eng.tpo.ir/uploads/2013statictic_word_tabdil_be_pdf_7454.pdf.

'Iran is Seeking "to Control Islamic World," Says Saudi Arabian Prince', *Associated Press* (02.05.17), www.theguardian.com/world/2017/may/02/iran-is-seeking-to-control-islamic-world-says-saudi-arabian-prince.

'Iraqi Prime Minister Meets with the Leader of the Revolution', *Khamenei.IR* (n.d.), https://farsi.khamenei.ir/news-content?id=36913.

'Iraq's Sadr Calls for Protest Against Bahrain Deaths', *World Bulletin* (03.16.11), www.worldbulletin.net/?aType=haber&ArticleID= 71168.

'Jami'ya al-tahdid al-Bahrayniya: Khitabna al-maraji'a al-fiqhiya fi al-Iyran al-'Iraq li dafa' al-durur 'n al-watan' (BCR: We Talked to Religious Authorities in Iran, Iraq, to Avoid Problems in the Country), *Al-Aafaq* (22.09.08).

Jeffery, S. 'The Arab League Summit', *The Guardian* (28.03.02).

Jeffrey, T. 'The Sunni-*Shi'ite* Cold War or Worse', *Human Events* (16.10.06), http://findarticles.com/p/articles/mi_qa3827/is_200610/ai_n17196736.

'Joint Statement on the Formation of the Islamic Military Alliance', *Embassy of the Kingdom of Saudi Arabia in the United States of America* (15.12.15), http://embassies.mofa.gov.sa/sites/usa/EN/PublicAffairs/Statements/Pages/Joint-Statement-on-the-Formation-of-the-Islamic-Military-Alliance.aspx.

Kalin, S. 'Saudi Arabia Winds Down 15-Month Anti-Corruption Campaign', *Reuters* (30.01.19), www.reuters.com/article/us-saudi-arrests-idUSKCN1PO2O1.

Kamrava, M. 'Mediation and Saudi Foreign Policy', *Orbis* 57:1 (2013), 159.

Karouny, M. 'Saudi Edges Qatar to Control Syrian Rebel Support', *Reuters* (31.05.13), www.reuters.com/article/us-syria-crisis-saudi-insight-idusBre94u0ZV20130531.

'Khamenei Declares Assad "Hero of the Arab World" during Syrian Dictator's Surprise Iran Visit', *New Arab* (25.02.19), www.alaraby.co.uk/english/news/2019/2/25/khamenei-declares-syrian-dictator-hero-of-the-arab-world.

'Khamenei Says Iran's Duty to Defend Syria's Assad', *New Arab* (02.03.18), www.alaraby.co.uk/english/news/2018/3/1/khamenei-says-irans-duty-to-defend-syrias-assad.

Khatib, L. 'Hezbollah's Ascent and Descent', *Turkish Policy Quarterly* 14:1 (2015), 105–11.

'King Salman Vows to Continue Yemen Campaign', *Al Arabiya* (28.03.15), https://english.alarabiya.net/en/News/middle-east/2015/03/28/King-Salman-arrives-in-Egypt-for-Arab-summit-.

Knights, M. 'The Houthi War Machine: From Guerrilla War to State Capture', CTC Sentinel, Washington Institute (September 2018), p. 17.

'KSA to Finance Morocco Projects Worth $1.25 bn', *Arab News* (18.10.12).

Lawrence, T. E. 'Faysal's Table Talk', Reort to Colonel Wilson, January 8, 1917, FO 686/6, pp. 121.

'Leader's Speech to Members of Ahlul Bayt World Assembly and Islamic Radio and TV Union', *Khamenei.ir* (17.08.15), http://english.khamenei.ir/news/2109/ Leader-s-speech-to-members-of-Ahlul-Bayt-World-Assembly-and-Islamic.

'Learn Lesson from Saddam's Fate: Ahmadinejad', *Mehr News* (16.03.11).

'Lebanese PM Hariri Resigns, Saying He Fears Assassination Plot', *BBC* (04.11.17), www.bbc.co.uk/news/world-middle-east-41870406.

'Lebanese Split along Religious Lines in Views on Saudi Arabia and Iran', *Pew Research* (06.01.16), www.pewresearch.org/fact-tank/2016/01/07/ the-middle-easts-sectarian-divide-on-views-of-saudi-arabia-iran/ft_15- 01-06_saudiarabia_iran_lebanon/.

'Lebanon Apologizes to Saudi over Nasrallah Speech', *World Bulletin* (08.11.15), www.worldbulletin.net/middle-east/lebanon-apologizes-to-saudi-over- nasrallah-speech-h157564.html.

لقاء اليوم- المخلافي: من يصدق صالح والحوثي 'واهم (Liqa alyoum- al-Mikhlafi: mun yosadeq Saleh u al-Houthi Wahem [Today's meeting – al'Mikhlafi: Who believes Saleh and al-Houth are 'the most important']) (20.11.15), www.youtube.com/watch?v= p4xcrxJDGhI.

الشيخ عبد الرحمن السديس كلمته عن الحرب في اليمن (lShaykh Abdul Rahman al-Sudais Kalimathu 'an Alharab fi Alyaman [Sheikh Abdul Rahman al-Sudais, his speech on the war in Yemen]) (28.11.15), https://youtu.be/yBKF7eYXusk.

Lynch, Colum, et al. 'Can a Young Saudi Prince End the War in Yemen?' *Foreign Policy* (20.11.19).

Mably, R. and Evans, D. 'Interview – Saudi Says Yemen Strikes Show Arab Resolve to Act Alone', *Reuters* (22.04.15), https://in.reuters.com/article/ yemen-security-saudi/interview-saudi-says-yemen-strikes-show-arab-resolve- to-act-alone-idINL5N0XJ2JZ20150422.

Macdonald, N. 'CBC Investigation: Who Killed Lebanon's Rafik Hariri', *CBC News* (21.09.10), www.cbc.ca/news/world/cbc-investigation-who-killed- lebanon-s-rafik-hariri-1.874820.

Macfarquahar, N. 'Behind Lebanon Upheaval, 2 Men's Fateful Clash', *New York Times* (20.03.05).

MacGinty, R. and C. S. Hamieh. 'Lebanon Case Study', in A. Harmer and E. Martin (eds.), *Diversity in Donorship: Field Lessons* (ODI, Humanitarian Policy Group, 2010), Report 30, 39–48, www.odi.org.uk/sites/odi.org.uk/files/ odi-assets/publications-opinion-files/5876.pdf p40.

Majed, R. 'Lebanon and Iraq in 2019: Revolutionary Uprisings Against 'Sectarian Neoliberalism', *TNI Longreads* (27.10.21), https://longreads.tni .org/lebanon-and-iraq-in-2019?fbclid=IwAR0o4MQi_a1BSYjYhe3BzKTKg SJSBvpodn2brxSfNfrhM1miOHiOGfBbz8w.

Malmvig, H. and Fakhour, T. 'Takes of the Unexpected: Will the Lebanese Uprising Stay Clear of Attempts at Geopolitization?' *POMEPS: Sectarianism and International Relations* (03.20), https://pomeps.org/tales-of-the-unex pected-will-the-lebanese-uprising-stay-clear-of-attempts-at-geopolitization-1.

Mansour, R. 'In Life and Death, Iraq's Hisham al-Hashimi', *Chatham House* (01.08.20), www.chathamhouse.org/publications/the-world-today/2020-08/life-and-death-iraqs-hisham-al-hashimi.

Mansour, R. 'Networks of Power: The Popular Mobilization Forces and the State in Iraq', *Chatham House* (2021).

'Mavaze 14 Mars by mozoue Arabistan Saudi gereh khordeh [The Positions of March 14 Are Tied to the Saudi Position], *Fars News Agency* (29.04.08).

Mazzetti, M. and M. Apuzzo, 'U.S. Relies Heavily on Saudi Money to Support Syrian Rebels', *New York Times* (23.01.16).

McDowell, A. and A. Bakr. 'A Saudi King Aims for New Sunni Bloc vs Iran and Islamic State' *Reuters* (05.03.15), www.reuters.com/article/us-saudi-mideast-brotherhood-idUSKBN0M127N20150305.

Memri (01.04.16.).

Mehr (Iran) (15.01.14).

Milani, M. 'Tehran's Take', *Foreign Affairs* 88:4 (2009), 88.

Muir, J. 'Historic Saudi-Syrian Beirut Visit Shows Arab Concern', *BBC News* (31.07.10), www.bbc.co.uk/news/world-middle-east-10825228.

Mukhashaf, M. 'Southern Yemen Separatists Want Saudi-Backed Government Overthrown', *Reuters* (21.01.18), https://uk.reuters.com/article/uk-yemen-security-southerners/southern-yemen-separatists-want-saudi-backed-government-overthrown-idUKKBN1FA0WT.

Naar, I. 'Bahrain Condemns Beirut Hosting Press Conference for "Hostile Personnel"', *Al Arabiya* (12.12.21), https://english.alarabiya.net/News/gulf/2021/12/12/Bahrain-condemns-Beirut-hosting-press-conference-for-hostile-personnel-.

'Nabil Rajab li Aafaq: al-Tabqa al-hakima bil Bahrayn tumaris al-t'athiir did al-Shi'a' (Nabil Rajab to Aafaq: Bahrain's Ruling Class Practices Apartheid Against Shi'ites), *al-Aafaq* (26.10.08).

نصيحة لأهل اليمن في مواجهة الحوثيين – ربيع بن هادي المدخلى (Nasiha lahl Alyaman fi Mwajhet al-Houthiyyn- Rab'i Hadi al-Madkhali [Advice to the People of Yemen in the Face of the Houthis – Rabie bin Hadi al-Madkhali]) (08.11.14), https://youtu.be/b4r3ecxN7l8.

N. N. 'Ma Taquluh Washington wa Dimashq 'an Muhadathat Burns', *al-Nahar* (14.09.04).

'Nasrallah: ISIS Is a "Real Existential Danger" to the Whole Region', *Al Akhbar* (15.08.14), http://english.al-akhbar.com/node/21153.

'Nasrallah: ISIS Would Be in Beirut If Not for Hezbollah Intervention in Syria', *Al Akhbar* (17.06.14), http://english.al-akhbar.com/node/20207.

Nasr, M. 'Hizbullah Implemented the Operation Professionally, Israel Is Floundering', *al-Diyyar* [Beirut] (06.01.15).

National Legislative Bodies/National Authorities, Iraq: Resolution No. 666 of 1980 (nationality), 26 May 1980, www.refworld.org/docid/3ae6b51d28.html.

Nawar, I. 'Untying the Knot', al-*Ahram Weekly*, No. 625 (2003), http://weekly.ahram.org.eg/archive/2003/625/sc5.htm.

Naylor, H. "'Rivals Tehran, Riyadh Pledge Billions to Lebanon's Army,'", *Washington Post* (04.11.14), www.washingtonpost.com/world/middle_east/rivals-tehran-riyadh-pledge-billions-to-lebanons-army/2014/11/03/1505b9d4-9cb4-4f22-af4a-d5a9ab867e5c_story.html.

Nehme, D. 'Top Saudi Cleric Says Iran Leaders Not Muslims as haj row mounts', *Reuters* (07.09.16), www.reuters.com/article/us-saudi-iran-mufti/top-saudi-cleric-says-iran-leaders-not-muslims-as-haj-row-mounts-idUSKCN11D0HV.

Nerguizian, A. 'Assessing the Consequences of Hezbollah's Necessary War of Choice in Syria', *Centre for Strategic and International Studies* (17.06.13), http://csis.org/publication/assessing-consequences- hezbollahs-necessary-war-choice-syria.

Nichols, M. 'Latest Houthi Missile "Bears Hallmarks" of Iran Arms Attacks: U.S.', *Reuters* (19.12.17), www.reuters.com/article/us-yemen-security-saudi-usa/latest-houthi-missile-bears-hallmarks-of-iran-arms-attacks-u-s-idUSKBN1ED2PC.

Niethammer, K. 'Voices in Parliament: Debates in Majlis, and Banners on Streets: Avenues of Political Participation in Bahrain', Mediterranean Programme Series, EUI RSCAS (2006/7), https://cadmus.eui.eu/handle/1814/6224, p. 17.

'No Changes in Border with Yemen, Says Prince Khaled', *Arab News* (07.03.10), www.al-monitor.com/pulse/politics/2013/08/saudi-russia-putin-bandar-meeting-syria-egypt.html#ixzz2d5UVLSNv.

'Nokhostin Mosaahebe-ye Tafsili-ye Rahbaraan-e Asa'ib Ahl Haq Dar Iran [First Detailed Interview of Asa'ib Ahl Haq Leaders in Iran]', *Fars News Agency* (02.09.14), www.farsnews.com/newstext.php?nn=13930811000718.

An Open Letter, *The Hizbullah Programme*, www.cfr.org/terrorist-organizations-and-networks/open-letter-hizballah-program/p30967.

Orkaby, A. 'Yemen's Humanitarian Nightmare: The Real Roots of the Conflict', *Foreign Affairs* 96:6 (2017), 93–101.

Osborn, A. 'Russia Uses Iran as Base to bomb Syrian Militants for First Time', *Reuters* (16.08.16).

Phillips, C. 'Sectarianism as Plan B', in Simon Mabon (ed.), *Saudi Arabia and Iran: The Struggle to Shape the Middle East* (SEPAD, 2018) www.sepad.org.uk/report/sectarianism-as-plan-b-saudi-iranian-identity-politics-in-the-syria-conflict.

Pierret, T. 'The Reluctant Sectarianism of Foreign States in the Syrian Conflict', *USIP* (18.11.13), www.usip.org/sites/default/files/PB162.pdf.

Pincus, W. 'US Military Urging Iraq to Rein In Guard Force', *Washington Post* (25.12.06), www.washingtonpost.com/wp-dyn/content/article/2006/12/24/AR2006122400551.html. [accessed 2 August 2015].

Pollock, D. and A. Ali, 'Iran Gets Negative Reviews in Iraq, Even from *Shi'ites*', Policywatch blog, Washington Institute for Near East Policy, Policy #1653 (04.05.10).

Qudat, B. 'Making up at Last', *Al-Ahram Weekly* (19–25.02.09).

Rayhab News, 'Iran: General Nowi-Aghdam Urges Recruits to Fight in Syria as Assad Stumbles', *Islam Media Analysis* (06.15).

'Record Protest Held in Beirut', *BBC News* (14.03.05), http://news.bbc.co.uk/2/hi/middle_east/4346613.stm.

'Refrain from Using Social Networking Sites' Appeal', *Gulf Daily News* (20.02.11), www.gulf-daily-news.com/ArchiveNews Details.aspx?date=02/20/2011&storyid=300029.

Reidar, V. 'Religious Allegiances Among Pro-Iranian Special Groups in Iraq', *CTC Sentinel*, 4:9 (2011), 5–8.

'Report – One Year Later: Assessing Bahrain's Implementation of the BICI Report' (2012), https://pomed.org/wp-content/uploads/2013/12/One-Year-Later-Assessing-Bahrains-Implementation-of-the-BICI-Report.pdf

Reuters Staff, 'Iran's Zarif Says Saudi, UAE Want "to Fight Iran to the Last American"', *Reuters* (20.09.19).

Reuters Staff, 'Lebanon's Hezbollah Condemns Gulf States for "Terrorist" Label', *Reuters* (03.03.16), www.reuters.com/article/us-mideast-crisis-lebanon-hezbollah-idUSKCN0W51RB.

Ricks, T. E. 'What Would a Saudi-Iran War Look Like? Don't Look Now, but It Is Already Here', *Foreign Policy* (28.12.17), http://foreignpolicy.com/2016/12/28/what-would-a-saudi-iran-war-look-like-dont-look-now-but-it-is-already-here-3/.

Riedel, B. 'The Return of Prince Bandar: Saudi's New Spy Chief', *Brookings Institution* (23.07.12).

'Riyadh Pushing for a Strong Independent Iraq', *Reuters* (17.08.17), https://gulfnews.com/world/mena/riyadh-pushing-for-a-strong-independent-iraq-1.2075708.

Roston, A. 'A Middle East Monarchy Hired American Ex-Soldiers To Kill Its Political Enemies. This Could Be The Future Of War' (BuzzFeed News, 16.10.18), www.buzzfeednews.com/article/aramroston/mercenaries-assassination-us-yemen-uae-spear-golan-dahlan.

'Rouhani Praises Iran's Role in Ensuring Security in Iraq', speech given by Hassan Rouhani at shrine of Imam Reza, Mashhad, *Islamic Republic of Iran News Network/BBC Monitoring* (06.09.14).

Ryan, C. 'The New Arab Cold War and the Struggle for Syria', *Middle East Report* 262 (2012), 28–31.

Sadeghi-Boroujerdi, E. 'Head of Ammar Strategic Base: Syria is Iran's 35th Province: If We Lose Syria We Cannot Keep Tehran', *Al Monitor – Iran Pulse* (14.02.14).

Salisbury, P. *Federalism, conflict and fragmentation in Yemen* (SAFERWORLD: October 2015), p12.

Salisbury, P. *Yemen: National Chaos, Local Order* (Chatham House, 20.12.17).

Salloulkh, B. F. 'The Sectarian Image Reversed: The Role of Geopolitics in Hezbollah's Domestic Politics', *POMEPS Studies* 38 (2020), https://pomeps.org/pomeps-studies-38-sectarianism-and-international-relations.

Salloukh, B. 'Syria and Lebanon: A Brotherhood Transformed', *Middle East Research and Information Project* 35 (Fall 2005).

Samaha, N. 'Hezbollah's Death Valley', *Foreign Policy* (03.03.16).

'Sanaa is the Fourth Arab Capital to Join the Iranian Revolution', *MEMO* (27.09.14), www.middleeastmonitor.com/20140927-sanaa-is-the-fourth-arab-capital-to-join-the-iranian-revolution/.

'Saudi Ambassador in U.S. Speaks on Military campaign in Yemen', *Al Arabiya* (26.03.15), http://english.alarabiya.net/en/webtv/reports/2015/03/26/Video-Saudi-ambassador-in-U-S-speaks-on-military-campaign-in-Yemen.html.

'Saudi Arabia's Aid Halt to Lebanon is Justified', *Khaleej Times* (15.12.21), www.khaleejtimes.com/editorials-columns/saudi-arabias-aid-halt-to-lebanon-is-justified.

'Saudi Arabia Condemns Ongoing Iranian Regional Interference and Aggression', *Embassy of the Kingdom of Saudi Arabia, Brussels* (09.11.16), http://ksaembassy.be/en/saudi-arabia-condemns-ongoing-iranian-regional-interference-aggression/.

'Saudi Arabia Intercepts Missiles from Yemen Heading over Riyadh', *Financial Times*, www.ft.com/content/6fe57680-536c-11e8-b24e-cad6aa67e23e.

'Saudi Arabia to Provide Jordan with $487 mln for Development Projects, *Jordan News Agency* (28.11.12).

'Saudi Arabia Recalls Ambassador to Syria', *BBC* (08.08.11), www.bbc.co.uk/news/world-middle-east-14439303.

'#SaudiCables: Ring-wing Lebanese Christian Leader Asked Saudis for Money', *New Arab* (n.d.), https://english.alaraby.co.uk/english/news/2015/6/22/saudicables-right-wing-lebanese-christian-leader-asked-saudis-for-money.

'Saudis Cut Off Funding for Military Aid to Lebanon', *New York Times* (20.02.16), www.nytimes.com/2016/02/20/world/middleeast/saudis-cut-off-funding-for-military-aid-to-lebanon.html.

'Saudi FM Urges Joint Arab Strategy on Iran', *Al-Arabiya* (03.03.09).

'Saudi King Eyes End to Syrian Killing, Pulls Ambassador', *Reuters* (07.08.11), www.reuters.com/article/syria-saudi-idUSL6E7J70FP20110807.

'Saudis Held Briefly by Yemeni Rebels', *Arab News* (25.04.10).

'Saudis Not Competent to Run Islam's Holy Mosques', *The Office of the Supreme Leader* (09.07.16), www.leader.ir/en/content/16203/The-Leader's-meeting-with-families-of-Mina-and-Grand-Mosque-tragedies-in-Saudi-Arabia.

'Section 6 Islam and Resistance: The New Hezbollah Manifesto' (11.09), www.lebanonrenaissance.org/assets/Uploads/15-The-New-Hezbollah-Manifesto-Nov09.pdf.

'Saudi's Jubeir: "Too Early" to Reopen Syria Embassy', *Al Jazeera* (04.03.19), www.aljazeera.com/news/2019/03/saudi-foreign-minister-early-reopen-syria-embassy-190304184023059.html.

'Saudi-Iran "Proxy Wars" Play Out in Embattled Lebanon', *France24* (31.10.21), www.france24.com/en/live-news/20211031-saudi-iran-proxy-wars-play-out-in-embattled-lebanon.

Schneider, T. 'The Decay of the Syrian Regime Is Much Worse Than You Think', *War on the Rocks* (31.08.16), http://warontherocks.com/2016/08/the-decay-of-the-syrian-regime-is-muchworse-than-you-think/.

'Security and Stability Top Priorities Now, Foreign Minister Says', *Bahrain News Agency* (29.03.11).

Shiban, B. 'Brothers in Arms – Dissecting Iran-Houthi Ties', *The Brief* (2.11.18), https://the-brief.co/brothers-in-arms-dissecting-iran-houthi-ties/?fbclid=IwAR3p8Ymp-NQKa37mY5b-5k89ETpYCfWLy0CspCll_MRHtxD9-dJGy2bcZg0.

Shokair, M. 'Russia Assures Arab Capitals of Curbing Iran Influence in Syria Before Normalization', *al-Sharq al-Awsat* (23.01.19), https://aawsat.com/english/home/article/1558211/russia-assures-arab-capitals-curbing-iran-influence-syria-normalization?utm_source=dlvr.it&utm_medium=facebook&fbclid=IwAR29MCNwYHSt1-yHmpMH7FKuOHDMwqkFLbevwu8QGm-6beYwGPeWa3DQaA8.

Sobh-e Sadeq (Iran) (01.26.14).

'A Statement by Bahraini Youth for Freedom', *CNN* (11.02.11), http://ireport
.cnn.com/docs/DOC-554209.

'Statement to the Security Council on Missions to Yemen, South Sudan,
Somalia and Kenya and an update on the Oslo Conference on Nigeria and the
Lake Chad Region', *United Nations Office for the Coordination of Humanitarian
Affairs*   (10.03.17),   https://reliefweb.int/sites/reliefweb.int/files/resources/
ERC_USG%20Stephen%20O%27Brien%20Statement%20to%20the
%20SecCo%20on%20Missions%20to%20Yemen%2C%20South%20
Sudan%2C%20Somalia%20and%20Kenya%2C%20and%20update%20
on%20Oslo%20Conference%20-%2010%20March%202017.pdf.

'Stop Meddling' Call to Tehran', *Gulf Daily News* (31.03.11).

Swisher, C. and D. Hearst. 'Exclusive: Saudi Crown Prince Wants out of Yemen
War, Email Leak Reveals', *Middle East Eye* (16.08.17), www.middleeasteye.net/
news/exclusive-saudi-crown-prince-wants-out-yemen-war-email-leak-reveals).

'Syria's Assad Visits Iran, Meets Khamenei', *Radio Free Europe* (25.02.19), www
.rferl.org/a/syria-s-assad-visits-iran-meets-khamenei/29790299.html.

Syria Comment, 'Sanctions on the Table', *Al-Arabiya* (05.03.09).

Syria Comment, 'Saudis and Syrians ... Brothers or Rivals?', *al-Hayat* (05.03.07).

'Syria Conflict: Cleric Qaradawi Urges Sunnis to Join Rebels', *BBC News*
(01.06.13), www.bbc.co.uk/news/world-middle-east-22741588.

'Syrian Army "Resumes Shelling Dier al-Zour"', *BBC* (08.08.11), www.bbc
.co.uk/news/world-middle-east-14441323.

'Syrian Opinions and Attitudes Towards Sectarianism in Syria – Survey Study', *The
Day After* (22.02.16), http://tda-sy.org/en/publications/english-sectarianism-
in-syria-survey-study.html.

'Syrian Opposition Leader Interview Transcript', *Wall Street Journal* (02.12.11),
http://online.wsj.com/article/SB1000142405297020383310457707196038 42
40668.html.

'Syria Regime Repays War Debt by Awarding Iran Huge Construction
Contract', *New Arab* (25.02.19), www.alaraby.co.uk/english/news/2019/2/25/
syria-regime-repays-ally-iran-with-huge-construction-project.

Telhami, S. Anwar Sadat Chair for Peace and Development University of
Maryland/Zogby International 2006 Annual Arab Public Opinion Survey
(08.02.07).

'Text of Bush Speech', *CBS News* (01.05.03), www.cbsnews.com/news/
text-of-bush-speech-01-05-2003/.

'UAE, Oman and Bahrain to Resume Flights to Syria', *Middle East Monitor*
(14.01.19), www.middleeastmonitor.com/20190114-uae-oman-and-bahrain-
to-resume-flights-to-syria/.

'UAE Reopens Syria Embassy in Boost for Assad', *Reuters* (27.10.18), www
.reuters.com/article/us-mideast-crisis-syria-emirates-idUSKCN1OQ0QV.

United Nations Security Council, Resolution 2201 (2015), http://unscr.com/en/
resolutions/doc/2201.

UN Security Council Resolution 1559 (02.09.04), www.un.org/News/Press/
docs/2004/ sc8181.doc.htm.

UN Security Council, 'Security Council Unanimously Endorses Findings of
Investigation into Murder of Rafik Hariri, Calls for Syria's Full Unconditional
Cooperation', *United Nations* (31.10.05), www.un.org/press/en/2005/sc8543
.doc.htm.

'US Intercepts Multiple Shipments of Iranian Weapons Going to Houthis in Yemen', *CNN* (28.10.16), www.sabanews.net/en/news339378.htm.

'The U.S's Claims about Fighting Terrorism Are Really Ludicrous: Ayatollah Khamenei', Khamenei.ir (26.09.18), http://english.khamenei.ir/news/5967/ The-U-S-s-claims-about-fighting-terrorism-are-really-ludicrous.

'U.S. Officials: Iran Supplying Weapons to Yemen's Houthi Rebels', *NBC News* (27.10.16).

'Voice of the Masses Radio', *Baghdad, Iraqi News Agency* (04.03.80), in FBIS (6 March 1980).

Wahab, S. 'Missile Attack on Riyadh "An Act of War" by Iran', *Arab News* (07.11.17), www.arabnews.com/node/1189476/saudi-arabia.

Watkins, A., R. Grim, and A. S. Ahmed. 'Iran Warned Houthis Against Yemen Takeover', *Huffington Post* (20.04.15), www.huffingtonpost.co.uk/entry/ iran-houthis-yemen_n_7101456.

'Weapons Bound for Yemen Seized on Iran Boat: Coalition', *Reuters* (30.09.15).

Wehrey. F. et al. *Saudi-Iranian Relations since the Fall of Saddam: Rivalry, Cooperation, and Implications for U.S. Policy* (Santa Monica, CA: RAND Corporation, 2009).

'Wide Variation in Favorability of Saudi Aabia and Iran in the Middle East', *Pew Research* (n.d.), www.pewresearch.org/fact-tank/2016/01/07/ the-middle-easts-sectarian-divide-on-views-of-saudi-arabia-iran/ ft_16-01-06_saudiarabia_iran/.

Wikas, S. 'The Damascus-Hizbullah Axis: Bashar al-Asad's Vision of a New Middle East', *Washington Institute* (29.08.06), www.washingtoninstitute .org/ policy-analysis/view/the-damascus-hizballah-axis-bashar-al-asads-vision- of-a-new- middle-east.

Wilkin, S. 'Shi'ites across the Middle East Decry Execution of Saudi cleric', *Reuters* (03.01.16), www.reuters.com/article/saudi-security-shiites/shiites-across-the- middle-east-decry-execution-of-saudi-cleric-idINKBN0UG0CQ20160103.

Wood, J. 'Saudi Arabia Cancels $4bn Aid Package for Lebanon's Security Forces', *The National* (19.02.16).

Wood, P. 'Life and Legacy of King Fahd', *BBC* (01.08.05), http://news.bbc .co.uk/1/hi/world/middle_east/4734505.stm.

Wong, E. 'U.S. Faces Latest Trouble with Iraqi Forces: Loyalty', *New York Times* (06.03.06), www.nytimes.com/2006/03/06/world/americas/06iht- military.html?pagewanted=all.

Wright, R. and P. Baker. 'Iraq, Jordan See Threat to Election from Iran: Leaders Warn against Forming Religious State', *Washington Post* (08.12.04), www .washingtonpost.com/wp-dyn/articles/A43980-2004Dec7.html.

'Yemen: From Civil War to Ali Abdullah Saleh's Death', *Al Jazeera* (05.12.17), www.aljazeera.com/programmes/aljazeeraworld/2017/11/yemen-north-south- divide-171129152948234.html.

'Yemen Rebel Missile Fired at Riyadh "Bears Hallmarks" of Iran', *BBC News* (20.12.17), www.bbc.co.uk/news/world-middle-east-42421289.

'Yemen, South Sudan, Somalia and Kenya and an Update on the Oslo Conference on Nigeria and the Lake Chad Region', *United Nations Office for the Coordination of Humanitarian Affairs* (10.03.17), https://reliefweb.int/sites/reliefweb.int/files/

resources/ERC_USG%20Stephen%20O%27Brien%20Statement%20to%20
the%20SecCo%20on%20Missions%20to%20Yemen%2C%20South%20
Sudan%2C%20Somalia%20and%20Kenya%2C%20and%20update%20
on%20Oslo%20Conference%20-%2010%20March%202017.pdf.
'Yemen: The Peace and National Partnership Agreement', *Jadaliyya* (23.09.14),
www.jadaliyya.com/Details/31248/Yemen-The-Peace-and-National-
Partnership-Agreement.
'Yemenis Will Not Allow Interference in Internal Affairs: Iran', *Tehran Times*
(08.06.11),   www.tehrantimes.com/news/242067/Yemenis-will-not-allow-
interference-in-internal-affairs-Iran
Zarif, J. M. 'Let Us Rid the World of Wahhabism', *New York Times* (09.13.16),
www.nytimes.com/2016/09/14/   opinion/mohammad-javad-zarif-let-us-rid-
the-world-of-wahhabism.html.

Wikileaks

95RIYADH712_a Iran: Meeting with Saudi Foreign Minister Saud Al-Faysal
(08.02.95), https://wikileaks.org/plusd/cables/95RIYADH712_a.html.
04MANAMA1814_a Saudi Statement on GCC Bilateral Agreements Concerns
Bahrain (06.12.04), https://wikileaks.org/plusd/cables/04MANAMA1814_a
.html.
05BAGHDAD3015_a Building a House ON Shifting Sands – Iran's Influence
in Iraq's Center-South (20.07.05), www.wikileaks.org/plusd/cables/05BAG
HDAD3015_a.html.
05MANAMA24_a King Focuses on Relations with Saudi Arabia in Meeting
with Ambassador (04.01.05), https://wikileaks.org/plusd/cables/05MAN
AMA24_a.html.
05MANAMA38_a Bahrain FTA: Full Speed ahead Despite Protests from Saudi
Arabia (05.01.05), https://wikileaks.org/plusd/cables/05MANAMA38_a.html.
05MANAMA71_a Minister of Interior Discusses CT, Saudi Arabia, Iran
with Ambassador (16.01.05), https://wikileaks.org/plusd/cables/05MAN
AMA71_a.html.
05MANAMA176_a CONTINUING SAUDI CONCERNS ABOUT BAHRAIN
FTA (07.02.05), https://wikileaks.org/plusd/cables/05MANAMA176_a.html.
05MANAMA280_a Bahrain Faces Budget Crunch Following Saudi Oil Grant
Cutback (01.03.05), https://wikileaks.org/plusd/cables/05MANAMA280_a
.html.
05MANAMA347_a GOB Reacts to Outward Signs of Shi'a Activism during
Ashura Observances (09.03.05), https://wikileaks.org/plusd/cables/05MAN
AMA347_a.html.
05MANAMA1182_a Bahrain Expects Continued Strong Relations with Saudi,
Hopes for Resumption of Oil Grant (16.08.05), https://wikileaks.org/plusd/
cables/05MANAMA1182_a.html.
05PARIS2660_a Saudi Crown Prince Visit Focuses on Lebanon, Close Ties
with Chirac, but Concludes No New Contracts (19.04.05), https://wikileaks
.org/plusd/cables/05PARIS2660_a.html.

06MANAMA4_a GCC Summit: Bahrain Focuses on Iran (02.01.06), https://wikileaks.org/plusd/cables/06MANAMA4_a.html.

06MANAMA409_a Luncheon with King Hamad (15.03.06), https://wikileaks.org/plusd/cables/06MANAMA409_a.html.

06MANAMA595_a U/S Joseph Discusses Iran and PSI with Bahraini FM (12.04.06), https://wikileaks.org/plusd/cables/06MANAMA595_a.html.

06MANAMA1849_a King Hamad Supports Gulf Security Dialogue (01.11.06), https://wikileaks.org/plusd/cables/06MANAMA1849_a.html.

06RIYADH9_a Saudi Views on Iranian And Syrian Activities in Iraq and Elsewhere (02.01.06), https://wikileaks.org/plusd/cables/06RIYADH9_a.html.

06RIYADH3312 The Saudi Shi'a: Where do their loyalties lie? (02.05.06), https://wikileaks.org/plusd/cables/06RIYADH3312_a.html.

06RIYADH9175_a Saudi MOI Head Says if U.S. Leaves Iraq, Saudi Arabia Will Stand with Sunnis (26.12.06), https://wikileaks.org/plusd/cables/06RIYADH9175_a.html.

07MANAMA650_a Bahrain Reacts Angrily to Iranian Territorial Claim on Bahrain (12.07.07), https://wikileaks.org/plusd/cables/07MANAMA650_a.html.

07MANAMA662_a Iranian FM Assures Bahrain of Full Respect for Sovereignty (17.07.07), https://wikileaks.org/plusd/cables/07MANAMA662_a.html.

07MANAMA669_a Future of Bahrain: Ambassador's Parting Thoughts (19.07.2007), https://wikileaks.org/plusd/cables/07MANAMA669_a.html.

08BAGHDAD239_a 'The Street Is Stronger Than Parliament:' Sadrist Vows Opposition To Ltsr (27.01.08), https://wikileaks.org/plusd/cables/08BAGHDAD239_a.html.

08BAGHDAD2812_a Karbala: Iran Exerts Heavy Influence through Tourism Industry (02.08.08), https://wikileaks.org/plusd/cables/08BAGHDAD2812_a.html.

08BAGHDAD3994_a (C), PRT Salah Ad Din: Iranian Involvement in Samarra (21.12.08), https://wikileaks.org/plusd/cables/08BAGHDAD3994_a.html.

08MANAMA420_Shi'a and Sunni Preachers Trade Insults, Government Steps in to Muzzle Sectarian Voices (24.06.08), https://wikileaks.org/plusd/cables/08MANAMA420_a.html.

08MANAMA541_a General Petraeus' Visit to Bahrain (13.08.08), https://wikileaks.org/plusd/cables/08MANAMA541_a.html.

08MANAMA835_a Iran: Bahraini Foreign Minister's Visit to Tehran (28.12.08), www.wikileaks.org/plusd/cables/08MANAMA835_a.html.

08RIYAD000768 Lebanon: Sag FM Says UN Peace Keeping Force Needed (14.05.08), https://wikileaks.org/plusd/cables/08RIYADH768_a.html.

09MANAMA438_a Bahrain's Shi'a Opposition: Managing Setarian Pressures and Focusing on 2010 Parliamentary Elections (22.07.09), https://wikileaks.org/plusd/cables/09MANAMA438_a.html.

09MANAMA642_a General Petraeus with King Hamad: Iraq, Afghanistan, Iran Nato Awacs, Energy (04.11.09), https://wikileaks.org/plusd/cables/09MANAMA642_a.html.

09MANAMA651_a Sayyid Ammar Al Hakim, Chairman of the Islamic Supreme Council In Iraq, Visits Bahrain (12.11.09), https://wikileaks.org/plusd/cables/09MANAMA651_a.html.

09RIYADH1684_a Saudis Say Syria 'Isolated for too Long' (30.12.09), https://
    wikileaks.org/plusd/cables/09RIYADH1684_a.html
09RIYADH447_a Counterterrorism Adviser Brennan's Meeting with Saudi King
    Abdullah   (22.03.09),   https://wikileaks.org/plusd/cables/09RIYADH447_a
    .html.
09SANAA1628_a Saada Conflict: A Proxy War of Words between Iran, Saudi
    Arabia (02.09.09), https://wikileaks.org/plusd/cables/09SANAA1628_a.html.
09SANAA1662_a Iran in Yemen: Tehran's Shadow Looms Large, but Footprint
    is Small (12.09.09), https://wikileaks.org/plusd/cables/09SANAA1662_a.html.
09SANAA2186_a Who Are The Houthis, Part Two: How Are They Fighting?
    (09.12.09), https://wikileaks.org/plusd/cables/09SANAA2186_a.html.
10BAGHDAD22_a Iraqi Views on Events in Iran and Impact on Iraq (05.01.10),
    https://wikileaks.org/plusd/cables/10BAGHDAD22_a.html.
Doc12139 *The Saudi Cables*, https://wikileaks.org/saudi-cables/doc12139.html.
Doc32628 *The Saudi Cables*, www.wikileaks.org/saudi-cables/doc32628.html.
Doc53032 *The Saudi Cables*, www.wikileaks.org/saudi-cables/doc53032.html.
Doc110212 *The Saudi Cables*, www.wikileaks.org/saudi-cables/doc110212.html.
Doc105956 *The Saudi Cables*, https://wikileaks.org/saudi-cables/doc105956
    .html.

Index